THE ETHICS OF AR

M000206294

The question of ethics and its role in archaeology has stimulated one of the discipline's liveliest debates in recent years. In this collection of essays, an international team of archaeologists, anthropologists and philosophers explore the ethical issues archaeology needs to address. Marrying the skills and expertise of practitioners from different disciplines, the collection produces fresh insights into many of the ethical dilemmas facing archaeology today. Topics discussed include relations with indigenous peoples; the professional standards and responsibilities of researchers; the role of ethical codes; the notion of value in archaeology; concepts of stewardship and custodianship; the meaning and moral implications of 'heritage'; the question of who 'owns' the past or the interpretation of it; the trade in antiquities; the repatriation of skeletal material; and treatment of the dead. This important and timely collection is essential reading for all those working in the field of archaeology, be they scholars or practitioners.

CHRIS SCARRE is Professor of Archaeology at the University of Durham. His previous publications include *Monuments and Landscape in Atlantic Europe* (ed.) (2002) and *The Human Past: A Textbook of World Prehistory* (ed.) (2005).

GEOFFREY SCARRE is Reader at the Department of Philosophy at the University of Durham. He is the author of *After Evil: Responding to Wrongdoing* (2004) and the editor of *Moral Philosophy and the Holocaust* (2003).

THE ETHICS OF ARCHAEOLOGY

Philosophical Perspectives on Archaeological Practice

EDITED BY

CHRIS SCARRE AND GEOFFREY SCARRE

CAMBRIDGE
UNIVERSITY PRESS

CAMBRIDGE UNIVERSITY PRESS
Cambridge, New York, Melbourne, Madrid, Cape Town, Singapore, São Paulo

Cambridge University Press
The Edinburgh Building, Cambridge CB2 2RU, UK

Published in the United States of America by Cambridge University Press, New York

www.cambridge.org
Information on this title: www.cambridge.org/9780521549424

First published 2006

Printed in the United Kingdom at the University Press, Cambridge

A catalogue record for this book is available from the British Library

ISBN-13 978-0-521-84011-8 hardback
ISBN-10 0-521-84011-2 hardback
ISBN-13 978-0-521-54942-4 paperback
ISBN-10 0-521-54942-6 paperback

Contents

Contributors

CHRIS SCARRE is an archaeologist specialising in the prehistory of Europe and the Mediterranean, with a particular interest in the archaeology of the Atlantic seaboard. He took his MA and PhD at Cambridge, UK, the latter a study of landscape change and archaeological sites in western France. He has participated in fieldwork projects in Britain, France and Greece and has directed excavations at Neolithic settlement and mortuary sites in western France. His early work was published in *Ancient France* (Edinburgh University Press, 1983). He is currently Deputy Director of the McDonald Institute for Archaeological Research, University of Cambridge, and editor of the *Cambridge Archaeological Journal.*

GEOFFREY SCARRE took his MA and MLitt degrees in Philosophy at Cambridge, UK, and a PhD in Philosophy with the Open University, 1986. For ten years from 1983 he was a Tutor-counsellor with the Open University and a Tutor in Philosophy. Since 1981 he has also taught in the Department of Philosophy, University of Durham, becoming a full-time lecturer in 1993. He became Head of Department in 2001 and Reader in 2004. In recent years he has taught mainly in the areas of Moral Theory, Applied Ethics and the Philosophy of Religion. His latest book, *After Evil: Responding to Wrongdoing*, was published by Ashgate in 2004. He has also edited *Children, Parents and Politics* (Cambridge University Press, 1989) and (with Eve Garrard) *Moral Philosophy and the Holocaust* (Ashgate, 2003).

JEFFREY C. BENDREMER is Staff Archaeologist with the Mohegan Tribe Historic Preservation Department, Connecticut, USA, and author of many articles on North American indigenous archaeology, tribal affairs, and archaeological ethics.

CHIP COLWELL-CHANTHAPHONH is Preservation Fellow at the Center for Desert Archaeology, Tucson, Arizona, USA.

ROBIN CONINGHAM is Professor of Archaeology at the University of Durham, UK. In addition to his research interests in Asian archaeology, he is an archaeological consultant and adviser to the Asia Pacific unit of the UNESCO World Heritage Centre.

DAVID E. COOPER is Professor of Philosophy at the University of Durham, UK. He has written widely on nineteenth- and twentieth-century German thought, and on collective responsibility and war crimes. He is the author of many books, including *Existentialism* (Blackwell, 1990), *The Measure of Things* (Oxford University Press, 2002) and *World Philosophies* (2nd edn, Blackwell, 2003).

RACHEL COOPER is Lecturer in Philosophy at Lancaster University, UK. She has published a number of papers in the philosophy of science.

SANDRA M. DINGLI is a Lecturer in Philosophy at the University of Malta and member of the Maltese historical guides association. She has edited several publications on creative thinking, including *Creative Thinking: A Multifaceted Approach* (Malta University Press, 1994). She is the author of *On Thinking and the World: John McDowell's Mind and World* (Ashgate, 2005).

T. J. FERGUSON owns Anthropological Research, LLC, a research company in Tucson, Arizona, where he is also an Adjunct Professor of Anthropology at the University of Arizona. He is the author of several books and numerous articles on the archaeology and ethnology of indigenous people in the Southwestern United States.

LEO GROARKE is Professor of Philosophy and Dean of the Brantford Campus, Wilfrid Laurier University, Canada. He has published extensively on ethics, aesthetics, logic and the history of ideas, and has a special interest in the ethics of political and social structures.

JULIE HOLLOWELL is Research Associate at the Department of Anthropology, University of Indiana, USA. She has published several articles on ethical issues in archaeology, in particular the problem of looting. She is a co-editor of *Ethical Issues in Archaeology* (AltaMira Press, 2003).

DOUGLAS P. LACKEY is Professor of Philosophy at Baruch College and the Graduate Center, City University of New York. His many publications include *Moral Principles and Nuclear Weapons* (Rowman and Littlfield, 1984), *The Ethics of War and Peace* (Prentice Hall, 1989) and *Ethics and Strategic Defense* (Prentice Hall, 1990).

ROBERT LAYTON is Professor of Anthropology in the University of Durham, UK. Among his numerous publications are *Anthropology of Art* (Cambridge University Press, 2001) and his edited volume *Conflict in the Archaeology of Living Traditions* (Routledge, rev. edn, 1994).

OLIVER LEAMAN is Professor of Philosophy and Zantker Professor of Judaic Studies at the University of Kentucky, USA. He has written and edited a number of books in the area of Islamic and Jewish Philosophy.

ATLE OMLAND is a doctoral student in archaeology at the University of Oslo, Norway, and has published papers on aspects of Nordic archaeology and on World Heritage issues.

MARK POLLARD is Edward Hall Professor of Archaeological Science and Director of the Research Laboratory for Archaeology and the History of Art at the University of Oxford, UK. He has a PhD in Physics and is a Member of the Royal Society of Chemistry. He is also a Fellow of the Society of Antiquaries and a Member of the Institute of Field Archaeologists.

KENNETH A. RICHMAN is Associate Professor of Philosophy and Healthcare Ethics at the Massachusetts College of Pharmacy and Earth Sciences, Boston, USA, and author of articles on early modern philosophy, bioethics and the philosophy of medicine. His book *Ethics and the Metaphysics of Medicine* is available from MIT Press.

SARAH TARLOW is Lecturer in Historical Archaeology in the University of Leicester, UK. Her books include *Bereavement and Commemoration: An Archaeology of Mortality* (Blackwell, 1999) and the edited volume *Thinking through the Body* (Kluwer, 2001), and she has written several articles on archaeological theory and on the archaeology of death.

GILLIAN WALLACE is a Research Associate in Wetland Geoarchaeology in the Department of Geography at the University of Hull, UK. She obtained her MPhil and PhD in Archaeology from the University of Cambridge. Research projects have included the 'Integrated Management of European Wetlands' (in which she focused on local perceptions of the environment, conservation and the development of responsible tourism), and the T-PLUS project, which investigated the origins of landscape use and settlement in the North Tyrolean Alps.

GARY WARRICK is Assistant Professor of Contemporary Studies, Wilfrid Laurier University, Canada. His research interests lie in Iroquoian archaeology, Ontario archaeology, colonialism and native peoples, and the history of the Grand River watershed, on all of which he has published.

JAMES O. YOUNG is Professor of Philosophy and Chair of the Department of Philosophy, University of Victoria, Canada. He has wide interests in philosophy and is currently researching the aesthetic and moral issues raised by cultural appropriation. He is the author of *Global Anti-Realism* (1995), *Art and Knowledge* (2001) and many philosophical papers.

Acknowledgements

We should like to thank the staff of Cambridge University Press, especially Simon Whitmore who commissioned the volume and Annie Lovett who saw it through the press, Nancy Ford who compiled the index and copy-editor Frances Brown. We are also most grateful to Katie Boyle for her invaluable assistance in resolving the copy-editing and bibliographical queries. Finally, we owe particular thanks to our contributors for responding patiently and cheerfully to our many queries.

CHRIS SCARRE,
GEOFFREY SCARRE

CHAPTER I

Introduction

Chris Scarre and Geoffrey Scarre

This book aims to promote dialogue between archaeologists, anthropologists and philosophers on significant ethical issues raised by the contemporary practice of archaeology. We believe that it represents the first attempt at an intellectual interchange between philosophically minded archaeologists and anthropologists, and philosophers with an interest in archaeology. But we do not think, in view of the growing sense of the importance of archaeological ethics and of the difficulty of many of the issues, that it will be the last.

The twenty-one authors of the chapters that follow comprise ten archaeologists, four anthropologists and seven philosophers. The two editors are an archaeologist and a philosopher. Since the 1980s there has been much good and innovative writing on the ethics of their discipline by archaeologists themselves and a number of substantial anthologies on the subject have appeared in print. That is just as it should be, since ethical problems in archaeology are the problems of archaeologists. It is researchers in the field who encounter the problems at first hand, and their reflections carry the authority of experience. To have to deal with a moral dilemma is a very different thing from abstractly theorising about it in one's study, and can involve a much steeper learning curve.

But whilst archaeologists may have the advantage of relevant experience, few are also trained moral philosophers, with the conceptual tools and analytical skills that have been developed within that tradition over centuries. Ethical thinkers in the west have been wrestling for more than two millennia with deep and difficult questions about what sort of people we should be, what kinds of acts we should perform or avoid, and how we should treat our fellow human beings. In recent years much attention has been devoted by the philosophical community to moral problems arising within such special contexts as the law, medical treatment and research, genetic engineering, business and the commercial world, and the management of the environment. Cooperation between philosophers and professionals in these and other areas has produced new insights and understanding that would otherwise have remained elusive. It is our conviction that similar happy results will flow from a pooling of their efforts by archaeologists, anthropologists and philosophers.

Whilst this book does not purport to cover every theoretically or practically important ethical question that faces archaeologists, or those with an interest in the subject, its scope is broad. Among the topics addressed are: archaeologists' relations with indigenous peoples; the virtues, professional standards and responsibilities of researchers; the role of ethical codes; the notion of value in archaeology; concepts of steward-ship and custodianship; the meaning and moral implications of 'heritage', local and universal; the question of who 'owns' the past or has a right to interpret it; the problem of 'looting' and the trade in antiquities; the repatriation of skeletal material and culturally significant artefacts; and archaeologists' treatment of the dead.

A major purpose of the book is to show how important moral ques-tions such as these can be approached in a more appropriate analytical manner than they sometimes have been. Thus the editors do not share the view expressed by Karen Vitelli, in the introduction to her 1996 collection *Archaeological Ethics*, that 'One need not be trained in philosophy, an expert in cultural property law, or even have followed closely the fast-growing body of literature on the subject, to be qualified to teach a course on archaeological ethics.' Vitelli rightly remarks that 'Any serious and conscientious archaeologist will discover that she or he harbours a wealth of relevant experience' (Vitelli 1996b: 21). But it would be naïve to think that experience, taken raw, can provide all the moral answers. One may be a serious and conscientious researcher, and a decent human being to boot, without necessarily finding it easy to appraise moral claims, weigh up and decide between conflicting interests, or determine the dutiful or virtuous thing to do – still less deliver a course on archaeological ethics. In our view, good intentions are not enough and any worthwhile writing in this area needs to be both well informed and philosophically rigorous. The experts we have invited to contribute to this collection approach their topics from a variety of perspectives but are all, we believe, well able to meet these exacting standards.

Ethics is concerned with the critical appraisal of human conduct and character. Moral judgements are sharply distinct in kind from factual ones. In the words of J. H. Muirhead, everything can be looked at from two points of view: 'We may take it simply as it is, seeking to discover how it came to be the thing it is, and how it is related to other things; or we may compare it with some ideal of what it ought to be' (Muirhead 1912: 414). We can say what a person is doing (description) or we can judge whether she ought to be doing it or how creditable her performance is (evaluation). Sometimes ethics is presented as if it were chiefly concerned with dampers on action: dos and don'ts, rules, limits and constraints. But that is a distorted image. Ethics is also about positive and attractive springs of action: values, goals and ideals, aspirations, and personal and social fulfilment. The subject of perhaps the greatest of all ethical treatises, Aristotle's *Nicomachean Ethics*, is the living of a human life in its best possible form. For Aristotle, ethics is about locating and attaining the highest goods available to us (identified by him with excellences of mind and character). People who keep their moral hands clean and satisfy the bare requirements of acceptable behaviour may be described as minimally ethical agents. In contrast, those who follow a more inspiring view of the ethical life not merely avoid the bad but energetically pursue the good.

These ideas carry over into professional ethics, though with an important caveat. Archaeologists should be seeking to realise the highest goods of their profession, whatever these may be. Deciding what they are is one important part of archaeological ethics; determining how they may *legitimately* be achieved is another. This second clause is the one that conveys the caveat. The problem is that the highest goods for the archaeological profession may not always be compatible with the highest goods for other groups of people. Thus, to take an obvious example, an ancient cemetery whose excavation would yield rich archaeological data may be a sacred site for an indigenous community. The archaeologists' end of knowledge is at odds with the local people's end of preserving and respecting the remains of the ancestors. Once upon a time – and not so many years ago – researchers too often assumed that the interests of science trumped all other interests. A classic instance is the series of excavations carried out by the cultural anthropologist Aleš Hrdlička in Larsen Bay, Alaska, in the early 1930s, in which several hundreds of skeletons and many thousands of mortuary items and other artefacts were removed to the Smithsonian Institution in the face of vehement and sustained objections by the local population. As Randall McGuire has remarked, for anthropologists and archaeologists of Hrdlička's stamp, the objects they uncovered 'were data, not mothers, fathers, aunts, and uncles' (McGuire 1994b: 182). Small wonder then that, in the words of another recent scholar, Hrdlička displayed 'a gruff and belligerent manner of dealing with native peoples

who appeared at the dig site to protest the disturbance of their ancestors'
(FitzHugh 1994: viii).

The ethics of any profession cannot be conceived in isolation from
ethics in general. Moreover we should be good persons before being good
archaeologists, philosophers, politicians or bus-drivers. No doubt a researcher like Hrdlička had a clear view of the goods he was seeking. He
was also *right* to think that the knowledge and understanding he sought
were goods worth having. But Hrdlička's was also a striking case of moral
tunnel vision. His brusque, not to say brutal, treatment of the local
protesters reflected not only a disproportionate weighting of his own
goals but also, one suspects, his unquestioning belief in the racial superiority of whites to Indians and the consequent right of the former to
exploit the latter. Such blatant racism amongst archaeologists and anthropologists is happily now a thing of the past. Yet we should beware of
resting on our laurels, however enlightened and egalitarian we believe
ourselves. As several of the writers in this book remind us, it is easy even
for well-intentioned researchers, through ignorance or inadvertence, to
show insufficient respect for native people and their traditions.

Attempts by archaeologists to formulate principles of ethics to guide
their practice have by and large recognised the importance of accommodating the goals of the profession to broader moral requirements. Whilst
doubts are sometimes expressed as to whether archaeological ethics can be
satisfactorily reduced to a neat system of general principles (see, e.g.,
Hamilton 1995; Tarlow 2001b), codes such as that propounded by the
Society for American Archaeology in 1994 at least provoke thought on the
relations between archaeologists' goals and the morally significant interests of those whom their activities affect. They also afford an opportunity
to reflect on the points of possible intersection or convergence of the
interests of archaeologists and others. For example, the fourth principle of
the SAA's code is headed 'Public education and outreach' and encourages
archaeologists to disseminate their findings to all who are interested in the
preservation and interpretation of the past, 'including students, teachers,
lawmakers, Native Americans, government officials, environmentalists,
service organizations, retirees, reporters, and journalists' (Lynott and
Wylie 1995: 23). The praiseworthy intention behind this provision is to
lessen the sense of an 'us and them' divide between archaeologists and
other constituencies, and to emphasise that the goods of archaeologists are
by no means exclusive to them.

We have divided the chapters in this volume into four sections,
although many of the themes intersect and overlap and these divisions

are to some extent arbitrary. Nor do all the authors find themselves in agreement on key issues. The emphasis throughout is on the obligations of archaeologists as practising professionals, though several of the chapters seek to balance these against the rights and obligations of other interest groups.

We begin with a group of papers focusing on the ownership of cultural objects. The very term 'cultural' implies that these objects possess a special status which removes them from the ordinary and everyday, and raises the question how 'ownership' in such objects is to be assigned and understood. James Young identifies four categories of potential owner for archaeological finds (excluding remains of the dead). These may be individuals (including both collectors and museums on the one hand, and the finders or archaeologists on the other); or some larger grouping such as a culture, a nation, or indeed humanity as a whole. He supports the claim of 'cultures' but not on the basis that any group inherits rights to objects which may be centuries or millennia old; cultural, ethnic, social and religious change make any such claim difficult to accept as a universal. Instead, he takes the view that no one has inherited a claim to many archaeological finds but that the ownership question should focus on the current value of those finds for living communities. This may in the case of specially significant objects mean indigenous or other special interest groups, though he argues that many finds might more properly remain with their discoverers. Furthermore, other principles must be invoked, including the need in most cases to ensure the preservation or conservation of an object, the desirability of public access, and the principle that separated parts of cultural property ought to be reunited. Where Young differs from some of the other contributors to this volume is in denying the utility of the concept that archaeological finds are the common heritage of all humanity. As he observes, although we may wonder whether archaeological finds should be 'owned' in the same way as ordinary personal property, at the end of the day decisions have to be made about who ought to hold such objects. The 'common heritage' question is none the less an important principle to which we return in the final section of this volume.

Oliver Leaman contrasts the legal ownership of cultural artefacts with the moral or political criteria that might be cited to justify such ownership. If cultural artefacts belong in some way to the wider community, legal ownership can never be absolute. At the same time, Leaman contests the view that ownership should be decided simply or largely on moral criteria of desert. He argues for the parallel between care of artefacts and care of children; parents are allowed freedom to bring up their children in a diversity of different ways, and other authorities only intervene in cases of neglect or abuse. In the case of artefacts, this would require some definition of the public good against which the proper care of artefacts could be measured. The difficulty of defining such a 'public good' leads Leaman to argue that if we were to contemplate removing an object from its owner then we would need to show not only that it would do better elsewhere than with its present owner, but that its present owner may represent a danger to the object's future. He cites various ways in which different kinds of ownership might be beneficial (for instance in spreading the products of different cultures around the world and placing monetary value on their survival) and concludes that a diversity in the ownership of artefacts is ultimately the best state of affairs.

The concept of cultural artefacts as private property to be bought and sold raises the key issue of commodification. This is addressed directly by Robert Layton and Gillian Wallace, who begin by defining cultural property as artefacts and buildings that embody the values and traditions of a community such that concern about their fate transcends legal ownership. Layton and Wallace hence agree with Leaman that ownership of cultural objects cannot be or should not be determined merely on the basis of modern Western concepts of private property. From an anthropological perspective, concepts of ownership vary considerably from culture to culture. Traditional societies may consider certain cultural objects as simply inalienable, their ownership vested not in an individual but in the wider community or clan. Furthermore, such 'ownership' may extend beyond physical objects to include oral performances or religious practices and beliefs. Here there is potential for conflict with Western principles such as copyright, which rely upon the existence of a durable object albeit one that may be a transcript or recording. At the same time, indigenous and other local communities may manage and benefit from the commodification of their culture and traditions through practices such as eco-tourism. The looting of archaeological sites by local communities could be considered in the same way: as the financial exploitation of a group's ancestral capital. As Layton and Wallace illustrate, the role of archaeologists in all this is ambiguous; they may sometimes be called in to provide evidence in support of local land claims, though by its nature archaeological evidence is rarely conclusive, and most archaeologists feel uncomfortable about the use of excavation to help resolve political disputes such as that surrounding the destruction of the Ayodhya mosque.

The final chapter in this first group considers the problematic issue of the looting of sites by local communities. Julie Hollowell examines the conflicting ethics of archaeologists seeking to preserve and manage archaeological resources for the future, and the needs of local communities to gain a livelihood. She calls the latter 'subsistence digging' and questions an archaeological ethic which may place the preservation of archaeological remains above the survival of (often impoverished) local people. The issue focuses once again on the ownership of archaeological materials, and on who has the right to control and exploit them. Hollowell warns against the sometimes distant and alienating stance taken by archaeologists, and stresses the need to pay much greater concern to the local communities who may consider archaeological sites as legitimate resources, left them by their ancestors, to be mined for profit. 'Subsistence digging' declines significantly where other sources of income and employment are available. The solution, she suggests, is for archaeologists to involve local communities much more closely in their work, and as far as possible to make the archaeological heritage the basis for the sustainable employment of local people.

The second part of this volume concerns the responsibilities of archaeologists towards other interest groups, including (though not restricted to) indigenous peoples and local communities. Jeffrey Bendremer and Kenneth Richman advocate the extension of human subjects reviews to archaeological projects. They accept that anthropologists generally approach their work with a desire to benefit the host communities, but observe that considerable harm has none the less resulted in many cases, owing to a lack of mutual understanding. Human subjects reviews (as used in regard to biomedical projects in the United States) would address the problem by requiring formal consent from the local community or the descendants of the people being studied before an archaeological project was given clearance to proceed. The basis for the approach lies in the ethical principles enshrined in the Belmont Report produced by the US National Commission for the Protection of Human Subjects of Biomedical and Behavioral Research in 1979 to guide biomedical research. This arose from discussions at a seminar held at the Smithsonian Institution Belmont Conference Center three years earlier. The key ethical principles recognised in the Belmont Report comprise respect for persons; beneficence; and justice. Bendremer and Richman also advocate involving local communities not only in negotiating the ways that archaeological projects may be carried out but also in the choice of research questions to be addressed by those projects. These proposals have particular resonance in a North American or colonial context, but could be applied more widely, wherever local communities can be involved in the planning and execution of archaeological fieldwork.

Bendremer and Richman focus on the practical mechanisms which might be installed to ensure that archaeological work conforms to ethical standards; Chip Colwell-Chanthaphonh and T. J. Ferguson take a different line, considering not the rules and procedures but the ethical basis for archaeologists' obligations towards both living and dead communities. They propose Virtue Ethics as the basis for these relationships. Virtue Ethics revolve around questions of character and trust, and place emphasis not on codes of practice or regulations but on the subjectivities of social interactions. Establishing mutual relations of trust between archaeologists and local or indigenous communities here again emerges as a key objective; but Colwell-Chanthaphonh and Ferguson argue that this can be extended to the dead, with whom we also have a relationship which leads us to cultivate respect for their remains and to treat them with dignity. The principle that archaeologists have direct obligations towards the deceased (not merely through the medium of their living descendants) opens the much wider issue of the appropriate treatment of human remains, to which we return in a later section of this volume.

Archaeologists have a growing awareness of the need to respect the wishes of indigenous communities amongst whom they work. This is borne out in most recent codes of ethics and in national legislation such as NAGPRA in the United States. As David E. Cooper argues, however, archaeologists have responsibilities which extend beyond these considerations, to professional integrity and 'truthfulness'. The desire for epistemic inclusion – the acceptance that archaeologists do not have the sole authority in dealing with and interpreting the past – may sometimes result in conflict between the results of archaeological work and the beliefs of local or indigenous communities. Cooper observes that the willingness by archaeologists to relinquish control over remains of the past (e.g. by returning the dead for reburial by descendent communities) must be carefully distinguished from the abandonment of archaeological interpretations in favour of a particular community's mythical beliefs about the past. The latter would be to abrogate the virtue of truthfulness. Respect for indigenous beliefs and interpretations should not lead archaeologists to abandon their archaeological understanding of the material they uncover.

The background to the NAGPRA legislation, and its implications, run through several of these chapters. Douglas Lackey addresses the issue head on, examining the ethical principles behind the aims and operation of the Act. Like Cooper, he argues that respect for indigenous beliefs and practices must be viewed alongside considerations of other and equally legitimate demands, including those arising from science and aesthetics. He questions whether the claims of indigenous communities to possess and perhaps rebury or destroy human remains or cultural objects should in ethical terms outweigh the desire to study or inspect (have access to) those remains. NAGPRA makes no reference to the competing demands of science or aesthetics, but simply seeks to return objects to their rightful owners. Lackey concludes that the ethical argument is not so simple, and that, on ethical grounds, competing claims cannot always be so easily dismissed.

The recurrent contention that archaeological or cultural remains cannot be owned absolutely in the same way as most other private property leads to the concept of 'stewardship': that archaeologists or others who possess these remains hold them in trust for the wider community. Attractive though this idea might be, Leo Groarke and Gary Warrick demonstrate its inadequacies, for 'stewardship' is exercised on behalf of another, but in this case that 'other' is hard to identify. Not only is the concept of stewardship vague, but it is impracticable, since it assumes that it is possible to manage the archaeological resource in the interests of all stakeholders, whereas in reality many of those will make conflicting demands (for preservation, ownership, redevelopment, etc.). It may be more appropriate to regard the archaeological profession as only one among several interest groups whose competing claims might more appropriately be decided in the political arena; archaeologists cannot at one and the same time be advocates for the archaeological resources and adjudicators in disputes about them. Furthermore, Groarke and Warrick argue that there is more to ethics than stewardship and that archaeologists' ethical obligations go much further than this and include commitments to honesty, openness and professional standards. They propose that the principle of stewardship should be coupled with a principle of archaeological professionalism.

Many see the ethics of dealing with the remains of the past as focused on the claims and obligations of living communities. An alternative view, however, argues that we also have obligations towards the dead themselves. This is the view taken by Colwell-Chanthaphonh and Ferguson in the context of Virtue Ethics, as we have seen. It is developed further in the two contributions to the third section of this volume. Geoffrey Scarre draws attention to the second principle of the Vermillion Accord, which requires respect for the wishes of the dead concerning the disposition of their remains, wherever those wishes are known or can be reasonably inferred. Archaeologists whose work disturbs remains of the dead frequently try to act with great sensitivity towards the feelings of descendent communities. It is a very different thing to claim that the wishes of the dead in their own right should be respected. Scarre argues that although we may believe that death is an end to existence, in another sense people can be injured after death if their posthumous wishes or desires are not respected. Dead people remain in many respects interest-holders, and their memory or reputation may be harmed by things which happen after their death. This does not mean that the interests of living archaeologists (or developers) may not often override the claims of the dead, but it raises an issue that requires further debate.

Sarah Tarlow also argues that dead people may be harmed by activities in the present, and emphasises the need for research on human remains (as in the sphere of medical research) to be justified by a demonstrably beneficial consequence. She furthermore points to the special responsibility that archaeologists have in interpreting or reconstructing the lives or physical appearance of dead individuals. Is it ethical to construct unflattering depictions of the humans who are being studied? The question is not simply one of honesty and accuracy (principles to which all archaeologists should subscribe) but concerns the dilemma posed by hypotheses or interpretations which may be more loosely tied to the archaeological evidence. Tarlow also observes that however much archaeologists seek to operate sensitively with regard to others, conflict is almost inevitable when dealing with people whose ethics are differently constructed from our own; that, in essence, there can be no absolute set of ethical principles that we can expect everybody to accept.

The final trio of chapters in this volume address the idea that cultural and archaeological remains cannot belong to private owners, local communities or interest groups in any absolute way since they must be considered the common heritage of humankind. Some forty years ago the Government of Malta proposed to the United Nations that the oceans should be regarded as the common heritage of everyone, and the concept has been applied to other extraterritorial entities such as outer space or Antarctica. Sandra M. Dingli argues that the same rationale should apply to archaeology, on the basis that the past belongs to no one, but is instead the shared cultural heritage of everyone, including future generations. This leads her to three important consequences: that the past must be managed for the benefit of all humankind; that it must be conserved for future generations; and (perhaps more controversially) that it should be used for exclusively peaceful purposes. She suggests that such an approach would also produce an enhanced understanding of archaeological sites and remains, leading away from politically motivated or trivialised interpretations to a more sophisticated reading of the past. It would also raise international awareness of the need to safeguard the cultural heritage against chronic problems of damage and destruction.

Atle Omland explores the same question of 'common heritage' through the medium of the UNESCO World Heritage concept and the designation of sites as part of that World Heritage. Despite various objections that have been raised against the World Heritage Convention, he argues that it provides a global ethical solution to the worldwide destruction of sites by establishing an international fund for their protection and by encouraging respect for the cultural heritage of others. Like Dingli, he sees World Heritage as an instrument for peace, and urges that cultural heritage be depoliticised to avoid its abuse by nationalist interests. Such an approach does not exclude the use of cultural heritage by local groups such as indigenous peoples seeking to maintain their identities, but Omland observes the dangers of 'essentialist' notions of culture and the exclusion of 'strangers' – refugees, stateless people and immigrants – that current approaches generally entail. A more inclusive understanding of the global cultural heritage would overcome these restrictions.

The final chapter considers in detail the criteria used for selecting cultural and archaeological sites for inclusion in lists of places or monuments to be protected and preserved. Robin Coningham, Rachel Cooper and Mark Pollard observe that one criterion that is frequently cited is that certain sites are 'unique' or 'valuable' in some special sense that sets them apart from the rest. The concept of uniqueness is particularly problematic and open to a wide diversity of interpretations; the 1980 ruling that Mohenjodaro and Harappa were not sufficiently different from each other for both to merit inclusion in the World Heritage list strikes many archaeologists as absurd. The preservation of the 'unique' timber circle of Seahenge by the removal and conservation of its timbers elsewhere raises further questions about the values and criteria (here academic rather than symbolic or aesthetic) that drive decisions about the archaeological heritage. The chapter returns us to the practical difficulties that lie behind the implementation of any ethical code for the ownership and protection of archaeological remains.

We expect that readers of this volume will be left not with solutions but with a series of questions. Although the chapters do not provide

tailor-made answers or quick fixes to specific problems about archaeological practice, we hope that they will stimulate wider reflection on the
key issues they raise. Do archaeologists have some privileged status in
dealing with the remains of the past or deriving meanings therefrom? For
what reasons should we consider cultural and archaeological remains to be
different from other kinds of material product or possession? Do we have
obligations to the dead themselves, and not just to their living descendants? Do the past and its remains belong to anyone (everyone?), or do they
have a value which transcends ordinary concepts of property? Is it ethically acceptable to use the archaeological record to support particular ideas
of identity or belonging? These are just a few of the questions that are
raised in the chapters that follow. We hope that readers will find many of
their conventional notions challenged, and be inspired to seek new and
deeper meanings for an ethics of archaeology.

PART I

The ownership of cultural objects

CHAPTER 2

Cultures and the ownership of archaeological finds

James O. Young

The question of who ought to own the artefacts archaeologists find has generated a vast literature. Lawyers, archaeologists, anthropologists, museum curators, aboriginal rights activists and others have written extensively on the question of who has a right to archaeological finds.[1] This literature has been part of the larger literature concerned with cultural appropriation. With very few exceptions, philosophers have had nothing to say about the appropriation of archaeological finds.[2] This is unfortunate since ethical questions lie at the root of the legal and public policy debates about ownership of archaeological finds. This chapter is designed to provide the ethical framework required for the resolution of some of these debates. I am particularly interested in the suggestion that a culture can have a claim on archaeological finds. My hypothesis is that, some of the time, a culture has a rightful claim on archaeological finds.

CANDIDATE OWNERS

At least four types of candidates can be identified as possible rightful owners of archaeological finds. The first possible owners of find are individuals. These individuals could be either individual people or institutions such as museums. Individual owners could be those who have found artefacts or those who have fairly acquired them from the individuals who have. Alternatively, a find might be owned by a culture. So, for example, one might hold that some find belongs to the members of Greek culture. One also hears the suggestion that archaeological finds are part of

---

1 In addition to works cited below, some of the most noteworthy contributions to the literature include Battiste and Henderson 2000, Brown 1998, Handler 1991, and Nason 1997. Two law reviews have devoted entire issues to the ownership of tangible cultural property, including archaeological finds. See *Arizona State Law Journal* 24 (1992), 1–562 and a Special Issue of *University of British Columbia Law Review* 29 (1995), 1–345.
2 The exceptions: Dummett 1986, Thompson 2003, and Warren 1999. See also Wylie 1995.

the patrimony of a nation. This is the view adopted by the Government of Mexico, which claims ownership of all pre-Columbian artefacts in the country. Similarly, in Scotland and Denmark all archaeological finds belong to the Crown (Gerstenblith 1995a). The same view is implicit in the 1970 UNESCO Convention on the Means of Prohibiting and Preventing Illicit Import, Export and Transfer of Ownership of Cultural Property. Finally, certain pieces of tangible cultural property are held to be the common inheritance of all humanity. This is the view adopted in the 1954 Hague Convention for the Protection of Cultural Property in the Event of Armed Conflict. The Preamble to this document refers to some cultural property (which will include certain archaeological finds) as 'the cultural heritage of all mankind'.[3] The 1972 UNESCO Convention for the Protection of World Cultural and Natural Heritage takes a similar stand. It classifies certain items of tangible cultural property as 'the heritage of all the nations of the world'.[4]

Let me begin by discounting the suggestion that the whole of humanity is the rightful owner of archaeological finds. I am not unsympathetic to this suggestion. As we will see, it will often be difficult to identify an individual who has, or group of individuals who have, a clear claim to have inherited certain archaeological finds. In such instances we may want to say that everyone has as good a claim as anyone else. If everyone has an equal claim on some item, we may say that it belongs to everyone or, alternatively, to no one. The trouble with this suggestion is that it has, in practice, very little value. We are seeking guidance in answering questions about who ought to possess artefacts that cannot be possessed by everyone. The proposition that something is the patrimony of all does not assist us in answering this question. Although one can wonder whether archaeological finds are owned in the same way as ordinary personal property is owned, at the end of the day we have to determine who ought to have them. The people who ought to have them might as well be called the owners. (Notice that artefacts are different from items of intellectual property. All of humanity can possess some item of intellectual property in a way that they cannot possess some amphora or a stele.)

Although I will defend the suggestion that cultures own some archaeological finds, I do not want to deny that individuals and nations can also own them. Sometimes, I think, an individual can acquire a right to archaeological finds simply by appropriating them from a state of nature.

3 Found at http://www.icomos.org/hague/HaguePreamble.html.
4 Found at http://sedac/ciesin.org/pidb/texts/world.heritage.1972.html.

At the same time, I will attempt to establish the limits on this right. The suggestion that a nation is the rightful owner of certain archaeological finds can also be defended in some contexts. Sometimes, however, it seems that a culture will have a stronger claim on finds than a nation. Consider Mexico's claim to own all of the pre-Columbian artefacts within its borders. Mexico, like many nations, is a multicultural state. It is composed of the descendants of the conquistadors as well as the descendants of the indigenous population. One of the indigenous cultures within Mexico may have much better claim on certain pre-Columbian artefacts than does the nation as a whole. A similar point can be made about the US, Canada and many other nations. An aboriginal culture in one of these countries may have a stronger claim on a find than the nation as a whole. (In the case of culturally homogenous nations, the situation will be different.) The principal aim of this chapter is to establish when and on what basis a culture has a legitimate claim on particular articles of cultural property, including archaeological finds.

Before going any further, a preliminary point needs to be addressed. I have spoken of cultures, but one might wonder about how a culture is to be defined. One might even wonder about whether the concept of, say, Greek culture can be defined. I certainly assume the concept of some specified culture can be defined. I need to assume this because a definition of some culture specifies membership in the culture and thus identifies the people who may have a claim on some archaeological find. I do not believe, however, that a culture can be defined by giving necessary and sufficient conditions. That is, I do not believe that necessary and sufficient conditions can be given for membership in a given culture. (So I am not an 'essentialist' about cultures.) Rather, I believe that a concept such as the concept of Greek culture is (in Wittgenstein's sense of the word) a family resemblance concept. Someone is a member of a culture who has enough of an amorphous set of cultural traits. So, for example, one cannot define Canadian culture in terms of some shared set of beliefs, practices, customs and values. Rather, someone belongs to Canadian culture who has enough of a pool of traits: fanaticism about ice hockey, commitment to universal health care, suspicion about American foreign policy, and so on. Of course, matters are more complex than this picture indicates. People can belong to more than one culture at a time. So, for example, someone might belong to Western culture, Greek culture, Cretan culture, Christian culture, and so on. I cannot here do justice to all of the issues raised in this paragraph. I will simply assume that it is possible to identify the members of a culture who are supposed to own some archaeological find.

TWO BASES FOR A CULTURE'S CLAIM ON ARCHAEOLOGICAL FINDS

We need to begin by asking what gives a culture a claim on archaeological finds. Let me begin by stating the obvious. Cultures do not make archaeological discoveries. Individuals or groups of individuals do. So it is hard to see how a culture can claim to have appropriated artefacts that exist in a state of nature. That being the case, it seems to me that two basic approaches are available.

The first sort of approach reflects on the history of some recovered artefact and comes to the conclusion that we can trace ownership of an artefact from its original owners to the members of some contemporary culture. This approach says that a culture inherits a right to certain artefacts from those who produced them or who were otherwise the last rightful owners.

The second sort of approach to the ownership of archaeological finds takes as its starting point the claim that the archaeological record of the past has value for all of humanity. On this view, no one has inherited a claim to many archaeological finds. Instead, we should focus on the current value of archaeological finds. The second approach encourages us to ask how finds can have the greatest value for all of humanity. Sometimes, at least, the answer to this question will be that a culture ought to have certain finds, usually one with certain affinities to the culture which produced the found artefacts. In my view, the second approach is the best. Many archaeological finds are in a state of nature and without owners. Nevertheless, since they often have great value for all of humanity, it is wrong to say that they can be appropriated by whoever finds them. Since not everyone can possess finds, we need to ask pragmatic questions. We need to know who will benefit most from possession of a given artefact.

My strategy will be to examine critically the suggestion that cultures inherit a right to certain archaeological finds. I will then explain why I believe that it is more fruitful to focus on the value that certain finds have for particular cultures. I will call the first approach the *inheritance approach*. The second I will call the *cultural value approach*.

THE CONCEPT OF INHERITANCE DOES NOT APPLY

The first problem with the inheritance approach is that it employs a concept, that of inheritance, that it has no application in the present context. Central to the concept of inheritance is the notion of respect for the final testamentary wishes of property owners. In contexts where the testamentary wishes of owners cannot be known or do not exist, the concept of inheritance does not apply. I suggest that archaeological finds often exist in such contexts.

Archaeological finds typically did not begin their lives as the property of a culture. Most of the things archaeologists dig up were the property of an individual person, a family, a clan, a religious community or a state. Generally, we can have no idea what their testamentary wishes might be. When we do not know the testamentary wishes of the last owners, they are in a position similar to that of people who die intestate. When people die intestate, certain procedures for deciding who inherits are followed. These procedures make counterfactual presumptions about who the beneficiaries would have been, had a last testament been formulated and recorded. It is highly unlikely that the intended beneficiaries of the last owners were the members of a culture as a whole. On the contrary, it is likely that an individual would have intended that property remain within his family. Probably this would be so, even when family members do not share his culture. I know that I would like my children to inherit my estate, even if they should move to Chad, profess Islam and speak Arabic. Religious communities would have liked to retain ownership within the communion and so on. A Greek from ancient Sparta would probably be horrified by the prospect of his property going to modern Athens, even if that is the seat of the closest surviving culture.

A culture might be thought to be the beneficiary of last resort. Archaeological finds often originate in the remote past. Consequently, it is often impossible to identify an individual owner's next of kin. Frequently states, clans and religious communions have ceased to exist. Consequently, none of these can be a beneficiary. This being the case, it might seem reasonable to adopt the counterfactual that original owners would have wanted a culture to inherit their property. This strikes me as groundless speculation. It seems just as likely that some individuals in the remote past would have wished their artefacts to be possessed by the wealthiest and most powerful people in the present. Perhaps they would have hoped that their property would be possessed by people who can ensure that it receives a wide audience. Perhaps the ancient Irish would have wished that archaeological finds go to America, where a majority of their descendants lives. There is no way to know which of these counterfactuals, or any of an array of others, is true. Indeed, according to some philosophers of language, one can reasonably doubt whether any of them is true. The situation is complicated further by the fact that we have no reason to believe that all members of a past culture would have the same default testamentary wishes. I conclude that cultures cannot inherit rights to archaeological finds.

Even if we grant that the concept of inheritance could play a role in grounding a culture's claim to archaeological finds, problems remain with the inheritance approach. In this section I identify a problem that arises since cultures evolve and change through time. It is not clear that a culture has a claim on any past culture to which it is not identical.

Cultures are constantly in flux. This partly explains why giving necessary and sufficient conditions for the identity of a culture through time is probably impossible. Nevertheless, it seems clear that after a sufficient degree of cultural change has occurred, one culture has ceased to exist and a numerically distinct one has come into existence. Consider, for example, the culture of the Greeks. There is no obvious sense in which modern Greeks share a culture with their ancient ancestors. Ancient and modern Greeks do not share a religion, a mutually intelligible language, economic activities or, for the most part, cultural practices. Certainly, cultural identity is not the same as ethnic identity. Even if it were, ethnicity is as fluid and easily blurred as cultural identity.

To complicate matters further, cultures can both merge and diverge. That is, two quite distinct cultures can have a common root while a single culture can have multiple origins. When cultures have diverged, a question will arise about which of the cultures has a better claim on artefacts produced by the original culture. Arguably, ancient Greek cultures have diverged into a variety of European cultures, giving many different cultures a claim on the cultural property of ancient Greece. When cultures merge other questions arise. Perhaps, for example, a modern Greek culture may be identified but ancient Greek culture was not unified. One may wonder about whether a composite culture inherits rights to the cultural property of all of its component cultures or none of them. In all probability, the ancient Athenians would have found anathema the suggestion that non-Attic Greeks had any claim on cultural property produced in Athens.

Since cultures can change, merge and diverge, the inheritance approach to cultural ownership faces another difficulty. Imagine that, contrary to what I think likely, some people or institutions in the past would have wished their property to be inherited by the people who share their culture. The trouble is now that it will often be difficult to identify a unique culture that can claim to have inherited a right to archaeological finds created in some past cultural context. In many cases no successor culture can be identified. In others, more than one can be found. In consequence, the inheritance approach is once again unable to ground a culture's claim on archaeological finds.

LOST AND ABANDONED PROPERTY

This section will examine how the loss or abandonment of property affects the debate about ownership of archaeological finds. Let us assume that a culture could be said to inherit certain archaeological finds. A culture's claim to have inherited certain archaeological finds, even if it could withstand my earlier objections, will often be undermined by the fact that such finds are abandoned property. If property is abandoned, those who originally owned it have forfeited their claim to it. One cannot inherit something from someone who has abandoned it. Finders of the property need not seek anyone's approval for their appropriation.

The strength of a finder's claim to property depends in large part on particular circumstances. Common law rightly draws a distinction between lost and abandoned property.[5] The crucial difference between abandoned and lost property is a difference between the intentions of the original owners. One who abandons property intends to give it up. One who has lost property has no such intention. Abandoned property is deemed in common law to have been returned to a state of nature and may be appropriated by the first person who finds it. From a moral perspective it seems clear that this is at least partly right. (It is only partly right because, as will emerge, under some circumstances, a culture may have a claim on abandoned property.) Any right to property is forfeited by a clear intention to abandon the property. Suppose I leave my old toaster out in the garbage for the city to collect. It is carted off to the municipal dump where someone recovers it. I cannot reasonably claim that this person has stolen my toaster. I cannot do so even if I subsequently learn that it is a valuable collectible, a rare 1962 General Electric Toast-O-Matic, worth a fortune. The case of lost property is different. A finder of lost property acquires a right against everyone – except the rightful owner of the property. If the rightful owner can be identified, then the finder loses all rights to the property. People who own property

---

5 For a good discussion of the bearing of common law on tangible cultural property, and citations of the legal authorities, see Gerstenblith 1995.

do not forfeit the right to the property by losing it. Now the question becomes that of whether archaeologists discover lost or abandoned property. Unfortunately, a single, simple answer to this question is not available.

Sometimes it is clear that archaeologists and others have wrongly appropriated property that has not been abandoned. Consider, for example, the War Gods of the Zuni people of the American Southwest. Each year members of the Zuni are commissioned to carve two War Gods (or Ahayu:da), which are believed to guide and protect the tribe. The carvers produce these sculptures with the intention of them becoming the communal property of the Zuni people and it is uncontroversially theirs. At the expiration of each year, the War Gods are moved to secret locations where they are left, exposed to the elements, to decay. The Zuni believe that the decaying War Gods return their powers to the earth (Blair 1979; Merenstein 1992). Over the years, many of the Ahayu:da were recovered and found their way into museums and private collections. This was clearly wrong. The Zuni had formed no intention to abandon their property. Consequently, they retained their right to it. (Fortunately, this story has a happy ending. The rights of the Zuni have been recognised by American courts and the vast majority of the War Gods have been returned to the custody of the Zuni culture.)

Other archaeological finds seem more like abandoned property. Imagine a situation, quite common in the nineteenth century and even in much of the twentieth, where archaeologists recover artefacts about which the local population does not care in the least. (The local population may be assumed to be the inheritors of the culture of those who produced the property in question.) Suppose that some sculptures and works of architecture are lying about neglected and even abused by the local population. They break off pieces of statuary for use in building cottages and fences. (They do so, not out of necessity, but because reusing the stone is easier than quarrying new building materials.) This situation differs from the one in which I throw away my Toast-O-Matic. The people in question have formed no explicit intention to abandon property. Nevertheless, the actions of the local population amount to an abandonment of any claim to have inherited the artefacts produced by their ancestors' culture. Under the circumstances, archaeologists do not seem to act wrongly if they cart off everything they can find.

Once a proprietary right to something has been abandoned, it generally cannot be recovered if someone else has established a claim. Suppose that archaeologists carry off finds to a foreign country. At the time the property is exported, the local population cares nothing for it and has abandoned it. Even were they to be in possession of all available information about the artefacts, let us imagine, they would still not have objected to the export. They may have changed religion since the artefacts were created and regard the artefacts as worse than worthless: blasphemous pagan monstrosities, perhaps. (Imagine that the vast majority of Afghans agreed with the Taleban's view of pre-Islamic artefacts, such as the sculptures of the Buddha at Bamiyam, destroyed in March 2001.) Suppose now that the local population subsequently changes its views about the exported property. Now, the population values it. Under the circumstances, if its claim to ownership of the property depends on its having inherited a right to it, its change of heart comes too late. The situation is analogous to my abandonment of my Toast-O-Matic. After you have recovered it from the dump, and discovered its value, it is too late for me to reclaim my ownership on the grounds that I inherited the toaster from my grandmother.

The case just described is similar to that of the most celebrated and controversial instance of the appropriation of tangible cultural property. I refer to Lord Elgin's removal of the Marbles from the Parthenon, beginning in 1801.[6] By all accounts, the locals were quite happy to knock off pieces of the Parthenon for sale to tourists. When the House of Commons investigated the removal of the Marbles, it asked about the views of the Greeks. An eyewitness reported that, 'Among the Greek population and inhabitants of Athens it occasioned no sort of dissatisfaction . . . so far from exciting any unpleasant sensation, the people seemed to feel it as the means of bringing foreigners into their country, and having money spent among them.'[7] Whatever the status of the Parthenon Marbles, many museums may claim to be holders of property that was abandoned by its original owners. When property is abandoned, it may be freely appropriated. Some archaeological finds seem to fall into this category and this further undermines the inheritance approach to cultural ownership of archaeological finds.

VALUE TO A CULTURE AS A BASIS FOR OWNERSHIP

What I have said so far should have revealed the limitations of the inheritance approach to cultural ownership of archaeological finds. I will

6 For a discussion of the circumstances of the removal of the Elgin Marbles, see Merryman 1985.
7 Report from the House of Commons Select Committee on the Earl of Elgin's Collection of Sculptured Marbles, 25 March 1816, pp. 433–4.

turn now to a consideration of the cultural value approach. In many contexts it is recognised that the value some artefacts have imposes limitations on property rights in those artefacts. I want to go further and claim that, in some cases, the great value an artefact has for some group can carry with it a right to ownership.

It is widely recognised that the great historical or aesthetic value of certain artefacts places limitations on ownership rights. Suppose I were to buy a supremely great painting: one of the masterpieces of Rembrandt, say, or Vermeer. It is clear that my moral rights to the painting are severely limited. I ought not to tamper with the work. I am obliged to care for the painting in a way that I am not obliged to care for less valuable items. Minimally, I ought to ensure that scholars have full access to the work. I may be obliged to ensure that the work is publicly exhibited. I may even be under an obligation to offer the work to a public institution, with the expectation of fair compensation. All of these obligations are imposed by the value that the painting has for humanity. If a work of art has sufficiently great value, I act wrongly in letting it moulder away in my basement. The laws in many jurisdictions explicitly recognise that the value of cultural property can place restrictions on possessors.[8] For example, many jurisdictions have laws that control what may be done with architecturally significant buildings. They may not be demolished or even modified. Other jurisdictions have restrictions on the export of cultural property. The moral intuition underlying these laws is the belief that the value some item has for an entire community gives the community some claim on it.

Sometimes an artefact is valued more highly by some group of people than it is by others. Sometimes the group of people for whom an artefact has special significance is a culture. Stonehenge, for example, has value for all of humanity, but it has a special value for the English. An artefact can have such great value that it becomes tied up with the well-being of a culture. Melina Mercouri, a former Greek minister of culture, held that the Parthenon Marbles had special significance for Greeks: 'You must understand what the Parthenon Marbles mean to us. They are our pride. They are our sacrifices. They are a tribute to the democratic philosophy. They are our aspirations and our name. They are the essence of Greekness.'[9] Mercouri's prose is a little purple, but she is in effect claiming that the Parthenon Marbles have a greater significance for Greek

8 For an excellent discussion of how the social value of artworks and other items places limits on the rights of private owners, and how this is recognised in law, see Sax 1999.
9 Found at http://www.culture.gr/4/41/411/e41106.html.

culture than they have for others. Furthermore, she is suggesting that this gives Greek culture a claim on the Marbles.[10]

We now have the premises needed to establish a culture's claim on certain items, including certain archaeological finds. The first premiss states that the social value of an item can be so great that it is something that ought to be the property of a community. Sometimes this community is all of humanity, as is the case with certain basic scientific ideas. Sometimes a subset of humanity has a particular claim on certain items. This is the second premiss in the present argument. The subset of humanity can be the members of a culture. When this is the case, the culture has a claim on ownership of the item in question. The conclusion may be called the *cultural property principle*: when some archaeological find has significance for the members of some culture, they have a claim to own the artefact. The strength of this claim is proportional to the degree of significance an item has for members of the culture. (As we will see below, this is not the only principle that bears on questions of the ownership of archaeological finds and other artefacts.)

The cultural significance principle may not be as widely applicable as may at first appear. Members of certain cultures sometimes claim that virtually everything produced by past members of the culture is vitally significant, often on the grounds that they are sacred. A member of the Hopi Cultural Protection Office has been quoted as saying that, 'Even something like a digging stick could have a ritual use, but we're not about to say what it is' (Brown 2003). One is often sceptical about claims of this sort. If the cultural significance principle is to ground a culture's claim on some archaeological find, the find must have genuine, substantial and enduring significance for a culture. I am also inclined to say that the principle does not apply when the significance an artefact has for a culture is artificially cultivated. A politician might, for example, whip up enthusiasm for some new archaeological find as a means of harnessing chauvinistic sentiment for his own ends. Under such circumstances, the significance an item has for a culture ought to be discounted. In any case, when the significance some item has for a culture has been artificially cultivated it is unlikely to be substantial or enduring.

The argument leading to the cultural property principle is subject to an obvious objection. Someone might hold that the fact that I find something valuable does not give me a claim on it. I might value your watch

---

10 A lawyer who adopts this view is John Moustakas (1989).

very highly. I may even value it more than you do. But I still do not have any claim on your watch. The fact that a culture values archaeological finds discovered by others may seem to give the culture equally little claim on the finds.

I have two responses to this objection. The first point is that individuals do not have a claim on something merely because they find it valuable. Only when something has a high degree of value for a large group of people does the value of an object become a factor in determining who ought to possess something. Archaeological finds can have a degree of value for a culture sufficient to ground a claim to them. Even this will strike some people as a position which is far too consequentialist. Some people will say that the legitimate claims of those who appropriate items from a state of nature ought not to be overridden by something like the cultural significance principle. To such people I offer my second response. This involves drawing attention to the peculiar nature of archaeological finds. Those who discover archaeological finds do not produce them. They are not earned in anything like the same way you earned the money to buy a watch. So while I believe that the discoverers of archaeological finds acquire some claim on them, I do not believe that the claim is so strong that it cannot be overridden. (Perhaps suitable compensation is due if the claims of finders are overridden.)

The suggestion that a culture has a claim on artefacts it finds valuable (usually ones its members have produced) is sometimes attacked by means of a *reductio ad absurdum*. This suggestion is held to lead to the conclusion that every item of cultural property ought to be returned to its original culture or, at any rate, the surviving culture closest to the original. It is held to follow that every Monet ought to be returned to France, every Haida carving to the Queen Charlotte Islands, every shard of Attic pottery to Greece. This view is absurd, as is any position that entails it. Nevertheless, it may appear difficult to explain why a culture has a claim on some items of tangible cultural property but not on others.

The proposal advanced here is capable of explaining why a culture has a claim on some artefacts but not others. Sometimes the value of an item for a culture is sufficient to ensure that the cultural significance principle trumps other applicable principles. Sometimes, because the value of some property for a culture is relatively low, a culture does not have a claim on certain items. Consider this example. Sitting on the mantelpiece in my front room is a stone arrowhead that my mother dug from her garden in suburban Vancouver. I do not believe that I am morally obliged to deliver this artefact into the keeping of some local First Nation. I certainly do not think that any local band has inherited a right to the arrowhead. For a start, when my mother dug it up, it was abandoned property in a state of nature. More importantly, my arrowhead is a pretty undistinguished and commonplace specimen. It has no particular significance to any aboriginal culture. If it were a rare and unusually beautiful example, or had considerable ritual significance, the situation might be different. As it is, I do not act wrongly in keeping it. I own it.

APPLICATION OF THE CULTURAL SIGNIFICANCE PRINCIPLE

An example will serve to illustrate the application of the cultural significance principle. Arne Magnussen exported certain culturally significant manuscripts from Iceland in the early eighteenth century. Magnussen was born in Iceland, but immigrated to Denmark where he worked in the Royal Archives. Over the course of his life, he acquired a collection of Icelandic manuscripts. Among these was the *Flatejarbók*, which records the journey of Leif Eriksen to North America, and manuscripts of sagas that are central to Icelandic cultural identity. Magnussen acquired these manuscripts fairly. He bought them from individuals who, so far as one can tell, were not coerced. On his death, he bequeathed his library to the University of Copenhagen.

From the perspective of the inheritance approach, the University of Copenhagen had an impeccable claim to the manuscripts. Nevertheless, Icelanders objected to their appropriation. (I take it that Icelanders constitute a culture as well as a nation.) Icelanders did not inherit a claim to the *Flatejarbók* and other manuscripts. Their sole claim on the manuscripts was the great significance they have for Icelandic culture. After a series of lengthy and not always harmonious negotiations, Denmark agreed, in 1971, to return the *Flatejarbók* and other especially significant manuscripts to Iceland. In view of the huge aesthetic and historical significance of these manuscripts for Icelandic culture, this strikes me as the right decision. Given that Iceland has the resources to preserve the manuscripts, they ought to have been in the possession of Icelanders. It does not matter that Icelanders did not inherit a right to the *Flatejarbók*. It does not matter that, at a certain point in their history, Icelanders did not much care for medieval manuscripts. Even the fact that modern Icelanders can scarcely be said to share a culture with the Vikings does not undermine their culture's claim on the manuscripts.

Similar considerations apply to archaeological finds. Stonehenge is not exactly an archaeological *find*. It would be rather hard to miss. Still, it will illustrate the point. Modern English culture is in no way identical to the culture that produced Stonehenge. Moreover, Stonehenge was almost certainly abandoned property. No one cared about it for centuries. Nevertheless, Stonehenge has a special significance for the English. This significance gives the culture as a whole a claim on the monument. Stonehenge was for sale as recently as 1915, when it was sold for £6600. It would have been a travesty had an American tycoon bought it and had it relocated to Druidworld in Florida. Subject to suitable compensation to the buyer (a point to which I will return), the English would have had a strong claim on restitution of the monument.

So far my comments may not seem to have much application to the resolution of questions about ownership of most new archaeological finds. Occasionally a new find will immediately be recognised as having special significance for a culture. In the unlikely event that Excalibur is dug up, it certainly ought to remain in England. Despite the fact that it was used to resist the incursions of the ancestors of many present inhabitants of England, it would have a special significance for English culture. Most finds, however, are comparatively mundane and contribute only to the incremental growth of human knowledge of the past. They have no great significance for any culture. The cultural significance principle still applies to finds of mundane items. Given, however, that the principle states that the claim on a culture is proportional to the significance of the find to the culture, a culture's claim on mundane finds will be rather weak. Still, when no other basis for a claim exists, the cultural significance principle may be enough to establish a culture's claim.

OTHER PRINCIPLES FOR THE ALLOCATION OF ARCHAEOLOGICAL FINDS

The cultural significance principle is not the only principle that ought to be taken into account when determining who ought to possess archaeological finds. At least four other principles can be identified. All of them need to be taken into account in determining who ought to possess archaeological finds.

The paramount principle is the conservation principle: possession of archaeological finds ought to be vested in those best able to preserve them. Unless an object is preserved, it is of value to no one. Consequently, possession of an object ought to be vested in those who are best able to preserve it. Sometimes the persons best able to ensure the preservation of an archaeological find are not members of the culture in which it originated. When this is the case, appropriation of the object is, in general, not wrong. Indeed, it may be morally required.

Under some circumstances, the preservation principle can be overridden by other principles. The case of the Zuni War Gods has already been mentioned. In this case, the conservation principle is trumped by the proprietary principle, described below. The Zuni own the sculptures in question and they may let them rot, if they so choose. If these sculptures had greater aesthetic significance across a range of cultures, we might arrive at a different conclusion.

A decision about possession of archaeological finds made on the basis of the preservation principle is not final. As we have seen, some items will have a special significance for the members of certain cultures. Especially when this is the case, decisions about possession of an item made on the basis of considerations about preservation are subject to review. Imagine the following situation. An artefact has special significance for the members of some culture, but at a given time they do not have the resources or expertise to preserve it. Subsequently, they may acquire these resources and the requisite expertise. (Those who have appropriated the object may, in some circumstances, be obliged to assist another culture in acquiring the resources and expertise.) The question of who ought to possess the item ought then to be reopened.

The next general principle is the access principle. An archaeological find ought to be in the possession of those who are willing and able to make it accessible to all those persons for whom it has value. This principle complements the preservation principle. There is little point in preserving archaeological finds unless they are made available to an audience for which they have value. This audience will include scholars but also the general public. The access principle can, in different situations, be used either to undermine or to support a culture's claims on certain finds. In some cases, it will be important that finds be available to a wider audience than simply members of a single culture. In other cases, it will be most important to ensure that members of a culture for whom a find has special significance have ready access to it.

It is worth noting, in the context of a mention of the access principle, that the basements of the museums of the world are full of undisplayed and unstudied archaeological finds. An artefact that languishes in the basement of the British Museum might be a prized exhibit in the Queen Charlotte Islands.

Many objects are more valuable when their integrity is ensured. This observation leads to the integrity principle. According to this principle, steps ought to be taken to ensure that separated parts of cultural property are united. The property united can be either an individual work or a collection whose value is enhanced by its unity. A work of art, for example, has greater aesthetic value if its parts are displayed together. Consider *Boy with a Ball*, owned by the National Gallery of Washington, and a figure in the Louvre, previously described as an Atlas or a Hercules. In 1970, it was noticed that the two bronzes were stylistically similar. Closer inspection revealed that a projection on the National Gallery's bronze fitted perfectly into a slot on the hand of the Louvre's sculpture. The two pieces were revealed to be parts of *St Christopher Carrying the Christ Child with the Globe of the World*, attributed to Bartolomeo Bellano. The National Gallery of Washington's part of this sculpture is now on permanent loan to the Louvre and the aesthetic value of the reunited sculpture is greater than the value of the separated parts. The reunification of this sculpture is a model application of the integrity principle. It would apply equally to the case of archaeological finds.

The integrity principle will often support the conclusion that archaeological finds ought to be left *in situ*. The aesthetic or historical significance of certain finds is frequently greatest when they are seen in their original context. This is particularly true of finds of architecture and large sculptures. There is an obvious tension between the integrity principle and the preservation principle. Often, finds cannot be left *in situ* without risking or even ensuring their degradation. It is sometimes suggested that, when finds are removed from the places they are found (perhaps on the basis of the preservation principle), they ought to remain close to where they are found. I see no reason for thinking that this ought to be a principle governing the disposition of archaeological finds. If finds ought to remain close to where they were found, this must be a conclusion reached on the basis of one of the principles identified here. One of these might be the cultural significance principle.

Finally, I suggest that we need what might be called the proprietary principle. The interests of those who find lost or abandoned artefacts, or who fairly acquire them from those who do, must be taken into account when questions about ownership of archaeological finds are considered. Indeed, I believe that the interests of the finders must be taken quite seriously. People who make archaeological finds have performed a valuable service that needs to be recognised. Professional archaeologists do not, perhaps, aim at more than advancement of their science, but private individuals who make finds deserve to be compensated. This compensation can take the form of ownership of the find. When the cultural significance principle trumps the proprietary principle, as it can, the compensation will take another form. Quite apart from the compensation owed finders for their service, there is a prudential reason for taking their interests into account. If their interests are disregarded, they will have no incentive to publicise finds and less incentive to seek and protect archaeological finds.

CONCLUSION

Questions about who owns certain archaeological finds are often complex and difficult. Here I have simply suggested that a culture can sometimes have a strong claim on possession of certain finds and that its claim will generally have to depend on the cultural significance principle. Even when applicable, this principle will not provide a culture with a claim to all finds its members find valuable. The principle has to be weighed against other applicable principles and this will often be a difficult process.

ACKNOWLEDGEMENTS

In the course of writing this chapter I profited from the comments and criticisms of Colin Macleod and the editors of this volume.

How are issues of ownership different in historical contexts.?

If a descendent group can be identified through dv...g

census/church records ovn ownership.

Should they own ownership further

How is the situation further

complicated if connection is

claimed through oral history?

Should the goal of archaeology be to make artifacts available for display.

* little regard for archaeological context

CHAPTER 3

Who guards the guardians?

Oliver Leaman

There was a time when collecting artistic and archaeological artefacts was widely regarded in a very positive light. Both private and public collectors saved objects so that the public could experience those objects and the scholarly community study them. A good indication is the title of a recent book (published by the Hayward Gallery) by the British National Art Collections Fund which provides funds for museums in Britain to buy works of art. It is called *Saved!* But gradually this activity came to be questioned. Much of the material in museums was acquired by dubious methods, it has been argued, and is presented in patronising ways. For example, 'primitive' communities are presented through their artefacts as exotic and we often treat important religious symbols as just things to be gaped at as representatives of a very alien way of life. We may even display their dead as items for public entertainment and study in ways that would lead to questions were we to be dealing with corpses from our own culture. On the other hand, the recent von Hagens 'Bodyworks' display of dead bodies in a variety of poses suggests that breaking taboos in this area is a potent source of audience attraction. Even though the bodies come from people who have voluntarily consigned them for display, or so we are told, one might wonder what point is made by their manipulation into unusual poses and public display. An even more potent issue is raised in the case of bodies that have been acquired perhaps by dubious means, certainly without the consent of who they were when alive, and perhaps in contravention to the cultural beliefs of the community from which they came. Related issues arise for artefacts that are collected by museums and individuals. Issues arise such as who has the right to own such objects, and how they should be displayed and preserved. It will be argued here that the present rather messy lack of resolution of these issues is not without its cultural advantages.

There have in recent years been protracted disputes about whether artefacts ought to be returned to their original owners. In many cases the original owners are no longer alive and it may be that the artefacts are so old that the whole notion of an original owner is obscure. Those now living in the territory may not even want the artefacts, if they are of no great monetary value. On the other hand they may, and they may claim with some degree of plausibility that the artefacts have great religious and/ or national value, so that the grounds for restitution are prima facie even stronger. The most famous such case in Britain has been the case of the Elgin Marbles, parts of the Athens Parthenon now residing in the British Museum. They were removed from their original site by Lord Elgin in the nineteenth century after he had come to some arrangement with the Turkish authorities who then ruled Greece. The Greek authorities have argued that the Marbles ought to be returned to Athens, where they will be reunited with the city from which they came and where they will be well looked after by the appropriate authorities. These provisos are interesting, since they imply that the issue is not just one of ownership but also one of who is going to look after the artefacts best. Can rights to ownership be abrogated by poor guardianship? Can the inability of the British Museum to display the Marbles in their original setting, or something close to their original setting, disqualify the Museum as the owner of the Marbles?

The precedent of returning the Marbles is quite horrifying to museum authorities, of course, since much of what reposes in their possession has a similar provenance to the Elgin Marbles, or a much patchier one. The fact that there may be official bills of sale is not that relevant, since it is accepted that contracts made under duress are not valid, and a much more recent phenomenon is the forced sale by Jews of art at low prices to Germans. The original owners and their descendants have rights to those artefacts despite the 'legality' of the contract, since they would not have freely sold their artefacts had they not been forced to do so. This is even more clearly the case where such property was confiscated, despite the legality of the confiscation at the time. This seems a reasonable question to raise: would the original owner have freely entered into a contract to make the sale unless undue pressure was applied?

This question works for Jews in the twentieth century who were dispossessed of their art, but is more complicated for the Elgin Marbles. Who originally owned the Acropolis? Certainly not the Greek republic, but the Greek state might be assumed to have taken over the rights of preceding regimes in the Athens area with respect to what used to be there. It is worth noting here though that the builders of the Acropolis would possibly have been horrified at the notion of a Greek state and its power over Athens itself, the significance and independence of which is symbolised by the Acropolis from which the Marbles were taken. Would the Greek government have a stronger case if the gods were still worshipped in Greece, perhaps as the official religion of the country? They cannot plausibly claim to value the objects as religious objects; clearly the issue relates to the much wider question of who if anyone should own what. If there is to be property, and individuals and organisations and states are allowed to have it, then they need to ensure first that they are entitled to have it. Within a system of law this is of course a legal question, but it is also moral. Who deserves to own a rare and beautiful painting, for example? If I own it and restrict its audience to my friends and me, we might object that this important cultural resource was being unfairly restricted. If I use it as a table or a dartboard, it is being badly treated or even destroyed. Yet we do not normally take property away from people just because they abuse it: were that to be the case then incompetent gardeners would lose their gardens, bad drivers their cars and so on. Perhaps they all should, but there is good reason to think they should not, especially when the consequences of incompetence are limited.

Perhaps the relationship we are interested in is not so much that of owner/owned as guardian/treasure. We do allow pretty incompetent parents to look after their own children, and quite often other people's children also, but if their incompetence reaches a certain level, the children are removed from them. Although prima facie parents have primary responsibility for their children, they can be relieved of this by displaying signs of inadequacy. We might have a system whereby artefacts are looked after by whoever owns them with the proviso that they can be taken away if they do not do a good job, the sort of system we have with children, and also animals. What is different about children and animals, as compared with other sorts of things that we control? The obvious answer is that these are conscious organisms that can suffer, and we cannot allow people to treat them as inanimate objects. On the other hand, cultures trying to get back their artefacts often claim to regard them almost as living things, as parts of their culture and lifestyle that are so intimately linked with them that their loss is a palpable harm to the body politic. Interestingly, in cases where artefacts are returned with no problem on either side it is often because the country that has them is either embarrassed about owning them or makes little use of them. A good example is the recent agreement of Italy to return some Eritrean architectural objects that clearly were acquired during the colonial period, hardly a time for Italians to be proud of, but also because the Italians did not make much use of them. So their return hardly mattered, not to the Italians in any case.

An important fact about <u>artefacts is that they cannot suffer</u>. Apart from *cant they?* this, a problem with treating artefacts like children is that it would put the state in a paternalistic relationship with its citizens over issues that do not relate to life and death, health and happiness. It is reasonable to expect the state to monitor my treatment of my child, whether she is well fed and healthy, since she could so easily be otherwise and I could be the cause. Yet should the state have the right to check up on my management of artefacts, to see if the air conditioning is working properly, perhaps, or that they are not placed in direct sunlight, or misused? This point about artefacts being like children is an interesting one and leads to questioning whether there is just one notion of ownership. It is often argued that one reason why collections should not be made of cultural products is because those products are still capable of playing a role in the social life of the culture from which they come. The fact that they are old does not matter, and in fact may lead to them being even more important. What right has a collection to hold on to those things if they play a significant role still in their culture? This notion of a culture being owned by a community is an interesting one, and in some ways quite novel. Native American culture might be thought to be a part of American culture and so it might be thought to be entirely appropriate for American museums to contain examples of that culture. When critics of such ownership describe it, they suggest that crass museum directors are intent on ripping the heart out of local cultures and then display the artefacts in a cold and isolated environment, so that there is no context in which members of the public can understand the real role that they possess. There is certainly a good deal of crassness in the insensitive presentation of such material, but this is not an issue about ownership, but rather about how that ownership should be translated into display.

In the foyer of Lexington Theological Seminary is a Sefer Torah, a scroll of the law, written in Hebrew and displayed open at a particular place and reposing in a glass case. No doubt the seminary has legal ownership of this object, but it is certainly being displayed in ways that resemble only very distantly its normal use in synagogues only a few miles away. There scrolls like this are used in services and the law is read from them every week. But the display in the seminary is not disrespectful: the scrolls are not in a cocktail bar, for instance, and Christians might be expected to be interested in artefacts from a religion that predated their own. This brings out the useful point that perhaps ownership and display issues are not that unrelated. If something is poorly displayed, it raises the issue of whether it ought to be owned by the displayer. This issue is certainly relevant if the artefact is kept in a way that damages it physically, but is also relevant if it is displayed in ways that imply disrespect for it and the community of which it was a part. On the other hand, one would not want to say that the artefact would need to be displayed in line with its normal use since that would mean it could not be displayed at all.

Of course, a very important caveat here is that the question of owner- ship in general is very complicated. Some people argue that taxation is unacceptable since it interferes with the basic right of the individual to own property. Other thinkers dispute the notion of private ownership and would no doubt be amenable to the idea that important cultural objects should all be publicly owned if owned at all. This is not the place to examine all these different arguments, but they are clearly highly relevant to the topic of who should own or look after cultural artefacts. If there is to be completely unfettered private property then we clearly cannot argue with the right of collections to own cultural artefacts, since why should such possessions be treated differently from anything else? In the United States NAGPRA (Native American Graves Protection and Repatriation Act, Public Law 101–601, 104 Statute 3048 (1990) (codified at 25USC 3001– 3013 (Supplement V 1993)) does not cover private collections of Native American bones, for instance, although it does affect public collections. It returns artefacts connected to the remains of Native Americans to the community from which they were taken, including the remains themselves.

But if we think that ownership of property does need to be justified in terms of other moral or political criteria, then it is a live issue as to whether cultural property was really come about fairly, and if it is now being looked after properly. This notion of being fairly acquired is not as simple as it looks. If I go to a yard sale and spot a valuable bowl being sold for 25 cents and buy it, have I fairly acquired it? If I think that a particular stock on Wall Street is undervalued and buy it, and then it goes up in price, have I fairly acquired it? We would normally say yes. There is a very entertaining short story by Roald Dahl in which an antique dealer comes across a valuable piece of furniture, but he is intent on buying it as cheaply as possible from the simple farmer who owns it. He says he will return to pick it up, they agree on a (low) price and the dealer says it will really only be good for firewood. When he returns he finds that the owner has literally transformed it into firewood by chopping it up! Which of course he had every legal right to do, given his ownership of it.

We are critical of owners of property who allow their property to deteriorate, and not only owners of cultural artefacts. Someone who does not adequately look after anything is liable to be criticised for waste. In the case of cultural artefacts it is also an issue of something perhaps quite rare or even unique disappearing. A cynical owner of rare possessions might destroy some of them in order to increase the value of the others, of course, although one hopes this is not something that owners of public collections would contemplate. They do sell things, on occasion, and also decide not to display things, leading to the question of whether they are the right custodians of them. But as we know, collectors may be carrying out a very important function just by preserving things that are no longer of particular public interest, perhaps because they have just gone out of fashion. Even if they never come back into fashion, the collector is carrying out an important task by looking after them and no doubt writing about them also.

We are beginning to see now that there are some distinct arguments that can be discerned:

1 legal ownership of cultural artefacts is the only relevant category of possession;
2 legal ownership of cultural artefacts can never be absolute since they belong to a wider community;
3 legal ownership is largely irrelevant, what is relevant is desert;
4 human relics fall into a special category and should/should not be treated like everything else.

At the moment we have some variety of these views being held often at the same time in different permutations, and that makes the whole issue rather confusing.

Let us try to work out some rules for good behaviour in collecting. First, the ideal position is where the artefact is not far removed from its original environment, but is left there after having been excavated and placed within both its original natural context, in so far as this is possible, and together with other related objects that form its cultural context. Let us admit frankly that this is often not feasible. It may be that the country in which the artefact exists is intent on destroying it, or on stealing it and selling it on the international market, or is not capable of displaying it properly. In the latter case a strong case should be made for helping the country and providing the resources and expertise necessary for this to happen. In a kleptocracy this is a waste of time, and similarly in a hostile environment the only plausible strategy may be rescue rather than anything else. To suggest this is not to be imperialist or colonialist but merely to recognise the facts. Many former colonies frankly acknowledge the importance of the transfer of much of their earlier documents and artefacts to the imperial country since this has preserved them from almost certain destruction. There has in recent years been a particularly nasty trend in civil wars to attack the cultural heritage of communities that are perceived as hostile. The best example of this is the bombardment of the main library in Sarajevo, the repository of so much important cultural material particularly of the Islamic heritage of Bosnia. It is interesting that in a war resources should be spent in destroying what was primarily a cultural facility, but it should be hardly surprising, since in the history of the twentieth century cultural artefacts were always closely identified as objects of hatred. The Nazis preserved a few Jewish things in order to preserve an account of what they hoped would be an extinct race in the fullness of time, but apart from those things, they set out to destroy whatever else they could. In situations like that rescue is the only feasible strategy. A good example of this is the store of Afghan antiquities set up in Switzerland with the blessing of UNESCO, where cultural objects exported from Afghanistan (in theory illegally) could be 'rescued' and await repatriation to Afghanistan when security is restored, and a more amenable government in place. Of course, the previous regime was hostile to many such antiquities and had little compunction in either selling them or even destroying them. Actually, when one considers the long history of destruction of Buddhist objects in what is today Afghanistan by a variety of iconoclastic rulers it is remarkable that anything has survived!

There are difficult cases here. If a country is unable to look after its artefacts as well as a foreign country, does that mean that the latter should take them over? We suggested earlier that this might be seen as the worst kind of paternalism and imperialism, and no one likes to be told that they cannot handle their own affairs, especially if it is true. We need some notion here of an artefact as belonging much more generally to the world than to the country in which it happens to be found. It is not difficult to find such a notion, since many countries do restrict their inhabitants' use of their private property if that property has cultural significance. It may be their house, it may be their pictures, but there will often be restrictions on their use and sale. The state justifies this intervention into the area of private property by saying that the right to dispose of one's property as one wishes is limited by the public good. So one needs some concept of the public good on a universal scale to justify restricting what the individual property owner may do. Even if the owner in the case of a museum has the best of educational or curatorial purposes in mind, an argument needs to be established that their ownership and manipulation of the artefacts are really in the public good.

The principle worth considering here is that if a museum wishes to own an object, and keep on owning an object, it has to show that it has a well-developed plan to make that object generally available to the public in a meaningful way. This is especially the case if there is a possible claim by someone else to possess the artefact. For example, most countries impose restrictions on their citizens, and others, in their ownership and treatment of artefacts that are held to be significant culturally in some way. Often houses are designated as historically important, and the owner cannot just do what she wants to it. Objects are sometimes not allowed to be exported, or not before an exhaustive process of looking for a local buyer is completed. These all represent violations of the liberty of the individual to do what she wants with her own property. From a liberal perspective restrictions on liberty are justified in terms of potentially greater liberty consequent on such restrictions. So we would have to argue that preventing someone from exercising their liberty to sell something they own is less serious than preventing the public at large from experiencing that object. Once the object has gone elsewhere or been irretrievably changed no one is then free to see it, and so a liberal argument could be found to justify and explain the restrictions on ownership of historically significant artefacts and art objects.

Opponents may say that in general museums that get to own objects do not display them all the time (absence of space) or even ever, and that most such objects repose forever in the vaults and are only ever seen by scholars. Are we justified in keeping objects in that way? Exactly the same point may be made when a child is taken away from its parents and put under the control of the local authority, or the state or whichever social agency arranges these things. This can also result in a worse state of affairs than if the child is left with the parents, and that is why the decision to remove a child is not taken lightly. Alternative forms of parenting are often not successful; they may be even more abusive than the parents and the child may end up in a worse situation than he would have otherwise. Since everyone knows this, the onus is very much on the agency that wishes to remove the child to argue that it is really in the child's best interests. This gives us a good model for dealing with the artefact case. If we are going to remove an object from its owner then the onus is on us to show that it would not only do better than with its present owner, but that its present owner in some way represents a danger to the object's future. This might not be so much that he is going to mistreat it, but that if his purchase of the object encourages illicit pilfering of sites, and so a market for such objects, it may encourage further pilfering and the general destruction of such sites.

This has an interesting correlative in the case of children, of course. Many people in prosperous countries who cannot have children themselves acquire them from people in poorer countries, or from poorer people in their own country. It is a benign activity on the whole to match up families with children they cannot look after and do not want to look after with families who are prepared to look after them. But it leads to a market in such children, with fees, different prices and all sorts of quasi-legal and legal obligations between the parties. The state intervenes also by insisting on some adoption and naturalisation formalities. Who owns a child that was born in China, say, and has been legally adopted by an American couple, after a certain amount of money has changed hands? Not the original parents, one might say – they may have had the child purely in order to sell it after all – but difficult situations do arise where the natural parents renege on a deal, or where they later on try to assert their rights to the child. When prospective parents see a child not being well looked after, and they have the opportunity to 'save' it, and take it away with them to a country where it will be much better cared for, it looks very much as though that is what should happen. The similarity with artefacts is quite clear. Yet as we have seen, the question of ownership is not decisively settled by considerations of who would best look after the object in question. On the other hand, it might be said that the best owner has a strong claim on the object if the issue of whom it legally belongs to is in doubt.

The claim of the putative 'best owner' is harder to make than one might think. The Greek government might claim that the Elgin Marbles are at present displayed entirely inappropriately, out of context, and yet it would be difficult to argue that they are physically more at risk now than were they to be attached (or reattached) to the Parthenon in Athens, or if they were put in a museum in Athens. On the other hand, the point about context is more than a minor one. NAGPRA calls for the restitution of human remains to their original context, in so far as this can be managed, despite the fact, and it surely is a fact, that they may be more likely to be damaged or even destroyed in those surroundings. The view here is that the rightful owner morally of something has the right to use it as he wishes, and some damage is inevitable if an object is actually part of a living tradition rather than just an exhibit in a museum. (It might be thought that this legislation is based on the idea that it is wrong for anyone to own bodies, or parts of bodies. But that cannot be the case, private owners are excluded from the law anyway, and it is not just bodies that are returned from public collections, but everything that goes along with the bodies and is part of the burial ceremonial ritual. It is worth adding that other bodies such as Egyptian mummies are not part of the legislation, and there are no plans for returning them to Egypt.) Of course, damage may also occur in a museum: exhibits disappear and are stolen, and inappropriate curatorial methods may harm them. On the other hand, although we rightly criticise the ways in which the smuggling of artefacts deprives countries of their cultural heritage, there is a lot to be said for the spreading out of such artefacts. This is helpful to public education, at the very least, but also prevents a disaster in one place from totally wiping out a cultural tradition. As we have seen, there has been a long tradition of wiping out not just people but their cultures as well, so the dispersal of people and their artefacts is a highly pragmatic measure that makes the survival of some examples of both at least more likely.

If we accept that the owner of an artefact does not have the right to do anything she wishes to it or with it, then how do we assess that treatment? Does this mean that all owners of artefacts, both public and private, need to be inspected to see that they are doing the right thing? We should follow the analogy of artefacts with children here. No one bursts into my house to check that I am not mistreating my children unless there is evidence that I am. That seems reasonable; we have to assume that most parents do their best to look after their children and do not require regular inspection. On the other hand, if my child fails to thrive or appears to have unexplained bruising, then this may be grounds for investigation. Similarly in the case of artefacts, if museum workers are seen in the pub lighting cigarettes with what appear to be medieval manuscripts we might want to investigate them. With respect to private owners of artefacts, the state might wish to intervene if there was evidence of imminent or past harm to artefacts, on the grounds that restricting the liberty of some is permissible in order to preserve or increase the liberty of the community at large to enjoy a relationship with those artefacts. But does not the fact that those artefacts are in private hands restrict the public anyway, since they may not be available generally to public view? It does, but private ownership increases the value of artefacts and makes it more likely that they will be conserved properly. A mixture of private and public ownership is probably the right way to go, since the state is unlikely to wish to divert the resources necessary to own, preserve and display all of a country's artefacts. In any case, private owners can indulge private interests, and thus preserve material that an official body might discard as insignificant. This is useful since it can lead to a much broader definition of what counts as worth collecting as compared with some official consensus on the topic. Whatever imperfections result as a consequence of private ownership of artefacts, and there are many of these, there is no doubt that there are considerable advantages also. Governments have generally recognised this by offering tax breaks and other incentives for private owners of cultural artefacts, to acknowledge their preservation efforts and possibly the granting of public access to them.

It is then generally accepted that there is no absolute right to do whatever one likes with cultural artefacts, although the restrictions differ from country to country and even between regions of the same country. There is today often a suspicion of the motives behind the urge to collect. Lord Elgin was, as far as we know, governed by financial concerns to a large degree when he decided to remove the parts of the Parthenon that subsequently became the Elgin Marbles. Belzoni played a large part in discovering and popularising Egyptian antiquities, and really approached the area like an entrepreneur interested in making a quick buck. This buccaneering spirit is much disparaged today, but to a degree it has been adopted by the museum sector. Museums conserve, preserve and display, and these all seem like positive actions, but they may contain material that is of dubious provenance. Many museums in former colonial countries possess rich collections from their colonies, often of considerable religious or cultural significance. There are many paintings and sculptures in museums all over the world that originate in Jewish property from Europe that was acquired in questionable ways. It is difficult for the owners and their descendants to establish their right to this property since the records are often deficient and there has been little serious effort to discover the original owners anyway. Then we have issues of what is displayed and how it is displayed, what sorts of issues of hegemony are involved here, and how far does the broad community in which the museum is situated find its concerns and interests reflected in the museum? What is the community that the museum addresses, the people who live nearby, fellow citizens in general or indeed the whole world?

It would not be difficult to construct a list of requirements for a museum that would outline what it needed to do in order to fulfil its function ethically. A problem is that each museum's list would be different. Some would argue that museums should not display artefacts that have or had a symbolic meaning connected to a foreign culture, since this is condescending with respect to that culture. Some would argue that dead people should not be exhibited. An exhibit in the Liverpool Museum of a mummified hand of a child had been removed when I was last there because it was the hand of a child. In the next glass case there were mummies of adults, but for some reason it was held to be insensitive to display a limb from a child's body. Some would argue that the artefacts should only be displayed or indeed held on to if their provenance is beyond challenge, and if there are no issues about exploitation, colonialism and so on tied up with their ownership. In recent years the right of guardians to look after anything has often been challenged, and the self-confidence of curators has taken a knock. Yet one could well argue that this critique has gone too far. There is a lot to be said for continuing the rather imperfect system that leaves the precise details of looking after artefacts to both the individuals in the private sector and the professionals in the public sector, and we get to this argument through the comparison of artefacts with children.

As we have already seen, the welfare of children is given such a high priority by the state that children will be removed from their natural parents if there is evidence of ill-treatment. But the state will not actively check up on parents' treatment of their children unless there is some prima facie suspicious evidence. We know that some children are brought up in very strange ways. Some religious communities, for example, do not allow their children to watch television or even eat with members of other religious groups. Some parents who are racists may well infect their children with their prejudices. Some parents spend a lot of effort feeding their children with what they take to be healthy food, while others do not even think about it. One of the advantages of this relative laissez-faire approach is that it recognises the fact that we really do not know how children ought to be brought up. Different people have different views, and it is in our interests to have different experiments in living going on at the same time, since then we shall be better able to make informed judgements. We do limit parents here, and certain experiments in living are held just to be so potentially or actually harmful to the child that they cannot be tolerated. Yet the home in which the child is brought up is on the whole an unregulated place and the state will not intervene unless it has some reason to do so.

Exactly the same argument can be used for the guardianship of artefacts. Of course stolen property should be returned, if it can be, and artefacts exhibited sensitively, but this does not mean that there is only one way of carrying out these desirable policies. One of the advantages of the present system of ownership of artefacts is that there is a wide variation in approaches, and so no general orthodoxy prevails. Private collectors who indulge their personal passions and exclude the public from what they collect will eventually create collections that have a tendency of finding their way to the public anyway. They die, they try to preserve their estates from tax, they wish to be awarded honours or receive the plaudits of the critical world. More importantly, they can follow their own path; they are not limited by what is currently fashionable or valuable. Usually they will, but the private collector may preserve material that would otherwise be consigned to the rubbish heap. Later on it may be thought to be significant, or more significant than was previously thought. What is regarded as important periodically changes, and so it is a good idea not to try to define for all time what is important.

No consensus then exists as to what should be collected, or how it should be displayed or preserved. Even were it to exist in the public sector, it would be unlikely to prevail in the private sector, perhaps a good reason in itself to have such a sector. Stolen property should be returned, and it is worth noting that on the whole there has been no attempt to do so as opposed to it being the case that this is difficult. For example, the huge Mauerbach collection in Austria of confiscated Jewish property was replete with documentation identifying owners, yet nothing was done while there was a possibility of tracing those owners until it was too late. Many items from the Nazi period are now in private and public collections and could have been returned to their rightful owners or their descendants. This need not make all collectors or museum employees feel guilty, though the fact that there are such cases means that increased vigilance should be used to prevent them in future, not that we should all feel that we have dirty hands. It is often said that trade in cultural artefacts is the third largest illegal industry, after drugs and arms smuggling, and auctions in the west of such material are often notable for their relaxed attitude towards provenance. A more rigorous approach by potential buyers to where the material actually comes from would have a radical effect on the market itself, and do something to ensure that collectors are not dealing with stolen property.

This is an important aspect of what it is to be the guardian of artefacts, but not the most significant. As I write this in April 2004 the Brooklyn Museum is about to present itself as a new and exciting institution. It has apparently given up trying to attract Manhattanites to its exhibits and is going to try to bring in more local residents. So the security guards and curators have apparently had 'greeter' training and the explanatory labels are much shorter and simpler than in the past. A particularly popular exhibition in 2002 was 'Star Wars' that displayed a series of costumes and drawings from the movies. Some have criticised this as the shallow attempt at gaining popularity at the expense of scholarship, but others argue that it will bring more people in and they will then possibly go to visit the more serious side of the museum's work, the fine art, the archaeological material and the rest of the collection. Other museums take different approaches, and indeed in the past the Brooklyn Museum took a different approach. It may well take a different approach in the future from its present policy. There is no one strategy that is acceptable here; in many ways it is preferable to have different curators going in different directions, and then we shall be able to observe this variety and come to some informed attitude on the best direction. We can then argue that the diversity of forms of proprietorship of artefacts is ultimately the best state of affairs. It leads to a diversity of ways of collecting and exhibition, and that reflects the essentially contested nature of guardianship itself.

CHAPTER 4

Is culture a commodity?

Robert Layton and Gillian Wallace

The commodification of culture poses questions concerning value, ownership and ethics both in terms of those marketing culture and, more
specifically, with regard to the role of anthropologists and archaeologists
in facilitating or challenging the process. Here we look at ethical issues
that arise in two contexts: where there is tension between the status of
artefacts as commodities and as cultural property, and where rights to
cultural property are contested.

Culture consists of learned patterns of thought and behaviour that are
characteristic of a particular community. Culture includes beliefs, values,
language, political organisation and economic activity; also technology,
art and material culture. A commodity is an item that can be freely
bought and sold through the market economy. In a narrow sense, commodities are raw materials or primary agricultural products, but the term
can be extended to any useful or valuable thing that has a price, payment
of which transfers ownership from the seller to the buyer. All commodities (even raw materials) are cultural artefacts in the sense that demand
for them is culturally constructed. The market economy is itself a cultural
phenomenon.

Although culture is shared, anthropologists no longer think of it as a
'collective consciousness' (Durkheim 1915) but rather follow Bourdieu's
(1977) concept of *habitus*, which stresses the interaction between ideas and
their material expression. When Bourdieu attempted to discover the
structure of culture among the Kabyle people of Algeria, he found each
individual carried a slightly different mental model. Bourdieu termed this
mental schema the individual's *habitus*. Bourdieu investigated the processes that prevented individual habituses from diverging so far that no
one could understand anyone else. In the traditional Kabyle house, for
example, men sit on a raised area at the back, women in a lower area in
front. Children, he argued, grow up in a cultural environment that
predisposes them to think of men as superior to women. When children

become adult and build their own houses, they therefore reproduce the material structures in which they grew up (Bourdieu 1977: 35, 60; 1990: 136–40). Bourdieu concluded that ideas and their material expression are mutually reinforcing. Neither can exist without the other. The 'structured structures' of the adult's *habitus* lead to the production of material forms that have a 'structuring' effect upon the minds of the next generation.

Commodities are normally private property. There are many cases, however, where interests in the fate of artefacts embrace a wider community than the legal owners. *Cultural property* consists of artefacts and buildings that embody the values and traditions of a community to such an extent that concern about their fate transcends legal ownership. (On the difficulty of defining cultural property more precisely, see Nicholas and Bannister 2004: 328.) When, for example, a rare medieval manuscript is put on the market by an impoverished member of the British aristocracy, people lacking the means to buy it may still decry the manuscript's sale to a collector from the United States, and argue it should remain in the UK as it is an object of value in terms of heritage. The concept of cultural property was well expressed with regard to Scottish monuments in 1881: 'They belong to Scotland because they are inseparable features of her individuality, and they belong to Scotchmen in general in a sense which they can never belong to the holders of the lands on which they are placed [i.e. private landowners]' (Anderson 1881, quoted in Jones in press: 102).

As culture changes, so material expressions of its former state can increase or decrease in value. Where members of different communities come into conflict, cultural property may be attacked as a means of intimidation or a sign of contempt. Between 1991 and 1995, as the state of Yugoslavia disintegrated, Orthodox Christian Serbs invading Croatia sought to eradicate cultural property signalling Catholic Croatian identity in the contested landscape (Šulc 2001). Churches and folk museums were particularly targeted. The destruction of graves and registers of birth, marriage and death was intended to eliminate evidence of long-term Croat residence. Within a few months, Bosnian Croats were destroying Muslim property – mosques, religious schools, bathhouses – in the part of Bosnia-Hercegovina they hoped to (re)integrate into Croatia (see Tanner 1997: 285–94, and Barakat and Wilson 2001).

On 6 December 1992 the 450-year-old Babri Mosque, in the north Indian town of Ayodhya, was destroyed by Hindu fundamentalists. The fundamentalists claimed the mosque stood on the foundations of a Hindu

temple marking the birthplace of the legendary Hindu hero-king Rama
that had been destroyed by Muslim invaders. During September and
October 1990 L. K. Advani, a senior leader of the BJP (a Hindu nationalist political party), led a procession through several states, campaigning
for the demolition of the mosque and its replacement with a temple. On 6
December 1992 Hindu fundamentalist volunteers broke through a police
cordon and completely destroyed the mosque. The number of people
who died in the ensuing riots is difficult to determine, but contemporary
newspaper reports put the figure at around one thousand (see Rao and
Reddy 2001). Advani's strategy was to discredit the Congress Party
government in the eyes of the Hindu majority by forcing the government
to protect the Muslim minority. The BJP did indeed become the leading
party in the right-wing governing coalition that came to power after the
next general election.

Anthropologists and archaeologists have the power to shape the ways in
which cultural traditions are transmitted and transformed. Foucault (e.g.
1972 and 1977) drew attention to the relationship between meaning and
power. He highlighted the hidden role of power in the way that we speak
or write about the world, let alone how we act. A discourse, he wrote, is not
'an innocent intersection of words and things' (Foucault 1972: 49). Each
discourse (such as the technical language used in an academic discipline)
shapes the way we experience the world. The conventions of a discourse
specify the objects it talks or writes about by giving them names such as
madness or witchcraft, prehistory or stone age. Discourse defines the topics
that are worth discussing and, most importantly, who can speak on them
with authority. In response to the kind of concern highlighted by Foucault, the 'Writing Culture' school of anthropology in the USA (Clifford
and Marcus 1986) advocated ethnography as a dialogue between the
anthropologist and the subject community, in which both contribute to
the construction of anthropological writing. Indigenous and archaeologists' interpretations of the significance of the remains of a particular
tradition may be different, but they can also influence each other, as, for
example, when indigenous guides are employed at tourist sites, or where
indigenous archaeological sites are nominated for the World Heritage List.

Sim (an archaeologist) and West (a native Tasmanian) describe their
collaboration in the interpretation of prehistoric campsites on islands in
the Bass Strait, between Tasmania and mainland Australia (Sim and West
1999). Sim's aim was to investigate whether isolated Aboriginal populations had remained on the larger islands after they were cut off by the
rising postglacial sea level, or whether mainland people used water craft to

voyage to the islands. Sim was therefore primarily interested in the antiquity of shell middens on smaller islands that could have provided stepping stones for people voyaging from the mainland. West's aim was to document the antiquity of mutton-bird exploitation, particularly on those islands that the Aboriginal community was leasing from the Tasmanian government for commercial mutton-bird harvesting. The term 'mutton-bird' (*yolla* in the Tasmanian Aboriginal language) covers a number of species, but refers principally to the short-tailed shearwater, *Puffinus tenuirostris*. West knew well that the mutton-bird had been a staple part of the Aboriginal economy in colonial times, but Aboriginal land claims to these islands had been challenged as opportunistic attempts to convert the leases into ownership in order to develop a non-traditional activity. He needed archaeological evidence to support oral history. Had West not become involved, the mutton-birding sites would not have been excavated in such detail, and other archaeological findings would not have become known to the Aboriginal community.

Although Bourdieu tended to emphasise inertia in the transmission of culture, *habitus* entails a constant renegotiation between succeeding generations. Can we talk of the 'true' meaning of, say, rock art? Both archaeologists and indigenous people use their interpretative skills to deduce the significance of rock art produced in the past, and can influence each other's readings. (For an excellent case study from the American Southwest see Stoffle *et al.* 2000.) In the course of dialogue between social scientists and indigenous people, technical language becomes part of everyday discourse. Aboriginal people in the Northern Territory of Australia learned to describe themselves as the 'traditional owners' of their land: a technical term defined in the 1976 Aboriginal Land Rights Act. Many indigenous groups now speak of the importance of preserving their 'culture'.

Does the production of archaeological knowledge always benefit humankind generally? Archaeologists' valuation of artefacts affects their value in the antiquities trade. What happens where a community is divided, e.g. over the mosque at Ayodhya? Can archaeology reveal the 'true' history of a site, or will there always be a need for interpretation and therefore politics? What if the researcher is commissioned by the indigenous community, or by opposing commercial interests: is she bound to provide an interpretation that is favourable to her employers' interests (Toussaint 2004)? Who holds intellectual property rights over knowledge that has been jointly produced through collaboration between archaeologists and indigenous people (Nicholas and Bannister 2004: 330)?

OWNERSHIP AND COPYRIGHT OF INDIGENOUS ART

Ownership and copyright of indigenous art illustrate several issues raised by the commodification of cultural property: the ownership of designs, the authenticity of production and the ownership of ideas. Copyright is a Western principle, which confers the right to produce and distribute specific creative works. In Australian Aboriginal society rights to produce and display artistic designs, and to sing song cycles associated with ancestors, are vested in clans. Such rights are means of expressing membership of the clan, with the consequent rights to enter and care for sacred sites on clan land, and the right to be asked permission by members of other groups who want to camp and forage on that land. The only ways others can gain the right to produce a clan design are either by adoption into the clan or through alliance with a 'brother' clan. If an Aboriginal person were to produce or wear a design to which he was not entitled, that would amount to theft of the owner's title to land and his spiritual inheritance.

Michael F. Brown (1998: 196) points out that copyright laws are based on the assumption of an individual, romantic genius who deserves rights in his work for a sufficient time to profit from them, not enduring rights in collective property held by indigenous people. The differences can be summarised as follows:

Western copyright	Traditional rights
1 Exclusive rights to market the product	Exclusive rights to land with which design associated
2 Right vested in individual artist	Right vested in group (clan)
3 Freely alienable	Very limited alienability
4 Specific design	Indefinite series of designs created within 'ancestral template'
5 Limited semantic content	Levels of meaning progressively revealed
6 Must be in permanent medium	Includes transient oral performance and body painting
7 Limited time span	Indefinite duration

Western copyright is clearly orientated towards the exclusive right to produce and sell commodities. Although traditional Aboriginal rights are also vested in a subset of people within the community (the clan), there is a stronger sense of cultural property. The rights of individual users are circumscribed by obligations to a wider community; rights are not freely alienable and they persist indefinitely. Western copyright does not protect transient oral tellings of a community legend or performance of a traditional song. It is the anthropologist who acquires copyright in a performance by recording it in a durable medium (Barron 1998; Janke 1998).

Although indigenous rules of production apply to traditional art produced for sale, the ability to enforce them is limited once the artefacts have become commodities held outside the community. This has posed some interesting ethical issues. The most notorious case is the one dollar note issued in 1966, when Australia switched to a decimal currency. The note reproduced a painting of a mortuary ceremony by David Malangi, a painting that had been purchased by the Parisian art collector Karel Kupka (Barron 1998: 57; cf. Myers 2002: 68). When the new notes reached his community, and Malangi discovered his clan design had been reproduced without his permission, he went to court claiming payment for the right to reproduce his design. Although he lost the case, Malangi did later receive some payment (Sutton, Jones and Hemmings 1988: 179). It was only in the 1960s that Aboriginal people in the Northern Territory gained the right to manage their own wages; it may not have occurred to the white owner of Malangi's painting that the artist would ever see a bank note. At the time, the Governor of the Reserve Bank of Australia explained they had not considered paying Malangi because they assumed he was a long-dead traditional artist (Barron 1998: 57).

A more recent case concerns the reproduction of Johnny Bulunbulun's painting of his clan waterhole on T-shirts sold in Darwin. Like David Malangi, Bulunbulun was from Arnhem Land, to the east of Darwin. When he saw the image he had painted marketed on T-shirts in Darwin shops, Bulunbulun initiated legal proceedings, saying that he had been unable to paint since he became 'victim of the theft of an important birthright'. Ironically, his claim to copyright was challenged on the grounds that the design was a traditional one, and not Bulunbulun's original design. Witnesses called on his behalf (the Curator of Aboriginal Art at the Northern Territory Museum and a former community adviser) argued that Bulunbulun's realisation of the design displayed his unique artistic skill. Happily, Bulunbulun won his case; the T-shirts were removed from sale and returned to the artist. Golvan notes that T-shirt manufacturers have responded by producing designs which 'may appear to be works of Aboriginal art but are in fact caricatures . . . One of the more depressing manifestations . . . has been the invention of the X-ray koala bear' (Golvan 1992: 229) – the koala is not native to the region where 'X-ray' art is produced.

This raises the related question of authenticity. At least two allegedly Aboriginal writers have been revealed as white Australians. Mudrooroo, who wrote six novels and four books of poetry, turned out to be Colin Johnson, white except for one Afro-American grandparent; Wanda Kool-matrie, who wrote an autobiography, was revealed as Leon Carmen, a middle-aged white taxi driver (*Guardian* 24 February 2001). The alleged Aboriginal artist Sakshi Anmatyerre, who had sold paintings to the Sultan of Brunei and Paul Hogan, was revealed to be an Indian from Calcutta, who had changed his name from Farley French in 1992. More disturb-ingly, the famous artist Elizabeth Durack, a friend of the anthropologist Phyllis Kaberry, created a black 'alter ego' Eddie Burup, in whose name she painted Aboriginal art. When she confessed, she received support from some senior Aboriginal men in Western Australia, who argued she was possessed by the spirit of an Aboriginal artist.

How broadly, then, can cultural property rights be defined? Brown (1998) reports that a consortium of Apache tribes have demanded exclu-sive control over all Apache cultural property, which they define as 'all images, texts, ceremonies, music, songs, stories, symbols, beliefs, customs, ideas and other physical and spiritual objects and concepts' relating to the Apache (Brown 1998: 194). Brown protests that such all-embracing, permanent vesting of cultural property in a group is precisely what we would resist if it were claimed by commercial companies. He does not point out that Western drug companies are busy patenting the active ingredients of traditional medicines, and that the basmati rice developed by peasant farmers in Asia over many centuries is now patented by a US cereal company.

During the 1950s, a group of American Boy Scouts in Colorado called themselves Koshare (a pueblo term for a sacred clown) and reproduced Zuni ritual masks to use in their 'mock' Indian dances. The Zuni lodged a complaint with the Commissioner for Indian Affairs and threatened to exclude non-Indians from all their dances. Their complaint was upheld; the masks were confiscated and given to the Zuni (Merrill *et al.* 1993).

The Fourth World Association, based in Sweden, is currently campaigning against Western neo-shamanism (http://www.algonet.se/~f4world/sham.html). Their publicity states:

European-Americans have stolen Native lands, Native resources, Native children, Native cultural images, and more recently Native profits. Now, they are taking Native spirituality, too. All of these thefts constitute violations of Native sovereignty – the inherent right of indigenous nations to govern themselves, and keep the lands, cultures, and economies belonging to them.

The Association argues that within the Western consumer culture, indigenous ritual items and ceremonies are trivialised into tools for personal advancement or goods that can be traded and sold on an international market. They cite the case of Michael Harner's Foundation for Shamanic Studies in the USA. Harner, they argue, 'developed his own concept of "core-shamanism" by collecting and recombining indigenous spiritual concepts and shamanic healing methods from all over the world. The result is a hotch-potch of different spiritual concepts based on the system of western psychology and without any reference to the original indigenous communities.' While we certainly do not wish to accuse archaeologists who interpret prehistoric art as shamanistic of malpractice, we do point out that – for example – the model of shamanism Lewis-Williams (2002) applies to the interpretation of Upper Palaeolithic art in Europe also synthesises aspects of shamanism taken from lowland South America, western North America and southern Africa.

TRADITION, TOURISM AND ANTHROPOLOGISTS AS TRANSLATORS OF EXPERIENCE

Tourism promotes the commoditisation of culture (Greenwood 1989). Tourist companies are quick to market rituals and tradition as a means of gaining customers; 'colourful age old' traditions are in themselves a means to an end, even though some tourists seek the authentically significant rituals, not just aesthetically pleasing performances. Greenwood discovered this effect during his work in a Basque village. Local rituals which are important to community identity became transformed in meaning when viewed by outsiders such as tourists (Greenwood 1989). Such performances are, as Nuttall (1997) puts it, 'deprived of understanding'.

Smith *et al.* (2000: 2) point out that globalisation threatens to have a permanent, negative impact on the indigenous peoples who comprise 6 per cent of the world's population. Yet although indigenous peoples are undoubtedly threatened by increasing communication and misappropriation of symbols and concepts, there is also some hope for the enterprising. Various Native communities in Alaska have claimed ownership over their heritage and material culture so that the past is becoming a lucrative and sustainable resource to be harvested for the present and future. Athabascan hunters and fishermen offer tours lasting several days to tourists who are willing to pay dearly for the opportunity to experience the 'subsistence lifestyle' of their hosts (Nuttall 1997: 233). Other Alaska Native communities are also hosting guests as an alternative to declining economic options, and tourists have options ranging from day trips to longer stays. One of the Athabascan tour companies controls access to their community, and visitors are guided by local people (Nuttall 1997).

Although these Alaskan examples show Native peoples commodifying the presentation of their own heritage without losing control, anthropologists and archaeologists can translate values and views of indigenous peoples to policy-makers, politicians and personnel in governmental and non-governmental organisations. Such was the case for the Integrated Management of European Wetlands (IMEW) Project.

The IMEW Project was funded by the European Commission's 5th Framework Programme. Previous 5th Framework projects had been orientated specifically towards natural science. The IMEW Project broke the mould by being conceived and managed by anthropologists. Three of the five research groups within the project relied on anthropological methods such as the use of focus groups, semi-structured interviews and ancillary ethnographic material, including visual culture, participant observation of daily life and newspaper clippings.

The purpose of the IMEW Project was to investigate the real and perceived conflict between local people and natural resource conservation. The project found that local people on the whole strongly favour conservation, even when the protected species has a negative impact on traditional fisheries. In this sense, both local people and outsiders value nature conservation. Yet the meaning of nature is different for locals and outsiders, and this can sometimes lead to conflict. One Finnish informant talked about the burgeoning tourism on Lake Pihlajavesi, saying that visitors were both welcome and good for the economy but that in order to keep in balance with nature local people should teach tourists to 'understand the meaning of silence'. Both this informant and local tourism providers spoke out strongly in favour of interpreting their culture to tourists. Indeed, informants in all four wetlands studied during the IMEW favoured the visitors who were willing to engage with what Wallace (2002) calls 'eco-cultural tourism'; that is, a responsible form of tourism where leakage of profit to outsiders is curbed in favour of local people designing, managing and interpreting their natural and cultural heritage. This form of tourism is particularly apt for people living in marginal places which otherwise would have only limited appeal (Russell and Wallace 2004; Wallace and Russell in press). Eco-cultural tourism is one way for indigenous and other local communities to take charge of, and benefit from, the globalising trend to commodify culture.

Interestingly, tourism in the areas of the IMEW Project is affecting the development of material culture in different ways from wetland to wetland. In Finland many of the tourist souvenirs centre on the protected Saimaa ringed seal (*Phoca hispida saimensis*). This seal is a symbol of local identity even though actual sightings are so rare that a recreational fisherwoman said seeing one is 'a significant happening'. The seal none the less appears on T-shirts, swim towels, postcards and local business signs. It is sometimes viewed as a predator by locals but most often is a symbol of solitude, of Lake Saimaa and as a symbol of the rural past (Tonder *in press*). A nostalgic song by the composer and singer Juha Vainio that describes the friendship between an old fisherman and the seal was very popular upon its release in the 1990s. The recent use of the seal by environmentalists and local companies as well as tourism entrepreneurs, however, transforms this traditional meaning of the seal into that of a 'cute little creature'. So it is that an animal too can be a cultural commodity which is highly marketable to visitors, particularly when it is a symbol of local identity and the focus of cultural practice and folklore, yet subject to reinterpretation in the discourse of outsiders.

From the local perspective, the main cause of conflict during development is rules made by outsiders such as managers and policy-makers that are inappropriate or impractical for the local context (Bell *et al.* 2004; Hampshire *et al.* 2003). This leads to a cycle of mistrust. One of the most powerful findings of the IMEW Project was that ecologists who are commissioned to monitor the populations of protected species often, in the view of local people, miscount the actual number. This was particularly the case for the Finnish wetland, Lake Pihlajavesi, although accusations of mismanagement prevailed also in the Danube Delta in Romania and to a certain extent Lake Kerkini in Greece.

The feeling of disenfranchisement on the part of local communities is significant. Many local people do not have the power to communicate their understanding of the natural and cultural resources of the landscape to outsiders, whether visitors or those whose decisions affect overall management of protected areas. Time and again local people interviewed during the IMEW Project expressed frustration at their lack of training in how to host people and effectively relate their views to institutions and policy-makers. As an agro-tourism provider in Greece said, 'It is one thing taking my tractor and going to the fields to plough for five hours and another thing to plough for three hours and spend the other two to convince you that what I fed you is good, the best thing you have eaten in your life.' Despite these difficulties, hosts in all four wetlands studied are using local cuisine as one starting point for introducing and interpreting local customs to visitors. Tourist art is closer to the acceptable end of the continuum of marketing culture than the antiquities trade (to which we next turn). Tourist art is already a burgeoning cottage industry in some parts of the Romanian Danube Delta and could be more widely encouraged in the future.

Each of the four wetlands has a rich archaeological heritage. To date only Finland commodifies this heritage, principally in the form of a tote bag with prehistoric rock art symbols. Wider production of tourist art, particularly that based on historic and prehistoric symbols and icons, will only happen through the cooperation and mutual understanding of archaeologists, anthropologists and the different stakeholders from the local communities.

Anthropologists working for the IMEW Project submitted policy recommendations to Brussels concerning future management of the field sites. They urged dissemination of local understandings of the environment and recognition of ways in which local people would like the tourism industry to proceed, through development from the local to the international level. In this sense, anthropologists are acting as intermediaries or interpreters of meaning. While this is also the case in traditional ethnographic studies (as the 'Reading Culture' School recognised), the stakes are much higher in applied anthropology: conservation of natural and cultural resources is a game with high financial value to those nations, states and local communities committed to their long-term protection. Anthropologists cannot halt globalisation but they can work with local communities to ensure that indigenous values are respected.

As replicas of popular motifs get transmitted throughout the world via tourism, trade and popular media, globalisation creates demand for supposedly traditional items. How else could a herbal salt scrub produced by a company in Oregon, USA, have registered 'Celtic Sea Salt' as part of its label (for other examples, see Nicholas and Bannister 2004: 335)? While this claim recalls the appropriation of shamanism, it is less clear who exactly are the custodians of Celtic culture. Arguably the very notion of Celtic culture was created by archaeologists. European Bronze Age armlets and earrings are likewise reproduced as popular jewellery items that are often reinterpreted as they are copied and reproduced by the jewellers. Value here lies in the aesthetic qualities of the motif, rather than the symbolic meaning and mystical power often claimed to reside in 'Celtic' objects. In the Bronze Age jewellery example, the connection between present-day populations and Bronze Age societies is even more tenuous. Yet what about communities that have strong continuity with the archaeological artefacts of the past? One can more readily make the case that Peruvian communities, from which artefacts are replicated or outrightly sold (cf. Alva 2001) to tourists, own the rights to reproduction.

COMMODITY AND MEANING IN THE ILLICIT ANTIQUITIES TRADE

The antiquities trade is one of the most powerful manifestations of culture as a commodity. Not only are meanings of material things transformed, objects themselves are removed and sometimes smuggled to their final destination far away from the original place. It is consistent with the concept of *habitus* that variation in the meaning of material culture may even vary among people within local communities. Rock art in Tanzania is seen by some local people as important for rituals, particularly the paints that are seen as containing magical powers for medicinal use. The same rock shelters, however, double as guest houses for hunters, honey collectors and traditional healers, with the smoke from fires used for these temporary habitations being quite destructive of paintings (Mapunda 2001: 51). Likewise, ancient buildings around the world are or have been dismantled so that the materials can be used to build newer structures (Hollowell-Zimmer 2003). Thus some people may value heritage aspects of material culture whilst others may destroy the same thing in order to derive new, practical use from ancient remains.

Archaeologically speaking, the crime of the illicit antiquities trade is its undocumented destruction of contexts. Objects lose meaning when removed from their original resting place without being first documented. Indeed, even when documented, a piece of material culture is subject to new and different labels when it is placed in an archaeological display. A Byzantine coin, for example, might have spent most of its original life in a money pouch. As an antiquity it is most likely to be displayed in a museum case or a collector's coin display board. Thus the meaning of things inevitably changes as material culture moves from one realm of use to another, irrespective of whether or not these realms are documented. However, this does not belittle the dire implication of the illicit antiquities trade.

Brodie and Doole (2001) point out that no distinction should be made between licit and illicit antiquities, since objects that are obtained illegally in one country may sometimes be sold legitimately in another. The monetary value of the trade is difficult to estimate and there is no easily accessible register of damage caused by looting (Brodie and Doole 2001). Qualitatively, the destruction is horrific. Statues at Ankor Wat in Cambodia have been either beheaded or totally removed. Ironically, looters have also taken replicas of statues which were placed there when the originals were removed for a museum display (Brodie *et al.* 2000). Parts of the throne room at Ninevah that were documented and left for future generations to enjoy have likewise been ripped out and sold in recent years (Renfrew 2000).

Local people are sometimes exploited by outsiders as guides or labourers. This renders the illegal antiquities trade little better than the drugs trade. In both cases the producers are generally poor, seeking to better their position through the sale of goods whose value is determined by relatively wealthy addicts in the west. In this sense local people are the 'producers' of illicit antiquities, as poorly compensated in relation to the middlemen and sellers abroad as are the South American coca growers. Local producers appear commonly to have taken up their role when they have no other subsistence options. Some local people in St Lawrence Island, Alaska, would choose factory jobs over pothunting but for a lack of permanent employment. Local opinion of pothunting on St Lawrence Island varies: some enjoying the occupation (cf. Jolles 2002) and others feeling that it is yet another way non-indigenous outsiders appropriate culture (Hollowell-Zimmer 2003; Zimmer 2003).

The use of material culture as a commodity is sometimes perceived by local people to be an ancestral contribution to the present-day population's well-being. One informant from St Lawrence Island summarised this idea by saying, 'Our Ancestors left us these things so we could survive in a cash economy' (Hollowell-Zimmer 2003: 50). Modern Etruscan tomb robbers view the ancient Etruscans as their guardians and defenders against the injustices of state and church. The ancients are not angered by tomb robbers but guide them to buried treasure so the robbers can escape from poverty unjustly imposed on them by those in power (Thoden van Velzen 1999: 188–9). A similar sentiment has been expressed by local peasant farmers in Belize who tunnel into Mayan temples (Matsuda 1998a, as cited in Hollowell-Zimmer 2003). Some local people in Peru have assisted outsiders in raiding Moche graves (Walter Alva pers. comm.). The latter case is interesting, for some looters changed their attitudes from disregard to curatorship after finding local pride through a myth created by archaeologists surrounding a spectacular (and documented) find, 'El Señor de Sipán' (Alva 2001).

Some local people choose to protect their material past and perceive value in terms of heritage. This was the case in most parts of Iraq until the United Nations sanctions necessitated diversification of livelihoods in order to make ends meet. The Iraqi case shows how poverty promotes the destruction of contexts, even when the material past is usually highly valued by local people as a resource to be preserved.

National governments may also value their country's past. Greece values the material culture of the past highly, perhaps because it is truly a form of commercial capital, given that cultural tourism comprises a significant percentage of the gross national product. Other countries also value material culture and claim ownership over all archaeological materials. In such cases, individuals are often allowed to possess objects but it is the state that controls the movement of objects (Vitelli 1996), as they are deemed the nation's cultural property.

Turkey, for example, also places high monetary value on its material culture heritage. For some time it has had a policy of attempting to recover stolen antiquities. Many of the antiquities Turkey sought to repatriate are sitting in museums (Rose and Acar 1996). A few years ago, the legal fine for looting in Bulgaria was 12 US dollars. While this is a paltry sum compared to the hundreds to thousands of dollars local middlemen might receive in return for the sale of Roman coins and other portable valuables (Bailey 1996), and while the Bulgarian or other governments do not have the funds actively to patrol for the prevention of looting, such legal penalties do prove that a government values the documentation and conservation of its citizens' collective past.

 Curators sometimes straddle a fine ethical line between courting wealthy benefactors who will donate either collections or money towards acquisitions, and opposing illegal trade in antiquities. In the United States federal tax law facilitates these relationships. Benefactors receive substantial tax breaks from donating antiquities (Vitelli 1996a), even when the material culture comes from undocumented contexts (Renfrew 2000). One also can surmise that at least some benefactors derive pleasure from having peers and members of the public admire the material culture that they acquired.

Morphy (2000; cf. Bourdieu 1984) points out that value in the Western world is an assignation that closely connects with class. As items are reproduced so too does the marker by which antiquities and replicas are judged get raised. This may in turn increase demand for antiquities, particularly from economically advantaged people. It is indeed the latter group who ultimately should be held accountable for the destruction of archaeological contexts and misappropriation of cultural heritage. This group seeks the 'authentic' at any price in order to display and enjoy 'the exotic' on their living room walls and in other areas within their homes (cf. Graburn 1976).

Major auction houses hold seasonal bids for antiquities (Renfrew 2000) and this too perpetuates demand from the wealthy. One idea for curbing the illicit antiquities trade is to have nations sign and enforce the UNESCO treaty, which bans the trade of illicit antiquities. Another more radical idea is to allow for material culture to be legally sold after it has been excavated and published (O'Keefe 1997). No matter the provisions for curbing the illicit sale of antiquities, it is certainly the case that the trade itself is driven primarily by the interest of wealthy collectors (Alva 2001) including, sadly, some museum curators (cf. Brodie and Doole 2001). Academics may indirectly profit from antiquities in so far as some get employed on the basis of expert knowledge of material culture (Watkins 2000a).

Julie Hollowell-Zimmer (2003) ponders ways in which archaeologists can combat the antiquities trade. She reports that the greatest success stories have occurred in participatory projects, where local communities work long term with archaeologists to halt looting. Joe Watkins (2000b), seeking to advance collaboration between indigenous communities and archaeologists, advocates projects where both parties share and learn from one another. Attitudes cannot change overnight but education and co-operation are perhaps a key to turning the tide towards context preservation or, at the very least, documentation that is satisfactory to both native communities and archaeological anthropologists. Here again, the value of dialogue in the interpretation of culture is underlined.

POTHUNTING, METAL DETECTING AND THE VALUE OF PORTABLE ANTIQUITIES

Pothunting is one of the most rampant and culturally acceptable forms of context destruction. As a general term, pothunting is used as a term which describes the general removal of portable antiquities from their context, whether pottery, lithics or metalwork. Pothunting is a pastime that is done individually, in groups or with family members. This is at least the case in developed countries. Some of the valuables recovered may eventually be shown to a local archaeological authority, but even if the location of recovery accompanies such a report it may still not be formally documented. This is because standard databases for recording goods which are recovered and stored by individuals are only just coming into use (see below).

Since the 1970s, nations with high per capita incomes and ample leisure time have had a burgeoning trend in metal-detecting (cf. Addyman 2001). People use metal detectors to search for metalwork much as people scan tilled fields or desert surfaces for shards of pottery or lithics. The number of goods recovered through this pastime is difficult to assess. One probable figure for the annual number of items in one English county alone, Kent, is roughly 100,000. Metal detecting clubs are popular also in North America and in other parts of Europe (Addyman 2001).

Laws in England and Wales such as the Treasure Act 1996 encourage metal detecting. Under this law, any person may recover coins or objects made of gold as well as any other additional items found with the metallic remains. The goods recovered may become public property, but not before the person who found the items is paid the equivalent of market value (Redmond-Cooper and Palmer 1999, as cited in Addyman 2001). Landowners and their agents may search for, find and sell antiquities from private property they own or manage. These laws and customs are quite different from those in Scotland and Northern Ireland, where all portable antiquities must be reported and sometimes relinquished to the relevant local authorities (Addyman 2001). The Scottish approach has however also caused problems. Siân Jones describes the long battle fought by the Scottish community of Hilton of Cadboll to have a local Pictish monument returned. For them, the monument's removal by a local landowner and its subsequent presentation to the National Museum of Antiquities was iconic of the Highland Clearances. When the Museum of Scotland refused to return the original, a replica (or 'reconstruction') was carved. To everyone's astonishment, as the date for erection of the replica approached, nearby excavations revealed the base of the original carved stone slab still buried in the ground. The local community mounted a campaign to prevent its removal, and negotiations with the organisation Historic Scotland were still underway in 2003 (Jones 2003), although the National Museum of Scotland has recently offered to put excavated fragments on display in the village (Jones in press: 112).

The variation in legal outlook regarding portable antiquities even between these closely linked countries is interesting. Culture in the form of portable antiquities, though highly valued by all states of the United Kingdom, is a bankable commodity in only certain parts of Great Britain. The Treasure Act makes the undocumented removal of portable antiquities in England a legal pastime where in other countries the same action is both condemned and illegal. It combines interestingly with the Portable Antiquities Scheme, which was established for all of England and Wales in 2001 to provide a medium for portable antiquities and their contexts recovered by metal detectors and other individuals to be recorded by archaeologists. Both the Treasure Act and the Portable Antiquities Scheme were created partially through the archaeological community acknowledging that portable antiquities are a commodity for which members of the public will continue to search in their leisure time. Both archaeologists and pothunters value 'portable culture', and because they have worked together on this common interest many finds have been reported and documented in England and Wales since the Portable Antiquities Scheme and Treasure Act were created. The same is also true in other states where archaeologists and local treasure hunters maintain good relations, which is fortunate considering that many governments cannot afford to reimburse pothunters the value of looted goods (cf. Abungu 2001; Gado 2001). It is, however, disturbing to find that some antiquities dealers argue they value the past as much as archaeologists; the only difference is their wish to make a profit from it (Watkins 2000a).

KENNEWICK MAN

In 1996 two men watching boat races found part of a human skull on a stretch of the Columbia River owned by the United States Army Corps of Engineers. Subsequent searches found a near complete skeleton. The remains were originally thought to be those of a nineteenth-century trapper, and when they were described as 'Caucasoid' in form that attribution appeared unproblematic. Subsequent dating of the skeleton, which became known as 'Kennewick Man', has shown it to be roughly 9300 years old (Watkins 2000b), rendering its supposed ethnic affiliation far more contentious.

The Native American Graves Protection and Repatriation Act (NAGPRA), passed in 1990, was designed to protect Native American human remains. Under NAGPRA, tribal communities may legally petition for the return of burial goods, skeletons and other cultural objects to which they are linked. Thus museums and individual collectors alike may have to return goods. Public agencies must report new discoveries; permits must be obtained from pertinent Native American tribes for new excavations on tribal or federal land of human remains or cultural objects.

Shortly after Kennewick Man's discovery eight anthropologists sued the federal government in order to study the remains, which are being stored in the Burke Museum in Seattle. This suit was upheld by the US District Court in Portland. In reaction to the court's decision, the Pacific

Northwest tribes of the Umatilla, Nez Perce, Colville and Yakama went to the 9th US Circuit Court of Appeals, which in 2004 ruled in favour of the anthropologists. The tribes decided not to contest this decision and, likewise, the US Justice Department decided not to ask the US Supreme Court to review the case before the statute of limitations for an appeal expired. At present the anthropologists are working with the US Army Corps of Engineers on the details of the study (*Tri-City Herald*, 22 July 2004).

As Pardoe has pointed out, it is the oldest skeletal remains that have most significance as cultural property for indigenous communities (Pardoe 1991). The older the evidence of human occupation, the stronger the claim to indigeneity. One of the points of controversy was whether the Pacific Northwest tribes could claim ancestry with the remains. A Umatilla religious leader addressed this issue of antiquity and ancestry by writing, 'If this individual is truly over 9,000 years old, that only substantiates our belief that he is Native American. From our oral histories, we know that our people have been part of this land since the beginning of time. . .' (Watkins 2000b: 136). The controversy surrounding Kennewick Man brings to the fore some of the debates about ownership of the past. Whilst the skeletal remains themselves are a type of commodity, it is control over the commodity which remains the key issue between the different stakeholders. In one sense this issue touches a raw nerve for the archaeological community and the debate about the peopling of North America. On the other, the Native American communities ask yet again whether remains to which they feel connected are going to be appropriated in the name of science. It is not without irony that the two communities who in a previous section combine to combat illicit raiding in fact also at times polarise against each other when the interests are not mutual. In some senses, this issue is further addressed using another case study in the next section.

ARCHAEOLOGY AND NATIVE TITLE IN AUSTRALIA

Australia was colonised on the notorious legal premise that hunter-gatherers could not own land because they neither fenced nor cultivated it. It was not until 1993 that the Australian Native Title Act finally acknowledged that Australia had not been 'empty country' when the British colonised it, and that precolonial rights to land could have persisted till the present. The court ruling that gave rise to the Native Title Act found that 'where a clan or group has continued to acknowledge the laws and (so far as practicable) to observe the customs based on the traditions of the clan or group, whereby their traditional connection with the land had been substantially maintained, the traditional community title of that clan or group can be said to remain in existence'. It was, however, also found that 'a native title which has ceased with the abandoning of laws and customs based on tradition cannot be revived for contemporary recognition' (Keon-Cohen 1993: 189). Indigenous sites and artefacts have played a crucial role in establishing continuity of residence and custom. As material evidence of collective rights, archaeological material again became cultural property.

Sections 13 and 61 of the Native Title Act stated that it is essential to demonstrate the claimants' connection with their traditional land, according to traditional law. (Land that has been legally handed over to someone else by the government can no longer be claimed. This excludes private property, and public land such as National Parks.) The Native Title Act also allows for the surrender of title in exchange for compensation, and this led some mining companies to negotiate deals with the Aboriginal owners of their mining leases, in order to pre-empt lengthy court cases.

Bradshaw (2000) documents the processes that led Hamersley Iron to develop a consultation programme with Aboriginal communities whose traditional lands fall within or were threatened by mining leases. Thanks to Hamersley Iron's Heritage Program, in Western Australia Aboriginal staff have gained skills in archaeological survey methods, site recording and assessment. Bradshaw concludes that the significance of archaeology to indigenous people is inversely related to the strength of living traditions. Where oral tradition is strong, it gives a greater sense of continuity from the past than does evidence recovered from excavations. Where people have been displaced to towns, excavations in their traditional country can provide useful evidence of past habitation. Even in the north of Western Australia, however, native elders pressed more strongly for excavations of rock shelters that might be disturbed by mining than did archaeologists, who would have preferred to leave artefacts *in situ*.

The first two Native Title claims to be heard in court were at opposite ends of Australia: the Miriuwung-Gajerrong claim in the cattle ranching region of northern Australia and the Yorta-Yorta claim in the heavily colonised Murray River region of southern Australia. Archaeologists were called upon in both cases, to provide evidence that the claimant group had continuously occupied the area since before European colonisation. In the Miriuwung-Gajerrong case, archaeologists successfully demonstrated that the community had sustained a hunting-gathering economy since long before colonisation, had continued to practise rock art according to traditional laws that required persons only to paint in their inherited country, and had maintained inter-group relations through traditional trade in (for example) stone for spear points (Fullagar and Head 2000: 28–30).

Not surprisingly (given the cost of a successful claim and the intensity of colonisation) the other, Yorta-Yorta claim failed. Although a large number of archaeological sites were located, the judge, Mr Justice Olney, ruled that there was no evidence to link them with the claimants, and no evidence that the claimants possessed unbroken links with the Aboriginal inhabitants of precolonial times (Fullagar and Head 2000: 31–2). Harrison (2000) and Murray (2000) argue that Australian archaeologists have spent too much time searching for evidence of the undoubtedly newsworthy, oldest Aboriginal sites, and neglected the less exotic subject of colonial archaeology. Many contemporary native Australians, particularly those whose traditions have been disrupted through forced removal to boarding schools, attach more importance to recovering the recent past through old photographs, written archives, genealogies and archaeology. Murray (2000: 65) writes, 'positing the existence of research agendas which do not coincide with the expressed interests of Indigenous Australians raises the question of whether such agendas can be ethically pursued by archaeologists in the face of Aboriginal opposition'.

Archaeology and Ayodhya

Australian Native Title claims are not the only context in which archaeologists have been called upon as expert witnesses. Archaeology has, for example, played a key role in the Ayodhya dispute, where the prior existence of a Hindu temple on the site of the mosque was alleged to justify the mosque's demolition. The Indian archaeologist B. B. Lal began research on the archaeology of sites named in the Ramayana epic in 1975. He conducted two seasons of excavations at Ayodhya. It was, however, not until October 1988 that Professor Lal reported he had uncovered what he interpreted as a series of brick-built pillar bases adjacent to the mosque. Lal surmised that a number of carved black stone pillars incorporated into the mosque might originally have stood on these bases. Proponents of the argument that the first Mughal emperor had destroyed a Hindu temple in order to build the mosque capitalised on Lal's report to support their case. The pillar bases appeared to continue under the mosque and it was argued that the motifs carved on the pillars incorporated into the mosque were of Hindu origin.

During the campaign to demolish the mosque another group of Indian archaeologists claimed to have discovered further evidence for the prior existence of a temple (Sharma *et al.* 1992). A 'hoard' of about twelve pieces of stone sculpture was reportedly found in a large pit about 9 metres from the mosque. Yet more stone objects were said to have been found during the mosque's destruction. Some were allegedly sealed within the walls. The most significant of these were a statue of Rama and a stone plaque carrying an inscription recording the construction of a temple dedicated to Rama (see Lal 2001). These objects were not found under controlled archaeological conditions: 'The area was crowded with a frenzied mob adamant on breaking every single brick of the structure' (Mandal 1993: 50). It also seems odd, as Mandal comments, that if the emperor Babur really destroyed a temple to Rama, he should have sealed a statue of Rama and the intact inscription in the walls of the mosque he built in its place.

The campaign to build a temple on the site of the mosque went to the Allahabad High Court, where the judge hearing the case ordered a controlled excavation in an attempt to determine whether or not a temple had previously stood there. The archaeologist Nayanjot Lahiri, among others, has pointed out that, even if there had been a temple, this would not justify destruction of the mosque. Lahiri (*Hindustan Times*, 2 October 2003) also argues that archaeologists are not accustomed to digging for 'proof' of a hypothesis. They deal with probabilities and fragments of the past. Some of the artefacts excavated at Ayodhya under the court's direction, such as female figurines and votive tanks, can indeed have a religious meaning, but they are ubiquitous objects that are frequently encountered in sites of folk worship. The multicultural character of northern India's history has resulted in the same artistic motifs and architectural styles being adopted by different faiths. There is nothing specifically 'Hindu' or 'Buddhist' or 'Jaina' about fragments with floral decorations, such as lotus petal motifs and the lotus medallion. One square slab found during the excavations has a *srivatsa* motif that is frequently found on the chest of a Jaina *tirthankara*.[1]

The seventeen rows of pillars partially located by Lal in the 1970s proved to be associated with a 50 metre wall and were perhaps the remains of two pillared halls, but there was no convincing evidence they belonged

---

1 A *srivatsa* is a geometric motif often depicted on statues of Jaina saviour figures, or *tirthankara* (Michael Carrithers, pers. comm.).

to a Hindu temple. In medieval north India Buddhist and Jaina temples, and mosques, were all pillared. No statues or inscriptions diagnostic of a particular religion were associated with them.

CONCLUSION

In this chapter we have explored some ethical issues that arise where there is a contest between treating artefacts as commodities or as cultural property. We drew attention to the importance Bourdieu attributed to material culture in the transmission of *habitus*. While even commodities are cultural artefacts, certain objects, monuments and buildings can embody the values of a community, becoming cultural property. Traditional culture may be legitimately commodified through tourist art and eco-tourism. It may also be appropriated by outsiders who market indigenous images without the artists' consent, or who dig up antiquities for illicit sale. If money can be made from marketing indigenous art and literature, fakes and forgeries will be perpetrated. Archaeology contributes to the creation of that value. The extent to which the descendent community can claim rights to its inherited cultural property, and the point at which images become freely available to enterprising commercial interests, is debated.

Culture is negotiated and argued over. We have explored ethical issues where different communities dispute the significance of artefacts as cultural property. We cited examples of conflict between Serbs, Croats and Bosnians following the disintegration of Yugoslavia in the early 1990s, and Hindu–Muslim conflict in northern India over the history and fate of the mosque at Ayodhya. Cultural property may be destroyed during conflict between opposed cultural communities. Archaeologists can contribute to and become embroiled in violent events, as at Ayodhya.

We noted Foucault's argument concerning the role of discourse in shaping perception of its subject matter. The writing of professional ecologists can seem alienating to local communities, who have their own discourse concerning their environment. The way that archaeologists write about artefacts can determine popular evaluations, and archaeologists' research agendas may lead to the neglect of issues that the living heirs to past cultures consider more important. We looked at cases of successful cooperation between archaeologists and native people, where both parties contribute to the other's understanding. Archaeologists can provide expert testimony, intervening in legal contests such as the quest of Aboriginal communities in Australia to have their native title recognised, or the claim that a Hindu temple once stood on the site of the Ayodhya mosque. The case for demolishing the mosque at Ayodhya gained momentum from the archaeologist Lal's report of finding the foundations of an earlier pillared building beneath. The case of Kennewick Man exemplifies how an object can be constructed as an artefact in three competing discourses. Local native people regard ancient bones as part of their indigenous inheritance, archaeologists treat bones as a source of scientific data, and extremists in the dominant population see Kennewick as evidence that an ancient white race preceded Native Americans, who cannot therefore claim to be truly aboriginal.

CHAPTER 5

Moral arguments on subsistence digging

Julie Hollowell

The undocumented excavation of archaeological materials for the commercial market, often called 'looting' by archaeologists, clearly damages the archaeological record and conflicts with contemporary principles of archaeological ethics. This chapter reflects upon the ethical divide between archaeologists and 'looters' with a particular focus on attitudes surrounding one form of undocumented excavation, 'subsistence digging'. It may upset some archaeologists to discuss subsistence digging so openly, as if doing so gives credence to the activity itself, but I take the stance that everyone concerned with working towards solutions to what is, for archaeology, a troubling dilemma benefits from a closer look at the situation and trying to understand the social, economic and historical standpoints involved.

Practising archaeology in today's world requires dealing with a range of interests, often in the spirit of compromise and negotiation, and a willingness to respect other legitimate points of view. The past certainly does not serve only one purpose or one group of stakeholders (Wilk 1999). Archaeologists are often called upon to balance ethically or to negotiate their own interests and definitions of conservation, significance, stewardship or appropriate management with those of others.

Perhaps more so than anyone, owing to their position of expertise and their claim to be stewards of the archaeological record, archaeologists have an obligation to examine and clarify the philosophical arguments that underlie their attitudes towards subjects such as looting, the commercial use of artefacts, subsistence digging, collecting or other practices, which they deem unethical (Wylie 2003: 5–6). This kind of moral inquiry, which involves the process of looking closely at the moral arguments underlying one's convictions, has at least two important purposes (Moody-Adams 1997: 111; Salmon 1997: 59). One is better to understand the person or position with whom or with which one disagrees. Another is to encourage the kind of self-scrutiny 'which may lead one to see oneself, one's relations to others, and one's place in the world in a different way' (Moody-Adams 1997: 120), thus opening up the possibility of considering alternative approaches to a seemingly unsolvable dilemma. When it comes to a particular problematic situation, ethical differences can sometimes be resolved, or at least a better or less harmful course of action determined, by a deeper, less partial understanding of the specific conditions under which people make certain moral choices (Salmon 1997: 48).

LOOTING

My discussion examines attitudes about a particular kind of 'looting', which I will call 'undocumented digging' – the act of taking objects from the ground – sometimes referred to as pothunting. This makes a distinction between looting which directly impacts upon the archaeological record, and that which involves objects already long removed from sites, but called 'looted' because they were stolen from a museum, crossed borders illegally or were implicated in some other illicit activity. It is important to distinguish among different kinds of looting because, although there are overlaps among these situations, they represent different problems and are likely to call for different approaches. If the real objective is to protect what remains of the archaeological record, it makes sense to focus on what is happening 'on the ground'.

Many archaeologists have argued long and hard against looting and the commercial use of artefacts (Brodie *et al.* 2001; Coggins 1972; Elia 1997; Gill and Chippindale 1993; O'Keefe 1997; Renfrew 2000; Smith & Ehrenhard 1991; Tubb 1995). The Society for American Archaeology's (SAA) Principles of Ethics and other professional codes speak strongly against any support for such activities and give clear arguments as to why (Lynott and Wylie 1995). In actuality, and in spite of what is written in any professional code, archaeologists' attitudes about undocumented digging range, as Matsuda noted, from empathy to vilification (Matsuda 1998a: 88), and many have had close encounters of more than one kind with these activities in the field (see Green *et al.* 2003 for a particularly candid account). Written accounts of interfaces between archaeological practice and looting, which are all too few and far between, are important because they shed light on the nuances and complexities of these situations and the consequences of various ways of responding.[1] As Wylie

---

1 For examples described by archaeologists see Alva 2001; Brodie *et al.* in press; Early 1999; Green *et al.* 2003; Munson and Jones 1995; Harrington 1991; McEwan *et al.* 1994; Pendergast 1991, 1994;

suggests, a systematic, empirical evaluation of the negative and positive consequences of different approaches to dealing with an ethical dilemma such as undocumented digging is a much-needed next step (2003: 9–13; 1996: 178–80), but will not be tackled here.

The term 'looter' lumps together people with diverse motivations and interests, including those who engage in a legal hobby that defines, for them, a close, sometimes even a hereditary, connection to a particular place (see Colwell-Chanthaphonh 2004; LaBelle 2003) and others who see digging and its profits as socially acceptable and justifiable in the face of government neglect (Migliore 1991). In some places, undocumented destruction of archaeological sites goes hand in hand with government corruption (see Carleton *et al.* 2004; Sandler 2004; Stark and Griffin 2004), the cultivation of an 'outlaw' image (Early 1999) or an individual's status as a 'local expert' (Smith 2005). Almost all discussions of looting have focused on its illicit nature (Brodie *et al.* 2001; Schmidt and McIntosh 1996; Tubb 1995; Renfrew 2000), though not all undocumented digging is against the law.[2] My concern here is not with the licit or illicit nature of the activity, except to the extent that legal mechanisms and the policies of institutions reflect certain moral standpoints and have diverse consequences.

Calling someone a 'looter' is meant to instil shame and shows strong moral opposition to the unauthorised taking of things from archaeological sites (McIntosh 1996). On the other hand, the label can be downright lionising to those who identify with its outlaw connotations, and others see it as a word used by the state to mark its authority. As far as I know, diggers never refer to themselves as 'looters'. Migliore (1991) describes how diggers in Sicily perceived themselves not as looters or criminals, but as treasure hunters who have been marginalised by the state. Use of such a loaded, one-sided term can be counterproductive to dialogue and the search for mutually beneficial solutions. The fact that, in the late 1980s, some archaeologists publicly called St Lawrence Islanders – some of whom legally dig on private property for goods to sell – 'looters' and 'cultural cannibals' still hinders dialogue and relations between

---

Schmidt and McIntosh 1996; Staley 1993; Stark and Griffin 2004. Many more examples are reported by journalists (Kirkpatrick 1992). For a particularly cogent account, see Smith 2005.

2 In most of the United States, for example, it is perfectly legal for landowners to dig into old sites on their lands for artefacts and sell them, unless they are from a burial context. Most states in the USA now have laws protecting even unmarked burials, and a few have successfully restricted digging on private land by requiring a permit for intentional archaeological excavations (Canouts and McManamon 2001). While many archaeologists would, on ethical grounds, call this, and any unauthorised alterations to sites or their contents, 'looting', others who adhere to a strictly legal definition do not (Hutt *et al.* 1992: 11).

archaeologists and community members, especially since, only fifty years before, archaeologists were packing up and leaving with crates of human remains.

SUBSISTENCE DIGGING

My discussion in this chapter is limited to 'subsistence digging': where people dig to find archaeological goods to sell and use the proceeds to support a subsistence lifestyle. David Staley employed the term to describe the digging on St Lawrence Island (Staley 1993), and Dave Matsuda used it in his ethnography of diggers in Belize (Matsuda 1998a). St Lawrence Islanders now use the term to refer to their own activities. Focusing on a particular kind of undocumented digging helps begin to differentiate among the various forms these activities can take and the motivations behind them.

Subsistence digging is the major source of newly excavated materials on the market. This form of 'looting' plays an important social and economic role in many countries around the world. It is often a local response to specific political and economic needs and situations. The term is not neutral. Use of the word 'subsistence' in this context euphemises the negative connotations of 'looting' and invokes a discourse of self-determination and economic justice, one that is associated today with struggles of peoples all over the world to maintain access to resources important to local livelihoods (Nuttall 1998; Young 1995).

Subsistence harvests once were defined as non-commercial, but no longer. Even economists realise that many subsistence activities require substantial inputs of cash and sometimes generate cash as well. Digging for artefacts is consistent with the ideology of subsistence in many ways and has much in common with other hunting or gathering practices (see Hollowell 2004:101–3; Krupnik 1993). It even has aspects of the thrill of the hunt. Yet unlike *renewable* subsistence resources, there is no such thing as a 'sustainable harvest' of the archaeological record. Furthermore, the ethical lines between what is considered subsistence use of a resource and a use that would be considered extravagant are far from clear or unanimously drawn. These issues come up again below, because they underpin some of the moral arguments used to support or oppose subsistence digging.

Two sources provide the primary frame for my discussion of the diverse moral claims that surround subsistence digging. One is a conversation on the electronic mailing list of the World Archaeological Congress. The other is my ethnographic study of legal subsistence digging in the Bering Strait region of Alaska, where Native residents have for generations been digging for long-buried walrus ivory, whalebone and worked artefacts as a way of generating needed cash or commodities to use in trade (Hollowell 2004). Studies of subsistence diggers by Matsuda (1998a, 1998b) and Paredes-Maury (1998) offer additional support for moral arguments that underlie the activities of diggers, as does information from shorter accounts and journalistic sources. The situation in Alaska is especially interesting because it offers a case where digging and selling archaeological materials is not illicit. Removing the issue of illegality puts the focus on the role that rights and ethics play in arguments for or against undocumented digging. In general, the more information that archaeologists or local communities have about the varied contexts in which subsistence digging occurs, the better informed their decisions and responses can be.

THE WORLD ARCHAEOLOGICAL CONGRESS DISCUSSION

In December 2003, a flurry of correspondence on the subject of looting erupted among archaeologists on the World Archaeological Congress (WAC) electronic mail distribution list, which circulates messages among WAC members. This cyber-storm was prompted by an e-mail from Sam Hardy, who had submitted a rather controversial proposition to the membership and Executive Council at WAC5 (the fifth quadrennial meeting) in Washington, DC, several months before. The proposition, which Sam had framed in accordance with principles stated in the United Nations Universal Declaration of Human Rights, took the position, in simple terms, that a person has a 'right to loot' and to sell artefacts for subsistence purposes if other alternatives for livelihood are not available (Hardy 2004). WAC is recognised as a liberal body in the spectrum of archaeological organisations. Still, the proposition was, according to Hardy, strongly opposed.[3] In mid-December, Sam sought further explanations for the reactions from the WAC membership list to what he thought was a well-constructed argument.

---

3 I would be remiss not to mention that a very different proposition, submitted to the same body, which supported the carrying of weapons by archaeologists in areas of widespread looting, was reportedly roundly rejected on the premise that defending the archaeological record did not justify endangering human life (K. A. Pyburn, pers. comm. August 2003).

The ensuing emails elicited a range of responses and quite a bit of discussion. It goes without saying that the particular background, values and experiences of a respondent affect that person's standpoint. Here I am interested in the range of moral stances these archaeologists took in critiquing or justifying subsistence digging, or what Hardy calls the right to loot.

The reader should keep in mind that Hardy's proposition grows out of the trying times surrounding war and destruction in Afghanistan and Iraq. Like myself, and others, he was haunted by the fact that humanitarian aid for the millions in Afghanistan appeared to come only after the destruction of antiquities (Hardy 2003). Second, as several contributors to the web discussion pointed out, supporting someone's right to loot under certain circumstances should not be considered tantamount to a blanket support for looting itself.

I have drawn below from the WAC discussion list and other sources to delineate some of the main arguments that emerged in support of and in opposition to subsistence digging. I describe each of these moral arguments and how they justify certain positions, examining some of the points for and against each argument, based on my own research on subsistence digging in the Bering Strait region of Alaska, other ethnographic accounts of subsistence digging, and additional reports of digging activities in scholarly and popular sources, including newspapers and magazines. The objective here is neither an apology for nor a condemnation of looting or subsistence digging, but the closer scrutiny of diverse moral positions in light of some of the evidence. The topic would benefit from further clarification of various arguments and the incorporation of additional evidence from a much wider range of voices, especially those of subsistence diggers.

THE ECONOMIC JUSTICE ARGUMENT

The primary moral argument that Hardy and others used in support of subsistence digging or the 'right to loot' is based on principles of economic justice. This ethic allows that under certain conditions of poverty or lack of other means of livelihood, people are justified in using archaeological goods as an economic resource. An even broader ethic underlies this one: that concern for things, whether artefacts or archaeological sites, should not come before concern for human life. Mark Kenoyer, an archaeologist who works in Pakistan, put it this way: 'Why should we expect the

Pakistanis to care about archaeology when they're worried about staying alive?' (Kenoyer 2002).

All evidence points to a strong relationship between digging for the market and a lack of viable economic alternatives (Heath 1973; Hollowell 2002, 2004; Matsuda 1998a, 1998b; Paredes-Maury 1998). Reports of digging continue to emerge from developing regions, where carving out a living is a constant challenge, and one major find can provide the equivalent of a family's annual income (Beech 2003; Heath 1973: 263; Stark and Griffin 2004). In many cases, increases in site digging are directly linked to a deterioration of local economic conditions and opportunities, often due to uncontrollable events such as drought (Brent 1994; Lawler 2003), political instability (Blumt 2002; Matsuda 1998b; Paredes-Maury 1998), major changes in the local economic base (Hollowell 2004), or any combination of these. The area around Blanding, Utah, for example, became infamous for pothunting after the shutdown of uranium mines left many local residents unemployed. In these situations, one valuable find can incite widespread digging. This was the case in south-eastern Iran, where drought, desperate economic conditions and the discovery of a lucrative site attracted whole families (Lawler 2003). Typically, the vast majority of diggers are those most directly affected by civil unrest and economic upheaval – local residents. In Israel, it is reported that 99 per cent of artefact diggers are shepherds or inhabitants of nearby villages, many of whom lost their livelihoods in the wake of the Intifada (Blumt 2002). Matsuda reported similar results from his research in Belize (Matsuda 1998a, 1998b).

War triggers the social disintegration and loss of livelihood that precipitates subsistence digging. Families uprooted by war and forced to leave behind their lands and all their assets turn to carrying off portable antiquities in an attempt to ensure their own survival.[4] War also encourages other less justifiable forms of looting. Often both sides engage in opportunistic digging and theft of cultural property, frequently with the complicity of insider officials or the military. This has been true in Iraq where local villagers and professional looters alike inundated sites and started digging on a massive scale. Still, according to reporters, digging

---

4 According to an art collector who has been offered goods from various parts of the world over the years, this explains much of the influx on the art market of goods from specific war-torn regions during times of disruption (P. Lewis, pers. comm. 19 February 2005). It follows that collectors feel that they are providing aid to those in need when they purchase these objects.

has been much more widespread in southern Iraq because of the endemic poverty in that region (Carleton *et al.* 2004).

The vacuum created by economic disintegration also attracts organised crime and black-market entrepreneurs to the artefact market who often employ area residents as diggers (Brent 1996; Heath 1973; Matsuda 1998b). In the Ukraine, for example,

Mafia groups . . . are pursuing a lucrative sideline in archaeology, looting valuable artefacts to be sold on the black market, in addition to their traditional criminal enterprises . . . Some of the mafia families have employed archaeologists to work directly for them, after making them an offer that they can't refuse . . . The economy here is very depressed, people need the money. (McLeod 2002)

In a case like this, would the economic justice argument support the right to dig for some and not others?

There are probably more situations than we would like to think where entire communities see the looting of sites as a legitimate route to financial gain and an act of social justice, in open defiance of laws that are perceived as indifferent and unresponsive to local concerns. This attitude was evident in Sicily, where Migliore (1991) found that people perceived the government not as a protector of archaeological heritage, but as an entity that was diverting what should be local wealth to foreign archaeologists. In these cases, the apathy or the disapproval of government can be interpreted as unwillingness to 'confront the fact that there are indigenous peoples among them – oppressed by land speculation and resource-hungry militaries, constrained from extra-local commerce, and lacking political power – who dig their ancestors' remains to put food on the table' (Matsuda 1998a: 90).

An economic justice argument also lends ethical weight to the 'right to dig' when it is conceptualised in terms of class struggle, one that pits wealthy archaeologists and governments against poor producers, rather than as merely a cultural one, over heritage preservation. According to Matsuda, many subsistence diggers in Belize saw things in this light. Archaeologists arrived each year with elaborate equipment, treating local people as low-paid workers with little or no chance of advancement. They returned to fancy homes and well-paid careers made possible by artefacts and information excavated and extracted with government permission, while those who used the proceeds of their digging to buy seed corn, medicine, clothing and food were considered villains (Matsuda 1998a: 93). To paraphrase Anne Pyburn, archaeologists 'take the gap between vernacular perceptions of the world and ours to be cultural gaps', or gaps in understanding, as if 'they' don't understand the importance of heritage, when the differences are to a great extent economic – and often not by choice but by necessity (Pyburn 2003: 171).

A major problem with the economic justice argument is its lack of clarity about who would be eligible for the 'right to loot'. What circumstances, if any, are dire enough to warrant digging into an archaeological site? Should we attempt to distinguish between 'better' and 'worse' diggers based on intentions and consequences, on whether the money they receive from digging is used to buy food, computers, cigarettes or methamphetamines? How would anyone draw the line between subsistence digging as a necessity for livelihood and when it is merely a supplement to an adequate standard of living?

Evidence shows that people dig for a wide variety of reasons. In some places, digging for artefacts is part of the seasonal round, done in conjunction with other subsistence activities (Hollowell 2004; Matsuda 1998a, 1998b; Paredes-Maury 1998). In Belize, the amount of digging in any one year was said to be more closely related to the success or failure of that year's crops than to auction house prices (Matsuda 1998a: 94). In northwestern Alaska, families go digging together on weekends for recreation, children dig for fun and curiosity, people dig to help pay the bills, or to buy groceries and equipment for subsistence hunting. In many cases eliminating digging altogether would increase the economic hardship communities already face. Subsistence digging is a way to convert locally available resources into cash, material goods and opportunity – those things so many of us desire in today's world. In China, Arctic Alaska, Latin America and elsewhere, people have acquired the capital needed to start a business, attend college or medical school or start a new life after fleeing a war-torn country by selling excavated goods.

Framing the right to dig as a question of economic justice certainly carries moral weight, but in most cases the dilemma of subsistence digging – and at least part of the solution — appears more generally related to a straightforward lack of alternative economic opportunities. In the Bering Strait, when jobs with a more reliable income were available in a community, such as working on the construction crew of a water and sewer project, even the most inveterate diggers stopped digging. There were still people who preferred the independence and flexible hours of digging or who dug mainly for recreation, but, to the dismay of dealers, the major suppliers of the market were preoccupied during the digging season.

DIGGERS AS VICTIMS OF A GLOBAL MARKET

A corollary to the economic justice argument is the notion that subsistence diggers are victims of a global market, exploited by the demands and desires of dealers and collectors, who are the real villains. Ample evidence for this comes from the reports that diggers typically receive a very small percentage of the final market value of their finds (Alva 2001; Coe 1993; Pendergast 1994). But a less typical example comes from St Lawrence Island, which represents a legal market for artefacts. In this case, diggers demand and obtain consistently high returns for their goods, now that they have access to the estimates in Sotheby's catalogues. This seems to be evidence that a *legal* market, with fewer intermediaries and less risk, offers higher returns to subsistence diggers, but we do not have enough cases really to evaluate this claim.

A corollary to this argument appears to be that if diggers were to receive higher prices, they would dig less. At least on St Lawrence Island, this does not appear to be the case. Higher prices for artefacts do not slow down the digging; if anything, they incite more people, including groups of kids, to head out with hopes of hitting a jackpot. At a closer look, while arguments about how little or how much diggers are paid for artefacts may appeal to an ethic of economic justice, they are irrelevant to concerns of protecting the archaeological record, except that they might indicate what the value of an economic substitute would need to be to persuade people to stop digging.

The main thrust of the 'global victim' argument, however, is to apologise for the activities of subsistence diggers and place the blame for undocumented digging on other parts of the market, notably wealthy collectors, who are seen as the 'real looters'. Much has been written from this moral perspective (Elia 1997; Renfrew 1993), but we are only beginning to acquire ethnographic descriptions that are detailed and broad enough to clarify how various participants in specific markets for archaeological goods manipulate supply and demand (see Brent 1996; Coe 1993; Hollowell 2004; Kersel in press). My research into the St Lawrence Island market suggests that the market is driven less by the needs of diggers or the desires of collectors than by dealers, who create and manage both the supply and the demand. It is the job of dealers to promote the market and cultivate taste for objects, and they do so with the (unwitting) help of museums, art historians, archaeologists and the media. I also know artefact dealers who argue that they have provided economic benefits to local people that far exceed what archaeology has had to offer and sadly in some cases this is true.

Finally, the portrayal of small-scale producers as victims of globalisation obscures their efforts to rework capitalist and global structures to meet local needs (Haugerud *et al.* 2000: 11). The subsistence diggers I know of in the Bering Strait are not blind victims of the desires of collectors, overpowering dealers, or supply and demand. They need ways to participate in the global economy and procure desired goods, and selling artefacts is one of the best options they have. They are constrained, however, by having few sources of capital or other locally available resources that they can turn into cash, and very limited choices of how to market their goods.[5] For most, a decision to dig for the market is clearly related to a lack of other more stable or reliable economic alternatives. As one St Lawrence Islander said, 'Our ancestors used ivory to make the tools they needed for survival. We have a different use for ivory today, but it is no less important for *our* survival' (Crowell 1985: 25).

THE ETHIC OF NON-COMMERCIALISATION

The primary moral argument archaeologists wield against subsistence digging maintains that commercial use of archaeological materials should not be allowed because these activities incite further undocumented destruction of the archaeological record. Many professional codes of ethics directly invoke an ethic of non-commercialisation, while at the same time recognising the potential for archaeologists to enhance the commercial value of archaeological objects indirectly, through their activities and associations (SAA 1996: Principle 3).

One of the underlying principles of the non-commercialisation argument is the idea that the archaeological record should not be treated as a commodity, either because it cannot be owned or because it is owned by all of humanity (Warren 1999). Keane (2001: 66) reminds us that contestations over what should and should not be alienable go much deeper than simple economics. We need to peel away the layers to reveal who claims what aspects of the archaeological record as inalienable and for what purpose(s). This will be further discussed below, in conjunction with the argument that archaeological materials belong to 'all of humanity'.

---

5 This may change, as people on the Island are on the verge of engaging in e-commerce.

Indigenous peoples have their own ideas about inalienability and appropriate uses of the archaeological record, which can overlap or conflict with those of the state or those of archaeologists.[6]

Plenty of evidence exists documenting the link between a market for artefacts and the destruction of archaeological sites (Brodie *et al.* 2001; Heath 1973; Matsuda 1998b; Early 1999; Renfrew 2000; Schmidt and MacIntosh 1996; Stark and Griffin 2004; Tubb 1995).[7] Nevertheless, many social and legal attitudes either work against an ethic of non-commercialisation or raise a double standard. US private property laws, with their differential treatment of public and private property, are one example. A number of states and countries support overt or quasi-legal marketing of artefacts where this is good business. In both Israel (Blumt 2002) and Alaska (Hollowell 2004), attempts to restrict the sale of archaeological goods to tourists have met vocal opposition from both retailers and the state. Archaeological writing or research and media accounts of new discoveries also stimulate and promote the market and undocumented digging (Heath 1973: 259; Matsuda 1998a). Art exhibitions and coffee-table books significantly increase the commercial value of the objects they display (Peers 1989). They influence taste and desire and directly motivate digging by encouraging dealers to obtain a supply (Heath 1973: 259–61; Matsuda 1998b). Museums frequently confront double standards in their practices relating to acquisitions, tax credits and insurance values (Barker 2003). And, of course, an ethic of non-commercialisation directly opposes the interests of collectors, who defend their right to engage in a free market. Add to this the historical fact that just forty years ago archaeologists were still purchasing objects to fill holes in institutional or even personal collections from the parents of some of the same people who are digging today.

Collecting antiquities is still seen as a form of status and social capital, but those who aspire to an ethic of non-commercialisation hope that one day it will be considered immoral and antisocial, much like wearing fur or smoking cigarettes (Elia 1997: 97). Social attitudes do seem gradually to be changing. Human skeletal material is now rarely commodified, and in

---

6 An Indigenous perspective might, for example, find the public display of images of human skeletal material from an excavation just as appalling as the commercial use of cultural artefacts from an archaeological context, or more so.

7 Non-commercial uses of excavated materials also have a substantial impact on the archaeological record. The reuse and recycling of archaeological material for the construction of houses, walls or roads or for household use have existed in most cultures for millennia (Padgett 1989; Alva 2001: 94; Hamann 2002; Karoma 1996; Paredes-Maury 1998).

more and more cases is treated as the inalienable property of cultural descendants and repatriated accordingly (though some museums probably continue to make trades 'in the name of science'). Museums, even some art museums, are refusing to purchase objects without a known, documented archaeological provenance. But in spite of archaeologists turning their backs on its existence, a commercial market for artefacts continues to thrive, and a policy of avoidance has not been very productive (Vitelli 2000). Rather than spending energy fighting a multi-million dollar market that deals with objects already out of the ground, archaeologists might want to focus on protecting what remains of the *in situ* archaeological record (Bauer 2003; Hollowell 2002; Lynott 1997: 594).

Not surprisingly, international art dealers argue against non-commercialisation. One argument used in this context is that an unrestricted trade in already excavated antiquities would actually deter site destruction because an increased supply of legally available objects would satisfy collector demand, thus decreasing the demand for objects from the ground (Merryman 1994). Israel is putting these ideas into action, trying to prevent further destruction of archaeological sites while having a market for antiquities. How is this working? The evidence from situations where a legal or quasi-legal market for archaeological artefacts exists indicates that the kind and range of marketable objects seems to expand to fill untold new product niches (Blumt 2002; Hollowell 2004; Prott 2003).[8] Nor has the lack of restrictions on the trade in Bering Strait archaeological materials slowed the digging, or changed the desire of collectors for newly excavated, 'never-before-seen' objects. More studies are needed that look at the effects of various laws, policies and political conditions, and their consequences for subsistence diggers and for the archaeological record (rather than for national patrimony).

Tom King (1985, 1991, 2003) and others have suggested that archaeologists ought to compromise their ethics and coopt the illicit market by working with diggers to allow the sale of artefacts that have been documented according to archaeological standards. But in my experience, digging according to archaeological standards would be far too slow and painstaking a method of extraction for most subsistence diggers, in terms of both returns from digging and the techniques used. Also, many

---

8 In Alaska, tourists can purchase a fragment of an 'ancient Eskimo artefact' glued on a card or a whalebone sculpture made from what once was part of an ancient house. In Israel, small sherds and other objects fill shops as souvenirs of a trip to the Holy Land (Blumt 2002; Kersel 2002).

subsistence diggers work independently, on a finders keepers basis; others work as members of a team. To whom would the objects found belong and how would the proceeds be shared or distributed? With the individual digger? A landowner? The whole community? Would it not be just as beneficial to hire diggers as excavators or site stewards, pay them more than they are likely to get from digging, and encourage new relationships with archaeology and ways to benefit the community in the process?

Allowing a trade in excavated materials raises the important question of which is more important, the information or the material object. Lynott (1997: 596) has argued that archaeology must keep all material results for future re-examination because, unlike other sciences, there is no possibility of replicating research results once a site is gone. But how realistic is this? Does everything need to be kept, or just a representative sample? Would selling the few, unbroken objects that might be marketable really make a difference? What if certain high-end objects were sold with the caveat that they would still be available for study? The consequences of these and other arrangements that articulate with the market deserve careful evaluation. It might be possible to find some moral common ground by rewarding collectors for not destroying context, yet allowing artefacts to be sold.

IMPROPER MANAGEMENT OF CULTURAL RESOURCES

Another major argument used against subsistence digging is that it exemplifies mismanagement of a non-renewable cultural resource. Just what comprises proper management, however, depends on who is doing the managing. Archaeologists may consider themselves experts in this area, but evidence suggests that subsistence diggers also regard archaeological sites as a resource they are managing, at least in discourse with outsiders. Heath (1973: 263) and Paredes-Maury (1998) both found that *huaqueros* in Costa Rica and Guatemala respectively spoke of antiquities as a resource to be exploited, like other natural resources. An article in the *Nome Nugget*, written by a St Lawrence Islander, exemplified the very different local approach with the title of 'St Lawrence Island "Digs" Resource Management' (Silook 1999). Obtaining a fair price and maintaining better control over their resources are major concerns.

From other perspectives, the management techniques of archaeologists have seemed just as exploitative or inappropriate as those of subsistence diggers. Archaeologists are 'just one more user-group either trying to convert archaeological resources (or Aboriginal heritage) into cash or influence, and whose impacts need to be managed' (Murray 1992: 13). Community members have rarely had input into the interpretation of findings or the questions the research addresses. Very few projects return information to the community about their lands. When a project is over, it leaves behind no sustainable activity and no way for people to partici-pate in the management, protection or tourism benefits of the sites next to them (Paredes Maury 1998).

This accurately describes a relationship of 'scientific colonialism', one in which data are extracted from a community and turned into knowledge elsewhere, without either the intellectual or the economic benefits returning to those closest to its source (Galtung 1974: 295–300; Zimmer-man 2001: 169). In a growing number of instances, archaeologists have begun to reverse the legacy of scientific colonialism and have worked with communities to help them create appropriate management plans that address local needs and make conservation more rewarding than digging. The results show that, under certain conditions, undocumented digging greatly diminishes.[9]

LACK OF SUSTAINABILITY

One of the most vocal perspectives on the WAC web discussion, used to support the argument that subsistence diggers are mismanaging resources, was the argument that subsistence digging is an unsustainable solution to creating an adequate standard of living. 'Mining the resource just uses it up' (Price 2003). This attitude emphasised the fact that *in situ* archaeo-logical resources are non-renewable; there is no sustainable yield. People need to find ways to live off the interest of the cultural capital these resources represent, instead of the capital itself. An ethic of sustainability also aligns the plight of the archaeological record with that of endangered

---

9 One example is the archaeological project in the community of Agua Blanco (Ecuador) that worked to address pressing economic needs defined by the community itself. The close involvement of archaeologists with community concerns fostered mutual respect and new attitudes towards archaeology. An incentive to protect sites came from turning conservation of sites into a profitable economic venture with more stable forms of employment than subsistence digging could offer (Howell 1996; McEwan *et al.* 1994). In other cases, long-term involvement and advocacy by an archaeologist in the community has made a difference (see Alva 2001; Atwood 2003; Goodale 1996; McIntosh 1996).

species, an argument that carries a great deal of moral weight among many publics. There is a potential double standard lurking here. Are we holding the subsistence digger, who may have few other economic options, to a higher standard, while the mining of precious metals and other non-renewable resources continues to support unsustainable lifestyles in uneven ways all over the planet? Indigenous landowners in Papua New Guinea who are pro-logging have found themselves the subject of a similar critique and have clearly stated that they will continue to exploit their natural resources until they have alternative, equally productive ways of generating an income (Filer 1996: 296–7).

Subsistence diggers are aware of the limited supply of archaeological resources. I have heard people in the Bering Strait discuss the benefits of conservative digging. They talk about sites as if they were banks that hold their inheritance. If digging proceeds slowly, not only will the resource last longer, but, since people believe that prices will continue to rise, there will be greater benefits for the future.[10]

What happens when the resource does run low? In the art market (and the tourist market as well), when the supply of a specific kind of artefact dries up, dealers shift to creating taste and demand among their consumers for other more available but equally rare or curious objects (Becker 1982; Moulin 1987; Thompson 1979). Such has been the case with Malian terracottas (Brent 1996), Cycladic figurines (Gill and Chippindale 1993) and Apulian vases (Elia 2001). This economic principle of substitutability also works at the other end of the commodity chain. When the supply of archaeological resources becomes depleted, diggers will need to substitute other (not necessarily more sustainable) sources of income, as they have had to do in the past.

The substitutability of resources elucidates the processes by which many archaeological objects become commodities in the first place. On St Lawrence Island, for example, people started digging in earnest for artefacts in the early 1900s after the collapse of the global market in whale baleen (with the demise of hoop skirts and buggy whips, and the invention of spring steel). The trade in baleen had made the Islanders relatively wealthy, but now they needed a substitute commodity to exchange for Western goods. Traders found a market for old ivory, curios and 'specimens' (as you've guessed, some customers were museums) and started to deal in archaeological goods (Hollowell

---

10 Some of this discussion ensued when a digger was asked why backhoes were not used at digging sites. There are, of course, places where people do use heavy equipment to mine sites.

2004: 189–93). More recently, global bans on other forms of ivory caused custom carvers to turn to archaeological ivory from the Bering Strait as one of the few remaining legal substitutes,[11] increasing both the value of and the demand for these excavated materials. Some of the same policies put an end to walrus hunting by non-Natives. Many of those Natives who had once been well-paid guides turned to digging to supplement their incomes. Whole tusks have now become harder and harder to find, but regional dealers have recently created new markets for bulk whalebone and fragments of artefacts.

DAMAGE TO THE ARCHAEOLOGICAL RECORD

From the standpoint of archaeologists, the number one concern with undocumented digging is not the lack of a sustainable yield but the irretrievable loss of contextual information about the past embedded in the archaeological record. This argument extends to the fact that undocumented digging deprives others and future generations of this information and the knowledge that could be derived from it.

There are not many worthy counterarguments here. The fact that the archaeological record does not matter or is irrelevant to certain people suggests that archaeologists have not done a good job of explaining their ways of meaning-making, or of showing consideration for those of others. Most collectors, dealers or diggers are not aware of the kinds of information that can be gleaned from finding an object *in situ* or from other contextual elements of the archaeological record. Many think of archaeology as it existed in the early part of the last century, when it hardly differed from what we call looting today (Hinsley 2002), and the objective was to fill the shelves of national museums. Thus even the most erudite collectors wonder why archaeologists would ever need another such-and-such, and dealers believe that a site name, estimated depth and a polaroid amount to adequate archaeological documentation. To an archaeologist this seems almost unbelievable, but this distancing is a mark of the professionalisation of the discipline, the inaccessibility of research findings, and the refusal to associate with certain 'tainted' elements.

---

11 Archaeological walrus ivory from the Bering Strait is used today in scrimshaw, knife handles, guitar inlays, jewellery, and other custom crafts. Some dealers ship it to Bali to be carved by workers who once carved elephant ivory.

Undocumented digging, however, is not the primary cause of damage to the archaeological record. In many places, erosion, agriculture and development rank higher in terms of destructive impact (Canouts and McManamon 2001: 100). Are we applying a double standard when we vilify relic collectors or subsistence diggers as 'looters' simply because developers, by jumping through the proper hoops, have the authority of the state on their side? There is also the argument that 'we can't dig it all'. This, however, neglects to take into account the singular and unique information about particular pasts at stake in sites all over the world, no matter what threatens them, and amounts to an apology for the status quo. There is no place, for example, comparable to St Lawrence Island, where undocumented excavations have brought many beautiful objects to light, but very little information about the people who used and created them.

Unfortunately, just the presence of an archaeology project can unintentionally cause damage to the archaeological record by stimulating undocumented digging. A quantitative study of eighty-four projects conducted in various (non-US) locations found that projects that included more public outreach reported higher incidences of looting in the area (Hollowell and Wilk 1995). Clearly, archaeologists need to prepare for these consequences and do a better job of convincing people that archaeology is 'for everyone's benefit' (Price 2003).

ARCHAEOLOGY AS A PUBLIC GOOD

This moral argument asserts that all forms of undocumented digging amount to stealing from our common world heritage since the record of the past belongs to all of humanity. Thus no particular person or group can own it or has the right to sell pieces of it. Archaeologists, then, hold the position of professional stewards of the archaeological record, envisioned as a public good, held 'in the public trust' for all of humanity. Such heady universalisms beg further scrutiny (see Wylie 2005; and Dingli, Omland and Young, this volume). What interests do they serve? What actions do they justify? Certainly not everyone benefits equally from the public good that is archaeology.

Arguments appealing to broad statements about the 'public trust', 'common good' or 'all of humanity' can mask nationalistic desires to retain cultural property. Claims related to 'the public trust' by the state in some cases have even been used to justify the seizure of private lands for archaeo-tourism or other forms of commercial development. In this paradigm, the expertise of archaeologists is enlisted by the state to manage its cultural resources in the name of the public trust in exchange for career positions and legitimacy. This explains some of the distrust of archaeologists, who are seen as in collusion with the state, which has too often abused the 'public good' argument.

Merilee Salmon (1997: 59) suggests that the use of a 'common good' argument can easily obfuscate and override the need to balance competing rights or to deal with troublesome issues of justice and fairness. 'Public good' arguments are in fact often used by governments to justify their authority to make decisions against the will of less powerful voices that stand in the way of nationalist agendas and 'progress'.[12] This ethic (typical of the cost/benefit analysis many governments follow) alleges that the harm done to a small group is justified by an outcome that brings more benefits to a greater number of people.

Double standards also exist in access to objects and information supposedly held in public trust. Collectors argue that artefacts lie unseen in locked dark basements and reports are never published, and feel that they are better stewards and give objects more care and exposure than most museums. The concept of the public trust is also problematic from the perspective of cultural groups who have culturally specific ideas about forms of knowledge that should or should not be accessible to the public (Ouzman 2003).

As Matsuda asserts, concepts of public trust and nationalistic debates over cultural property are for the most part irrelevant to subsistence diggers because they do not 'include indigenous voices, create alternative modes of subsistence or provide for the survival of indigenous lifeways and belief systems' (Matsuda 1998a: 94). He identifies the real issues as the unequal power and economic relationships that compel people to turn to subsistence digging as an economic alternative and remove from them their own ability to manage their cultural resources.

CULTURE AND HERITAGE LOSS

Another moral argument used by archaeologists is that subsistence digging and selling artefacts represent the loss or abuse of cultural heritage. Two related circumstances are usually blamed: an ignorance of the value of archaeology and the lack of a meaningful connection to heritage or the

---

12 One example is the flooding of huge tracts of Native lands in Canada to provide hydroelectric power to Canadian cities (Waldram 1988).

past. This argument assumes that if subsistence diggers understood the value of archaeology and heritage, they would stop digging. According to Walter Alva, once the residents of Sipán began to feel that archaeology was valuable to their identity and their political situation, they made a choice to stop looting (Alva 2001: 95; Atwood 2003). This took but a mere twenty years of building trust and understanding.

It is true that the knowledge produced by archaeology lacks relevance from the standpoint of many subsistence diggers. David Pendergast (1994) noted that the Maya feel archaeology has little to offer that concerns their lives. He blamed this dissociation and the lack of an ethic of site preservation on the failure to include living people in the process of knowledge creation in archaeology. Pendergast dentified this sense of detachment, along with the lack of other economic choices, as the main causes of subsistence digging (Pendergast 1994: 2–3).

But people are also detached from archaeology because they have other uses for the past and other, often more personal, ways of connecting to the past, such as oral histories, traditional skills and even the act of digging itself, ways that may not be valued by archaeologists or that are not meant to be shared (see Smith 2005). Only recently have oral histories been recognised by archaeologists as valid sources of information, and they are still regarded as a subsidiary to the archaeological record (Zimmerman 2001: 173).

Can heritage or culture be 'lost' (or gained) and could subsistence diggers possibly be blamed for that loss? As Larry Zimmerman observes (2001: 178), the past cannot really be lost or 'saved'. Selling objects is not equivalent to selling one's heritage, and to imagine otherwise amounts to fetishising objects.[13] On St Lawrence Island, digging for artefacts is part of every Islander's heritage, an activity that can actually strengthen one's connections with the past. Artefacts are regarded as gifts left by the ancestors that, if they allow themselves to be found, are meant for use in today's world. Similarly, in Belize, people conduct ceremonies before tunnelling into ancient sites and call the artefacts they find *semilla*, or seeds the ancestors have left to supplement their income (Matsuda 1998a: 92). Still, some St Lawrence Islanders do imagine the diaspora of archaeological artefacts in terms of 'culture loss', caused by the lure of the

---

13 The idea that cultural identity is literally embodied in material objects goes back to at least the turn of the century and the salvage period of collecting when people believed they were saving the past by taking cultural objects away from their sources and storing them in museums (Boas 1940; Clifford 1988: 234; Cole 1985; Dominguez 1986). Colonialist though these practices were, today objects stored in museums gain new agency when reconnected with source communities (Peers and Brown 2003).

market or a colonialist legacy of 'white people ripping us off'. People wonder out loud if future generations will hold them responsible. Elders sometimes talked about the digging as causing harm or disturbance and blamed social problems in the village on 'all the holes people have dug out there'. There are times when diggers distance themselves and claim not to be related to the people whose former lives they disturb.

CULTURAL AFFILIATION

Should a different ethic apply to diggers who have a cultural affiliation to those whose objects they seek? Does the fact that the diggers on St Lawrence Island are mining their own culture somehow make it more acceptable? After all, it is their heritage; they can do what they want with it. Dealers use this argument, because if the Natives themselves are digging and *they* don't have a problem with it, it vindicates the market (see also Pendergast 1994: 3). Archaeologists generally feel that cultural descendants have a stronger claim to the past than others (NAGPRA is evidence of this). Diggers who consider themselves cultural descendants are likely to agree, at least when it is beneficial to them, but concepts like heritage, identity and cultural affiliation are slippery, polymorphous forms of cultural capital that take varying shape depending on particular situations. Some even argue that any claims based on special cultural relationships are essentialist or even racist (Warren 1999). In this case they become an apology for the status quo, one that does not really address either the fate of the archaeological record or that of subsistence diggers. Still, believing that one has a direct connection can increase the intrinsic value of digging, and perhaps this could carry over to archaeology.

TOWARDS AN ARCHAEOLOGICAL ETHIC

The breadth of the arguments outlined above certainly speaks to the complexity of the issue of subsistence digging. Archaeologists represented in the WAC discussion touched upon all of the arguments, and many mentioned or discussed more than one. While all the participants seemed willing to see the issue from other perspectives, there were widely divergent and sometimes cynical views about how an explicitly archaeological ethic might interface with the dilemma of subsistence digging in practice. Some also had a strong feeling that the archaeological perspective was the 'right' one and a slight unwillingness to consider compromise, as if it would appear to condone looting. Without

some common ground these attitudes could inhibit working with subsistence diggers or communities to find mutually beneficial solutions, so
I want to conclude by discussing some principles that might underlie an
explicitly archaeological ethic and how these might articulate in practice.

From the standpoint of archaeologists, it should be clear that it is not
the act of undocumented digging in and of itself that is unethical, but
rather its consequences – the destruction of the archaeological record. If
the consequences cannot be avoided, they must be mitigated. Archaeologists are uniquely familiar with this framework already, because it describes most of the work done under the heading of cultural resource
management, where the portions of a site not sampled under agreed-upon
significance criteria meet the same fate as, or one worse than, those
confronted by the shovel of a subsistence digger.

Next, it should also be apparent that an archaeological ethic regarding
subsistence digging must take into account both the integrity of the
archaeological record *and* the human condition of subsistence diggers
and be careful *not* to put the welfare of artefacts or the archaeological
record above the welfare of living people and an understanding of their
situations. The tendency to privilege the archaeological record is a disciplinary fallacy, a nearsightedness caused by the training archaeologists
receive and their own position of privilege. Furthermore, the categorical
imperative and the precautionary principle[14] insist that we assess the wider
positive and negative consequences of actions and consider the potential
harm archaeologists and others could do by enforcing their ethic, *or* as a
result of other unintended or unintentional acts. Here again the consequences of various laws, policies or practices on living people (we may be
on the verge of including once-living people here as well; see Scarre
and Tarlow, chapters 11 and 12 this volume) ought to outweigh consideration of the archaeological record. More specifically, the consequences of
these acts on subsistence diggers receive additional weight because their
marginal economic and political status exposes them to greater potential
harm.

An ethic that aspires to uphold the integrity of the archaeological
record appears to be incompatible with subsistence digging as we know
it, if, as Lynott (1997) suggests, archaeologists should not compromise the
ethic of non-commercialisation, e.g. by allowing the sale of materials after
documentation. Nevertheless this is certainly an area where compromise

---

14 Note Bannister and Barrett 2004.

could occur, albeit with careful evaluation of the potential and actual effects on the archaeological record and the various participants in the market. Another highly possible compromise would be to negotiate set-asides of sites or areas designated as significant, much in the manner of CRM work, where any digging would require the use of archaeological techniques. I have seen this succeed firsthand, under rather challenging conditions.

The compromises suggested above are to the integrity of the archaeological record, but how might the activities of subsistence diggers align more closely with an archaeological ethic? The only possibilities appear to be that diggers either adopt archaeological techniques in their digging or cease digging altogether. The first requires working with and being trained by archaeologists; the second means finding a substitute subsistence activity; and either would require incentives to change, including a viable and more sustainable replacement for the income generated by undocumented digging. Whatever course of action, the lives of the diggers should improve and not worsen as a result.

What is archaeology's role in these scenarios? In the second scenario, perhaps none. Since it is likely that subsistence diggers will stop digging when more stable and reliable forms of income are available (Hollowell 2004: 94; Matsuda 1998a; Posey 1990: 14), an applied anthropology or development project, not necessarily related to archaeology, could ostensibly provide new means of subsistence for former (reformed?) diggers to replace the lure (and thrill) of digging. In times of dire conditions such as war or social unrest, this might be the best recourse. Hardy and others suggest instituting basic aid programmes or, where feasible, providing jobs, perhaps on the lines of the civilian conservation corps organised in the USA in the 1930s and 1940s, that would provide some stability and a steadier income than artefact digging or other forms of looting (Hardy 2003; Ouzman 2003). Realistically, the places that need this most are likely to be those that cannot afford or safely manage it (see Norton 1989; Stark and Griffin 2004). Still, it seems important for development agencies to recognise the potential connection between economic recovery or community development and archaeological heritage protection.[15] This would be most effective if the money would get directly to who would otherwise be looting.

---

15 Funds for site protection efforts in Iraq have come from several foundations, including $750,000 from the Packard Humanities Institute (Carleton *et al.* 2004).

The suggestion that subsistence diggers lay aside their digging practices and become site stewards or adopt archaeological techniques has several worthy precedents that prove this can be a viable option with benefits on several levels (Alva 2001; Atwood 2003; Howell 1996; McEwan *et al.* 1994; McIntosh 1996). These projects offer incentives that make doing archaeology or conserving the archaeological record more valuable than digging it up. The primary incentive, at least at first, is likely to be an extrinsic monetary one, since diggers need, at the least, to replace their subsistence digging income. These arrangements oblige diggers and archaeologists to work closely with one another, something that is unlikely to succeed if either strongly views the behaviour of the other as 'wrong' or unethical. The relationships formed in the process are an opportunity to overcome the feeling of dissociation or detachment that Pendergast described as fostering looting, and a chance to increase the intrinsic value of the archaeological record and make archaeology a more meaningful enterprise. The challenges for archaeologists include rethinking approaches to research design, recognising local expertise, involving community members in the production of knowledge and decision-making, returning benefits to the community, and, in general, making archaeology relevant to community needs. Gupta's (1998) findings from the field of conservation and development are very apt here. In situations where people have turned to resource degradation, different ethics can replace predatory practices if two conditions can be met. First, conservation must become more economically viable than exploitation; and second, local communities must be recognised and rewarded for their unique contributions to knowledge about the resources.

A particularly productive approach treats archaeological preservation as a form of development, much like applied anthropology, with the goal of placing the planning, profits and decisions in the hands of those people in the community who live with it and can protect it. K. Anne Pyburn's work with the Belizean community of Crooked Tree is an example of this paradigm (Pyburn 2003), and Green *et al.* (2003) present a thought-provoking case study of a project based on principles of participatory development.

Archaeo-tourism projects can also offer meaningful employment and make the preservation of sites a more profitable and sustainable venture than digging them. One example is the village of Agua Blanco in Ecuador, where archaeologists employed subsistence diggers first as excavators and later in the development of a community museum (McEwan *et al.* 1994). Visitors to Agua Blanco today are led on tours of unexcavated sites near the village by local residents. More studies of archaeo-tourism projects are trickling out (Crosby 2002; Rowan and Baram 2004), and these will hopefully provide information about the uneven consequences of these various commodifications of the past on the archaeological record, local economics and relations of power (see Kohl 2004). For example, in situations where local diggers do not benefit directly from these ventures, or there are insufficient jobs to go around, they could easily end up stimulating digging (Stark and Griffin 2004).

I have delineated moral arguments on subsistence digging, a practice that creates an ethical dilemma for archaeology, and have critically examined some of the evidence for and against them. To a large extent, my purpose has been to reflect to archaeologists the range of positions they and others hold on this problematic issue, some of the justifications in support of them, and the double standards they evince. This opened up the possibility of locating several potential approaches to the dilemma that benefit both archaeology and subsistence diggers and are based on an explicitly archaeological ethic. Finally, I want to reiterate the need to include the communities and individuals most affected in this conversation, and to develop methodologies that also meet their needs and make archaeology a more meaningful endeavour in the process.

PART II

Archaeologists and the li

CHAPTER 6

Human subjects review and archaeology: a view from Indian country

Jeffrey C. Bendremer and Kenneth A. Richman

> Into each life, it is said, some rain must fall, some people have bad horoscopes, others take tips on the stock market. But Indians have been cursed above all people in history. Indians have anthropologists.
> Vine Deloria, Jr. (Standing Rock Sioux) *Custer Died for Your Sins* (1969)

Many Native Americans view anthropologists as a curse, as people who are not to be trusted, people with ulterior motives, people who steal culture, language, images and things (Deloria 1992, 1995, 1999; Thornton 1998; Watkins 2000b; White Deer 1997). This view stems from the historic relationships that have provided anthropologists, university professors, museum professionals, art dealers and antiques dealers with livelihoods often to the detriment of Native people and communities.

There are a number of unfortunate tensions inherent in the longstanding relationship between Native peoples and anthropologists. Anthropologists generally express feelings of affection and affinity for indigenous cultures and most approach their work with a desire to benefit their host communities. Despite these good intentions, however, great harm has often been brought to indigenous communities who did not agree with or fully understand the goals, methods or long-term ramifications of participation in anthropological studies. In addition to the divergent interests of the host community and the anthropologist's career interests, there are additional tensions between paternalism and community autonomy. These arise as a result of differing conceptions of what constitutes benefit for a host community.

As a result of similar dynamics, the biomedical research community in the United States established human subjects reviews to ensure informed consent of participants, ethical research protocols and the appropriate use of information gathered. Following the adoption of federal regulations and guidelines, institutional review boards (IRBs) now monitor most biomedical research in the USA. Social and behavioural research, which includes the kinds of work cultural anthropologists commonly conduct in the United States and abroad, have increasingly come under the review umbrella. However, there are numerous areas of anthropological inquiry that are not covered by human subjects reviews. These include most archaeological investigations.

Despite the fact that archaeological projects rarely undergo review as human subjects research, many archaeological projects have profound effects on living persons. The most severe effects on living Native Americans have, until recent legislation, stemmed from the indiscriminate excavation, long-term storage and public display of human remains, grave goods, sacred items and objects of cultural patrimony. Even after the institution of the Native American Graves Preservation Repatriation Act (NAGPRA), many Native Americans still find that archaeologists continue to alienate contemporary communities from their histories, sometimes in direct contravention of local custom, tradition and law.

The application of human subjects review to archaeological projects could provide redress for some of the deleterious effects of this area of inquiry. For example, the descendants of the subject population could be given the courtesy of informed consent on behalf of their ancestors. Archaeological methods could be reviewed for ethical considerations and the uses of the archaeological information would be disclosed and assessed for its impact on the contemporary community and their descendants. This process would allow Native beliefs and values to take centre stage. It would, for example, take into account the degree to which ancestors are viewed as active participants in the lives of contemporary people. In addition, this process would protect the privacy of tribal members. For example, the medical information of identifiable living descendants could be protected when genetic information derived from archaeological human remains suggests that living descendants have inherited health conditions.

INDIAN COMMUNITIES AND ANTHROPOLOGISTS

Many have found the long, complex relationship of anthropologists and American Indians exploitative and disturbing (Bendremer, Wozniak and Thomas 2002; Downer 1997; Ferguson 1996; Lurie 1988; McGuire 1997; Thomas 2000; Trigger 1980, 1989; Trope and Echo-Hawk 2001). King describes his own, all too common perspective:

many times we have been betrayed. Our honored guests have shown themselves to be no more than peeping Toms, rank opportunists, interested in furthering their own careers by trading in on our sacred traditions. Many people have felt anger at the way our communities have been cheated, held up to ridicule, and our customs sensationalized. (King 1997: 115)

According to Grobsmith (1997: 36), 'Some Indian students argued that anthropologists were exploiters and thieves of culture, stealing and revealing secrets to bring them academic fortune.'

Beginning in the nineteenth century, anthropologists have methodically extracted cultural information and material culture from indigenous peoples and from the land. In keeping with the Western scientific tradition, anthropologists have taken for granted that the collection of this information as well as archaeological and/or ethnographic materials was a worthy and productive endeavour. In fact, the rationale for much of these activities was the mistaken assumption that they were 'salvaging', documenting and preserving the cultures of 'disappearing' societies (Dippie 1982; Garza and Powell 2001; McGuire 1997). Think of Indiana Jones, who battles against profiteering looters with the refrain 'that belongs in a museum!' It made little difference whether this 'ethic' and its goals conflicted with the local norms and ideologies of Native participants and their communities (Bordewich 1996: 185–94; White Deer 1997; Zimmerman 2001) or rejected or marginalised indigenous histories and oral traditions (Echo-Hawk 1997, 2000). Native participants often saw these archaeological activities as essentially indistinguishable from those of looters who plundered burial, sacred and important historical sites for pleasure and profit:

The anthropological world has been quick to condemn pothunting, but in their effects, the 'professional' excavation of 'sites' and removal of artifacts to university museums seem hard to distinguish from the pothunter's practice. In both cases, important materials are alienated from Hopi, or from the collective spiritual patrimony of Hopi ancestry. (Whitely 1997: 184)

Furthermore, as an integral part of their discipline, anthropologists and archaeologists have taken it upon themselves to represent societies other than their own (McGuire 1997; Zimmerman 2001). Many assumed that Native Americans 'did not know their past, had no interest in that past, or were unable to preserve it' (Deloria 1973: 31–2, in McGuire 1997: 64). This is a continuation of a long tradition of colonialist exploitation of Native societies:

How did it happen that anthropologists came to think of themselves as having a mandate not only to study but to speak for Indian peoples? At the turn of the century, as anthropology was emerging as an organized university-based discipline, it took as a central mission the study of exotic nonliterate peoples. Such study had a long tradition in European thought, as exemplified by Herodotus, Snorri Sturlusson, Marco Polo, and assorted missionaries, travelers, and adventurers. (Wax 1997: 55)

Many anthropologists continue to approach native people for cultural information while expecting those same participants to be passive recipients of anthropological knowledge and interpretation. According to Lippert (1997), 'many Indians were made to feel like interesting specimens rather than people' (see also Bentz 1997). The activities of anthropologists and archaeologists ultimately had the effect of reifying, objectifying and decontextualising the study participants and their societies. This effect was especially evident when archaeologists chose to study human remains, sacred sites, sacred objects and/or religious beliefs (Deloria 1989; Garza and Powell 2001; Grimes 2001; Thornton 2001; Trope and Echo-Hawk 2001; Watkins 2001; Zimmerman 1997a).

In addition to speaking for Native people, anthropologists and archaeologists also presume to speak for the dead:

Archaeologists often claim to speak for past peoples, however remote. Implicit in this claim is the notion that they, as practitioners of a science, are the only ones capable of doing so. Native Americans do not accept this and challenge the very authority of archaeological knowledge. (Zimmerman 1996b: 214 in Vitelli 1996b)

As social scientists, anthropologists often work under the assumption that 'only scholars have the credentials to define and explain American Indians and that their word should be regarded as definitive and conclusive' (Deloria 1992). There is little regard for whether information is regarded as secret or sacred, or is otherwise regulated in Native society. Native people typically have no binding power or control regarding anthropological data despite their obvious interest in the disposition of traditional cultural information and properties (see Zimmerman 1996b).

Complicating this dynamic is a central tenet that views archaeological resources as belonging collectively to the wider society and not to local inhabitants or even to the descendants of ancient peoples. In addition, archaeologists have declared themselves 'stewards' of this communal past (Chippendale and Pendergast 1995; Hamilton 1995; Lynott and Wylie 1995; McGuire 1997; SAA Code of Ethics 1996; AIA Code of Ethics 1990; Zimmerman 1995, 1996b). However, the claim that archaeologists can act as impartial caretakers of a common past denies the indigenous community's overriding interests in the disposition of their individual heritage as well as the politics inherent in archaeology (Kohl and Fawcett 1995).[1] To say that archaeologists conserve historical and cultural properties better than Native people is arrogant at best and serves further to disenfranchise these communities from their ancestors and their own heritage. This can result in an increased sense of powerlessness in these already marginalised communities:

In the United States, archaeologists and anthropologists have been the authorities on Native American pasts, and this authority has given us power over those pasts. Courts of law and government commissions call us as expert witnesses and have often given our testimony more weight than that of tribal elders . . . We often assert this authority in books, articles and exhibits we prepare for the general public. We make the archaeologist the hero of the story and either split Indian peoples from their past or treat them as artifacts of the past. Rarely have our public presentations given an Indian point of view of the past or treated the past as part of an ongoing native cultural tradition. (McGuire 1997: 65)

Further exacerbating this dynamic is the sheer volume of archaeological projects and the poor record of providing good scientific or social rationales for proceeding other than furthering an archaeologist's career. Fagan (1996) comments on this tendency to engage in disruptive projects that are scientifically unnecessary:

Clearly, an overwhelming case can be made for less excavation and more analysis of previous work. However, our scholarly culture rewards people for new and original research, sometimes defined in the narrowest terms as participation in an active fieldwork program. (Fagan 1996: 249)

Researchers in other disciplines commonly share data for secondary analysis. However, this is only practical if the structures of reward, including tenure and grant funding, are appropriately tuned. Even the most concerned and thoughtful academic archaeologist must satisfy the expectations of editors, deans and department chairs in order to maintain a place in the profession.

---

1 Although it is often rather straightforward, it can sometimes be difficult for the anthropologist to ascertain just what the interests of the 'indigenous community' or 'Native American community' are, because these communities can speak with many divergent voices. In our experience, however, a consensus can usually be reached readily through open discussion, flexibility and examples of good faith.

Although the deleterious aspects of archaeology are ubiquitous, these dynamics are by no means universal. Anthropologists are perceived to have accomplished some good with respect to Native communities.[2] Furthermore, there has been some progress in recent years in the areas of human remains, grave goods and sacred objects (McGuire 1997). This is largely due to NAGPRA, which passed in 1990 owing to the increased influence of various tribes and despite the fact that 'The anthropological community lobbied hard against passage' (Zimmerman 1997a: 105).

> After centuries of discriminatory treatment, the Native American Graves Protection and Repatriation Act finally recognises that Native American human remains and cultural items are the remnants and products of living people, and that the descendants have a cultural and spiritual relationship with the deceased. Human remains and cultural items can no longer be thought of as merely 'scientific specimens' or 'collectibles'. (Trope and Echo-Hawk 2001)

As a practical matter, however, there has been little change in archaeological research methods and applications in many parts of North America. Native Americans are still rarely permitted to participate in the interpretation of cultural data,[3] to critique the resulting literature, to access collections of material culture easily, or to say how cultural information is disseminated (Bendremer and Fawcett 1995; Swidler *et al.* 1997). This results in a people's disenfranchisement from its own history, knowledge and material heritage. It perpetuates long-standing dynamics where whole nations were denied self-determination and command over their destinies. As McGuire remarks, 'In this larger set of relations the archaeologist's authority over Indian pasts is simply one [more] aspect of their lives that has been taken from their control' (McGuire 1997: 65).[4]

---

2 'While some Indians fought diligently to keep anthros [*sic*] out, others were equally adamant about the fundamental role anthropologists played in preserving their aboriginal heritage and culture. They had been raised without the benefit of learning their language and traditions, and they protested that a wealth of Native American heritage would have been lost to them were it not for recorded myth and ethnographic descriptions of religious and cultural life' (Grobsmith 1997: 36).

3 A significant exception is an ethnohistoric research project in Arizona's San Pedro River Valley funded by the National Endowment for the Humanities, principal investigators T. J. Ferguson and Roger Anyon (see Colwell-Chanthaphonh and Ferguson 2004).

4 'Most Indian people cannot escape the larger history of white–Indian interactions because that history dwells in the relations of their day-to-day lives. It lives in the regulations, bureaucracies, poverty, and discrimination that deny them the ability to determine their own lives and futures. In this larger set of relations the archaeologist's authority over Indian pasts is simply one aspect of their lives that has been taken from their control' (McGuire 1997: 65).

ETHICAL CODES AND THE SOCIAL SCIENCES

The National Research Act (Pub. L. 93–348) was passed by the US legislature on 12 July 1974. This legislation created the National Commission for the Protection of Human Subjects of Biomedical and Behavioural Research, which was asked to delineate the ethical principles that should be followed for research in biomedical and behavioural research involving human subjects. Among other tasks, the commission was to consider:

1) the boundaries between biomedical and behavioural research and the accepted and routine practice of medicine; 2) the role of assessment of risk-benefit criteria in the determination of the appropriateness of research involving human subjects; 3) appropriate guidelines for the selection of human subjects for participation in such research, and; 4) the nature and definition of informed consent in various research settings. (Belmont Report 1979, Summary)

Following a four-day meeting at the Smithsonian Institution's Belmont Conference Center in February 1976 and monthly meetings over a period of about four years, the deliberations of the Commission were summarised in the Belmont Report. The report describes the basic ethical principles that should be applied to research with human participants as well as guidelines for addressing the ethical problems of human subjects research.

The Belmont Report (1979) identifies three overarching ethical principles: (1) a principle of respect for persons; (2) a principle of beneficence; and (3) a principle of justice. *Respect for persons* mandates that we should not use people, and that we respect individual dignity and autonomy.[5] Informed consent is required under the principle of respect. *Beneficence* can be understood as the requirement that chance of benefit outweigh risk of harm. Beneficence also requires that researchers avoid harm in general, which can also be described as a duty of non-maleficence.[6] The concept of *justice* requires that burdens and benefits be distributed fairly. The significance of these principles will become clearer as we see how they relate to other ethics statements.

The regulation known as 'the Common Rule' came into effect in the USA in 1981, and has been modified in later years. The Common Rule specifies that activities meeting certain specifications must be approved by

5 The theoretical support is found in the second formulation of Kant's categorical imperative, which requires that we treat humanity, whether in ourselves or in others, always as an end in itself and never as a means only (Kant 1959: 46).

6 The medical version of non-maleficence is familiar: *primum non nocere* (first do no [net] harm).

an institutional review board (IRB). IRB review is designed to ensure that research is consistent with the ethical principles outlined in the Belmont Report. Of course, cultural anthropology by US-based researchers doing field research with contemporary human communities in the United States and abroad requires human subjects review by an IRB.[7] Archaeological research has not been put under the scrutiny of the Belmont Report *per se* because it is not taken to satisfy the Common Rule's definition of human subjects research. According to the Common Rule:

(f) *Human subject* means a living individual about whom an investigator (whether professional or student) conducting research obtains

1 Data through intervention or interaction with the individual, or
2 Identifiable private information. (Section 102)

Archaeologists are most likely to collect identifiable information about individuals who are no longer living, or about groups as a whole rather than about individual people. If archaeologists interact with living individuals or intervene in a community setting, it is unlikely to be the direct subject of their inquiry. Even so, other, non-governmental codes of ethics have been adopted by professional associations in efforts to set standards for archaeologists. We will examine two of these codes here.

The Code of Ethics of the American Anthropological Association (1998) incorporates a standard similar to the Belmont Report's principle of respect for persons when it calls for anthropologists to put the interests of their research subjects (and objects) above anthropology's interest in data collection:

Anthropological researchers have primary ethical obligations to the people, species, and materials they study and to the people with whom they work. These obligations can supersede the goal of seeking new knowledge, and can lead to decisions not to undertake or to discontinue a research project when the primary obligation conflicts with other responsibilities, such as those owed to sponsors or clients. (AAA 1998)

This significant statement is followed by four examples of more specific obligations that fall under this general statement. These are 'To avoid harm or wrong', an obligation of non-maleficence; 'To respect the well-being of humans and nonhuman primates', which emphasises *people* and

---

7 Human subjects review is mandated through funding agencies that are part of the federal government in the USA, including the National Institutes of Health. However, many institutions require that research with institutional affiliation be reviewed independent of whether the research receives funding from an agency that requires review.

some of the *species* mentioned in the general formulation; 'To work for the long-term conservation of the archaeological, fossil, and historical records', which emphasises the *materials* mentioned in the general formulation; and 'To consult actively with the affected individuals or group(s), with the goal of establishing a working relationship that can be beneficial to all parties involved' (AAA 1988). This last example, combined with the mention of sponsors and clients, implies that anthropologists have an obligation to avoid conflicts of interest that could lead to harm.

In requiring that all parties benefit, this last item introduces concerns of justice. According to the Belmont Report, the principle of justice is violated when some benefit or right 'to which a person is entitled is denied without good reasons or when some burden is imposed unduly' (Belmont Report 1979: 4). Violation of a person's safety, dignity or privacy would be a violation of the principle of justice if imposed unduly. This shows that the principles of justice and of beneficence overlap in application. However, justice is the primary issue when those who bear the burden of research (i.e. the research subjects or participants) do not also benefit.

The Belmont Report's principle of beneficence requires that human subjects be protected from harm and that efforts be made to secure their well-being. This is most often implemented through efforts to maximise benefits and minimise possible harm. The American Anthropological Association explicitly promulgates this idea: 'Anthropological researchers must do everything in their power to ensure that their research does not harm the safety, dignity, or privacy of the people with whom they work, conduct research, or perform other professional activities' (AAA 1998). Here dignity of persons is combined with safety issues, where dignity falls under the principle of respect, and safety under the principle of beneficence. Again, this shows how the Belmont principles can overlap. (Of course, they may also compete, as when potential research participants refuse to consent to a study that would bring them benefit.)

The AAA Code does not specifically include informed consent or respect for autonomy in the statement of the anthropologist's primary obligations. Instead, it treats informed consent separately, and does not use the word 'autonomy'. This distinguishes the AAA's Code from the Belmont Report, which states that individuals should be treated as autonomous agents and that persons with diminished autonomy are entitled to special protections (Belmont Report 1979: 4).

Not surprisingly, when we move from the AAA Code to the Society for American Archaeology's eight Principles of Archaeological Ethics (Society for American Archaeology 1996, hereafter the SAA Principles), respect for persons, respect for communities and respect for ownership drop into the background. In naming the object of study 'the archeological record', the Society essentially removes these issues from the picture. This makes sense given the history of archaeology, and there are many good ideals in the SAA Principles. However, as our view from Indian country shows, this conception of archaeology is inadequate.

SAA Principle Number 1 (Stewardship) states that 'It is the responsibility of all archaeologists to work for the long-term conservation and protection of the archeological record by practicing and promoting stewardship of the archaeological record.' 'Stewards' are described as 'caretakers of and advocates for the archaeological record for the benefit of all people'. The SAA Principles, therefore, assert the inherent value of objects and information. People are only considered in the calculation of a just distribution of benefit from the objects. Therefore, archaeologists can advocate on behalf of the archaeological record in opposition to the explicit wishes of interested individuals and groups. They can also act on conceptions of benefit or its just distribution different from the conceptions prevalent in affected communities. The SAA Principles fail to address these possibilities and essentially empower the archaeologist to adjudicate any conflict.

SAA Principle Number 2 (Accountability) reflects the AAA's Code in its call 'to consult actively with affected group(s), with the goal of establishing a working relationship that can be beneficial to all parties involved' (SAA Principles). This introduces an element of respect for communities and individuals. However, the next principle erodes this element. Principle Number 3 (Commercialization) discourages the use of 'archaeological objects' for 'personal enjoyment or profit', on the basis that the archaeological record is for the benefit of all. We see an assumption that the archaeological record is not initially owned by anyone, so that treating archaeological objects 'as a matter of personal possession' (SAA Principle 5, Intellectual Property) is impermissible. This makes sense where there really is no claim to the record. This might be the case with, to create an example, the geological record of the moon. But when we consider archaeology of Native American lands, particularly involving first nations still in existence, the SAA Principles ignore legitimate claims. It is arguable, consistent with the principles of the Belmont Report, that the descendants of the inhabitants of a land may refuse to allow archaeological work (consistent with respect for persons) and have a greater claim to any benefit that may derive from excavation should any occur (consistent with justice) unless there is reason to suspect that the archaeological project under consideration would move human knowledge forward by leaps and bounds (consistent with beneficence). This is contrary to the SAA Principles, which promote the idea that the general public has a right to information, a right that supersedes the claims of individuals or local communities.

'Native Americans and other ethnic, religious, and cultural groups' are mentioned in SAA Principle 4 (Public Education and Outreach). This principle explicitly promotes cooperation with those 'who find in the archaeological record important aspects of their cultural heritage', as well as with the general public. This is the most explicit recognition in the Principles that there may be people who have special relationships to the archaeological record and its objects. Nevertheless, in describing Native Americans as one of the 'many publics [that] exist for archaeology', this principle reinforces the message that the archaeologist is responsible for the archaeological record and that others should stand back and wait as their own cultures are curated, interpreted and displayed for them.

These considerations show that the principles of the Belmont Report can be used to elucidate some of the deficiencies in ethical codes promoted by the professional societies. Human subjects IRBs use the Belmont principles to evaluate methodologies such as sampling procedures, research instruments, inclusion of underrepresented or marginalised populations, dissemination of information, informed consent procedures, etc. to ensure that research participants are safeguarded. In addition to biomedical research, this approach has been widely applied to good effect throughout the social sciences and is a fact of life for cultural anthropologists. North American archaeologists, however, have yet to adopt this level of ethical accountability even though they often interact with Native Americans and profoundly impact their lives and communities.[8]

NEW MOVEMENTS

Archaeological projects have not undergone human subjects reviews because they rarely meet the legal definition of human subjects research.

---

8 We are certainly not the first to bring this into question. For example, Johnson argues that: 'protesters say, in effect, that the responsibility acknowledged, but not always met, by the ethnographer toward the people studied is a responsibility that the professional archaeologist must also meet' (Johnson 1973: 129).

However, there have been profound ramifications for contemporary Native individuals and communities given that many anthropologists, and archaeologists in particular, have conducted their fieldwork without regard for Native American sensibilities or interests. 'This approach promotes an *etic*, rather than *emic* perspective,[9] and privileges the rights of anthropologists to study and investigate over the indigenous group's rights to control their own historical, cultural and intellectual property' (Bendremer, Wozniak and Thomas 2002). The scant literature on this topic describes this as an imperial or colonial relationship (Biolsi 1997; Smith 1999). As a result, archaeological inquiry has been particularly damaging to Native societies who view their ancestors and histories not as remote or academic, but more as a vital and real presence in the contemporary world.

The existing laws and codes of conduct for archaeologists (see Cassell and Jacobs 1987; Watkins 2000b) are insufficient to protect Native American communities. Generally, the best these regulations have to offer are requirements that archaeologists consult with or consider the opinions of Federally Recognized Tribes (Section 106), interested or affected groups (Society for American Archaeology Code of Ethics 1996; Watkins *et al.* 2000; Society for Professional Archaeologists 1995) or local communities (Archaeological Institute of America Code of Ethics 1990). An often-used definition of consultation is as follows: 'Consultation means the process of seeking, discussing and considering the views of the other participants, and, where feasible, seeking agreement with them regarding matters arising in the Section 106 [consultation] process' (36 CFR 800.16(f)). From this, it is evident that 'consultation' implies that the decision-making authority resides not with the Native community, but with the archaeologists. At best, the results of consultation depend on the disposition, sensitivity, goals and experience of the anthropologists or officials involved and their understanding of and respect for Native sovereignty, belief systems and self-determination (Anderson 1995; Grimes 2001; O'Brien 1989; Tsosie 1997; White Deer 1997).

Increasingly, archaeologists are calling for safeguards of Native American interests and increased participation by the tribes. For instance, Zimmerman writes:

---

9 The terms *emic* and *etic* were borrowed from the expressions phonemic and phonetic in linguistics. In the social sciences, the terms have generally come to refer to an insider's or Native's perspective (emic) versus an outsider's or observer's perspective (etic).

Quite simply, anthropologists must learn to share control of the past. This means that an archaeological view cannot be seen as the only legitimate view of the past. In practice, this means working with indigenous peoples to formulate both research questions and methods. (Zimmerman 1997a: 105)[10]

These calls have led some archaeologists to advocate a number of practical approaches for ethical archaeological studies to provide relief to Native American communities. For example, Watkins, Pyburn and Cressey (2000: 73–81) suggested seven steps for applied archaeologists:

1 Identify the community with which they will be involved.
2 Form partnerships beyond archaeology.
3 Understand the legal boundaries involved in the process.
4 Communicate effectively.
5 Recognise the diverse decision-making structures.
6 Place the goals of the project ahead of personal and private goals.
7 Be aware of social and gender issues.

Zimmerman (2001: 178) advocates 'Ethnocritical Archaeology' where 'archaeologists and indigenous people share construction of the past'. Loring (2001: 190) suggests 'Community Archaeology' which 'address[es] the interests and needs of the Innu community and their notions of the past while exploring the ancient tenure of the land'. Colwell-Chanthaphonh and Ferguson (2004: 23) suggest 'an ethic of collaboration' guided by Virtue Ethics.

As seen above, a number of archaeologists advocate inquiry in order to pursue the self-defined vital interests of Native American communities. This is based upon the recognition that cultural data, past or present, belong to members of a society and/or its descendants. In fact, the World Archaeological Congress First Code of Ethics, accepted in its entirety by

---

10 Consider also:

> In this era of aboriginal self-government, it is not for the outsider to set the rules of conduct on our lands and in our communities. It is the right and responsibility of researchers to respect and comply with our standards. (King 1997: 118)

> Creative approaches must be discussed and debated by aboriginal communities, academic institutions, and individual researchers to reach a working relationship that neither constricts the advancement of knowledge nor denigrates the aboriginal communities' legitimate authority over the integrity of their own intellectual traditions. (King 1997: 118)

> Indians were no longer to be studied as research subjects for some do-gooder's Ph.D. dissertation topic without some accountability to the Indian community; they were to hold to the self-deterministic values that encouraged development from within the community rather than accepting the impositions of outside agents. Any interference or intervention by an outsider had better be genuine, have been sought by the tribe, be approved by local tribal authorities, and mean more than a passing summer's recreation and another meaningless article. (Grobsmith 1997: 37)

archaeologists in Australia, states this in no uncertain terms. This code identifies obligations:

1 To acknowledge the importance of indigenous cultural heritage, including sites, places, objects, artefacts, human remains, to the survival of indigenous cultures.
2 To acknowledge the importance of protecting indigenous cultural heritage to the well-being of indigenous peoples.
3 To acknowledge the special importance of indigenous ancestral human remains, and sites containing and/or associated with such remains, to indigenous peoples.
4 To acknowledge that the important relationship between indigenous peoples and their cultural heritage exists irrespective of legal ownership.
5 To acknowledge that the indigenous cultural heritage rightfully belongs to the indigenous descendants of that heritage.
6 To acknowledge and recognise indigenous methodologies for interpreting, curating, managing and protecting indigenous cultural heritage.
7 To establish equitable partnerships and relationships between Members and indigenous peoples whose cultural heritage is being investigated.
8 To seek, whenever possible, representation of indigenous peoples in agencies funding or authorising research to be certain their view is considered as critically important in setting research standards, questions, priorities and goals. (World Archaeological Congress 2001)

This code flatly contradicts the SAA Principles by recognising that some archaeological objects belong to indigenous peoples (5). It goes beyond the SAA Principles in acknowledging the existence of methodologies different from those of academic archaeology (6), and by recognising the importance of the unique relationship between indigenous peoples and the archaeological record (1, 2, 3, 4 and 5).

Consistent with these ideas, Powell, Garza and Hendricks (1993: 29) advocate an approach they refer to as 'Covenantal Archaeology' where 'programs train tribal members as archaeologists and ethnographers – so they may take over direction and management of their cultural heritage' (Garza and Powell 2001: 37–56). Watkins (2000b: 177) advocates 'Indigenous Archaeology' where native communities control the 'quality and quantity of archaeology'.[11] As a result, there is a small but increasing

---

11 'I do not see a truly indigenous archaeology developing until there is a major change in the way that archaeology views ownership and protection. Only when indigenous groups are able to

number of archaeological projects that operate under the authority of tribal governments, tribal historic preservation offices or tribal museums (Alexander 1996; Bendremer 1996; 1998; Bendremer and Fawcett 1995; Bendremer and Wozniak 2000; Bendremer, Wozniak and Thomas 2002; Cohen and Swidler 1995; Hantman, Wood and Shields 2000; Kluth and Munnell 1997; Swidler *et al.* 1997; Watkins 2000b).

HUMAN SUBJECTS REVIEW AND ARCHAEOLOGY

In cultural anthropology, applying human subjects review through IRBs has created a mechanism for ethical and collaborative approaches to research in Indian country. However, no such mechanism is presently available for Native American archaeology. It is of first importance that archaeologists begin to adhere to the tenets of human subjects reviews guided by the Belmont principles in conjunction with the ethics codes of their professional associations.

Archaeological projects have impacted Native communities in some devastating ways. For many societies, the ancestors are much less remote and abstract than they are in the European tradition. Often, the living community is more like an extension of the ancient community, with the contemporary people responsible for decisions regarding the past. Avoiding informed consent procedures is a violation of these prerogatives and, as such, also violates the AAA code and the SAA Principles. It further disrupts already marginalised and vulnerable communities, which are afforded special protections under human subjects review.[12]

In the view of some, even the application of human subjects review and informed consent would not fully alleviate the problems that archaeology poses for Native Americans:

If one is continually investigated by anthropologists or sociologists, all of whom share a common universe of disclosure where fundamental questions have already been decided, informed consent is somewhat akin to firing the warning shot immediately before the fatal bullet is sent on its way.

(Deloria 1980: 270, quoted in Grobsmith 1997: 44)

control not only the physical manifestations of their culture but also what should be protected and how "protection" is defined will indigenous archaeology flourish' (Watkins 2000: 178).

12 '[I]ssues of informed consent, particularly with minorities or those classified as "vulnerable" human subjects (for example, pregnant women, prisoners, and mentally disabled informants) are carefully scrutinized by review boards to maximize the protections to which citizens, especially those who historically have been at risk for exploitation, are entitled' (Grobsmith 1997: 43).

It is our belief, however, that human subjects reviews would go a long way in providing relief for American Indian communities that have been, first, subject to genocide by European colonists and, then, subjects of intrusive, long-term study by the intellectual descendants of these colonists. This would be especially true if a mechanism were instituted that allowed Native Americans to determine research questions and methods as well as final disposition of the information.

What would human subjects review look like for archaeology? Human subjects reviews performed by Institutional Review Boards (IRBs) would examine research protocols, guided by the Common Rule and by the Belmont Report. Qualified academics would examine methods, instruments, documents (including consent forms and scripts for recruiting participants) and other technical aspects of the projects reviewed. IRBs are also required to have non-scientist members, and members unaffiliated with the sponsoring institution. As a group, IRBs develop expertise in assessing risks and benefits. They are exposed to the best practices at their institutions, and can raise the scientific quality of research being done as well as the ethical character of that research.

In a typical case, a researcher planning a project fills out forms intended to help the researcher and the IRB identify ethical issues posed by the research, with emphasis on the level of risk carried by the study. The forms are submitted to an IRB representative with copies of the consent documents, a description of the research protocol and other relevant documents. A large percentage of social science projects are approved as 'exempt' (meaning the project does not require detailed review even though it did need to be submitted). Others qualify for 'expedited review', which can be accomplished without waiting for the next full IRB meeting. Projects carrying greater than minimal risk require full IRB review. (See Office of Human Research Protections 1993 for details.) IRBs have the obligation and authority to stop research affiliated with their institutions that does not merit approval. Researchers have responsibility to submit proposals for human subjects research for review, and to stop an impermissible project even if the subjects give consent. Thus the IRB, the researcher and the research participant (subject) each have veto power.

Institutional Review Boards provide a forum for peer review of research protocols to promote good research and minimise unnecessary risk to subjects. Indeed, although IRBs are directly obligated to potential research subjects, most IRBs approach reviews with an eye to seeing how research can be done well and ethically rather than with an eye to finding ways to stop research. At their best, IRBs improve both the ethics and the science of the projects reviewed. In so far as doing research well improves the contribution a project makes, ethical concerns and scientific concerns converge: promoting scientific quality is an issue of beneficence (Richman 2002).

Since the IRB is charged with the protection of human subjects (research participants), it is very important that their deliberations take into account Native perspectives and sensibilities. There are a number of mechanisms available to provide the necessary insight. As mentioned above, these include United States government regulations that call for a non-scientist member and for a member from outside the institution. Lay members of affected communities and academics from these communities can be called upon to participate. It should be noted that the researcher, sometimes an individual with the significant knowledge about the values and interests of affected individuals or communities, is excluded because of the possibility of a conflict of interest for the IRB to rely on the researcher's perspective.

Another important mechanism that can be instituted to account for Native interests would be a separate Community Advisory Board (CAB) composed of members of the affected community group. Creating such a board for review of archaeology research would provide an additional way for academics to hear the voices of indigenous peoples. A CAB can help researchers anticipate and understand the needs and interests of the community in order to ensure successful ethical research (Strauss *et al.* 2001). In addition, the use of CABs is an excellent way to implement obligation 8 of the World Archaeological Congress First Code of Ethics (see above).[13] CABs have been used to advise researchers directly, but they could also serve as resources for IRBs seeking community input on the permissibility of specific research protocols. CABs could be given authority to stop research that they deem impermissible after reasonable consideration (even if the research has received IRB approval). The burden should be on the researcher to show that the benefits of the research are worth the burdens. In our experience, IRBs and CABs do a remarkably good job of supporting researchers while protecting human subjects. When such bodies meet, the deliberation process reveals both problems in research and solutions to those problems that individuals, even the same individuals, miss when working alone.

---

13 CABs have also been used to gain 'buy-in' from community members and to improve recruitment rates. This is not impermissible as long as it is not coercive and the three Belmont Principles, respect for persons, beneficence and justice, are satisfied.

Our discussion has centred on Native Americans and US policy. The values of respect for persons, beneficence and justice are not peculiar to the American context, but should be applied worldwide. Our immediate recommendations are limited, however. They apply to research where there are identifiable living persons with a stake in the disposition of the artefacts and information being studied. Native Americans offer clear examples of individuals and communities whose stakes in the practice of archaeology have often been ignored. The use of IRBs and CABs in archaeology will vastly improve the protection of research subjects, both at the level of individuals and at the level of communities. It will also foster accountability and enforce ethical standards for archaeologists where few such mechanisms exist today.

CONCLUSION

Vine Deloria, Jr. is said to have remarked 'that anthropologists were the only group he had ever known who had their "brains sucked out of [their] skulls"' (Grobsmith in Watkins 1997: 47). In part, this sentiment was a reaction to a field of inquiry which has unilaterally proposed to study, categorise, acquire, analyse, store and display another's precious heritage and ancestors. Because the endeavour of anthropology, in many of its forms, deals with some of the most fundamental issues of who we are and where we come from, it is impermissible to approach anthropological research in a cavalier or unilateral manner. In doing so, anthropologists have done great harm (while also providing some benefits) to Native Americans over the years.

Regarding the harm done, it is the responsibility of the current generation of anthropologists to begin to mitigate past wrongs and to put in place ethical procedures that ensure that we maximise benefits to indigenous people and minimise harm. It is imperative that we ensure protections for subject populations, especially marginalised, at-risk populations, consistent with existing professional codes and the National Research Act. For these reasons, archaeological projects should be subject to human subjects review just as cultural anthropological studies are. In this way, the anthropological community would better protect the Native people on whom we rely for our professional lives and livelihood and could help empower these communities to take control of their heritage, identities and futures.

CHAPTER 7

Trust and archaeological practice: towards a framework of Virtue Ethics

Chip Colwell-Chanthaphonh and T. J. Ferguson

In the autumn of 1922, an English archaeologist sat in the damp darkness of an underground tunnel studying by candlelight the seal of the royal necropolis etched into a heavy stone doorway. After years of searching the deserts of Egypt in vain, he hoped, at last, that this was the object of his desire. Feverish with anticipation, the young archaeologist broke through the ancient stone and peered into the gaping space. 'At first I could see nothing, the hot air escaping from the chamber causing the candle to flicker', he would later write, 'but presently, as my eyes grew accustomed to the light, details of the room emerged slowly from the mist, strange animals, statues, and gold – everywhere the glint of gold.' When the archaeologist's companions, burning with curiosity, asked him if he could see anything, he replied in a whisper, 'Yes, wonderful things.'

Howard Carter's discovery of Tutankhamun's tomb is fixed in the public imagination largely because of the spectacular material wealth found with the pharaoh's earthly remains (Carter 1923; Hoving 1978). Surely 'King Tut' would not be widely remembered today if Carter had only found a humble grave with a few undecorated ceramic sherds. Although most archaeologists oppose the popular stereotype of object hunter, they have built a professional identity that revolves around the possession and study of things. The museums around the world brimming with artefacts undeniably prove this point (Barringer and Flynn 1998). It is also notable that some of the earliest debates concerning professional ethics centred almost exclusively on the welfare of artefacts and sites. In 1961, after a decade of deliberation, the Society for American Archaeology's Committee on Ethics and Standards published its 'Four Statements for Archaeology', a proclamation about the profession's basic principles (Davis 1984: 15). Even though the 'Four Statements' declaration asserts that the value of objects is 'their status as documents, and is not intrinsic', the proscriptions for behaviour that follow focus almost entirely on collecting things, recording things, studying things, sharing things, writing about things, selling things and storing things (Champe *et al.* 1961).

A great deal has changed, however, since 1961. While archaeologists have continued to affirm the information value of objects, they also have begun to recognise that their discipline does not unfold in a social vacuum. Issues of commercialisation, relations with native peoples, public outreach and intellectual property have compelled archaeologists to consider how their profession encompasses more than objects because it entails myriad social and intellectual relationships. A robust literature written about these topics indicates the increasingly sophisticated awareness archaeologists have about these matters (e.g., Green 1984; Fluehr-Lobban 2003; Messenger 1999; Swidler *et al.* 1997; Tubb 1995; Woodall 1990; Zimmerman *et al.* 2003b). Professional associations of archaeologists have responded to these issues by promulgating ethical codes of conduct and principles that define obligations to colleagues, sponsors and the public.

Codes of conduct are law-like statements or rules about what archaeologists shall and shall not do in their professional practice. The code of conduct espoused by the Register of Professional Archaeologists in the United States, for instance, makes thirty-one specific statements concerning professional morality and responsibilities to the public: to colleagues, employees and students, and to employers and clients (see Vitelli 1996b: 253–60). This code explicitly spells out ethically acceptable conduct. For example, the archaeologist shall 'Actively support conservation of the archaeological resource base', and shall not 'Engage in conduct involving dishonesty, fraud, deceit or misrepresentation about archaeological matters.' Codes are limited, however, because they cannot cover every possible ethical dilemma and rarely address how archaeologists can sustain meaningful social relationships. They are often interpreted as fixed rules that simply define what constitutes an ethical agent. Karen D. Vitelli has written how, in her experience, the recent surge of codes has stifled classroom discussions, as students seek out the 'right answers' in the codes, 'assuming that those codes are absolute rules of appropriate behavior that professionals simply learn to live with, without questioning' (Zimmerman *et al.* 2003a: xiii).

Codes of conduct provide useful guides for professional practice but the specificity of their statements is such that they cannot possibly cover all potential ethical quandaries. Some organisations have therefore elected to issue statements of ethical principles rather than codes of conduct. Principles define general and fundamental propositions that affirm the tenets of the profession, which can be adopted to guide action in a wide variety of specific settings. The Society for American Archaeology has taken this tack in publishing the 'Principles of Archaeological Ethics'. This statement of eight ethical principles conveys contemporary concerns for both the archaeological record and the people affected by archaeological practice (Lynott 1997). At the heart of the SAA's 'Principles' is an ethic of stewardship, which entails being 'both caretakers of and advocates for the archaeological record'. Archaeologists are urged to take on a stewardship role not only for themselves, but for 'the benefit of all people'. As Mark J. Lynott and Alison Wylie (1995: 29) have written, 'As advocates for the record, so conceived, archaeologists must be concerned not only with the interests of their colleagues and the discipline of archaeology as we now know it (specifically, its scientific research goals as now defined), but also with the interests of the full range of publics, some of whose heritage is bound up in this record.'

Some professional organisations combine both principles and codes in a single statement. The 'First Code of Ethics' of the World Archaeological Congress begins with eight principles that describe ethical obligations to indigenous peoples, and then sets out seven rules that the members of WAC agree to adhere to in their archaeological investigations (World Archaeological Congress 1991). In this formulation, there is a general principle 'To acknowledge the importance of indigenous cultural heritage, including sites, places, objects, artefacts, human remains, the survival of indigenous cultures.' A specific rule then establishes that WAC members 'shall negotiate with and obtain the informed consent of representatives authorised by the indigenous peoples whose cultural heritage is the subject of investigation'.

Principles and codes of ethics in archaeology are important because they simultaneously reflect and shape the discipline's values and ideals (Davis 2003; Smith and Burke 2003). The Society for American Archaeology's principles were developed in a specific historical context, arising from the need to distinguish between competing interests, inspire critical self-reflection and resist demands for external regulation (Wylie 1999). The fact that virtually every national and international archaeological organisation endorses ethical principles or codes testifies to their institutional utility (O'Keefe, 1998). This ethical guidance is not without controversy, however. Peter Pels (1999) has argued that the anthropological endeavour is based on an inherent 'moral duplexity' because scholars have opposing obligations to both the people they study and the agencies that fund their work. In short, Pels asserts that anthropological conduct has been necessarily corrupt, and that its 'dual mandate' makes the profession incapable of designing an unequivocal ethical code. Commenting on this argument, Murray L. Wax (1993: 130) has suggested that the problem is not merely with anthropological practice, but more with contemporary ethical systems, such as Kantian and Utilitarian viewpoints that 'focus upon detached and independent social atoms rather than upon human actors organically related to each other'.

An alternative to principle- and rule-based ethics is a system of thought revolving around virtues. Instead of beginning with questions of obligations and oughts, Virtue Ethics begins with questions of character, focusing on relationships and the subjectivities of social interaction. Many philosophies worldwide, from Chinese to Hopi thought, reflect the core concerns of Virtue Ethics (Brandt 1954; Huang 2003). In Western moral philosophy, Plato and Aristotle launched expressions of Virtue Ethics, which remained the predominant approach in European culture until the Enlightenment when it fell into disfavour (MacIntyre 1966). Virtue Ethics was largely neglected until G. E. M. Anscombe's (1958) seminal paper, 'Modern Moral Philosophy', which reanimated Virtue Ethics and provided a counterpoint to the utilitarian and deontological theories then in vogue. At the time, mainstream moral theories disregarded vital issues at the heart of Virtue Ethics – moral motivation, character, moral wisdom, familial relationships, moral education, the role of emotions in moral life and the virtues themselves (Crisp and Slote 1997). Applying Virtue Ethics in archaeology provides an alternative not only to the inflexibility of principles and codes of ethics, but also to the Utilitarian and Kantian approaches that underlie them (Colwell-Chanthaphonh and Ferguson 2004). Unfortunately, Virtue Ethics is too often excluded from discussions of archaeological ethics altogether (e.g., Greenawalt 1998; May 1980; Wylie 2003).

In this chapter we closely examine one feature of Virtue Ethics – trust – as a beginning point to illustrate the value of a professional ethics based on concepts of virtue, instead of rules. Trust is an essential aspect of positive social interaction, and while many scholars have obliquely revealed its merits, few have expansively reflected on its place in archaeology. The first part examines the nature of trust in rather broad terms, looking in detail at philosopher Annette Baier's notions of trust. The second part explores how trust relates more directly to archaeology. By applying the moral philosophy of Virtue Ethics to archaeology, ultimately we hope to show the richness as well as the complexity of virtues, and their potential role in defining the moral landscape of archaeological practice.

THE NATURE OF TRUST

Moral philosopher Annette Baier has been deeply concerned with the role virtues play in our everyday lives. She has written extensively on Virtue Ethics, employing what some might call a 'feminist metaethics', to address the fundamental issues of caring, love, interrelatedness and trust that may guide our behaviour. For Baier, trust and trustworthiness are particularly salient aspects of human interaction because society could not exist without the kind of relationships of trust nurtured between a child and her or his mother. In Baier's influential paper 'What Do Women Want in a Moral Theory?' (1997), she examines in depth how trust binds the concepts of love and obligation (see also Baier 1994). Baier, unlike Anscombe (1958), wants not to do away with *deontic* notions (e.g., duty, obligation and moral oughts) of morality but to link them with *aretaic* concepts (e.g., virtue, excellence and character). To convince us that trust is valuable and can function as this bridge, Baier recognises that she must first demonstrate that trust is connected to and can elucidate the concepts of obligation and love.

Baier suggests that very few people will doubt that love involves trust. She assumes that if we examine trust and distrust, and love 'in all its variants', we will intuitively see the connection. Initially, one may imagine several variants of love that do *not* appear to involve trust, or involve little trust, such as unconditional love, blind love, unrequited love and love people have for non-human animals. One might say that a parent can love a child, even if there is no trust between them. That is the nature of unconditional love – there are no conditions, including trust. However, even in these instances, some kinds of trust are at stake. For instance, there must be trust in *one's own judgement* about the other as worthy of love. Also, there is trust that the other actually *is* a being with certain kinds of traits that merit love. Moreover, one's love for others is usually deeply bound up with trust of a person's goodwill or mutual affection. Therefore Baier suggests not that trust is linked with love only, or even mainly, as a condition, but that it is frequently inextricably tied to love.

Connecting trust to the concept of obligation, Baier admits, is more controversial. She initially claims that obligations involve trust because someone must ensure that obligations are met. That is, someone must judge other people's actions, decide if obligations are fulfilled, and if not, perhaps chastise or punish those persons in some way. And this judgement of others, the power of manipulation and coercion, requires trust – trust that these individuals will be fair and honest. Indeed, it seems to us that it is difficult to have an idea of obligation without an idea of judgement or trust. For even in evaluating one's own obligations, one must be willing to make self-judgements and thus maintain self-trust. This kind of trust seems crucial to all suites of other-regulatory attitudes, including love.

After establishing the link between trust and obligation, Baier criticises modern moral theorists for what she sees as a misallocation of trust. She argues that contemporary theorists have focused too much on 'cases where more trust is placed in enforcers of obligations than is placed in ordinary moral agents, the bearers of obligations' (Baier 1997: 274). As a case in point, she discusses how contractarians place a disproportionate amount of trust on enforcers. This seems to be a valid point for contractual obligations, but may be more problematic for other obligations considered by modern ethical theories. For instance, Peter Singer's (1975) consequentialist argument for giving equal consideration to all sentient beings is not a statement on how to punish those who eat meat, for instance, but an argument to steer the agent's action. But Baier is certainly correct in her more general argument that trust is a central feature of our moral relationships. Moreover, we must carefully consider which persons in a moral equation we are placing in our trust. Baier wisely suggests that moral agents cannot place their trust blindly, but must use the right kind of trust, at the right time, for the right reasons. Indeed the virtue of trust can easily become a vice when used indelicately.

These brief comments about Baier's multifaceted essay highlight the ways in which trust is an important aspect of ethical judgement. Baier, in short, effectively illustrates that trust is an important feature of (some kinds of) love and obligation. Indeed, recall that she merely wanted to begin to show that trust is connected to and can elucidate these two larger concepts. Baier's ideas have implications for moral theory in general, and archaeological ethics in particular. One important point is that scholars need to consider fully the ways in which *aretaic* concepts such as trust can be used in conjunction with *deontic* ideas such as obligation. A second point is that Baier brings our attention to how ethics can be agent-focused as much as act-focused. In other words, Baier is much more concerned with the agents themselves than in deciding which acts are morally required for specific situations. Baier would agree with other philosophers, such as Michael Stocker (1976), who focus on sustained action instead of single acts. Being a good person – and a good archaeologist – requires one to be concerned with more than just a moment of crisis or a single isolated act, but with behaviour extending over the years that is enacted daily. A third point about Baier's philosophy is largely unstated in her writing, but clearly underlies much of her thinking. While she never uses the Greek term *eudaimonia*, it is clear that Baier is concerned with not only how humans can prosper in the present, but also how humans can thrive far into the future. Baier does not want society just to get by, but to excel and flourish. Her discussion on child rearing brings to our attention that if we want society to flourish now and in the future, we must attend to how young people are morally instructed, a contention Plato (1992) raised several thousand years ago.

Baier's philosophy of Virtue Ethics is not so far away from the realities of archaeological practice. Archaeologists, after all, should be deeply concerned with illuminating the role of the virtues, agency and ethical training in their professional lives. When we examined the archaeological literature we found abundant evidence of these concerns, and particularly the virtue of trust. Joe Watkins (1999), for example, has clearly demonstrated an interest in sustaining virtues through an emphasis on respect and dialogue. As Merrilee H. Salmon (1999: 308) has noted about Watkins' work:

Drawing on his own experience, Watkins urges archaeologists to develop an ongoing broadly-based relationship with those who have differing interests in cultural properties instead of trying to communicate only when there is a dispute about the disposition of archaeological materials . . . Although Watkins does not refer explicitly to any ethical theory in his article, his proposal exemplifies the views of A. Baier and other contemporary metaethicists in its emphasis on trust rather than formal codes or principles of utility or justice, as the fundamental basis of ethical behavior.

Watkins is not alone in his position, as can be easily seen in the important work *Native Americans and Archaeologists*, an edited volume that examined the contested relationship between the two key stakeholders of the past. In that book, archaeologist Larry J. Zimmerman (1997b: 52) suggested that, 'Many have discovered that if a relationship of trust can be built, archaeology may gain increased access to materials and sites.' Rose A. Kluth (1997: 118), for her part, advocated that, 'There must be trust on both sides, or it will never work. Archaeologists must invite Native Americans to observe what they do and to communicate in a way that will be beneficial to both parties. It also follows that Native Americans must begin dialogue with archaeologists, in a manner that is respectful to our teachings.' Native American contributors to the volume framed interactions in similar terms. Leonard Forsman (1997: 107) of the Suquamish Indian Tribe noted that, 'Respect and trust from the

Indian community are earned through understanding Indian values and traditions and by a commitment to honor native interests through actions.' Cecile Elkins Carter (1997: 154) of the Caddo Indian Tribe in Oklahoma wrote that archaeologists could do much to build positive relationships with tribes by notifying them of discoveries, communicating in plain language and questioning the greater outcome of their work. 'For now', she wrote, 'there are steps that each individual involved with archaeology can take to promote trust and demonstrate that your work has relevancy for Native Americans.' Reba Fuller (1997: 183–4), a member of the Tuolumne Band of Me-Wuk Indians in California, noted that she knew of one project that failed precisely because some participants lacked trust and respect, and so argued that 'trust must be established and, henceforth, must reflect continuity. When good faith efforts are made to communicate (development of trust), the consulting parties should be able to enter into agreements addressing site preservation and/or proper mitigation measures and procedures for the disposition of human remains and cultural items (reflecting continuity).'

TRUST IN THE PRACTICE OF ARCHAEOLOGY

Although many people concerned about the ethics of archaeology have commented on the importance of trust, what, more precisely, is the nature of trust in archaeological practice? In this section we will pursue this question by defining and discussing five categories of trust relationships archaeologists enter into through their work. We then consider the distinction between entrusting and trusting, the interplay between goodwill and trust, the importance of power in trusting relationships, and how we might test the virtue of trust.

As Baier (1994: 98) has pointed out, everyone participating in society enters into trusting relationships on a daily basis: from asking directions, to walking alone at night, to eating at a restaurant. Moreover, besides these brief and mundane encounters of trust, most people have long-lasting and deep-seated relationships of trust with friends, family members and other individuals. While archaeologists are undoubtedly subject to these forms of trust – by virtue of being human – they also enter into unique trusting relationships owing to the very nature of archaeological research. Hence, one place to begin is by identifying some of the various trust relationships archaeologists explicitly and implicitly develop when they engage in their craft (Table 7.1).

Table 7.1. *Categories of trust relationships*

Trust relationship	Description
1. Professional trust	The collegial trust among archaeologists, including the rapport among peers, and students and their teachers.
2. Public trust	A trust relationship between professional archaeologists and the general public. Two subgroups can be defined: the actively involved public and the uninterested public.
3. Descendant trust	The relationship between archaeologists and the descendants of the people under study.
4. Governmental trust	Trust existing between professional archaeologists and the individuals in government and the institutions they serve.
5. Generational trust	A nebulous relationship between living archaeologists and (a) earlier generations of deceased people buried in archaeological sites, and (b) the future generations who will have a stake in the past.

These five categories generally describe the archaeologist's trust with other archaeologists (in an academic and contract setting), the general public (avocational archaeologists, the lay public and the non-interested public), peoples whose culture is under examination (typically, but not necessarily, Native Americans in the United States), the government (which is responsible for overseeing many archaeological projects), and past and future generations who are associated with archaeological sites or who may (or may not) have an interest in archaeological knowledge and materials. It is also worth observing that many of these groups have existing trust relationships independent of archaeologists. For instance, the public has its own trust relationship with the government, and the government has a special trust relationship with Native Americans (Wilkens and Lomawaima 2002). Hence, there is a complex web of trust existing between all these different groups that indubitably affects the relationship archaeologists have with others.

The last group, 'past and future generations', might cause some readers to pause. Many archaeologists objectify the dead as 'human remains', thereby denying the essential humanity of the people buried in archaeological sites and giving little thought to ethical responsibilities to these deceased people. Our native colleagues tell us that all of the people buried in archaeological sites are someone's ancestors (Nichols *et al.* 1999; Echo-Hawk and Echo-Hawk 1994; Riding In 2000; Ferguson 1996). The living have an interrelationship with the deceased and should therefore cultivate respect for these remains and treat them with dignity. That deceased people have rights is recognised in modern societies by the sanctity of graves in consecrated cemeteries, and by the legal status of wills (McGuire 1994b). The failure of some archaeologists to extend this approach to the deceased people of other cultures is somewhat inexplicable but is beginning to change. The Vermillion Accord of the World Archaeological Congress, for instance, calls for archaeologists to respect the 'wishes of the dead concerning disposition' (Day 1990: 15).

In considering future generations, we freely admit that it is difficult to cognise the desires and needs of people yet to be born. Baier (1994: 127) also found cross-generational trust a problematical issue, and for the most part her account simply ignores it. However, archaeologists cannot so easily dismiss generational trust because they often claim that their efforts are undertaken specifically for future generations. For example, as Ruthann Knudson (1991: 5) has argued, 'The complex temporal aspect of archaeological resources is significant in their "nonrenewable" label . . . these presently useful and past-reflecting resources are a "bank" of unique values for future recreationists, believers, and scientists.' Or, as Frank G. Fechner (1998: 387) stated, 'cultural assets are attributed to certain states, but these states have the duty to keep and to protect them in the interest of the whole humankind for future generations'. The very notion of 'preservation' seems to imply that we are saving the archaeological record *for* some future time, *for* future generations.

Following from this, it becomes clear that in some contexts many of the divisions presented in Table 7.1 fade or become recombined. For instance, the 'public' generally defined as non-archaeologists may include 'future generations' or 'descendants'. Indeed, the 'general public' constitutes a challenging concept when examined closely. Public trust, as a legal and moral framework, is a complex phenomenon and difficult to extrapolate into unambiguous categories. Essentially the 'public' may be defined as anyone who is not a professional archaeologist, but even professional archaeologists, as citizens and living beings, comprise a part of the public. However, if the public is used as a reference to every person living and future, the term becomes essentially meaningless. As Francis P. McManamon (1991: 123) pithily observed, 'the general public is a big category; it includes just about everyone'. If 'the public' is used to refer to any *non-professional*, the problem arises that many non-professionals enter into specific trusting relationships with archaeologists such as descendent communities and government employees; this is further complicated when one must define what constitutes a 'professional' archaeologist.

McManamon (1991: 123–4) resolved the problem of delineating the 'general public' by further subdividing this category, based on survey data, into: (1) those that are fully scientifically literate, (2) those that are informed and interested in science, and (3) those who are entirely uninformed and uninterested. More recent research on the general public confirms the applicability of these categories (Pokotylo and Guppy 1999).

McManamon's tactic mediates several of the problems articulated above, and provides him a workable approach to the 'general public' as a particular constituency of the archaeological past. As our aim is to outline the basic trust relationships archaeologists enter into, we collapse McManamon's first two categories into involved public trust, and contrast it with uninvolved public trust. The former refers to those in the 'general public' (i.e., those that are not in any of the other categories) that have a specific or vested interest in the archaeological past. This includes avocational archaeologists, volunteers on Earthwatch excavations, avid readers of *Archaeology Magazine* and the like. Uninvolved public trust includes individuals who are uninterested in the past generally or the archaeological past in particular, which might include, for instance, young children. These categories were created in part because it seems that there is a much more explicit trusting relationship with the interested public than with the uninterested public. In the former, archaeologists have clear obligations to be honest, not to take advantage of the latter, and actively include them in research, preservation issues and the dissemination of research results. For those who are disinterested, there is a much more implicit trusting relationship, in part because there is almost no relationship to speak of.

An important aspect of all these categories is the way in which relationships involve an implicit or explicit sense of trust (Baier 1994: 110–14). Where there is an explicit agreement of trust between two groups, a much stronger and definable obligation exists. Conversely, if only an implicit trust is present, then the nature of that kind of trust is less compelling and rigid. The relationship between a contract archaeology firm in the United States and the State Historic Preservation Office – a governmental trust relationship – is most often explicit because it is defined by laws and contracts. The commitment of trust that archaeologists make to future generations, in turn, is often implicit in the rhetoric of preservation, ill defined as to what this trust relationship might entail. Archaeologists, then, enter into both implicit and explicit trusting relationships, and they are important because they inform us about the type and level of trust that exists between groups.

In the practice of archaeology, trust centres on not only inter-personal relations but also objects and knowledge (Wildesen 1984: 4). A large part of these types of trust consists of the archaeologist being trusted to explore, preserve or examine material culture, and from these endeavours advance the knowledge of humanity. Employing Baier's (1994: 101) distinction between *entrusting* and *trusting*, this trust based on objects can be further elucidated. Baier points out that many things we value cannot be cared for by a single person, and therefore we often must entrust the things we value to other people to guard. Heritage resources easily fit this description, as no person can single-handedly watch over the immeasurable number of artefacts in the ground. Baier uses the three-place predicate – A trusts B with valued thing C – and notes that this might not easily depict many situations. And yet, this does, quite nicely, fit with governmental trust; for instance, in our table: the government (A) entrusts archaeologists (B) with heritage resources (C). This brings us back to the explicit–implicit discussion raised earlier. While the government often entrusts archaeologists with heritage resources, the responsibilities of professionals are frequently directed through work permits and review processes. At the same time, archaeologists are often free to conduct research as they see fit, so long as their efforts do not exceed their legal permits. Hence we see a dualism here whereby the government explicitly entrusts archaeologists with heritage resources through permits and reviews, yet also implicitly trusts them to do good research. While we do not have space to explore all five trust relationships identified above in this way, a brief look indicates the clear importance not only of working out the nature of the trust relationships archaeologists involve themselves with but also of examining what is being trusted to whom.

Throughout her book Baier (1994) raises the issue of goodwill as being an essential component of trust. Goodwill is important because we must use it when making and receiving promises, and because trust of an implicit nature allows for individual discretion (Baier 1994: 118). In some kinds of trust (especially implicit ones), a person must rely on goodwill because by trusting we become vulnerable, and consequently open to injury. As we begin to build a trust with someone or some group of people, we depend more and more on their goodwill not to betray our trust. Thus, in order for trust to thrive, so must goodwill. Baier's argument is persuasive, and if extrapolated, addresses some of the conflicts found in archaeological practice. Goodwill was evidently lacking, for example, between many archaeologists and Native Americans in the United States prior to the 1990s (e.g., Deloria 1992; Meighan 1992).

Goodwill was often absent between archaeologists and Native Americans during the burgeoning controversies that led to passage of the Native American Graves Protection and Repatriation Act (NAGPRA) and, as a consequence, little trust was formed (Quick 1985).

Notably, not only must goodwill be present, but each group must also *interpret* acts of goodwill as benevolent. Consider, for example, the study of human remains (see Mihesuah 2000). Archaeologists who have argued for the full and thorough study of human remains seem to believe that this action is one of goodwill. These studies, an archaeologist might reason, are intended to recover the 'lost' information about the past and thus elevate Native American experiences as an integral part of human history. These archaeologists then perceive the study of human remains as an act of goodwill towards Native Americans. However, many Native Americans interpret the study of human remains as the antithesis of goodwill because they view any disturbance of deceased ancestors as sacrilegious and spiritually reckless. Thus the same action – the study of human remains – is understood in opposite terms by different groups of people. Quite often, one could argue, both Native Americans and archaeologists offer goodwill through their actions, and only their behaviour is construed in ways not intended. As David Hurst Thomas (2000: 120) has written, 'Most are trying to do the right thing.'

The spectre of power, related to goodwill, also underlies any discussion of trust. Inequalities of power are suffused throughout archaeological ethics. For nearly all of the twentieth century, power, and hence control, over the archaeological record has largely been in the hands of archaeologists (McLaughlin 1998). As Thomas (2000: 257) intimated, 'The lingering issues between Indians and archaeologists are political, a struggle for control of American Indian history.' The clash over 'resources', ancestral sites and graves, is not only about history and the past. Many struggles are about who controls things now – in the present. This is true not only in the United States, but also in countries such as Canada, Australia and Honduras (Herle 1994; Mortensen 2001; Mulvaney 1991). It was not until the indigenous peoples movements of the late 1960s that we began to see the power archaeologists exert seriously challenged (Fine-Dare 2002). In the United States this confrontation climaxed with the enactment of NAGPRA in 1990, the effects of which are still unfolding as archaeologists and native peoples adjust to the new property and human rights codified in the law. Unlike in the past, Native Americans in the United States now have ownership and control over ancestral human remains, sacred objects, and other items of cultural patrimony in existing museum collections, or found on Federal land after 1990. As the recent Kennewick Man case demonstrates, the legal parameters of NAGPRA are still being defined in litigation, but NAGPRA has indubitably shifted the locus of power between archaeologists and native peoples (Watkins 2004).

Despite the significant shift in power stemming from ownership and control of important parts of the archaeological record, archaeologists in the United States are still allotted more control and power over heritage resources and the past they represent than any other group. National, state and local legislation continues to afford archaeologists a key role in protecting cultural resources, and archaeologists consider this activity to be part of their ethic of stewardship (Lynott 1997: 594–5). In the same ways that Native American groups are less powerful than archaeologists, the public and future generations also have less influence than archaeologists in how heritage resources are managed and used. This is evident, at least, in regard to the artefacts, sites and knowledge claims in archaeologists' work.

Unbalanced levels of power affect the trust relationship between archaeologists and other groups. Baier (1994: 147) addresses the issue of power with an example from the United Nations. She argues that less powerful nations cannot trust more powerful ones because little prevents stronger nations from domination. And because weaker nations are susceptible to attack, they have no reason to cultivate genuine goodwill – which is so imperative to trust – in a hostile environment. Baier rightly points out that less powerful nations have every reason to try to gain leverage, while more powerful nations have almost every reason to sustain unequal relationships. In other words *inequalities foster distrust* because feelings such as goodwill and a readiness to become vulnerable seem almost ridiculous in such contexts.

The parallel with archaeologists and Native Americans is quite clear. Archaeologists are in many, but not all, respects like the powerful country and Native Americans like the less powerful one. Prior to recent shifts in power, archaeologists have had little incentive to commence a trusting relationship with Native Americans. From a self-centred viewpoint, a trusting relationship with Native Americans might have entailed vulnerability and loss of power. Conversely, Native Americans had many reasons to suspect the motivations of archaeologists, and not to trust them out of fear of losing what little power they had. In short, there is a correlation between power and trust: the greater the disparity in power between two coequal groups, the less trust is likely to exist. Trust cannot develop in an atmosphere of inequality – or at least it can develop only with great difficulty and only if there is some dimension of the relationship not characterised by inequality – and power is the source behind that inequality.

A final issue we consider is how we might test the levels of trust in a given relationship. Baier (1994: 120–6, 140) repeatedly makes the point that trusting relationships are not intrinsically good; they are dependent on what results from them. The British prime minister might have a high degree of trust in MI6, but this particular relationship is ethically bankrupt should it promote vices and wrongdoings. In an archaeological example, two groups might build on their trust with one another to the detriment of a third party. For example, archaeologists and like-minded government officials might work towards a strong trusting relationship to protect themselves against an increasingly powerful Native American group. Or Native Americans and archaeologists might form an alliance to protect sacred areas with archaeological resources from development by governmental agencies and private companies interested in strip mining. Baier posits that two other features in a trusting relationship might indicate its moral weakness. The first is when the truster must use coercion to maintain the trusting relationship. Trust, in other words, is not genuine or defensible if it is forced. The second is when the trustee must use concealment in order to fain a grounded trust. From these two features, Baier (1994: 123) proposes a test, 'for the moral decency of a trust relationship', where the prolongation of the relationship does not depend upon either threats or concealment. Although each party must contemplate the degree of intimidation or false pretence in a relationship, the important point is for scholars to realise that trust also requires the virtue of moral wisdom, to know when to use the right kind of trust, at the right time, for the right reasons.

TOWARDS A FRAMEWORK OF VIRTUE ETHICS

'At the dawn of the twenty-first century ethics in archaeology are not simple', Randall H. McGuire (2003) recently wrote. 'They are very complex, conflicted, and confusing. Today, ethical questions and dilemmas are more about relations among people than about things.' As archaeologists increasingly see their profession as more than a search for things, they need a professional ethics that provides the right kind of vocabulary and questions to guide their understanding of social interactions. More than a rule-based system of ethics or a compilation of ideal principles, archaeologists will need to contemplate on the very nature of their relationships with colleagues, publics, descendent communities, governments, and past and future generations. While we do not disregard the value of codes of ethics and utilitarian philosophies, we regret that the archaeological discourse has so long neglected the subject of the virtues, character and excellence. In this chapter, we have attempted to provide an alternative perspective to rigid notions of moral action by beginning with a question about cultivating trust, a virtue, instead of questions of duty and obligation.

The philosophy of Annette Baier was a key starting point for this inquiry. She has demonstrated that trust is a vital aspect of moral life, and that trust successfully mediates between *aretaic* and *deontic* notions. Baier is instructive also because she shifts our focus to agents and sustained action instead of single acts. Although archaeologists, like all humans, must follow general virtues, by the nature of their work they also must understand the unique relationships they form and the consequence these interactions have for their ethical standpoints (Wylie 2003: 5). The value of examining the virtues is apparent even as we try to define the boundaries of professional ethics. A discussion of the kinds of relationships archaeologists form allows us to see the web of implicit and explicit trusting relationships that intersect. An added layer of complexity to these interactions is the way in which some stakeholders entrust archaeologists with objects and knowledge in addition to trusting archaeologists as people. Thus archaeologists have special obligations to cultivate meaningful relationships with people, as much as to care for artefacts and heritage sites. Trust, we find, is not independent of other social phenomena, as it is interconnected with expressions of goodwill and the dynamics of power. Both of these play key roles in defining trusting relationships, and determining their success or failure. The degree to which a moral trusting relationship has been formed cannot be ascertained through a simple assessment; it depends on whether a trust is maintained through coercion or concealment, and whether a trust promotes *eudaimonia*. After all, the purpose of ethical practice concerns not a simple adherence to abstract ideals or rules, but rather the ways in which our behaviours may ultimately better the human condition.

CHAPTER 8

Truthfulness and 'inclusion' in archaeology

David E. Cooper

'EPISTEMIC INCLUSION' AND TRUTHFULNESS

A striking feature of archaeology in recent years has been its increasingly 'inclusive' character. By 'inclusion', here, I mean the bringing into various archaeological activities – from fieldwork to the dissemination of results – of persons or groups outside the circle of trained, professional archaeologists. One thinks, for example, of the increased participation of indigenous peoples in determining the fate of remains, human or artefactual. There are several factors that explain the policy of, and calls for, inclusion. These embrace broadly political and ideological ones – 'post colonial guilt' over insensitive intrusions by earlier European archaeologists, say, or a sense that various relevant 'voices' have been illegitimately 'marginalised' in the past. They include as well a larger perception of the remit of the discipline of archaeology itself. With the emergence of 'public', 'applied' and 'ideational' archaeology, the activities of its practitioners are bound to have a greater bearing than in the past upon matters apt to engage the interests and emotions of people outside the discipline – upon, for example, issues of 'social transformation' and 'social critique' (Politis 2002: 193) or the validity of traditional belief systems. A related factor has been a heightened perception of the importance of archaeology to and for people outside of the profession, an appreciation of the potential of archaeological findings and interpretations to arouse powerful, conflicting feelings in large numbers of people. The decision of the Third World Archaeological Congress to proscribe any discussion of the Ayodhya controversy strikingly illustrates this appreciation.

My concern in this chapter is not with inclusion at large, but with what I shall call 'epistemic' inclusion. With this expression, I refer to the idea that professional, trained archaeologists have no privileged, let alone sole, authority in establishing, interpreting and disseminating truths about the past that falls within their discipline's compass. One finds this idea proposed, in effect, in the World Archaeological Congress First Code of Ethics (see Appendix 1 of Tarlow 2001b), which issues the injunctions to 'acknowledge and recognise indigenous methodologies for interpreting', and to regard as 'critically important' indigenous peoples' views in 'setting research standards, questions, priorities and goals'. The same idea, too, clearly informs the recommendation by two authors that we explore the 'relevance' to South Asian archaeology of 'ancient thought', an 'indigenous conception of scientific method', and traditional 'sources of knowledge', including 'intuitive knowledge', 'authority' and tradition itself (Paddaya and Bellwood 2002: 308).

Policies of epistemic inclusion have already had an impact upon archaeological activities. In 1995, for example, the Hopi Cultural Preservation Office severely restricted the dissemination of a report on the results of a survey: this was because its Hopi advisers objected to a 'public release which would make [the report] available for scholarly research outside the auspices of the Hopi tribe' (cited in Tarlow 2001b: 253). Around the same time, the excavation of the Hatzic site in Canada, a place of spiritual significance to the Stó:lo people, required the participation of Stó:lo students in order to guarantee that 'both Native and academic interpretations of the site' would be presented (cited in Merriman 2002: 544). Such examples have analogies, of course, with ones from other areas of archaeological activity – with, for instance, the inclusion of indigenous people in deciding whether human remains shall be returned to their place of origin. In some cases, it may even be unclear whether it is epistemic or some other mode of inclusion that is being encouraged or tolerated. For example, some excavations have been abandoned on the mixed grounds that 'ownership of the past' entitles indigenous descendants to intellectual control of their heritage as well as to physical control over the sites (see Zimmerman 1995). Certainly the rhetoric invoked in support of epistemic inclusion – talk, for instance, of 'ownership of the past' and the significance of 'cultural heritage' – is familiar from defences of other modes of inclusion.

Despite the analogies, I suggest that the issue of epistemic inclusion is a special one, and not just one more instance of the wider issue of inclusion. (Nor, one might add, is it just one more instance of the general issue of the responsibility of scientists to the wider public – one which has, in recent years and in various areas, prompted calls for the inclusion in the scientific enterprise of non-professional participants.) The question of whether, say, indigenous people should have some control over interpretations of a site raises problems of a different order from that of whether they may exert control over the human remains discovered on the site. It is unfortunate, therefore, that some authors – usually ones sympathetic to epistemic inclusion – elide the issue of epistemic inclusion with quite different ones. Gustavo G. Politis, for instance, strikes me as guilty of subsuming the question of whether it is legitimate to 'reconstruct the past' as an 'instrument of social action', and to elaborate 'a discourse that is of use to indigenous . . . groups and the dispossessed classes', under the more general one of how 'the archaeology of colonialism' may be replaced by an archaeology 'of service to contemporary society' (Politis 2002: 230ff). To engage indigenous groups and the dispossessed in the epistemic enterprise of reconstructing the past, however, is a more problematic policy than to engage them in, say, reconstructing their ruined temples or villages.

The issue of epistemic inclusion necessarily involves the matter of *truthfulness* in a way that other inclusion issues do not. An archaeologist may regret relinquishing or sharing 'control of the past' by, say, returning human remains to their original site, while at the same time agreeing or at least sympathising with the decision to return them. But no archaeologists could agree to relinquish or share 'control of the past' by deciding to abandon or modify their understanding or interpretations of the past in favour of, say, an indigenous people's account of that past. If archaeologists have formed, on the basis of their investigations, genuine beliefs about the past, they cannot – assuming they are rational – at the same time give credence to ones that contradict these beliefs of theirs. There are, of course, a number of things they can do: they can *say* that they give some credence to the non-professionals' account, or agree not to disseminate and broadcast their own views, or publicly 'celebrate' the currency of the rival account, or undertake not to continue with research suggested by their views, and so on. But if archaeologists do any of these things, they naturally invite the charge of compromising themselves and failing in truthfulness.

It does little to ease the problem of epistemic inclusion if the archaeologist is a healthy 'fallibilist' who concedes not only that his or her own beliefs and interpretations are, like any empirical hypotheses, open to possible refutation, but that the rival, non-professional account just *might*, in principle, turn out to be true. For there will surely be cases where the archaeologist has very strong grounds indeed, as judged by the normal criteria for scientific enquiry, for accepting a certain hypothesis. And cases, too, where the rival account is one that, judged by similar criteria, can only be regarded by the archaeologist as an exercise in myth or superstition, one to be given no credence *whatsoever*. In such cases, to pretend to take with any seriousness the rival account, as one deserving to be considered alongside the archaeologist's own, and to do so by gesturing towards 'openness' and 'pluralism', would seem to be just that – a pretence, and hence an abdication from truthfulness. (One wonders, to recall an example cited earlier, whether the 'relevance' of 'unbroken [Hindu] tradition' to South Asian archaeology embraces that of the Manu flood story, in the *Satapatha Brahmana*, to explaining the origin of a people. And, if it does, one then wonders how those who concede its relevance reconcile this with their own, very different, 'professional' account.)

TRUTH AND TRUTHFULNESS

Someone will object that there is something very old-fashioned – pre-postmodern, at least – about the above remarks. For isn't the situation entirely changed once we appreciate the merits of 'constructivism' – 'the position reached by [some? many? all?] archaeological theorists in respect to claims about truth: that archaeologists, indigenous people, visitors to heritage sites and so on all construct knowledge and interpretations in a personally meaningful way' (Merriman 2002: 549)? Seen from the vantage point of constructivism, my remarks may seem to betray a nostalgic, outmoded faith that some accounts of the past may actually be true and others false, that some interpretations are valid, others not, and that some claims to knowledge are not merely 'personally meaningful', but object-ively warranted. For the state-of-the-art constructivist, it is implied, epistemic inclusion is no problem, for there are no truths about the past to compromise by welcoming in a plurality of diverse perspectives.

Here is not the place for a discussion of the merits or otherwise of constructivist and other allied conceptions of truth. Nor is there a need for such a discussion, since it would be irrelevant to the issue of truthful-ness in the context of epistemic inclusion. There are two main reasons for this. First, paradoxical as it may at first sound, truthfulness is independent of truth and hence can be characterised independently of any particular conception of truth. As Bernard Williams puts it, truthfulness is a *virtue*, or rather a pair of virtues – those of Accuracy and Sincerity, to use his labels. These are, crudely characterised, respectively the virtues of taking care that one's beliefs are warranted and 'a disposition to come out with what one believes' (Williams 2002: 45). In order for someone to be exercising those virtues of truthfulness it is neither necessary nor sufficient that his or her beliefs are true. A carefully considered and warranted belief may be false, while a casually accepted one may turn out to be true. Coming out with what is true may be an untruthful act (when one does not believe it to be true), while asserting what is false may be a truthful act (when one believes the assertion to be true). It is irrelevant, therefore, to judgements about a person's truthfulness or lack of it what 'theory of truth' one subscribes to, if any. Since even constructivist archaeologists will have beliefs about the past, their truthfulness – Accuracy and Sincerity – can be ascertained, according to how they arrive at and how they communicate these beliefs.

The second reason we need not ponder the credentials of constructivism as a theory of truth is that it is impossible, in my view, to formulate the position at a level that gives it a bearing on archaeological practice, or on any other empirical discipline, come to that. Consider, in particular, the claim that all statements about the past are 'interpretations'. If this means that all such statements presuppose very general conceptions of and structures of thought about the past, then, to begin with, this is not something that 'traditional' archaeologists have necessarily denied. Nor does it entail that different interpretations of the past are on a par: some may be very bad ones indeed. As the philosopher-archaeologist R.G. Collingwood – himself no enemy of a broadly constructivist approach to truth – remarked, an advance in archaeology frequently 'rests on an advance in the interpretation of evidence' (1993: 491). If, on the other hand, the claim means, more radically, that no statement about the past has greater validity than any other, since they are all 'mere' interpretations that simply reflect the particular predilections of individuals or groups, then archaeological practice is futile. There can no more be a disciplined attempt reasonably to interpret the past than there can be to interpret a Rorschach test drawing. If, as in the latter case, things can only be 'personally meaningful', then the lesson for archaeologists is not to be more inclusive, but to shut up shop. For they would be in a position like that of someone who mistakenly takes the Rorschach drawing to have a significance independent of the motley of meanings read into it by whichever people are asked to 'interpret' it.

Now that the issue of truthfulness has been uncoupled from that of the nature of truth – now that we see, in effect, that this issue is a moral one, not an epistemological or metaphysical one – the issue can be more accurately formulated than earlier. It is this: should the virtues of truthfulness be compromised by archaeologists when the exercise of these virtues conflicts with the interests of non-professional parties? For example, should Accuracy and/or Sincerity be abandoned or diluted if

the establishment and communication by archaeologists of certain warranted claims about the past threaten a community's 'sense of identity',
tied up as this is with rival and incompatible claims? (I suggest, inciden-
tally, that the matter of broadcasting or disseminating the archaeologist's
findings, as in the Hopi case, can be subsumed under the issues of
Accuracy and Sincerity. The latter, in Williams' sense, includes the
broadcasting of one's beliefs to those with an entitlement to know what
these are, and a failure to broadcast them will surely, in some cases, be
inimical to the ability of other interested archaeologists to practise the
virtue of Accuracy – for they are being 'kept in the dark' about findings
relevant to their own enquiries.)

TRUTHFULNESS AND VIRTUE

The rather stark, moral issue, as I have posed it, is rarely addressed in the
literature. As we have already seen, there is a tendency to mask the issue by
locating it in the context of vague and often irrelevant talk of 'openness'
and 'inclusiveness'. It is, perhaps, unsurprising that people have been
reluctant to pose it as I have done, for it is indeed an uncomfortable
issue. How, on the one hand, could self-respecting archaeologists be
willing to abandon or compromise truthfulness, for this is a virtue? And
wouldn't such an abandonment mark a reversion, in effect, to the 'nursery
stage' of historical thought, as Collingwood called it (1993: 491), by
returning intellectual 'control' of the past to dogma, sentiment, ideology
and tradition? But how, on the other hand, can the archaeologist – a
human being, after all – be indifferent to the interests, including self-
respect and a sense of identity, with which the exercise of the virtues of
truthfulness may come into conflict?

Uncomfortable as the issue is, it won't go away, either by masking it
in the manner already indicated or by the sleight of hand performed
by some philosophers when responding to Nietzsche's challenge to the
value of 'the will to truth' – to his question, 'Why truth, and not rather
untruth?' (see, e.g., Nietzsche 2001 [1882]: §344). The response has been
that his question is absurd, for given my recognition that one statement
is true, another false, I have no option but to believe the first. I cannot
'will' to accept the untruth. But this entirely misses Nietzsche's point,
which is not about truth at all, but about truthfulness. The 'will to truth',
he explains, is the will 'not to deceive' and 'not [to] allow oneself to be
deceived' (§344) – in effect, the will to Sincerity and Accuracy, to the
virtues of truthfulness. While I cannot will to believe what I recognise as

false, I most certainly can will not to discover what is true or, having anyway discovered it, to keep it under wraps or communicate to others what I take to be false. As Nietzsche himself recognised, when it is the issue of the will to truth*fulness* that is at stake, 'we stand on moral ground' (§344).

There are those, perhaps, who, even when they appreciate the issue for the moral one it is, hope for a speedier resolution of it than it allows. For example, there may be archaeologists, of 'the old school' at least, for whom the clear recognition that epistemic inclusion can require the compromising of truthfulness – a virtue – settles the matter. How can they and their colleagues legitimately be asked to act other than virtuously? But, for two connected reasons, the fact that truthfulness is a virtue does not settle the matter. To begin with, recognising that a practice, like being truthful or considerate, is virtuous does not determine how and when the virtue should be exercised. This is something that, as Aristotle taught us, requires judgement, wisdom even. Should one be truthful? Yes – but not, one would think, when this takes the form of telling a dying man about his son's arrest for raping a child. It might be urged that such a case is not *really* an example of untruthfulness, of a departure from a virtuous practice. But then the point can be reformulated as follows: recognising that something is a virtue does not determine just what *counts as* an exercise of it. Maybe, then, certain policies of epistemic inclusion in archaeology do not constitute illegitimate departures from truthfulness.

Second, there are lots of virtues. Socrates may have been right that there is a 'unity' to them – that, at any rate, they tend generally to 'pull together'. (Being truthful often requires courage, while courage – if it is not to degenerate into rashness or bravado – typically calls for an Accurate estimate of one situation.) But it would be utopian to imagine that, in no circumstances, do the virtues conflict – as when, for instance, kindness inclines us to be less than truthful, lest we cause pointless distress for someone, like the dying man in the previous example. Now it is not unreasonable to regard respect for people's sensitivities and for nurturing *their* self-respect as virtues. Like any virtues, they might conflict with others, including that of truthfulness. Hence it hardly settles matters to emphasise that truthfulness is a virtue, for the question remains whether, in situations where the demands of truthfulness conflict with those of other virtues, the former should determine how one acts. This point is, of course, related to the first one, made in the previous paragraph: for one important reason why an action may not be an appropriate exercise of a virtue is that, on an occasion when demands of that kind conflict, it is more pressing to exercise a different virtue.

Put succinctly, that truthfulness is a virtue cannot entail that we act appropriately and, all things considered, virtuously, only by manifesting what Nietzsche called an 'unconditional will to truth[fulness] . . . at any price' (2001 [1882]: §344).

Where, then, does the virtuous archaeologist go when caught between the demands of truthfulness and those of other virtues, in particular ones that, on the surface at least, motivate policies of epistemic inclusion? Is there a moral rule or principle perhaps, or a 'super-virtue', to which he or she can appeal in order to settle which of the virtues that have come into conflict should 'trump' the rest? Or is it, as Sarah Tarlow argues in her critique of the 'ethical codes' promulgated to govern professional archaeology, that such moral conflicts, 'historical and contextual' as they are, can only be responded to on 'a case-by-case basis', rather than through 'the application of a rule' (Tarlow 2001b: 245)?

But perhaps those two alternatives are too stark. Like Bernard Williams, I have spoken of the virtues of, and not of rules or principles of, truthfulness, and this indicates a wider sympathy – which I shall not, here, try to defend – for what has come to be called a 'virtue ethical' style of moral philosophy. Virtue ethicists place at the centre of moral reflection attention to the questions of what a good or virtuous person is like and how he or she might be expected to act. (See, e.g., Cooper and James 2005; Hursthouse 1999.) They have no expectation, however, that such reflections will yield anything like an algorithm or a principled decision procedure for determining the right course of action in 'hard cases', nor that there is any 'super-virtue' – Kantian 'respect for the [moral] law', say – that determines a rank order of the virtues. On the other hand, virtue ethicists would be suspicious of the suggestion that decisions can only be made on a case-by-case basis if what is intended is that, in each particular case, one must just 'see' or 'intuit' the right thing to do, without appeal to wider considerations. If Tarlow's point is that one should, of course, attend to the details of each case and that general rules are liable to be insensitive to relevant differences among cases, the virtue ethicist will not demur. But he will add that, whatever the particularities of a case, this does not exclude bringing to bear upon it wider-ranging judgements on virtuous character and the implications of this for behaviour. Indeed, he will add, this *cannot* be excluded if *reflection* on the case – and not simply 'intuition' or 'gut feeling' – is invited.

It will be useful to consider an example where a general consideration or judgement of this type might surely be relevant. The holiest and most popular shrine in Sri Lanka, Kataragama, has over the last century undergone a striking degree of 'Sinhalisation' (see Gombrich and Obeyesekere 1988: ch. 11). What for centuries had been a primarily Tamil Hindu religious site has been invested by Sinhalese Buddhist zealots with great significance for their own heritage and religion, not least through attributing to ancient Buddhist heroes responsibility for the founding and sanctity of the site. Now such an account of the past is, in principle, refutable by archaeological investigation. Should there be such an investigation? And, if there is and the evidence refutes the Sinhalese account, should it be broadcast? And, if it is broadcast, should the archaeologists nevertheless give a public display of 'openness' and 'respect' for the rival Sinhalese account? After all, it is clear that many Buddhists have a considerable emotional and ideological investment in the Sinhalised version of Kataragama's origins and history, so that rejection of that version is bound to offend against sensitivities. But it is surely at least relevant, and arguably decisive, to reflect that, first, the Sinhalised version seems to have begun as a fairly recent, self-conscious exercise in myth-making, and second, this version has been used, by zealots and politicians alike, to impugn another, and older, story about Kataragama that is of comparable emotional and ideological significance to another community of people, the Tamil Hindus. Had things been different – had the Sinhalese version been of ancient and popular pedigree, and not exploited, moreover, to marginalise another community – judgement on an inclusive attitude to the version would surely be affected.

The consideration just discussed is of a very general kind, its relevance by no means confined to the practices of archaeologists. In any area of enquiry, indeed of life at large, the fact that people have self-consciously fabricated an account of something in order to bolster the self-esteem of some at the expense of that of others, is always a good reason for criticising them and for being reluctant to extend 'respect' to their account. In the remaining sections of this chapter, I want to turn to two questions somewhat more specific to the issue of epistemic inclusion in archaeology. I do so, not in order, myself, to 'resolve' the issue, but because these questions are ones that need to be addressed if reflection upon it is to make progress.

PROFESSIONAL VIRTUES

The first question is a special instance of a more general one as to whether there are virtues that, if not peculiar to a certain profession, are at any rate especially characteristic of it and especially to be cultivated and exercised by its members. Specifically, are the virtues of truthfulness characteristic of archaeology, as an academic, scientific profession? If so, one might reasonably argue, then whatever attitudes towards epistemic inclusion may be legitimate for, say, politicians or representatives of indigenous communities, it cannot be welcomed by archaeologists – where truthfulness is compromised – without betrayal of the characteristic virtues of their calling.

How might one address this question? On the one hand, no one denies that there are certain rights and duties that go with membership of a given profession. I do not do wrong by having a few beers the evening before I lecture, but the pilot who drinks the night before flying a plane to Tokyo does. On the other hand, a pervasive axiom in modern moral philosophy is to the effect that specifically *moral* requirements are incumbent on human beings as such, irrespective of their particular 'stations in life'. *How* a virtue is to be exercised, or a moral obligation is to be discharged, will vary according to station. But *what* is morally virtuous or obligatory for one person is equally so for anyone. (The pilot's moral, as distinct from his contractual, duty to stay sober is but an instance of a universal imperative not to endanger lives.)

This modern view is indeed a modern one, contrasting with more ancient conceptions of virtue and duty. It would not, for example, have surprised the early readers of Plato's *Republic* or the *Bhagavad-Gita* to be told that there are characteristic virtues of the Guardian class or the *kshatriya* caste – ones that other groups in the societies described in those works are not under a similar obligation to cultivate and exercise. They, of course, have their own characteristic virtues to cultivate – industriousness rather than courage, say, or prudence rather than justice. Defence of the ancient view could, as with Plato, take the form of arguing that a society as a whole prospers most through this division of moral labour. Better that some people maximally manifest certain virtues, to the relative neglect of others, than that everyone should minimally manifest them all. For Plato, such a division is an integral aspect of what he calls 'justice' – 'keeping what is properly one's own and doing one's own job' (*Republic.* 433).

Unsurprisingly, in the light of that ancient viewpoint, there has been a tradition according to which there are characteristic virtues of the scholar – of the academic or the scientific enquirer: notably, the virtues of truthfulness – of assiduously striving to arrive at only properly warranted beliefs and of honestly, even fearlessly, communicating those beliefs to other enquirers. Such, to take a relatively recent example, is the line taken by Johann Fichte at the end of the eighteenth century in his lectures on 'the vocation of the scholar'. The special moral demands made upon the scholar are to 'supervise' progress in the acquisition of truth and to place his knowledge – above all, historical knowledge – at the service of others (Fichte 1988: c. 170). (For Fichte, one should stress, these are moral demands, and not (simply) ones that are appropriate as a result of some contract signed up to by the scholar when accepting an academic appointment.)

While the idea of the characteristic virtues of a profession may find rather little support within modern moral philosophy, with its 'universalistic' predilection, it still resonates, I surmise, with wider opinion. Newspapers, for example, can be relied on to castigate the sailor who jumps into the life-boat ahead of the women and children more severely than they do some male passenger who does the same. Or again, the journalist who selects, invents or distorts evidence for the sake of a good story is not 'the disgrace to her profession' that, say, the psychologist Cyril Burt is deemed by many to be for allegedly having done the same for the sake of saving a theory. Many people, that is, find it natural to suppose that there are virtues whose cultivation is especially incumbent on members of particular professions, including that of science.

The implication of the thought that archaeologists, *qua* scientists, should display the characteristic virtues of truthfulness is not a blanket rejection of policies of epistemic inclusion that threaten truthfulness. For, of course, other relevant parties – politicians, leaders of indigenous communities, guardians of a religious tradition, and so on – would presumably have their own characteristic virtues as well: ones whose exercise may, on occasions, understandably decide them in favour of such policies. Maybe, for example, dissemination of the truth about a certain ancient site really would dent a venerable religious tradition, the protection of which is the task of certain people. On the other hand, to accept that the virtues of truthfulness are characteristic of archaeology must surely make a difference to archaeologists' response to epistemic inclusion. At the very least, the sacrifice of truthfulness for the sake of epistemic inclusion must be cause for real regret on their part – not something to 'celebrate' in the name of 'openness' and 'inclusiveness'. Again, while it is compatible with their recognising truthfulness as their characteristic virtue that archaeologists should accede to their government's demand that their work be abandoned or its results unpublished, it would not be similarly compatible with this that the archaeologists themselves make such a demand on their colleagues, or indeed on themselves. Bowing to necessity is one thing; proactive betrayal of truthfulness another. (It was one thing, to take an analogy, for the ancient warrior or Japanese soldier of more recent times – inspired by his characteristic virtues of honour and courage – to lay down his arms by order of a king or emperor; another to surrender voluntarily.)

As the tone of my remarks may have indicated, I have more sympathy than many modern ethicists with the ancient, but still current, idea of characteristic professional virtues. Readers can estimate their own degree of sympathy, or lack of it. Indeed they need to estimate this if a question that is surely germane to the issue of epistemic inclusion is to be properly addressed.

ARCHAEOLOGY AND MYTH

There is a second question that also needs to be addressed, even though it is one whose resolution along the lines described below is itself unclear in its implications for the truthfulness versus epistemic inclusion issue. Earlier I portrayed – not unreasonably, one might think – the issue as arising, at least in a large range of cases, when what the archaeologist knows or believes about the past conflicts with beliefs that he or she can only regard as 'superstitious', 'mythical', at any rate as plain false. This is certainly how many archaeologists themselves construe the situation – not only those, like Collingwood, who contrast a 'dogmatic, nursery stage' of belief about the past with the knowledge attained by the archaeological sciences, but those more sympathetic to traditional beliefs. One reads, for example, in a recent review of an edited volume on Burmese archaeology that some of the authors are 'not biased against even folklore traditions', since they recognise that there are 'discrepancies between archaeological evidence' and 'oral history', and that there are real 'problems in assessing evidence' (Thwe 2003: 24). The authors referred to hold, in effect, that if the traditionalist's claims are to be 'respected', they must be rescued from the realm of mythology and shown to be supported by serious evidence in the manner that the archaeologist's claims are.

But there are reasons to think that this may not be the appropriate way of construing the apparent conflicts between the archaeologist's and the traditionalist's claims. Maybe they are not claims on, as it were, the same level, and do not express beliefs in a single sense of 'belief'. Maybe the conflicts, if that is what they are, are not of a type to which appeals to 'evidence' are relevant.

It has long been noted by anthropologists that allegedly superstitious and mythical 'beliefs' have some peculiar features. They do, at any rate, if considered as being like ordinary beliefs, only more exotic. For one thing, they seem happily to coexist with ordinary beliefs that, on the surface, plainly contradict them. (Many Sinhalese, it seems, find it no strain to locate King Mahasena at different points in history in order to accommodate both his identity with the Kataragama divinity, Skanda, and his recorded heroic exploits.) Relatedly, such 'beliefs' are peculiarly resistant to being revised, in the manner that ordinary beliefs are, in the face of new evidence that would seem conclusively to refute them. (Many Australians, it seems, do not revise their image of the ANZAC Gallipoli campaign – one of 'mateship and egalitarianism', a 'myth' that 'play[s] [a] symbolic role for Australia' (Coleman 2004: 6) – in the light of uncomfortable evidence produced by military historians.)

For reasons of this kind, some anthropologists and philosophers – notably Wittgenstein in his acidic remarks on *The Golden Bough* (1979) – have argued that we badly misconstrue allegedly mythical and superstitious discourse by assimilating it to ordinary propositional discourse. They argue, in effect, that such discourse does not even purport to state facts or truths about the past, or to express beliefs in the sense that ordinary statements do. To speak in Wittgensteinian terms, the 'language-game' to which it belongs is of a quite different kind, with a different function and role within a 'form of life', from that of propositional and scientific discourse. Mythical utterances, therefore, are not stabs, belonging to the 'nursery stage' of human thought, at stating how things are or were. Hence they do not stand to be refuted by later, more sophisticated accounts of the world and its past. Rather there is no level on which they directly compete with such accounts.

I shall not pursue the question of how, if one is sympathetic to this line of thought, mythical 'beliefs' should then be construed – of whether, for example, they are helpfully described as 'symbolic'. The question I do want to raise concerns the practical implications of the line of thought for the issue addressed in this chapter. The answer to that question is that different people will draw different conclusions.

Some will argue that, once the status of mythical 'beliefs' and discourse is properly understood, archaeologists' difficulties in accommodating to epistemic inclusion are significantly eased. They are not in the position of having to 'respect' or be 'open' to beliefs that compete with their own and which they can only regard as plain false. Rather they are in the position of, say, some modern physicists who have come to think that religious discourse does not compete with that of science – a perception that enables them to respect religion in a way that earlier scientists, for whom science and religion were rival claimants to the possession of truth, could not. To be sure, the archaeologist who submits to a policy of epistemic inclusion – to, for instance, those Hopi demands that the results of a survey remain unpublished (p. 132 above) – may regret the consequent restrictions on research and its dissemination. But at least he or she is not in the situation of having to suppress or moderate claims that they reasonably believe to be true in favour of ones judged to be plain false.

Others will argue, however, that on the approach just described all the accommodation is being done by the archaeologist, and intolerably so. If archaeologists are willing to appreciate that their claims do not compete with mythical 'beliefs', why cannot the spokesmen for those 'beliefs' – for, say, certain myths about the origins of a holy site – do the same? And if they do recognise that these 'beliefs' are at too different a level to be contradicted or threatened by the truths uncovered by archaeology, why do they not withdraw their objections to the uncovering and broadcasting of those truths? Just as some physicists feel able to respect religious discourse, once its character is properly appreciated, so of course many modern theologians (often of a Wittgensteinian hue) – who share that appreciation – now feel able to allow scientific accounts of the world to go unchallenged. Those spokesmen for mythical 'beliefs' who insist on policies of epistemic inclusion are, in effect, modern-day Bellarmines and Bishop Wilberforces, and it is they, at least as much as archaeologists, who should be educated into an understanding of the status of their own discourse.

Even if, then, merit is found in the Wittgensteinian treatment of mythical 'belief', this is not, by itself, going to provide a clear-cut resolution of the issue of truthfulness versus epistemic inclusion, for the implications of that treatment might reasonably be disputed. More generally, it has been my ambition, in the later sections of this chapter, not to resolve the issue, but to render salient the further issues into which it ramifies. While I have no confidence in what the proper resolution might be – or even in whether it lends itself to such a resolution – I am rather more confident, first, that it is ramified issues like those discussed which must be addressed in any attempt at a resolution and, second, that there is a very real issue at stake, one that we should not allow to be disguised by a flaccid rhetoric of the 'respect', 'openness' and 'inclusiveness' that archaeologists should be displaying.

CHAPTER 9

Ethics and Native American reburials: a philosopher's view of two decades of NAGPRA

Douglas P. Lackey

The social sciences were apparently conceived in sin: ethics demands that we treat people as subjects; social science requires that we view them as objects. No talk of *Verstehen*; no degree of sympathy, can close the gap, plaster over the chasm between observer and observed, between human beings willing their ends and human beings taken as means to knowledge. But for social scientists deep into their trade, the divide between knower and known becomes a piece of the landscape, part of the natural order. The observer looks, the observed is looked at. Nothing could be more surprising to seasoned social scientists than a contretemps in which the object of study looks the observer straight in the eye.

Yet this is precisely what happened in American archaeology in November of 1990, when George Bush I signed into law the Native American Graves Protection and Repatriation Act, NAGPRA. The specimen on the slide looked up through the microscope, stood up and shook a fist in the air. NAGPRA has no preamble. No statement is made about relations between archaeologists and Native Americans, between the curators and the tribes. But there is a presumption in the text, perhaps most evident in Section 7:

7(A) If the cultural affiliation of Native American remains and associated funerary objects with a particular Indian tribe or Native Hawaiian organization is established, then the Federal agency or museum upon the request of a known lineal descendant of the Native American or of the tribe . . . shall expeditiously return such remains and associated funerary objects.

7(B) If the cultural affiliation with a particular Indian tribe or Native Hawaiian organization is shown with respect to unassociated funerary objects, sacred objects, or objects of cultural patrimony, then the Federal agency or museum, upon the request of the Indian tribe or Native Hawaiian organization, shall expeditiously return such objects. . .

7(C) If a known lineal descendant of an Indian tribe or Native Hawaiian organization requests the return of Native American unassociated funerary objects, sacred objects or objects of cultural patrimony pursuant to this Act and presents evidence which, if standing alone before the introduction of evidence to the contrary, would support a finding that the Federal agency or museum did not have the right of possession, then such agency or museum shall return such objects unless it can overcome such inference and prove that it has a right of possession to the objects.

There is no mistaking the implication: archaeologists or anthropologists, amateur collectors or museums curators, are body snatchers, grave robbers, culture vultures, art thieves, desecrators of sacred ground – unless proven otherwise. This is not a side effect of their work; it is the work itself that has made them so. By way of penance, almost all American museums, universities and institutes that have anything to do with Native American or indigenous Hawaiian cultures have devoted years of hard labour since 1990 to compiling inventories, notifying affiliated tribes, packing objects and returning human remains. Native Americans, forced now to bear the burdens of victory, have spent the corresponding years in patient attendance at NAGPRA meetings, budget-breaking travel to distant collections, tedious preparation of formal claims, and emotionally exhausting burial ceremonies. NAGPRA was an earthquake that transformed perception and memory. Current international covenants regarding cultural property address only present wrongs and present crimes. With NAGPRA, the whole history of relations between social scientists and American indigenous peoples is called into question. And the burden of proof, case by case, rests on the scientists to show they are in the right.

HOW THE CONFLICT WAS MISCONSTRUED: DEONTOLOGICAL ABSOLUTISM VERSUS ETHICAL RELATIVISM

The discussions leading up to NAGPRA dramatised the repatriation issue as a conflict between ethics and science. But which ethics, and which science? Native Americans argued that right is right, and science be damned. Here is Perry Tsiadiasi, a Zuni and elder brother Bow Priest:

I want my fathers back. As the elder brother Bow Priest, I support the statement of the Bear Clan leader about the need for our War Gods to return to Zuni country . . . We want our fathers to be returned to our land . . . For the good of the people, I want our fathers back. (Fine-Dare 2002: 94)

The claim is a simple, deontological one: these are *our* fathers; so we have a right to have them on *our* land. In this text and many others we have possessive pronouns and an assertion of rights of ownership, or at least, of a right to stewardship. 'Who Owns American Indian Remains?', asks the title of the best anthology compiled about this subject (Mihesuah 2000). And indeed the text of NAGPRA works within the logic of ownership or stewardship: the guiding idea is that things should be returned to their rightful owners. The Zuni have a right to Zuni bones, and the curators who have them have a duty to return them. Loss of scientific knowledge does not figure in the argument, and no argument is given in NAGPRA that some compensating good will result from repatriation. Likewise the authors who have addressed repatriation as a basic human rights issue (Dombroski and Sider 2002: 189–96) have not specified any good that will come from repatriation, except the tautological good of rights-satisfaction. What is supposed to happen is the righting of past wrongs, the paying of debts to the dead, the establishment and maintenance of justice. The bottom line is: do it, because it is right.

Now, no doubt, in the particular case, we must do the right thing, because it is right. But laws and moral principles must have a rationale, and that rationale must be rooted in the good. There is no point to a law, no point to a moral principle, if adherence to it and connected principles does not, on the whole, serve the good and make people's lives go better. These rationales for law and moral principles must make sense. They must be consistently applied. They cannot themselves deploy only moral concepts, since these moral concepts would then need further justificatory rationales and we would have an infinite regress. Some non-moral values, material, aesthetic, religious, cognitive, must be brought in. The elder brother of the Bow acknowledges this when he says, 'For the good of the people, I want our fathers back.' What good is he talking about? And how is it served by repatriation of bones? The ethical argument based on ownership may not be invalid, but it is surely incomplete.

On 'their' side (the partition is artificial since there are many Native American scientists), the scientists argued that ethics is socially constructed and culturally relative, while science is fact-responsive and culturally transcendent. Here is Lynne Goldstein, Secretary of the Society for American Archaeology:

What are ethics? In general terms, ethics can be seen as a coherent system of values that specify a mode of conduct. The definition implies that there can be more than one system of ethics. A discussion of ethics is, by definition, a discussion of moral principles, with an underlying definition of Right and

Wrong. Such definitions are cultural, all anthropologists know this. There are many examples that demonstrate this point: the death sentence passed upon Salman Rushdie for his blasphemous novel *The Satanic Verses*; the differing perspective on abortion, and witch trials in colonial America. All the instances present a conflict between two (or more) systems of ethics. The important point we wish to raise here is that no particular system of ethics can be said to be absolutely right or wrong. Ethics are a cultural construction.

(Goldstein and Kintigh 1990: 585–6)

As a philosopher, I am touched and appalled by this quaint evocation of positivism, killed off in my own field by Quine and Kuhn forty years ago. To set the record straight, it is simply not true that there is 'one' science and 'many' codes of ethics; Newton's theory of gravitation is still *science*, even if it fails to describe the facts fully, and it is still *science*, though Einstein's General Theory, which is also science, conflicts with it. On the current scene, there are string theorists and particle theorists each with competing theories of everything. The fact that people disagree about what is to be done with Salman Rushdie proves nothing about the subjectivity of ethics, since it has been reliably reported to me that scientists at professional meetings also disagree with each other, yet do not infer from this the subjectivity of science.

I refuse to declare, 'Science is itself a social construct', as the phrase 'social construct' has an uncanny power to paralyse the human mind. Let me say instead that science *is* a human activity, and human activities make sense – must make sense – to those who engage in them. If scientific activity makes sense, it too has a rationale, and the rationale must refer to the good, or else we should stop doing science. As with the rationales of law and morals, the rationale of science must be consistent and consistently applied. And when we articulate the rationale of science, it may turn out that there are particular cases of scientific work where the rationale is weak or fails to apply, or is trumped by competing values.

To construe the NAGPRA conflict between Native Americans and social scientists as a conflict between ethical objectivism and ethical subjectivism does not get things right. The parties allege this, but it is not so. The real conflict, on examination, turns out to be a tension between the various dimensions of human good: religious, political, cognitive, aesthetic, material. Ethics is not a party to *this* conflict; rather it is above the conflict, arbitrating it. This is why, when we reach a considered ethical judgement, we must follow it. To get to the judgement, we must survey everything in human life, and why it matters. Then, when the judgement comes in, there is nothing more to be said.

A POOR ARGUMENT ON THE SCIENTIFIC SIDE

On 26 February 1993, the NAGPRA Review Committee held its fourth meeting in Honolulu, Oahu, Hawaii. One major question on the agenda was the disposition of human remains then in storage in the P. A. Hearst Museum of Anthropology, a part of the University of California at Berkeley. There was no dispute that the remains were exhumed in Hawaii in the 1880s, and subsequently transported to the museum. There was some question as to whether the remains were Native Hawaiian, or non-native Hawaiian, perhaps dead sailors, the museum said, washed up on the beach.

The museum was represented by Mike Smith, Assistant Chancellor of the University of California, Berkeley, and Tim White, Professor of Anthropology at Berkeley. When asked to articulate the museum's interest in these remains,

Mr. Smith responded that the Hearst was concerned about certain ambiguities in the law and did not want to violate the museum's mission by de-accessioning materials held in the public trust. . . Mr. White stated that the remains were important as part of the University's osteological collection. It was not so much that these remains would answer a specific research question, he continued, but rather the collection is important as a whole. He emphasized the need to keep the collection because research tools are constantly improving and thus important questions might be answered at a later date.
(NAGPRA Review Committee Minutes 1993: 4)

Smith's problem with repatriation involved concepts of property or stewardship. The museum, he says, is holding the remains 'in trust for the public'. But which public? The public of Berkeley, California? Surely that is too narrow, as obviously a wider public, including Native Hawaiians, has an interest in these remains. The American public? But the American public has already spoken through NAGPRA as regards the disposition of affiliated bones: they are to be returned to the indigenous peoples. *This* trust would not be violated by repatriation.

Professor White's argument refers to the scientific need to have a 'complete collection' of specimens for scientific study. But he does not indicate what studies are involved. If the studies are in that slightly crazed area of anthropology called craniotomy, then a replica of a skull will serve as well as the skull itself. If the studies are of disease patterns and transmissions, then often a replica of the bone will serve as well as the bone itself: the absence of evidence of rheumatoid arthritis in ancient human skeletons is as demonstrable from skeleton replicas as from the originals.

But now, what of chemical analysis? Here a replica won't do. But the original location of these remains was not known and without information about strata, chemical analysis will not provide the most useful form of data: that *these* chemicals were found at *this* spot at *this* time. Still, the chemical data might be of some limited significance. But if there are such data to be had, tests can be done *now*, the information recorded, and the specimen repatriated. Nothing in NAGPRA, the Review Committee noted, forbids the scientific study of remains, provided that such studies are not an excuse to delay repatriation.

We are left with Professor White's argument that there might be some *future* chemical test that will yield important data. Some dramatic improvement, for example, might be achieved in the dating of bones and artifacts. But improving precision in the dating of the remains will not help locate the original site, and knowledge of time will be debilitated by ignorance of place. The problem is widespread: the majority of remains in American collections were taken off the land as trophies, tossed up by farmer's ploughs, uncovered in floods. They are typically of unknown provenance, often delivered to bewildered curators in bags.

WHAT FORM OF SCIENCE ARE WE PROTECTING?

The difference between morphological and chemical analysis of specimens points up an ambiguity in the term 'science'. Science can refer either to scientific theory or to natural history. (The two areas sometimes overlap, as in contemporary cosmology, where the Big Bang Theory merges with the natural history of the early cosmos.) Scientific theories state laws which specify that a certain cluster of qualities is associated with some different cluster of qualities. There might, in fact, be no instance of either cluster: the law might say that resistance in a certain material will disappear at absolute zero, but neither zero temperature nor zero resistance is ever obtained. Natural history describes the particular events of the cosmos, notes their positions in space and time, and makes claims about causal relationships among the events. The two areas are parasitic on each other: without knowledge of particular events, theories cannot be confirmed, and without knowledge of general laws, no claim of causation between events can be sustained.

Nevertheless, there is a profound gap between the two. Though scientific theorising leans on particular events for confirmation, it uses particular events only as instances of *types* of events. Though natural history makes causal claims, it construes causal relations as existing between particular events, tokens, not types. Thus natural history requires samples of particulars, but scientific theory needs only examples of types. The difference must be kept in mind as arguments swirl about the use of particular specimens. If theory is at issue, then no particular specimen is crucial, since the loss of one can be replaced by another of the same type. If natural history is at issue, then each specimen is useful, but only if provenance has been properly determined.

THE HAWAIIAN CASE, FROM THE RELIGIOUS SIDE

The same 1993 meeting addressed by Smith and White was attended by numerous members of Hui Malama I Na Kupuna O Hawai'i Nei, an organisation of Native Hawaiians dedicated to the preservation of tribal culture and particularly interested to the repatriation of human tribal remains. Edward Kanahele said that his organisation intended to rebury the remains in order to return the bones to the earth and to right spiritual and moral wrongs. According to Mr Kanahele, reburial strengthens the connection between present-day people and the ancestors by allowing the spiritual power, the *mana*, and the ancestral bones, to flow back to the earth. He explained the Hawaiian belief that the spiritual strength, or *mana*, in one's house can be taken away by evil or negative thoughts. Thus bones need to be protected so that the *mana* can flow back into the earth. The earth will then reciprocate and help the living people. 'We see this spiritual force as something that benefits everyone', Mr Ayau added, 'even if these remains are not our people, we would be paying them equal respect.' (NAGPRA Review Committee minutes, February 1993, p. 4.)

Even in these few sentences, the background religious narrative is clear. A human being is formed from the earth, at birth separates from it, borrowing from the earth the living force called *mana* that provides for motion and life. At death, the body must be restored to the earth, so that the force borrowed is returned, to be used again. Furthermore, the remains must be returned to the point of origin; Hawaiian bones must come to rest in Hawaiian earth.

Outside the Native Hawaiian form of life, we can ask, 'Why doesn't the force just return of itself?' The Hawaiian can answer, 'Why should it?' Outside the Native Hawaiian form of life, we can ask 'Why can't the force be returned by the proper incantation?' The Native Hawaiian can answer, 'Why should it?' Given equal plausibility of available answers, the Hawaiian believes and acts according to the one that makes sense, and the one that makes sense in that culture, and many others, is that the force returns with the burial of the body.

But there are some questions that cannot be so easily fended off. If Native Hawaiian remains must be interred in Hawaiian ground (or else the *mana* will not return to the earth) then non-Native Hawaiians must be buried in non-Hawaiian ground, or else the *mana* will not return to the earth. Thus Mr Ayau is simply incorrect, relative to his own religious narrative, to say that everyone will benefit when non-Hawaiian remains are interred in Hawaiian ground. If this were true, then Hawaiian remains could return their *mana* by being buried in California.

Furthermore, the religious narrative is unspecific as to what parts of the deceased must be returned to the earth for the *mana* to be discharged. There seems to be no requirement that all hair, or all fingernails, grown in a lifetime be returned to the earth. Some pieces of a person do not get buried, and yet the *mana* is returned. But if not all pieces of the person need burial, then a small piece, perhaps smaller than a hair, could remain with the museum for future testing, without transgressing the logic of the narrative. NAGPRA does not permit this, but that is because NAGPRA works within the shallow framework of rights and not the deeper context of values.

The NAGPRA committee decided, and decided rightly, to repatriate the Hearst remains to Hawaii, where they were given into the custody of Hui Malama I Na Kupuna O Hawai'i Nei. But now we must refer not just to law, which is satisfied by repatriation, but to the rationale for the law, which is satisfied by reburial. Hui Malama I Na Kupuna O Hawai'i Nei is committed by its narrative to reburial, and there is no evidence that they have not done so. But there is also no evidence that they have, since all Hui Malama I Na Kupuna O Hawai'i Nei reburials have taken place in secret, in unmarked graves. Nothing in the narrative would imply that *mana* can be returned to the earth only by a secret burial. And if Hui Malama I Na Kupuna O Hawai'i Nei is concerned that the remains be undisturbed, having a public record of where they are will be helpful when locations are chosen for the Marriotts of the twenty-second century.

The 1993 Hearst/Native Hawaiian case is not a case of ethics versus science, but a case of religion versus science, where the religious case was strong and the scientific case was weak. The review committee hit the right ethical target, but it did not have a full ethical rationale for its actions. Being only charged with applying a law, it reached the correct ethical decision by a kind of happy accident.

The case for repatriation of the Hearst remains was strong. Now, what of Kennewick Man, the most celebrated of NAGPRA cases?

Kennewick Man was discovered on the banks of the Columbia River in July 1996. The remains, consisting of about 360 bone pieces forming 90 per cent of a compete skeleton, with a spear point lodged in the hip, were established by radiocarbon analysis to be about 11,000 years old, making Kennewick Man by far the most complete skeleton of such age found in North America.

Though the Kennewick site is near tribal areas, the Army Corps of Engineers took control of the Kennewick Man as the remains were found on a navigable waterway. Four Columbia Plateau tribes filed for repatriation of the bones under NAGPRA, and the Corps announced its intent to repatriate the remains in the fall of 1996. Eight prominent anthropologists filed suit against the Corps to block repatriation, and the remains, enjoined from study, were deposited in the Burke Museum. The court case, pitting the anthropologists against the United States, the Army Corps of Engineers and the four tribes filing as intervenors and appellants, ground forward for six years.

In the meantime, reports were leaked to the press that preliminary measurements had shown the skull was 'Caucasoid' in appearance. A facial reconstruction of the Kennewick Man, bearing an uncanny resemblance to Star Trek actor Patrick Stewart, was presented on public television. The Stewart face was reproduced on a number of white supremacist websites, sometimes with superadded red hair, in the manner of Kirk Douglas in the film *The Vikings*.

In 1998, the Army Corps of Engineers bulldozed the discovery site and covered it with concrete blocks, causing irretrievable loss of stratigraphic data. In 2001, the Secretary of the Interior, acting for the National Park Service and the Army Corps of Engineers, accepted arguments from the defendants that the Kennewick remains were 'culturally affiliated' with the four tribes. But in 2003, the District Court ruled in favour of the anthropologists. The defendants appealed, but in February 2004 the Circuit Court denied the appeal, Judge Gould ruling that appellants had failed to show that the Kennewick Man was the biological ancestor of any Native American now living, nor had they shown that the Kennewick Man was 'affiliated' with any presently existing Native American tribe.

It is not possible here to review the opinions of the Circuit and District courts, which run to 105 pages. But I believe that the cases were wrongly decided. Nowhere in the decisions did the courts consider the implications of NAGPRA Section 7(C), quoted above, which places the burden of proof as regards cultural affiliation on those who oppose Native American claims. In short, the tribes did not have to show (beyond a *prima facie* case) that the Kennewick Man was culturally affiliated. The burden of the proof rested on the anthropologists to show that he was not. Recall that the Kennewick Man had a spear point lodged in his hip bone. This places the Kennewick Man in a culture much closer to the four tribes than to the anthropologists, who do not often use spears. The tribal elders could say, 'He was a spear user, like us.' They called him the Ancient One.

In addition to an argument for repatriation stemming from the NAGPRA 'tilt', in favour of Native Americans, a second legal argument could be generated from the developing body of federal administrative law regarding experimentation on human beings. Since 1976, the federal government has required all scientists conducting studies on human beings (in federally supported institutions) to obtain informed consent from their subjects, a process supervised and monitored by independent local review boards. In the 1990s, the law has been commonly interpreted to include specimens preserved post mortem, which cannot be studied unless consent is supplied either by the subject before decease or by legal representatives after death. (Consent forms supplied to American subjects now regularly include explicit provision about future DNA testing of specimens, by implication testing after the death of the subject.) It is now understood that scientific study of a person need not require the present existence of a person. The Kennewick Man did not give consent, nor is it likely that he would have given consent for the study of his skeleton. Nowhere in the Kennewick Man documents have I found that any of the eight anthropologists submitted a study protocol to their Institutional Review Board.

From the standpoint of rights, the Kennewick Man should have been repatriated and reburied. But what of the ethical case? Should the Kennewick Man be reburied, all things considered? The value of the knowledge to be obtained must be weighed against the religious and cultural significance of reburial. In some Native American discussions, knowledge is 'useful' only if it helps solve current Native American problems. 'If the Society for American Archaeology ever gives a suitable answer as to the benefits for studying Indian skeletons, some tribes might be receptive to scholars who study remains' (Mihesuah 2000: 97). 'What have the anthropologists done for us?', Vine Deloria, Jr. was asking back in 1969.

By Deloria's and Mihesuah's standards, the anthropologists' case is weak. But the anthropologists are writing natural and human history, and their narrative is not just another religious story, one that happens to be told by white people. Religious narratives are concerned with significance and meaning. The scientific narrative is dedicated to separating fact from allegation, especially allegation tainted by hopes and wishes. This fact–allegation distinction is cross-cultural, since every culture distinguishes, at least in principle, 'he committed a murder' from 'people say he committed a murder'. The establishment of the basic scientific narrative is not theory free, but the descriptions generated are subjected to the discipline of historical method. They acquire from this discipline an objective character that the religious stories do not have. The objective narrative is valuable to all of us, immediately and emotionally, since emotions *demand* objectivity. One cannot be happy about so-and-so, unless so-and-so is the case.

On the religious side, the tribes presented oral histories to the court mentioning people that lived long before in the Pacific Northwest. But the narratives do not integrate anything like the Kennewick Man into a story of the universe in which the Tribes and the Man have related roles: they do not say, for example, that the Ancient Ones brought fire to the tribes. Of course, Native Americans believe, and rightly believe, that they had ancestors in 9000 BC. But so do all of us.

I conclude in the Kennewick Man case that the argument for science is strong and the argument for religion is weak. The scientific narrative has its own value, and scientific theory is more valuable still. To write, 'The fact that Indians exist allows these people [the anthropologists] to secure jobs tenure, promotion, merit increases, notoriety, and scholarly identity, all without giving anything back to Indian communities' (Mihesuah 2002: 97) is to lose sight of a fundamental human good. Native Americans at numerous NAGPRA Review Committee meetings have insisted on the value of 'spirituality', implying that there are more goods than material goods. One of those non-material goods is knowledge.

WEAK ARGUMENTS FOR REPATRIATING OBJECTS
OF CULTURAL PATRIMONY

The main focus of NAGPRA hearings, prior to passage of the law, was on the proper disposition of human remains. The retrieval of 'objects of cultural patrimony' snuck in almost as an afterthought. Nevertheless, some of the most contested NAGPRA cases have involved cultural objects. Here is the NAGPRA definition.

2(D) 'cultural patrimony' . . . shall mean an object having ongoing historical, traditional, or cultural importance central to the Native American group or culture itself, rather than property owned by an individual Native American, and which, therefore, cannot be alienated, appropriated, or conveyed by any individual regardless of whether or not the individual is a member of the Indian tribe or Native Hawaiian organization and such object shall have been considered inalienable by such Native American group at the time the object was separated from such group.

Given this definition, every object of any cultural importance not held by the tribes is not in the hands of its rightful owner, since by definition it could not have been rightfully sold or given away. And when one hears that items in current collections include trophies taken off Indian bodies after the massacre at Wounded Knee, the rights-based case for repatriation seems overwhelming. But let us ask again, what is the rationale for repatriation, beyond the issue of rights?

One argument is that the objects are necessary for the practice of Native American religion (Deloria 2000: 169–80). The freedom of religion argument was particularly pressed in the case for repatriation of the Zuni War Gods (Ferguson 1991). But it is scarcely credible that the Zuni, or any tribe, could not practise their religion without a particular material object, however vested the object might be with spiritual significance. Here is Professor Fine-Dare's account of the War Gods:

At winter solstice each year, when a new bow priest (also called a war chief) is initiated, leaders of the Deer Clan of the Zuni people carve and paint an image of the elder twin war god, Uyeyewi. Meanwhile, leaders of the Bear Clan carve Uyeyewi's younger brother, Ma'a'sewi, who, like his brother, is endowed with living powers that can be used to ensure safety, health, and success of the tribe by bringing rain or defending the Zunis against enemies or other trials.

(Fine-Dare 2002: 94)

It would appear that the *old* war god carvings are not part of the religion, as *new* ones must be carved each year. Religious rituals usually function with types, not tokens, and new examples can be and often are produced at will, and the power invested in one object can be transferred or reinstated in the next.[1]

The same argument about reproducibility of instances of types can be given in response to a related argument for repatriation of cultural objects, the argument that without repatriation of such objects the culture cannot survive. Consider the dispute between Hui Malama and the Providence (RI) Natural History Museum over the Native Hawaiian spear holder, given to the museum by retired sailors around 1810. The spear holder, 30 cm high and inlaid with mother-of-pearl, was claimed by Hui Malama under NAGPRA as a 'sacred object of cultural patrimony'. The attorney representing the museum replied, 'It is not a sacred item or item of cultural patrimony, but a utilitarian spear holder used by Native Hawaiian chieftains to hold spears on their canoes' (Smith 1998: A18). The NAGPRA review committee ruled in favour of Hui Malama, but the Providence Museum sued, arguing that repatriation of the item violated Fifth Amendment protection against 'uncompensated takings'.

That the spear holder is not a sacred object is clear, since Hawaiian chiefs had the power to dispense them as gifts. That these are products of this particular culture is clear, but whether they are 'central' items of cultural patrimony is not demonstrated. There were many such spear holders, and the Providence spear holder was not the first on which the rest were modelled, or a spear holder used in a historically significant battle. To say that Native Hawaiian culture, or any indigenous culture, cannot survive without these particular tokens is also not credible. Any culture that cannot survive without taking an object from a museum case is already dead.

The ethical resolution, then, turns not on religious or cultural grounds but simply on which group is likely to be the most responsible steward for the spear holder. In this case, both sides were manifestly irresponsible. The Providence Museum, it is credibly, or perhaps incredibly, reported, had a private offer of $200,000 for the spear holder, and had decided to sell it in order to fund 'other projects'. Hui Malama, we noted previously, has a history of secret burials of repatriated objects. In 1998 the Office of Hawaiian Affairs, fearing that a collision between NAGPRA and the Fifth

---

1 The exception, of course, is the sacred ground or the sacred mountain. In that case, only that very piece of ground will do. But the reclamation of sacred grounds is not part of the NAGPRA story, and I will not pursue the question of whether a sufficiently powerful priest can consecrate new ground.

Amendment might destroy the entire NAGPRA regime, bought off the Providence Museum with a cash payment of $150,000. The suit was withdrawn, and the spear holder was brought to Hawaii, where it was given to Hui Malama and promptly disappeared (*Honolulu Star-Bulletin, 15 July*, 1998). This, perhaps, is a good time to bring up the value of public access.

REPATRIATION, PUBLIC ACCESS AND ARTISTIC VALUE

In 1905, eighty-three Native Hawaiian objects were discovered in a cave on the Island of Hawaii. The items, now called the Forbes Cave Artifacts and worth several million dollars, were brought to Oahu and were given to the Bishop Museum, which houses the world's largest collection of Native Hawaiian artefacts. In 1994, Hui Malama applied under NAGPRA for repatriation of the objects, announcing their intention to rebury the collection. Despite the objections of several other Native Hawaiian organisations that the collection should be kept on view for educational purposes, the Bishop Museum 'loaned' the collection to Hui Malama in 2000, pending the outcome of several lawsuits regarding the objects. They have not been seen since.

I have already rejected the 'cultural survival' argument for the repatriation of such objects. What is seen under glass in a museum case is necessarily not part of any living culture. For educational presentations, in anthropology, replicas will serve as well as the originals. But the object in the museum case, or on the wall, can exhibit artistic value, and indeed presentation in a museum, with its dislocated context, encourages concentration on artistic features by the viewer, generating aesthetic experience and aesthetic appreciation. The aesthetic experience provoked by an object's artistic features, though generated within the culture, is available to people outside the culture and is important to people outside the culture. This is what is lost when such objects disappear from view. There is such a thing as the patrimony of humankind, as UNESCO puts it, a human cultural heritage. The actions of Hui Malama in the Forbes Cave Case, facilitated by NAGPRA, were viewed by many Native Hawaiians as an assault on their culture. That is too limited a charge. It is an assault on all of us.

I will expand on these points by answering objections from the other side.

(a) *The distinction between artistic objects and religious objects is artificial, or at least, specific to Western cultures.*

The distinction is real because some religious objects have no aesthetic features and some aesthetic objects have no religious features. But it is possible that the same object can have both aesthetic features and a religious function. No argument has been given that the aesthetic dimension is *less* important than the religious dimension. And no argument has been given that these objects can be restored to their religious function by burial in the ground.[2]

(b) *No non-Native Hawaiian can appreciate Native Hawaiian art. All aesthetic experience is an experience of meaning, which is available only to those who share the form of life.*

Understanding a culture not one's own is like understanding a second language: a difficult task but not an impossible one. The artistic features of a work of art result from intensifications of culturally specific experiences. They represent a cultural perspective. But to represent X from a perspective one necessarily transcends the perspective. Consider Constable's drawings, 'Salisbury Cathedral seen from the south' and 'Salisbury Cathedral seen from the west'. Each drawing is from a perspective. But that Salisbury Cathedral looked like this (to Constable) from the south is not a perspectival fact; it is an objective fact. Likewise that Salisbury Cathedral looked like this from the west (to Constable) is not a perspectival fact, but an objective fact. As objective facts, they are available to everyone, not just those who have seen Salisbury Cathedral from the west or from the south. Art objectifies as much as science does. The culture provides the perspective. The artist transcends it while incorporating it.

(c) *Aesthetic qualities are perceptual qualities, and the same perceptual qualities can be generated by good copies as by the originals. The museums should make perceptually indistinguishable copies, and return the originals to the tribes.*

Assume perceptually indistinguishable copies *can* be made. It seems inevitable that someday one will be able to travel to Orlando, Florida and enter a room perceptually indistinguishable from the Sistine Chapel.[3] Would the aesthetic experience provided by a visit to Orlando lack anything that would be provided by a visit to the Vatican? Yes it would.

---

2 Some of the artefacts contained human teeth as ornaments. But if all human teeth require reburial, Hui Malama should be raiding dental offices in Honolulu.
3 Lest it appear that this is just an American trend: in Mantua work is underway to create a life-sized replica of Mantegna's Camera degli Sposi, to spare the original from damage caused by the toxic breath of tourist groups.

Consider simply the descriptions of the two experiences: 'I saw a replica of the Sistine Chapel' versus 'I saw the Sistine Chapel.'

Paintings, statues, carvings, are tokens, not types, particular continuants with unique origins in space and time, and unique causal histories. They are, in Nelson Goodman's phrase, autographic objects, causally connected to the artist (Goodman 1968: 113–16). To experience autographic works is to be causally connected to their creators and to their points of origin. It is to stand in their presence. When people travel to the Vatican to be blessed by the Pope, whatever they hope to obtain from the blessing will come only if the Pope himself appears at the window, not some look-alike dressed as the Pope. Likewise when people travel to the Vatican to see the Sistine ceiling, whatever they hope to experience will come only if they see that ceiling painted by Michelangelo, not one contrived by the Xerox Corporation. That is why the originals must be in museums, and the copies in the shop.

NAGPRA, SKULLS AND GENOCIDE

The history of relations between Native Americans and European settlers is often described as 'tragic', a term that connotes inevitability and spiritual depth. In fact, there is nothing inevitable and nothing deep in the treatment of Native Americans by white Americans: what we have is a succession of free and brutal choices, expressing the shallow, vicious and duplicitous side of human beings. Against this background, NAGPRA was a necessary response. When I read Devon Mihesuah's account of a display box of Indian handbones in the windowsill of the ladies room in an East Texas museum (Mihesuah 2000: 96), I can only be ashamed of the persisting insensitivity of my own white people. One could only imagine the reaction of Europeans if a 'Museum of the Jews' opened in Berlin, complete with display cases of skulls from Auschwitz. Yet for the world's indigenous peoples, it is Auschwitz every day.

What is the difference between the tourist viewing a display case of skulls and the anthropologist studying those same skulls? The tourist is encouraged by the display to assume an attitude of domination: I am alive, you are dead; I am victorious, you are defeated (Hinsley 2002). The scientist takes, must take, to do the work, an objective attitude: this is the size, this is the weight, this is the date, this is how this skull compares with others. The objective attitude, we noted at the outset, is not the moral attitude, but it is not an immoral attitude either. The scientist does not consider himself better than the skull.

What is the difference between a tourist viewing a display case of skulls, and a museum-goer looking at a Native American headdress? Once again, the tourist is caught up with thoughts of domination; the museum-goer, perhaps vaguely, can feel only admiration: that some person, utilising the unique experience and special material resources of this particular culture, created such a splendid and expressive thing. By seeing the headdress, the viewer is connected to the creator and the creative act.

The consensus in the United States, even among museum administrators, is that the NAGPRA experience has been positive on the whole. Many legitimate, religiously based demands of Native Americans have been satisfied by NAGPRA. They might never have been satisfied without this legal power. But in the Kennewick Man case, NAGPRA collided with legitimate demands of science, and in the Forbes Cave Case, NAGPRA collided with the legitimate demands of aesthetic life. There is no magic ethical formula for adjudicating the requirements of religion, art and science. My purpose has been to establish the equal legitimacy of diverse fundamental demands.

CHAPTER 10

Stewardship gone astray? Ethics and the SAA

Leo Groarke and Gary Warrick

After much deliberation and debate, the Society for American Archaeology (the SAA) has 'strongly' endorsed 'Principles of Archaeological Ethics'. It 'urges' archaeologists to use these principles in establishing the responsibilities they have to archaeological resources, to those who have an interest in these resources and to those affected by archaeological work (SAA 2004; SAA Ethics in Archaeology Committee 2000).

In this paper, we discuss the implications the SAA principles have for the treatment of archaeological artefacts other than skeletal remains. We have excluded the latter from our discussion for a number of reasons: because skeletal remains raise complex issues that warrant extended discussion on their own; because these issues are investigated in other contributions to this volume; and because we have examined these issues in another context (see Groarke 2001).

According to the set of principles the SAA proposes, the basic principle of archaeological ethics is the following principle of stewardship:

The archaeological record, that is, *in situ* archaeological material and sites, archaeological collections, records, and reports, is irreplaceable. It is the responsibility of all archaeologists to work for the long-term conservation and protection of the archaeological record by practicing and promoting stewardship of the archaeological record. Stewards are both caretakers of and advocates for the archaeological record for the benefit of all people; as they investigate and interpret the record, they should use the specialized knowledge they gain to promote public understanding and support for its long-term preservation.

(SAA Ethics in Archaeology Committee 2000: 11)

Though we see the SAA's ethics of stewardship as an important attempt to clarify the ethical obligations of the professional archaeologist, we will argue that its principle of stewardship is in many ways problematic. If our arguments are correct, the principle of stewardship is an unsatisfactory basis for an archaeological ethics because it: (1) is vague and difficult to apply in practice; (2) confuses ethical and political concerns;

(3) has inconsistent implications in circumstances in which different groups vie for the control of archaeological resources; and (4) does not properly recognise those aspects of archaeological ethics which transcend (and sometimes limit) stewardship. These problems notwithstanding, there are important insights that can be salvaged from the SAA's ethics of stewardship. We will try to show how it could inform ethical principles which might be the basis of a better 'ethics in the field'.

THE PRINCIPLE OF STEWARDSHIP IS VAGUE

It would be unrealistic to expect an archaeological ethics to provide easy answers to the complex ethical controversies that are a hallmark of archaeology today. That said, a viable ethics should provide the working archaeologist with a framework which allows them systematically to identify, assess and balance the ethical considerations which are relevant to their practice. In so far as an archaeological ethics is an exercise in applied ethics, the ultimate test of its success is its ability to provide the practising archaeologist with a useful framework they can apply in the course of their archaeological work.

The SAA suggests that archaeologists should assess ethical issues by thinking of themselves as 'stewards'. Outside of archaeology, a 'steward' (derived from the Old English *stig* meaning 'hall', and *weard* meaning 'to watch over') takes care of other people or other people's property. Good stewards take care of things in ways that serve their masters' interests. The unjust steward described in the parable in Luke 16:1–13 is unjust because he fails to do so, acting in a way that puts his own interests above those of his master, who owns the property in question.

The notion that archaeologists are stewards is grounded in the conviction that they do not own the archaeological record, and are obligated to care for it in a manner that serves others' interests. This perspective is (as it was meant to be) a helpful antidote to an archaeological imperialism which characterised archaeology in the past. As historical examples of the sort discussed by Bendremer and Richman in chapter 6 demonstrate, the attitudes associated with this imperialism assume that it is the scientific interests of archaeologists that determine appropriate professional behaviour. In the service of these interests, individual archaeologists felt free (even obligated) to ignore myriad different interests that other stakeholders (individuals, descendants, communities, the public, etc.) have in the disposition of the archaeological record.

Though the SAA principle of stewardship usefully emphasises the responsibilities archaeologists have to others who have an interest in the archaeological record, it has many shortcomings when it is proposed as a way to clarify archaeological ethics. A number of commentators have tried to delineate its implications, sometimes in useful ways (see Joyce 2002; McGuire 1997; Rosenwig 1997; Smith and Burke 2003; Watkins 2003; Wylie 1997, 2000; Zimmerman 2000), but the principle is inherently vague and difficult to apply in practice. To see why, we need to compare the stewardship model of archaeology with other kinds of stewardship.

Outside of archaeology, a steward's basic obligation is to care for things in a manner that serves the master who owns the property that is cared for. In this way, the interests of this master determine the steward's obligations. If archaeologists are stewards, their fundamental obligation is a duty to care for the archaeological record in a way that serves the interests of those who own this record. The problem is that the SAA principle does not clearly identify these owners, and in this way fails to identify the 'master' whose interests will determine the obligations of the archaeologist-as-steward.

One might try to answer this objection by noting that the SAA principle of stewardship maintains that the archaeological record should be stewarded for 'the benefit of all', and that the corresponding 'principle of accountability' requires 'an acknowledgment of public accountability and a commitment to make every reasonable effort, in good faith, to consult actively with affected group(s), with the goal of establishing a working relationship that can be beneficial to all parties involved' (SAA 2004; SAA Ethics in Archaeology Committee 2000). These kinds of qualifications might be taken to suggest that the owner/master of the archaeological record is everyone, and that archaeologists are, by implication, obligated to serve the interests of all.

Instead of resolving the vagueness in the principle of stewardship, such a view makes the principle almost impossible to apply in practice, for it falsely assumes that it is possible to manage the archaeological record in a way that serves the interests of all stakeholders. If this were the case, the controversies that motivate the development of principles of archaeological ethics would not have arisen, for they are the result of circumstances in which different groups of stakeholders have contradictory views, interests and desires. To make the situation worse, these are not abnormal circumstances for practising archaeologists, but day-to-day realities with which they must continually contend.

Consider an example. Under the Ontario Heritage Act (RSO 1990), licensed archaeologists in Ontario, Canada, must gain the permission of landowners before entering their land in order to conduct archaeological work. If the property in question is an active farm or tree nursery, an archaeological site can be destroyed by deep ploughing or harvesting. Unless human burials are discovered, nothing can be done to stop a landowner from knowingly destroying an archaeological site through the earning of their livelihood. Even in cases in which a site can be demonstrated to have a direct relationship to some living descendent community, the landowner can deny access to both a licensed archaeologist and the members of this community. Looters who enter the site without permission may, on the other hand, take artefacts without being prosecuted (because prosecutions are rare – there is only one case in Ontario in which looters have been tried and convicted for violating the Ontario Heritage Act).

Putting aside the many issues that this situation raises, these are circumstances in which landowners, licensed archaeologists, Native people from descendent communities, looters and others have conflicting interests in the same archaeological site. Archaeologists have an interest in the study of these archaeological resources, landowners have an interest in using their land in a way that is not impeded by archaeological investigation, Native groups have an interest in recovering and protecting their heritage, and looters have an interest in gaining ownership of whatever they can find. In these and other circumstances, the groups which have conflicting interests in archaeological resources may include the deceased communities (or individuals) who produced the artefacts (or records) in question; descendent communities; communities which have religious or other interests in the artefacts; the owners of the property on which artefacts are located; the individuals who find the artefacts in question; those who purchase them; professional archaeologists; the scientific community; educators; and the general public.

In order to decide the obligations of the archaeologist *qua* steward, we would need to know which of these groups should be the master whose interests the archaeologist should serve. Some will argue that the wishes of those who produced archaeological artefacts should play a primary role in determining how they are treated. Others will argue that these wishes are difficult to determine, and that the wishes of descendants are more important and more tangible (Joyce 2002; Smith and Burke 2003; Watkins 2003; Zimmerman 2000). Still others will argue that descendants (who may be separated from their ancestors by thousands of years) are in no position to judge how best to respect their ancestors, and that the interests of science, education, the public or property owners should take precedence over such tenuous connections (Lepper 2000; Meighan 1984).

Such debates are further complicated by considerations which suggest that the master whose interests should be served by archaeology may vary in different kinds of circumstances. It is not clear that an artefact which was created as a sacred object should be treated in the same way as an object which was discarded as a piece of garbage. Some would distinguish archaeological objects which are privately owned – in most US states non-burial archaeological sites are owned by the private landowner (see Ferris 2003) – from those which belong to a community. In the United States, the Native American Grave Protection and Repatriation Act of 1990 (NAGPRA) explicitly distinguishes between the individual/family owner-ship of 'funerary objects' and the communal ownership of artefacts of 'cultural patrimony'. In some cases, the provenance of – and title to – an object may be open to different interpretations, and different individuals (including different individuals from the same community) may claim objects in contradictory ways.

In circumstances as different as these, it is plausible to suppose that the working archaeologist is obligated to serve different masters, though complex principles would have to decide whose interests deserve primary (secondary, tertiary, etc.) consideration in particular situations. In the present context, these are further issues which have to be resolved in deciding between the contradictory interests that competing groups have in the archaeological record. It is only by resolving these issues that one can clearly establish what master an archaeologist-as-steward ought to serve. One cannot do so by taking refuge in the well-intentioned but vague suggestion that archaeologists should serve others, or by invoking the impossible suggestion that archaeologists should serve everyone. Be-cause these are the strategies adopted in the SAA ethics of stewardship, it fails to give clear direction to working archaeologists and in this way fails to pass one of the essential tests that must be passed by any viable ethics of archaeology.

AN ALTERNATIVE WAY TO READ THE PRINCIPLE
OF STEWARDSHIP

One might try to avoid these issues by reading the SAA principle in a way that suggests that archaeologists should serve, not particular groups of stakeholders, but the archaeological record itself. Such a position is in some ways suggested by the wording of the SAA principle, which holds that 'Stewards are both caretakers of and *advocates for* the archaeological record' and 'should use the specialized knowledge they gain to promote public understanding and support for its long-term preservation'. On this reading, the principle of stewardship maintains that the archaeologist's primary obligation is an obligation to the archaeological record which supports it by advocating the recovery, study and preservation of the artefacts it is composed of.

This way of interpreting the SAA principle of stewardship is, however, problematic. To begin with, it makes the SAA principle a principle which is at odds with other principles which have been proposed as guides for archaeologists' behaviour. For these principles usually privilege archaeology's responsibilities to living descendants and communities over any generic responsibility to the archaeological record. Following the lead of the American Anthropological Association Code of Ethics in 1971, the World Archaeological Congress (see the Vermillion Accord 1989 and WAC First Code of Ethics 1990) set the template for archaeological codes of ethics developed in Canada, Australia, New Zealand and other jurisdictions (Rosenwig 1997). For good reason, these codes privilege obligations to living descendent communities over obligations to archaeological preservation, even to the point of advising archaeologists not to conduct archaeological work if it is deemed to have a harmful impact on living descendants (Joyce 2002; Smith and Burke 2003).

Both Native and non-Native archaeologists working in the Americas (e.g., Joyce 2002; Rosenwig 1996a; Watkins 2003; Yellowhorn 2000; Zimmerman 1996a, 2002) have criticised the SAA on similar grounds, arguing that its ethical principles put science first and people second. We would go even further, for we believe that alternative interpretation of the SAA principle is problematic in a more fundamental way – a way which raises the question whether we can even understand its suggestion that archaeologists should, as stewards, 'serve the archaeological record'.

It should go without saying that a steward can only steward in the interests of something which has interests. It follows that archaeologists can steward in the interests of the archaeological record only if it is the sort of thing that has interests. The archaeological record is, however, made up of artefacts and records which are inanimate objects that have no interests (perhaps some would argue differently in the case of skeletal remains, but we have left them for elsewhere). A broken ancient pot buried in the ground does not itself care whether it is destroyed, found, reassembled, studied, preserved or displayed. It is not the sort of thing that cares. The claim that archaeologists should, as stewards, serve such objects is, rather, an anthropomorphic fiction which reads into the archaeological record interests which it does not, as a collection of artefacts, have.

It is not archaeological artefacts, but people, who care whether artefacts and records are preserved, forgotten or destroyed. It follows that it is the interests of people, not artefacts, that are served when one attempts to preserve and protect the archaeological record. And once we recognise people as the bearers of interests, the previously outlined problems with the principle of stewardship return, for it fails to provide a clear account of the people the archaeologist-as-steward ought to serve.

Indeed, there is a way in which the alternative reading of the principle of stewardship makes it more rather than less problematic, for it suggests that archaeologists should serve the interests of those who wish to have the archaeological record preserved and studied (interests it falsely reads into this record). This implicit privileging of these interests is arbitrary. More problematically, it begs the questions which have been raised in debates about the disposition of archaeological artefacts – debates which question the priority of these interests. Still more problematically, this implicit privileging is inconsistent with the avowed goal of the SAA principles of ethics, which are supposed to be an alternative to the principle that it is the interests of archaeology and archaeologists (i.e. the interests of those interested in the preservation and study of artefacts) that should be the key consideration in determining the obligations of the working archaeologist. For all these reasons, the alternative reading of the SAA principle is problematic and cannot make it the basis of a viable archaeological ethics.

THE PRINCIPLE OF STEWARDSHIP CONFUSES ETHICS AND POLITICS

One might try to rectify the problems with the stewardship model of archaeology by adding to it a clearer account of the master (or masters) archaeologists-as-stewards are obliged to serve. Looked at from this point of view, it may seem that the principle of stewardship is incomplete rather than untenable, and that the SAA should not reject the principle, but undertake some coordinated effort to develop this account.

But moves in this direction only serve to highlight a deeper problem with the SAA approach to ethics. This is its failure to distinguish between two distinct kinds of ethical issues: (1) those which are properly viewed as matters of professional conduct and professional regulation; and (2) those which are more properly seen as political issues that need to be resolved, not in the course of developing a professional ethics, but in a political arena which shifts authority, control and decision-making powers from a profession to a broader arena that incorporates other stakeholders. Though this is an important distinction which is pertinent to the development of any professional ethics, it is not acknowledged in the SAA principles of ethics, and raises questions about the merits of any possible SAA attempt to develop a detailed account of the master(s) archaeologists-as-stewards are obliged to serve.

The kinds of contexts in which ethical issues need to be resolved in a political rather than a professional arena are readily apparent in the medical professions, which operate in a context fraught with controversial issues – abortion, stem cell research, euthanasia and so on. Medical practitioners are, to take one example, intimately involved in decisions to implement passive or (in some countries) active euthanasia. This does not, however, mean that the medical professions – and their codes of conduct – should decide the circumstances in which euthanasia is and is not appropriate. As the medical professions themselves acknowledge, practitioners who believe that this is so misunderstand their proper role in the resolution of such issues. This is not because these practitioners should not contribute to this resolution (as key stakeholders, they have an important role to play in the discussion of the issues) but because the resolution must take place in a political arena which properly recognises the role, interests and opinions of other stakeholders.

In the case of archaeology, archaeologists misunderstand their proper role in the resolution of the ethical issues that have arisen over the disposition of archaeological artefacts if they believe that they should decide these issues by constructing principles of professional ethics. As stakeholders, professional archaeologists should play an active role in the discussion of these issues, but they should be decided in an arena which recognises a wide variety of competing stakeholders, among them, indigenous groups, property owners, developers, educators and other communities with an interest in the past. In such a context, archaeologists should act as participants in discussion and debate, not as professionals who decide the issues. To the extent that they become the latter, they act not as stewards, but as the master of the archaeological record.

The suggestion that archaeologists should, as a profession, decide broad ethical issues that involve many other stakeholders is particularly problematic given that archaeologists have a vested interest in the outcome of such decisions. It is not, for example, surprising that archaeologists and archaeological associations like the SAA condemn the private sale of archaeological artefacts. Such transactions break up collections of artefacts, make them inaccessible for study and education, and place their care and preservation in the hands of non-professionals. For these reasons, one might plausibly argue against the sale of archaeological resources, especially as this would, if it were a widespread practice, greatly impact archaeology.

Though there is something to this argument, others will see the matter differently. Some indigenous peoples recover artefacts from ancestral sites in order to sell them on the antiquities market. This practice is sometimes called 'subsistence digging', because the money earned is used for basic necessities (e.g., gasoline for outboard motors or snowmobiles) or to support traditional subsistence lifestyles (Hollowell 2003; Staley 1993: 348).

A particularly controversial case is that of the Yupik community of Gambell on St Lawrence Island, Alaska. This community has mined old ivory and artefacts from ancestral village sites since the 1940s (a practice which was initiated with the sale of artefacts to archaeologists working on the island). The Yupik claim ownership of the sites and artefacts in question, asserting their exclusive right to excavate and sell their ancestors' material culture. Contrary to most aboriginal people, they regard sites and artefacts as economic resources, comparable to mineral resources. Entire families engage in the digging of sites and individual ivory carvings are allegedly sold for thousands of US dollars (Staley 1993). Because the Yupik village corporations own St Lawrence Island, US heritage legislation (e.g., the Archaeological Resources Protection Act) does not apply.

While the Yupik are not doing anything illegal (Staley 1993), the SAA Ethical Guidelines suggest that members of the SAA should condemn the Yupik as looters and commercial diggers. But why should a professional organisation like the SAA dictate how the Yupik should and should not use their ancestral heritage? This is a matter in which archaeologists have an interest, but they are one of competing groups of stakeholders and such an approach privileges their interests. In cases such as this, the proper treatment of archaeological resources is more reasonably seen as a political issue that should be decided in a political arena. The obligation of the archaeologist is not to resolve the issues, but to recognise and respect rules and decisions made outside of professional bodies like the SAA. The appropriate place to resolve such issues is in a political forum, which is open to other stakeholders who have different points of view.

This conclusion highlights some fundamental tensions in the SAA ethics of stewardship, which is motivated by a desire to recognise the role that outsiders should play in determining what is done with the archaeological record, but still suggests that these issues should be resolved by applying principles of ethics which are designed and applied by archaeologists. In cases of ethical controversy, this puts archaeologists in an untenable situation (politically, ethically and often practically), asking them to decide between competing points of views in cases in which they have a vested interest. We will do better to resolve these issues in a political arena, leaving the working archaeologist with a responsibility which is both more reasonable and more manageable, i.e. the responsibility to abide by standards established in a broader and more neutral forum.

THE PRINCIPLE OF STEWARDSHIP IS INCONSISTENT

One might try to rectify the problems with the principle of stewardship by conceding the point that decisions about ethical issues should be deferred to a more public, political forum. One might in this way eliminate some of the vagueness inherent in the SAA approach to ethics, but the problems, tensions and inconsistencies which make the principle untenable cannot be so easily resolved. To see why, we need to separate the following two principles, which are both incorporated within the SAA's principle of stewardship.

> *The principle of simple stewardship*: Archaeologists are not the masters of the archaeological record, and are obliged to deal with it in ways that serve others' interests.
>
> *The principle of archaeological preservation*: Archaeologists are obligated to: (1) 'work for the long-term conservation and protection of the archaeological record' and (2) 'promote public understanding and support for its long-term preservation'.

The SAA treats the principle of archaeological preservation as though it were an intrinsic part of the principle of stewardship, but it is an independent principle which needs to be considered on its own merits. Not surprisingly, the principle of preservation is one which is attractive to archaeologists (not surprisingly, because it is an interest in archaeological preservation that attracts them to archaeology). That said, it is a principle which is open to debate.

Particularly in contexts in which the benefits of preservation must be weighed against other interests, many hold that preservation does not trump every other value. Some communities may think that economic or other benefits outweigh the value of archaeological preservation (Staley 1993), and Zimmerman (1996a), Thomas (2000) and others argue that the political interests of contemporary indigenous people are more important than archaeological preservation. According to Riding In, native religious values are more important than preservation, a view that convinces him that archaeology is 'an oppressive and sacrilegious profession', and that 'the study of stolen remains constitutes abominable acts of sacrilege, desecration, and depravity' (1996: 238, 240).

In practice, indigenous interests in and use of the archaeological record may challenge the principle of archaeological preservation. In Australia, rock art sites that are thousands of years old continue to be used and repainted by local Australian Aborigines who tell archaeologists that the sites must be continuously reused (Bowdler 1988). Native peoples on the Northwest Coast of Canada (e.g., the Haisla) believe that memorial totem poles should be permitted to complete their natural cycle – i.e. to rot and fall and decompose. Masks, baskets and other artefacts used in ceremony are destroyed ritually (one might compare the deliberate breakage and burial of stone bowls in antiquity – bowls which archaeologists excavate and reconstruct) or left to disintegrate (Clavir 2002: 153–6).

The Zuni successfully repatriated dozens of their wooden *Ahayu:da* or 'War Gods' in the 1980s and 1990s. In accordance with Zuni beliefs, these carved poles must be exposed to the elements and allowed to return to the earth through a process of decay (Ferguson *et al.* 2000; Merrill *et al.* 1993). In Ontario, some Six Nations elders have maintained that archaeologists interfere with a proper natural process when they salvage burials and archaeological sites that are naturally eroding along a river bank or lakeshore. In Canada, provincial and territorial legislation, like NAGPRA in the United States, recognises limits on the value of preservation, requiring the repatriation of aboriginal skeletal remains and associated artefacts for reburial.

In a discussion of the principle of stewardship, the chairs of the SAA committee which formulated the SAA principles themselves recognise that there may be times when archaeological research 'may not be justifiable' (Lynott and Wylie 2000: 36). This demonstrates their sensitivity to such issues, but raises the question why the principle of archaeological preservation should be subsumed within a principle of stewardship, especially as the two principles form an inconsistent combination: one declaring that the interests of archaeologists should not determine arch-aeological practice, the other that the prime interest of archaeologists – preservation – is the core value that should guide decisions about arch-aeological remains. In combining the principles, the SAA principles declare that the interests of archaeologists are, and are not, the crux of archaeological ethics.

THERE IS MORE TO ETHICS THAN STEWARDSHIP

The issues raised by the principle of preservation suggest that the SAA principles of archaeological ethics do not fully embrace stewardship as an ideal. This is a problem, but not because stewardship is the be-all and end-all of ethical archaeology. A plausible ethics for archaeologists must better recognise the interests other groups have in the archaeological record, but it must also recognise that there is more to ethics than stewardship. In keeping with this it makes the other aspects of ethical archaeology an integral part of any principles used to guide the working archaeologist.

What are the other aspects of archaeological ethics? At the very least, archaeologists' commitment to care for the archaeological record in the service of others cannot weaken their responsibility to practise archaeo-logy in a way that is characterised by honesty, openness and an ongoing commitment to professional standards of investigation (it is in this regard surprising that the SAA principles of ethics do not more clearly reject actions like the falsification of archaeological records or the draw-ing of conclusions that are at variance with professional standards of assessment).

As a profession, archaeology needs to assert these responsibilities, both because they are a core element of professional practice, and because the nature of archaeological work means that archaeologists work in contexts in which a variety of stakeholders may wish to have sites and artefacts understood, categorised and interpreted in ways that suit their interests.

In Ontario, for example, 90 per cent of all archaeological work is carried out by consulting archaeologists who work for land developers. About five hundred new sites are discovered as a result of these activities each year, one hundred of them requiring some form of salvage excav-ation prior to development. About 80 per cent of the sites in question are pre-contact Native sites (Ferris 1998). Typically, a land developer is re-quired to complete archaeological work prior to development and hires an archaeological firm based on the lowest bid.

In such a context, a developer, the Ministry of Culture, Native people and other stakeholders (say, a municipality which has hired the developer to build a road) may have competing interests. The developer desires to have the required archaeological work done in a way that allows it to proceed as quickly and efficiently as possible. Delays in scheduling may result in significant financial losses. The municipality may need to have the road built to alleviate a pressing traffic problem. The problem may cost lives by causing accidents. Native groups may wish to protect their heritage. Particular interpretations of archaeological findings may have political ramifications or raise questions about their oral histories. Different Native groups may vie for the control of artefacts. The Ontario Ministry of Culture has a responsibility to protect archaeological resources for the people of Ontario.

In a context such as this, much may hang on the conclusions of a consulting archaeologist (all the more so given that the Ministry of Culture does not inspect their work in the field). The developer, the municipality, different Native peoples, the general public, etc. all have much to gain from particular points of view. There may, in view of this, be financial, social and political pressures that the consulting archaeologist has to deal with. In such a circumstance, there may be something to be gained by reflecting on the role of the archaeologist as steward, but it is as important to state clearly that an archaeologist's professional obligation is, first and foremost, an obligation to conduct an accurate and honest archaeological investigation.

In contexts such as these, one might usefully compare the working archaeologist to an auditor or accountant, whose independence must be zealously protected. It is only in this way that the profession of archaeology can fulfil its responsibility to come to reasonable archaeological conclusions. Especially in the highly politicised context in which archaeological work is often conducted, it is important to assert that such obligations cannot be overridden by the interests of employers or others who may benefit from particular kinds of findings. It is in such circumstances that a responsibility to steward the archaeological record in the interests of others reaches its limits, and is trumped by other professional obligations.

SALVAGING A PRINCIPLE OF STEWARDSHIP

Our account suggests that the SAA principle of stewardship has serious flaws when it is used as a basis for an ethics of archaeology. We have tried to emphasise four of these shortcomings: its inherent vagueness, which manifests itself in its lack of any clear mechanism for choosing between competing interests in the archaeological record; its failure to acknowledge the need to resolve disputes about artefacts in a forum controlled by archaeologists; its question begging commitment to a principle of archaeological preservation; and its failure to recognise central professional obligations which extend beyond (and sometimes limit) stewardship concerns.

These problems notwithstanding, we want to end this chapter on a positive note, by reiterating our earlier comment that the SAA principle of stewardship is motivated by important concerns. Especially in a context in which archaeologists have often failed to recognise that archaeological work can be constrained by other interests and concerns, it is important to assert clearly that this is so. We would not, therefore, wholly reject the principle of stewardship and instead propose that the SAA principle be replaced by a different principle of stewardship which is less susceptible to the kinds of issues we have raised.

The space at our disposal does not allow us to develop such a principle in detail, but we will suggest the following variant of the principle of stewardship as an alternative basis for a more viable archaeological ethics.

The principle of archaeological stewardship: *Archaeologists have a duty to practise archaeology in a way that respects the rights of individuals and groups and societies affected by their work; to recognise that the goals of archaeological research may be superseded by these obligations; and to respect and recognise the right of communities to regulate archaeology in this interest.*

Unlike the SAA principle of stewardship, this is a principle which does not attempt to combine stewardship with a principle of preservation, and much more clearly recognises that an ethical archaeology must deal with artefacts and promote archaeological research in a manner which recognises that it may legitimately be constrained and regulated by obligations to individuals, communities and groups. One of the primary duties of the individual archaeologist is, this suggests, to respect regulatory decisions properly located outside the archaeological profession.

To the extent that it establishes constraints on archaeological work, the principle of archaeological stewardship needs to be balanced by a further principle which sets appropriate limits on the extent to which the latter interests can impose on archaeological research. To that end we will couple our principle of stewardship with the following principle of 'professionalism':

Archaeological professionalism: *In the course of conducting archaeological work, an archaeologist is obligated to act in a way that adheres to reasonable standards of research and investigation.*

The principle of archaeological stewardship highlights archaeology's obligations to communities affected by archaeological research. There is a sense in which the principle of archaeological professionalism limits the obligations established by the principle of archaeological stewardship, for it asserts that archaeologists are obligated to conduct their work in an honest and unbiased way that reflects high standards of research and investigation. It is these professional obligations that stewardship cannot trump.

The principles of archaeological stewardship and archaeological professionalism are our attempt to balance two concerns which must be the basis of any viable archaeological ethics. One (the latter) embodies archaeologists' relationship to their profession, the other their relationship to a broader community of external stakeholders. It is by balancing these obligations that the working archaeologist can best exemplify ethics in the field.

PART III

Archaeologists and the dead

CHAPTER II

Can archaeology harm the dead?

Geoffrey Scarre

Death and the sun, said the Duc de la Rochefoucauld, are two things that cannot be looked at steadily. If our own death is a daunting prospect, many archaeologists, anthropologists and collection curators spend a large portion of their professional lives confronting death, or at least the dead. From an academic point of view, the study of the corporeal remains of human beings and of the mode of their disposal is a crucial source of knowledge of the human past. Yet from an ethical perspective the highly intrusive nature of much of this study raises problems. Whilst a bone may be no more animate than a stone, it is the relic of a man or woman who once thought and felt, was happy and sad, loved and feared as we do. To disinter or disturb it, or to subject it to chemical or physical analysis, is to take a liberty – not with the thing itself but with the person to whom it once belonged. Kant famously held that we should treat human beings as ends in themselves, never merely as means to our own or others' advantage. Using the dead as a research resource is prima facie inconsistent with this principle since it is hard to see how such treatment can be of any benefit to the subjects. Moreover, where the presumption is that an individual would not have consented to exhumation, study or exhibition of his body or bones, the exploitation can seem a major affront to his autonomy.

Recent years have seen an increasing awareness by members of the archaeological and kindred professions that human remains should be handled with ethical care. Few are now likely to dispute that human remains, whatever their age or ethnic origin, should be treated with a measure of respect. One much-cited ethical code, the Vermillion Accord on Human Remains, adopted by the WAC Inter-Congress at its meeting in Vermillion, South Dakota, in 1989, employs the word 'respect' or its cognates in five out of six of its constituent principles. Thus we are told (to quote the first two principles) that:

1 Respect for the mortal remains of the dead shall be accorded to all, irrespective of origin, race, religion, nationality, custom and tradition;
2 Respect for the wishes of the dead concerning disposition shall be accorded whenever possible, reasonable and lawful, when they are known or can be reasonably inferred.[1]

A problem, however, with these and similar statements is that they require a lot of unpacking before they yield much practical guidance. What does it mean to 'show respect' to the remains, or the wishes, of the dead? In some cultures, *any* kind of disturbance of remains counts as disrespectful. To defer to this hard-line position would rule out much archaeological activity at a stroke. (It would also provide a considerable impediment to much development and construction work that involves destroying sites where remains are present.) Even amongst Western-trained archaeologists, opinions differ as to what respectful treatment of remains requires. Most minimally, showing respect may be held to involve no more than not treating bones or body parts as junk or comic props or curios. On a more rigorous view, respect precludes not just irreverent handling but also all unnecessary disturbance of remains, and demands the restoration or reburial of all but the most crucially significant remains at the end of a research project.

Complicating the issues further is the need to consider not just the two-termed relation of researchers and subjects but the three-termed relation of researchers, subjects and (genetic or cultural) descendant communities.[2] The third principle of the Vermillion Accord holds that 'Respect for the wishes of the local community and of relatives and guardians of the dead shall be accorded whenever possible, reasonable and lawful.' Legislation in several countries has compelled those who uncover, study or preserve archaeological human remains to negotiate their activities with local communities claiming rights to the ownership or guardianship of those remains, and in some cases to return them to those communities

1 For the full text of the Vermillion Accord, see www.wac.uct.ac.za/archive/content/vermillion. accord.html. Other clauses of the Vermillion Accord, concerning the respect that should be shown to the wishes of 'the local community and of relatives or guardians of the dead', have proved more controversial, especially in view of the highly contentious Kennewick case. Larry Zimmerman (2002: 97) comments that 'What have mostly not changed since the Vermillion Accord are attitudes about the primacy of scientific approaches to the past, accompanied by some rearguard actions.'
2 Some would say that archaeologists are involved in a quadrilateral rather than a triangular relationship, with the general public forming the fourth corner. Although it is salutary to remember that the public has both financial and academic interests in archaeological research, we can ignore this extra complication here.

on demand. Since other chapters in this book explore the significance and justification of such legislation in some detail, I shall only draw attention here to the important distinction between treating the dead with respect *for their own sake* and treating their remains respectfully as a way of showing respect for the descendant communities. It is one thing to honour the ancestors and another to honour their descendants, though we do both at once when we treat the relics of the dead with due care and decorum. Plausibly, these represent concomitant obligations.

Cynics might suggest that some archaeologists or curators who treat human remains in a publicly respectful way only do so to avoid falling foul of the communities of origin, which might otherwise make life tough for them. Assuming an attitude of reverence that they don't really feel is good for business (and what they say and do in private may be different from what they say and do in public). No doubt there are those who fit this description but we need not suppose such attitudes to be common, still less typical. Archaeologists are as morally varied as any other group of people and many feel real sympathy for the dead they examine, especially when remains show evidence of horrific wounds or serious pathological conditions. Being interested in the people they were and the lives they led, they do not find it easy to view their remains as mere research data. Archaeology tries to make the dry bones live, and it is hard to think ourselves into the situation of past people without feeling towards them some of the interpersonal attitudes that characterise our relationships with the living. Human remains probably receive, on the whole, more sensitive treatment from archaeologists than they do from developers who, whatever their individual moral qualities, are not professionally interested in re-creating former lives. Moreover the contemporary discourse in which archaeologists are engaged indicates a widespread willingness to do right by all parties. It is now generally accepted that there are other morally significant stakeholders in the archaeological enterprise, though specific adjudications amongst competing interests are often contentious (inevitably, given the disparate character of those interests). Archaeologists whose work involves the disturbance of the dead increasingly feel a genuine respect for the communities of origin and sincerely wish to minimise distress to those who claim descent from or kinship with the deceased subjects of their research.

However, even the best-intentioned researchers may find themselves at odds with communities, both past and present, whose ideas about the proper preservation of the dead are in sharp contrast with their own. The complex funerary customs practised in many societies from prehistory onwards, the erection of elaborate monuments to the dead, and the taboos commonly associated with interference with burials and grave-markers, indicate the prevalence and power of beliefs that death marks a transition rather than a final end. Such practices as mummification or the encasement of a corpse in precious metals or jade, the building of pyramids, heart burials, etc., are justified by the conviction that it matters to the deceased how their remains are disposed of. Numerous contemporary native peoples of the USA, Canada, Australia, New Zealand and elsewhere believe that the dead can be affected for good or ill by the treatment of their physical remnants. In their view, inappropriate handling of these can seriously harm the deceased by, for example, preventing their spirits from finding rest. The ancestors may be dead but they are not gone. The belief that certain archaeological and curatorial practices are against the interests of the dead provides a solid reason for resisting them.[3]

In contrast, most Western archaeologists, anthropologists and museum keepers think that death is either extinction (as I think) or at least the termination of the capacity to be harmed or benefited by anything that is done to the physical body. This may seem to imply that the dead have no interests that need be considered in debates over the treatment of their remains. This view of the invulnerability of the dead is reflected in legislation such as the UK Human Rights Act 1988, which lays down that one must be alive to be a victim of a rights abuse. But if the dead cannot be harmed, then how can it matter to them what happens to their remains? It might be suggested that whilst, strictly speaking, they cannot be harmed by what is done to their relics, they can still be wronged by certain kinds of indecorous treatment of them. But to say this is only to shift the problem. How exactly does it wrong the dead to manipulate their remains in ways they can never be conscious of? (Besides, can something really be said to be wrong if it isn't even potentially the cause of harm?) Have we, perhaps, failed to break free of a superstitious fear that the dead might somehow get to know what we do to their bones and resent it?

---

3 In some cases concern for the ancestors and self-concern interlock in a way that is unfamiliar in Western culture. For instance, Native Hawaiians believe that they stand in a symbiotic relationship to their ancestors, who become *'aum_kua* (guardians) to their living descendants once they have been accorded *kanu pono*, a proper and righteous burial. So, 'Steal the soul and you steal the life of the land' (Ayau 2002: 179–80). In some Native American societies, e.g., the Pawnee, it is believed that disturbing the buried remains of the dead causes their spirits to become restless and harmful: 'Wandering spirits often beset the living with psychological and health problems' (Riding In 2000: 109).

But maybe we should change the perspective. Instead of thinking about the moral status of the dead, we could focus on that of living people who have reflexive desires for their posthumous future. Instances of such desires are very common. Thus people make wills because the scope of their concern for themselves and others typically extends beyond their own lifetime. In Western tradition, individuals are normally assigned both moral and legal rights to determine what happens to their goods and their bodies after death. If I bequeath my money to a canine rest-home and my body to medical science, then those are the destinations to which they should go. Although patently immoral or impracticable desires of the deceased for the disposal of their remains may fairly be ignored (so I cannot reasonably demand that my body should be eaten by my heirs or my ashes be scattered on the surface of Mars), the default position is that deceased persons' wishes should, in the absence of legitimate objections, be complied with.

Switching perspective like this can help to free us from the sense of paradox generated by the idea that there can be obligations to the dead *qua* dead. If instead we can think of our obligations as being to the *living*, then the conceptual strain induced by the notion that there can be duties towards the non-existent (or, at least, permanently unresponsive) is relieved. On this view it is you, the living you, I wrong if I agree to your deathbed plea to scatter your ashes at sea but afterwards put them on the roots of my rose-trees. Promises remain in force until they have been fulfilled, unless they are annulled by the promisee. Admittedly, there may occasionally be competing interests to consider. Imagine that Marcus has a rare bone condition and that medical researchers would gain potentially life-saving knowledge from a posthumous examination of his skeleton. But Marcus rejects their request to leave his body to science and demands a decent burial. Has Marcus an indefeasible right to have his own way? Once dead, he would be none the wiser if his remains were disposed of contrary to his wishes, and living people would benefit from the lessons that would be learned from studying his skeleton. Nevertheless, Marcus' autonomy would have been seriously flouted. Is this a conclusive reason for following his wishes to the letter? Whatever the answer to this, we cannot settle the issue simply by denying that Marcus' wish has any force. That move is inconsistent with allowing that the living have a right to a say in what happens to them and theirs after death.

But how universal a concession are we obliged to make here? Some might challenge the second principle of the Vermillion Accord on the ground that the rules and conventions formulated to govern mutual relations in our own society have no bearing on the inter-societal relations in which archaeologists are typically involved with their subjects of study. To disregard Marcus' desires for his corpse is to infringe the terms of the social contract by which he and we are tacitly bound. But there is no social contract linking Howard Carter, or ourselves, with Tutankhamun. Hence to disregard the Pharaoh's wish that his mummy and grave goods be left intact and untouched breaches no agreement, on this view. However, the claim that we have no moral responsibilities except to those with whom we are linked in a social contract is not very inviting.[4] Not only does it countenance all kinds of exploitative and self-seeking treatment but it implicitly locates the basis for moral respect not in the value of other human beings and their lives, but in what they can do to serve our own interests. The ultimate reason why we should honour the wishes of Tutankhamun or Marcus is that they are ends in themselves. If our obligation to treat others well is contingent on their capacity to act in a similar way towards us, then morality is reduced to social economics, and such notions as virtue, kindness, sympathy and fellow-feeling have little if any place in it.

If we reject the cold-blooded contractualist model of morality, it may seem that we have no more to explain in regard to our duties towards the dead. Only conceive of these as being really duties to the *living* (e.g., to accede to their wishes for their mortal remains, or to carry out the provisions of their wills) and they cease – apparently – to be puzzling or problematic. Our original difficulty rested on the fact that if death terminates the subject (or at any rate the subject's consciousness of being harmed or wronged), it is hard to see how posthumous events can have any adverse effects, in the absence of a suitable subject to suffer them. But there is no such problem if we take the living person to be the subject who is harmed or wronged.

Unfortunately, this cannot be the end of the story. We have made progress with our explanations, but not completed them. Actually, we have replaced one puzzle by another.

The new puzzle can be put like this. By identifying the living person as the subject who suffers the moral affront if certain acts are posthumously performed, we side-step the problem that the dead are either non-existent or in a state of permanent oblivion. But that problem does not go away. It reappears when we ask how a living subject can have any well-founded

---

4 The contractualist approach is also bad news for animals, which as non-contractors now lose all moral protection.

reflexive concern for her posthumous future if death is the actual (or effective – though I shall not keep adding this alternative) end of her as a subject. A living person has the status of subject only until death; so whom are we worrying about if we entertain anxieties about our posthumous state? True, if I care what happens to my mortal clay, I am concerned about something that is peculiarly and intimately mine. Still, my dead body is mine rather than me. (It would be silly to say that I shall survive death just so long as my corpse resists dissolution.) Once there is no *I* any more, it is obscure how I can be harmed or wronged by anything that is done to my physical remains. Note that it need not be irrational to be concerned about things that will happen after one's death. It is entirely reasonable to care about the fate of one's children or grandchildren when one is gone, or whether there will be a nuclear war, or about the long-term effects of global warming. The troublesome concerns are the reflexive or self-directed ones, because of their focus on an absent subject. It was the difficulty of making sense of these that gave rise to the celebrated argument of Epicurus that death cannot be an evil, since while we are alive death is 'not with us', and once dead we no longer exist to be subjects of misfortune (Epicurus 1926: 85).

In a recent article, T. M. Wilkinson maintains that an ante-mortem person can have interests that can be satisfied or dissatisfied after death. These might include interests in reputation, bodily integrity, privacy and 'not having one's remains desecrated' (Wilkinson 2002: 34–5). Wilkinson argues to the reality of posthumous interests from the premise that people commonly care about aspects of their posthumous fate. But this is a *non sequitur*, since we cannot infer that people have a real interest from the fact that they believe that they do. We are not infallible judges of our own interests. Many writers have noted how difficult it is to conceive of the finality of death. Heidegger observes that we think of others' death in terms of loss but that we cannot experience our own death as loss, or in any other way (Heidegger 1962: 282). Metaphorical descriptions of death as sleep or rest or a land of shadows indicate the problem we have in grasping the idea of a permanent, irreversible loss of consciousness.[5] The suspicion is that we slip into believing that we have interests that continue through death because we fail to grasp death for what it is, the end of us. We make the mistake of seeing dying, as it were, as a semi-colon in our existence rather than as the final full-stop. Yet if

---

5 For an insightful study of such misleading metaphors, see Fingarette 1996: 13–25.

death extinguishes the subject, it is hard to see how it can leave any genuine interests standing.[6]

Note that even if there were no genuine posthumous interests, there could still be some moral responsibilities in regard to human remains. Living people have a real interest in not being made unhappy. So even if Luke were wrong in believing it to be against his interests to have his remains 'desecrated' by research (since when such 'desecration' occurred, there would be no Luke any more), he could still be made very unhappy by the fear that his body might be mistreated after death. To prevent such unhappiness, there might be a persuasive moral case for prohibiting all research on remains except where subjects have given their express consent to it ante-mortem. Interestingly, whilst such a prohibition would disadvantage researchers, it has been argued that the widespread acceptance of the possibility of posthumous harm has certain important social advantages. Ernest Partridge remarks that 'the casual slandering of reputation and breaking of promises and wills after a person's death compromise and damage the moral point of view, at enormous cost to the moral order of society'. If we start by being careless about keeping the promises we made to people who are now dead, we may end up by taking a casual attitude to promise-keeping in general. Hence for the sake of the living and the good order of society, Partridge argues, it is prudent to pretend that a person's interests do not finish with his death (Partridge 1981: 258).

Whatever we think about the morality of the 'useful lie', we should not, I suggest, be too quick to dismiss the idea of posthumous harm as a fiction. In fact there is good reason to reject the claim that we have no posthumous interests in respect of which we can be harmed. In order to see this, we need to do some metaphysics.

Recall that the problem with posthumous interests is that they appear to lack a subject. In the words of Alan Fuchs, it seems that 'to be helped or harmed, one has to exist. There must be an existent self for self-interest, a living being for personal well-being' (Fuchs 1990–91: 349). The tactic of supplying a subject by construing the ante-mortem person as the bearer of the relevant interests looked at first as though it might meet the challenge. We breach our explicit or tacit agreements made with living people if,

---

6 For a vivid statement of what we mistakenly imagine death to be, see Adam Smith, *The Theory of Moral Sentiments* (1759): 'It is miserable, we think, to be deprived of the light of the sun; to be shut out from life and conversation; to be laid in the cold grave, a prey to corruption and the reptiles of the earth; to be no more thought of in this world, but to be obliterated, in a little time, from the affections, and almost from the memory, of their dearest friends and relations.' Smith describes this as a powerful 'illusion of the imagination' (Selby-Bigge 1897: vol. 1, 262–3).

following their demise, we flout their wishes for the disposal of their bodies or goods. However, the tactic proved insufficient to establish the genuineness of any posthumous interests. For a living person's concerns about her posthumous fate are still concerns about a non-existent subject. If 'to be helped or harmed, one has to exist', then all such concerns, however intensely held, must be misconceived.

My argument that they are not (necessarily) misconceived will proceed in four stages.[7] First, I will explain a distinction favoured by many modern metaphysicians between two kinds of change, *real* change and *Cambridge* change. Secondly, I shall show that while real changes can only occur to things that exist, non-existing things, including the dead, can be subjects of Cambridge change. Thirdly, I shall argue that Cambridge changes can be practically and morally significant changes. Fourthly, I shall apply the conclusions reached to showing how certain kinds of treatment of human remains can be morally wrong.

The difference between 'real' and 'Cambridge' change is explained like this. In the broadest sense, a change occurs at a point in time if and only if something begins (or ceases) to be the case then which previously had not (or had) been the case.[8] But we are intuitively disposed to distinguish between real changes in things and the purely relational changes that happen to them in consequence of real changes in other things. To cite a stock example: when Socrates died, his wife Xanthippe became a widow. Here we want to say that Socrates underwent a real change – he ceased to be a living man – but that nothing really changed in Xanthippe. In the contemporary jargon, Xanthippe underwent a 'Cambridge change'.[9] Whilst Socrates' dying transformed Xanthippe from a wife to a widow, this change was not a change *in* her (a change in her intrinsic properties) but a merely relational shift. Similarly, if John works hard to improve his chess skills and becomes a better player

---

7 Some, of course, may be misconceived for contingent reasons. It would be silly for me to care that no one wearing a green hat should ever walk on my grave. However, our present concern is with whether such a concern is even intelligible.

8 I adapt this formulation from Lowe (2002: 238). My understanding of kinds of change is much indebted to this author.

9 The term is usually attributed to Peter Geach, who identified it as a theme of interest to certain Cambridge philosophers of the earlier twentieth century (Geach 1969: 71–2). Note that not all relational changes are of the Cambridge kind: for instance, the change of an object's position in relation to another's is not. The analysis of locational change is contentious but one view is that it involves a change in an intrinsic relation, namely the distance between the two objects. For further discussion see Lowe 2002: 242–4.

than Jim, then Jim undergoes the Cambridge change of becoming an inferior player to John in virtue of the latter's real change.

It is evident that Cambridge changes can happen to the dead. Suppose that in 2010 Tolstoy begins to be surpassed in popularity as a Russian novelist by Turgenev. This is a Cambridge change affecting Tolstoy produced by a real change in something else, namely the collective object we call the reading public. A corresponding Cambridge change occurs to Turgenev from the same cause. Neither change, of course, involves any alteration in the intrinsic properties of either writer. It is a sound metaphysical tenet that a thing cannot undergo a change in any of its intrinsic properties unless it exists (for the obvious reason that only existent things can have such properties).[10] Cambridge properties, on the other hand, are relational properties whose acquisition or loss depends wholly on changes in other real things. Therefore they can be ascribed to things that no longer exist. We may conclude that *only* Cambridge changes are predicable of the dead.[11]

It might be objected at this point that it is hard to see how the dead can undergo relational Cambridge change when they no longer possess any intrinsic properties. It is one thing to talk about Cambridge change in a thing whose intrinsic properties have not changed (as in our examples of Xanthippe and Jim), and another to talk about such change in a thing which has no intrinsic properties. The thought here is that for a thing to enter into a relation with another, and hence instantiate a relational property, it must ultimately instantiate some intrinsic property which characterises it independently of that relation. Otherwise, what would serve to identify and individuate the thing that was entering into the relation in the first place? And the relational properties of a thing must be explained in terms of the intrinsic properties that it has, even if we are talking about mere Cambridge properties. So Jim has the property of being an inferior chess player to John in virtue of his own chess-playing skills; and whilst these need not change in order for him to

---

10 The definition of 'intrinsic' property is itself a matter for philosophical debate but we do not need to attend to the technicalities here. Brian Weatherson in the *Stanford Encyclopedia of Philosophy* characterises an intrinsic property as one a thing has by virtue of the way it is (Weatherson: http://plato.stanford.edu/entries/intrinsic-extrinsic/). He also quotes Stephen Yablo: 'You know what an intrinsic property is: it's a property a thing has (or lacks) regardless of what may be going on outside of itself' (Yablo 1999: 479).

11 For a much fuller defence of this claim, see Ruben 1988: *passim*. Ruben rightly remarks that a recognition that all posthumous changes are Cambridge changes 'will . . . help sort out what is involved in the long-running dispute concerning whether one can harm the dead' (Ruben 1988: 232–3, fn. 20).

undergo the relevant Cambridge change, he must still have them to be a chess player at all.

There is clearly something right about this objection. For a thing to undergo relational change, it must have intrinsic properties which individuate it and in virtue of which it can enter into relations with other things. Without intrinsic properties, there can be no relational ones. However, it is a mistake to think that a thing has to have the appropriate intrinsic properties at the time that it undergoes relational change. Consider the example of Tolstoy's relative loss of popularity. Tolstoy's posthumously changing from being more to being less popular than Turgenev occurs when neither he nor Turgenev has any intrinsic properties. But to explain the change we refer not to what Tolstoy now is but to what he *was*: what kind of books he wrote, his abilities as a story-teller, his manner of engaging his audience, and so on – in addition to facts about changing tastes in the contemporary readership. It would be impossible to explain how a posthumous Cambridge change could take place at time t if there were no changes in *any* intrinsic properties at t; but that condition is fulfilled by what happens at t to the living readers. No changes need happen in respect of Tolstoy's intrinsic properties at t – and indeed cannot, since none such then exist. But the proper way of characterising the change occurring at t refers to the properties that Tolstoy had ante mortem.[12]

One might suppose that Cambridge changes could have no practical or moral import. A natural thought is that harms and benefits must involve real changes to their subjects. How could a person be harmed or benefited by a change in something else that did not affect her own intrinsic properties? The thought may be natural but it is not correct. Real changes are not the only ones that can matter to us. People can reasonably care not just about their intrinsic properties but about their relational ones too. In particular, we like to appraise ourselves in our social context and to know where we stand in relation to others. Smith's pride at owning the best car in the street turns to ashes when Jones next door buys a Lamborghini. The fact that Smith undergoes 'only' a Cambridge change makes it no less intense. Similarly, Tim, who has

---

12 I am very grateful to Sophie Gibb for raising this objection and for discussing it with me. A more extensive discussion might go on to consider the case of fictional entities, which never have existed and yet which appear capable of undergoing Cambridge change. For example, in the age of Harry Potter we might say that Merlin is now only the second-most-famous wizard. An explanation of this change still needs to ascribe intrinsic properties to Harry and Merlin, albeit fictitiously in both cases.

stopped growing, is upset when his younger brother Tom overtakes him in height.[13] Cambridge changes can also please, as when Mary realises she is now the front-runner for the scholarship, following the withdrawal of the previous front-runner.

There are broadly two sorts of reasons why Cambridge changes and Cambridge properties can be morally significant. The first is that they can be the objects of desires, hopes, wishes, fears and other intentional attitudes whose fulfilment or frustration is important to us. If you take an innocent pride in being the grower of the biggest leeks on the allotment and I grow some bigger ones in order to spite you, then whilst neither you nor your leeks undergo real change, you feel hurt (as I intended) at losing your pre-eminence. The second is that Cambridge changes can give rise to further changes, including real changes, for better or worse. Suppose that Dr Black by his clever tongue can make and break the reputations of his faculty colleagues. By provoking (real) changes in people's attitudes, Dr Black (Cambridge) transforms admired professors into academic pariahs, and vice versa. When he changes Dr White from being the faculty darling to being the faculty demon, he not only causes him distress but puts his very job in jeopardy.[14]

What bearing has all this on the status and proper treatment of the dead? The answer is that it provides a way of dispelling the sense of paradox generated by the claim that people can be harmed posthumously when they no longer exist as subjects. Our discussion of Cambridge change shows how it could be a misfortune for Tolstoy to be overtaken in popularity by Turgenev in 2010, despite having died a hundred years earlier. The fact that Tolstoy is dead in 2010 is no obstacle to his undergoing a Cambridge change then, and we have seen that Cambridge changes are ones that we may care about deeply. (It is true that Cambridge changes occurring to the dead cannot cause further real changes in them. But they can cause real changes in other things, e.g., the thoughts

---

13 An alternative scenario is that Tim grows too, but more slowly than Tom. Can we still say, when Tom becomes taller than Tim, that Tim undergoes a merely Cambridge change? Tim, too, has changed in respect of an intrinsic characteristic. Nevertheless his becoming shorter than Tom is a function of Tom's change in respect of an intrinsic property, not his own, and in virtue of that is still a Cambridge change.

14 It might be wondered whether, instead of talking of a Cambridge change in Dr White, we would do better to talk about a real change in something else, namely Dr White's reputation. But the reification of such items as reputations offends against the principle of Ockham's Razor, that entities should not be multiplied beyond necessity. It is metaphysically more abstemious to parse talk of reputations in terms of the views and attitudes that people hold (though some metaphysicians think that any reification of such intentional attitudes is itself a step too far!).

and feelings of surviving relatives or friends, that may be objects of concern to the dead subjects ante-mortem.) Whether Cambridge changes are good, bad or indifferent for us is generally strongly dependent on our wishes and projects. If Tolstoy would not have cared about Turgenev's posthumously surpassing him in popularity (improbably, given the former's well-known hatred of the latter), then his doing so would not be bad for Tolstoy. However, it would be wrong to think that the goodness or badness for a subject of a posthumous Cambridge change always turns on whether it fulfils or frustrates his ante-mortem desires. For there are ante-mortem desires that are perverse and irrational on any count. Suppose that a depressive, self-hating individual hopes that his well-deserved unpopularity will continue after death. If it were posthumously revealed that he once performed an exceptionally noble and selfless act, it would be hard to argue that the resulting improvement in his reputation was bad for him.

Next, consider a man, Theseus, who is very anxious that his body should be undisturbed after it has been properly buried according to the customary rites of his society. Theseus' anxiety may stem from one or more of a number of sources: a fear that such disturbance would prevent his spirit finding rest, a desire that his privacy or his dignity should be posthumously respected, a conviction that tampering with remains is sacrilegious, or a dislike of his remains being pressed into the service of alien interests. None of these grounds is prima facie perverse or unreasonable, even if some of them might not be grounds for us. Some centuries after Theseus' death, however, archaeologists exhume his skeleton and remove it, along with his grave goods, to a laboratory for detailed examination. The changes that occur to the bones and other buried contents are real changes but they produce a change to Theseus of the Cambridge kind. From being a person whose remains lie intact in the grave, he becomes one whose remains no longer lie intact there.[15] The Cambridge

---

15 Note that I am not identifying Theseus with his skeletal remains. This is not the place to enter into a discussion of what constitutes the essence of a person but I hope it is fairly uncontroversial to assume that the preservation of bodily remains is insufficient for personal survival. I concede, however, that our Western concept of personhood, natural though it seems to us, may not be a cultural universal. Chris Scarre has observed to me that some societies appear to consider people not as bounded individuals with alienable possessions but as relational bundles in which both living persons and the things they possess or possessed form some kind of whole. If these conceptions are taken literally, they imply that there is survival of death in so far as parts of the 'bundle' (including, but extending beyond, corporeal remains) survive. And if surviving parts of the bundle are damaged, we have an easy answer to the question of how some forms of post-mortem harm are possible. But the notion of a 'literal' construal of the bundle idea is problematic.

nature of this change is not, if our foregoing argument was correct, a
reason for thinking it trivial or irrelevant. On the contrary, like many
other Cambridge changes it may be assigned substantial moral weight.
Theseus' keen ante-mortem wish that his burial should not be disturbed ceases to be satisfied at the moment when the archaeologists go to
work. This is a moment which, could he have foreseen it, he would
have anticipated with horror. Were the archaeologists to claim that they
were only disturbing bones (adding, if they were metaphysically minded,
that these were the only things they were subjecting to real changes), the
correct rejoinder would be that they were also causing a Cambridge
change to Theseus to which he would never have consented. The fact
that bones, being inanimate, are not the kind of thing that can be harmed
is beside the point. Theseus, their owner, *is* subject to harm; and he is
harmed when posthumous events take place that are contrary to his
reasonable desires.[16]

There is another potential objection to be tackled here. It might be
claimed that introducing the notion of Cambridge change to explain
how posthumous harm is possible is unhelpful, because it fails to solve
the root problem of the absence of the subject at the time when the
harmful event occurs. Certainly we can ascribe Cambridge changes to the
dead, as when we predicate a change in Tolstoy's popularity in the year
2010. But it is a further task to explain how such a change can be *harmful*
to Tolstoy when he no longer exists. Our other examples of morally
significant Cambridge changes concerned living people who can have
intentional attitudes (joy, sadness, disappointment, etc.) to the Cambridge
changes that happen to them. But the dead have no intentional attitudes.
Theseus is eternally oblivious to the fact that archaeologists have dug

---

To claim, for instance, that a certain shaman's magical equipment is part of *him* may just be a
vivid way of expressing the thought that it is intimately *his*, and that no one else must use or
tamper with it, even after his death. If we reject a metaphorical reading, then it is hard for us to get
a grip on what the bundle theory is claiming in terms that we can readily understand. One thing it
is not is a variant account of persons and personhood as *we* understand them, since for us it is an a
priori postulate that a person and her possessions are distinct existences. Alternatively we could see
it as the rejection not of our idea of personhood, but, more startlingly, of the idea of personhood
altogether. But now the radical incommensurability of the two conceptual schemes threatens to
make any dialogue on descriptive or moral issues impossible. For the purposes of this chapter, I
cut this Gordian knot of interpretation by remaining within the Western paradigm that firmly
distinguishes persons from objects.

16 Note that 'reasonable' here does not imply 'based on true assumptions'. If Theseus wants his
remains to be left alone because he thinks that disturbance will harm his spirit, while we may
think the premise wrong it would be arrogant for us to dismiss as irrational or unwarranted a view
that many reasonable human beings in other cultural traditions have upheld.

up his bones. The point of bringing in the idea of Cambridge change was that it promised to elucidate how non-existent things could change for better or worse. It is the last part of this promise that has still not been made good.

This objection is based on a misunderstanding of the proposal. Suppose that Tolstoy's popularity begins to be surpassed by Turgenev's in January 2010. Assume too that Tolstoy would have hated the thought of this happening. When the change occurs, Tolstoy is no more. That does not stop the Cambridge change from occurring. And nor does it stop it from being harmful to him. The harm of a harmful event is not temporally confined to the moment of its occurrence (think of such obvious examples as having an accident or being sacked from one's job; or of somewhat less obvious cases such as failing the exam on which one has spent months of preparation, where the shadow falls retrospectively, making the effort one has put in futile).[17] The bad state of affairs for Tolstoy commences in January 2010. But to say that that is when the harm begins is misleading. That date marks the start of the harmful condition, rather than of the harm. This can be *timelessly* ascribed to Tolstoy.

Thomas Nagel writes that 'it is arbitrary to restrict the goods and evils that can befall a man to nonrelational properties ascribable to him at particular times'. Rather, '[a] man's life includes much that does not take place within the boundaries of his body and his mind, and what happens to him can include much that does not take place within the boundaries of his life' (Nagel 1979: 6). People have hopes and wishes that may or may not be satisfied posthumously. Such future-oriented attitudes are a powerful clue to the social dimension of our existence; persons are essentially social animals, as Aristotle famously said, with a sense of their identity that largely resolves itself into a consciousness of their social roles and relationships.[18] It is hardly surprising that they see their own good and evil as inextricably linked with that of their community, and care what will happen in and to it once they are gone. Death may be the end of us in the literal sense, but what we were and did may resonate for long afterwards and posthumous events occur that

---

17 The latter is not, of course, an instance of backward causation. No event can alter the past but some events can retrospectively affect the significance of what has gone before. (See also note 19, below.)

18 Aristotle, *Nicomachean Ethics*, 1169b (Aristotle 1954: 238). What Aristotle actually said was: 'man is a political creature and one whose nature it is to live with others'.

fulfil or frustrate our lifetime desires. Hence Nagel's observation that things can happen to us outside the temporal limits of our lives. As another recent writer puts it, 'the dead are not just memories', since 'to the extent that you remain (if you do) part of a community, you remain a person, even though a dead person' (Brecher 2002: 115).

We may say, then, that it is bad, not at some particular time or through some particular interval, for Tolstoy that he loses the popularity race to Turgenev, but bad *tout court*. Imagine that, in another turn of fortune's wheel, Tolstoy recovers his position with readers in 2050. We should not say that the harm Tolstoy suffered was confined to the period 2010 to 2050. We should rather say that whilst it was bad for him that his popularity was eclipsed by Turgenev's for a time, the harm was not so great because the eclipse was temporary.

There is nothing very mysterious about the timeless ascriptions of attributes. If we remarked that Rembrandt was a great artist or that Heidegger's prose was obscure we would be taken aback if someone asked us *when* Rembrandt was great or Heidegger obscure. Saying that Rembrandt is great is not like saying that Rembrandt is in the studio. (Note too how odd it would sound to say that Rembrandt was once great but that he is not great now.) Of course, attributes that we timelessly ascribe may pertain to a subject on account of temporally situated features or factors. The paintings that make Rembrandt great and the novels that ground Tolstoy's popularity were produced at specific points in their creators' lives. Likewise posthumous events that have an overall significance for a life may have particular relation to specific acts, states, desires or projects.[19]

Although my examples in this chapter have not all been archaeological ones, I hope that the implication for archaeology should be clear: the disturbance and manipulation of human remains by archaeologists is morally problematic because, *pace* Sir Mortimer Wheeler and other archaeological cavaliers (and cavalier archaeologists), such treatment can

---

19 Reflections of this kind have led me to argue in previous writings that the timing of the harmful and beneficial effects of posthumous events should always be pulled forward to within the subject's lifetime. I now believe that timeless ascriptions of harms and benefits are often more in line with our intuitions, though I continue to think that events after death can bear positively or negatively on the things we do and the ends we pursue during life. Thus (to cite an example I have used before), an author is actually wasting, though he does not know it, the last ten years of his life if the sole copy of the novel that he is writing to guarantee his immortality is destroyed the day after his death. Here one might say that he is harmed during his lifetime *and also* timelessly, in that he fails to acquire the status he has so desired.

be harmful to the subjects.[20] Yet it does not follow that all archaeological work involving human remains should cease. The Vermillion Accord states that respect should be shown to human relics, and to the wishes of the dead concerning their disposition. This brings us back to the question of what precisely such respect requires. Does showing respect preclude all disturbance of the dead or only certain kinds of treatment of remains? If the latter, then what is permissible and what forbidden, and how do we distinguish?

Some would claim that it is always wrong to do harm, and that we should therefore never do anything that harms the dead. (Knowingly and deliberately harming a subject surely qualifies, if anything does, as a form of disrespectful treatment.) However, even if we are persuaded that the dead can be harmed, for the reasons set out in this chapter, we may not be convinced that causing harm is always wrong. Sometimes benefits to some are purchasable only at the cost of harms to others. Only moralists of the severest Kantian stamp hold that we should never cause a minor evil in order to avert a great one or produce a great good. Few people have moral qualms about systems of redistributive taxation that take wealth from the rich in order to provide some social cushioning for the less well off. More controversial is the scenario imagined by Bernard Williams in which a man, Jim, is given the option of shooting an innocent hostage as the ransom price of twenty innocent hostages who will otherwise be executed (Williams 1973: 98–9). Death by shooting can hardly be called a minor evil, yet many think that in the circumstances Jim should shoot the hostage.

These hard problems of ethical theory cannot be relegated to discussion in some philosophical ivory tower: their implications are too important for practice. We may never be in a predicament as harrowing as Jim's but we often face structurally analogous situations in which we have to weigh up competing interests. Archaeologists face a dilemma of this kind when deciding whether to conduct an excavation that disturbs human remains. (Only in those rare instances where they believe that the buried subjects would have had no objection is the moral picture simpler.) That such treatment can harm the dead is not, I suggest, an insuperable moral obstacle to it. But it should certainly give pause for thought. Before proceeding with an investigation, an archaeologist should think about

---

20 In a 1973 radio broadcast Wheeler disclaimed any sense of uneasiness about disturbing the dead, adding that, 'We do no harm to those poor chaps. When I'm dead you can dig me up ten times for all I care.' I owe this reference to Bahn (1984: 214).

the interests of the dead as well as of the living. Admittedly this is easier to propose than perform. How can researchers be sure they are being maximally fair to the interests of both the living and the dead? On what basis should they settle the relative importance to be accorded to the interests of living and of deceased people? Too often the convenient assumption is made that the interests of living archaeologists trump those of dead subjects. Conceivably this assumption is right, but if so it needs to be demonstrated by argument. Much further work is needed in archaeological ethics if these important issues are to be clarified, and the ways of archaeologists vindicated.

ACKNOWLEDGEMENTS

I am very grateful to Sophie Gibb and Chris Scarre for helpful discussion of the themes of this chapter.

CHAPTER 12

Archaeological ethics and the people of the past

Sarah Tarlow

That archaeological practitioners have ethical responsibilities to various present-day groups is almost universally recognised, even if there is some disagreement about the exact nature of those responsibilities, and over how competing claims can be negotiated. Much archaeological legislation, and most codes of practice, also recognise a responsibility to future generations, at least implicitly, in their defence of preservation, conservation and recording. However, the ethical relationship between modern archaeologists and the past people whom they study, and whom in one sense at least they represent, has hardly been considered.

How do, and how should, archaeologists relate to the people they study? There is certainly no agreement on the issue. While it is possible to construct a coherent case arguing that all our ethical responsibilities relate to the present and future, and that the past is a 'resource' to be deployed in line with political aims in the present, others, including myself, have argued that we owe a responsibility towards past people at least as far as concerns the ways we represent them, if not a duty of advocacy. This chapter will contend that ethics are ideological and culturally situated, rather than transcendent and universal, and that because of the pervasiveness of Western, scientific and medical beliefs about bodies, selves, life and death, modern archaeologists' attitudes towards past people may not be coherent and raise problems for our practice.

DO WE HAVE ANY RESPONSIBILITY TOWARDS PAST PEOPLE?

Archaeological ethics depends, at least implicitly, on the recognition that archaeological practitioners in their professional capacity have responsibilities to certain groups, individuals and values. There is, however, limited consensus on who those groups and what those values are, and how responsibilities are best discharged, especially when they appear incompatible with each other.

The ethical orientation of those concerned with archaeological practice has altered and expanded over the last thirty years. Codes of practice in the 1970s were principally concerned with defending the quality of archaeology at a time of increasing professionalisation as the discipline was being drawn into the commercial world. By the 1980s Raab was able to include not only fellow archaeologists and the client amongst the groups to whom practitioners have a responsibility, but also the public (Raab 1984: 58). This again relates to a general shift in the discipline towards 'public archaeology', recognising a need to communicate with and educate a wider public, and with the theoretical and critical attention given to this project within academic archaeology. In the 1990s and into the twenty-first century, the groups to whom we owe a responsibility have again been differently constituted, this time in a way that privileges groups claiming genetic or cultural descent from the people whose remains are the subject of modern study. Others have carried out more comprehensive surveys of the groups to whom we may owe a responsibility, including Pluciennik (2001: 30) who lists collaborative organisations, funding sources, government departments in both his own country and the place of fieldwork, the university and its students, other project members and more generalised or abstracted constituencies such as nations, 'archaeologists', the environment, the archaeological record, the people of the past and those of the future, both of the last two being heterogeneous groups of people.

Nevertheless, most archaeological ethical and legal codes, as well as most archaeological writing, limit their concerns to how we might address the needs of contemporary groups. It is easy to see how living people might be affected, materially or emotionally, by the impact of our research, and to acknowledge their welfare in our planning and practice. A general orientation towards the future is implicit in ethical principles of 'stewardship' and conservation, invoked for example by Lynott and Wylie (2000) and brilliantly critiqued by Hamilakis (1999). The interests of people in the future, whether conceived narrowly as the research community or more broadly as the people of the world, are protected by our current preference for a cautious, preservative archaeology, minimising intervention. If we 'use up' archaeological resources of a particular place or period through destructive research now, there will be nothing left for our successors. Thus, future people, as yet unborn, are the beneficiaries of our ethical conduct now. Protection of the well-being of present and future groups is therefore the main concern of contemporary archaeological ethics, as formulated in codes and regularised through normative practice. What of the past?

THE PARTICULARITY OF ETHICS

This chapter proceeds from an understanding of ethics as ideological, mutable and cultural. I will suggest that we have not formulated a consistent and coherent position in relation to the appropriate treatment of past people. This is partly because the appropriate ethically analogous situations are not always clear, and partly because the contextual ethics for dealing with a modern human body, which underlie much of our implicit and explicit ethical codes, is of limited relevance when dealing with past people. How do we, and how should we, treat past people? Do we indeed have any ethical responsibility at all towards them? Making a coherent philosophical case that past people should be the subjects of our ethical concern is fundamental to the intention of this chapter, but complex and controversial. There are two (or more) grounds arising from contemporary, Western academic thought on which such a claim can be based: first is the argument that Geoffrey Scarre (2003) has recently made, that those engaged in researching the past through archaeology do indeed have an ethical responsibility to past people, based not on some idea of what we owe 'the dead', either as worthy bones or as spiritual ghosts, but on the idea that practices in the present which egregiously flout the values and dignity of past peoples impacts upon them *as living beings* and therefore 'we need to consider the possibility that archaeological investigation does some form of retrospective harm to its objects'. It is therefore unnecessary to share, for example, Tutankhamun's own religious beliefs about the consequences of harm to his body after death to recognise a duty to his remains, because maltreatment of his body would be deeply inimical to a project that was of great importance to him during life (Scarre 2003).

The second line of argument adds to Scarre's discussion another reason for accepting that our research on and writing about past people do have an impact upon them: the important implications of adopting a relational understanding of social identity; that is to say an understanding that people are constituted in part by the way that they relate to others, and that identities are formed by interactions and the understandings of others. 'No man is an *Island*, entire of it self; every man is a piece of the *Continent*', reflected John Donne (Meditation xvii). A 'self' is not entirely invented and performed by a single agent, but is the result of meanings, roles and expectations ascribed by others within cultural contexts. All of us therefore participate in one another. In contemporary social situations my identity is formed by ascriptions regarding gender, age, class and so on as well as idiosyncratic and individual factors. In the case of past people they are constituted as social beings by people in the present, including archaeologists and historians whose research practices attribute meanings to their being and practices in the past. Because social existence is not necessarily the same as or coeval with 'life', people can and do have an existence after death, not necessarily in any spiritual sense, but through their continuous creation and re-creation by people in the present. Our practices themselves then animate the (often) forgotten dead and in one sense bring them into being. However, it is not only scholars who 'create' past people this way; they also continue to have a social existence because of the way they live in the imaginations and cultural productions of wider contemporary society: novelists and novel-readers, TV audiences, film-makers, 'descendants', museum-goers and so on.

Because modern people through their acts of scholarship and imagination give existence to past people, those past people should not be regarded as dead or static but, as social beings, capable of being affected by action or discourse in the present. Because past people then could be said to have existence, although not sentience, in the present, as well as because of the retrospective effect of present practices on past peoples discussed by Scarre, past people could also be considered, alongside sponsors, descendants, academics and so on, as participants in archaeological research in the sense of having a legitimate interest in the research we undertake and its results. Throughout this chapter I will be referring to 'past people' and not to 'the dead' in order to evoke the sense of their social existence.

The large role played by archaeologists and historians, however, in providing material for the cultural after-lives of past peoples is in itself, I think, sufficient reason to claim that we have a responsibility to past people and that there should be an ethical duty to be 'responsible' in the way we produce them. Yet we are not creators; we are not fiction-writers making people out of nothing but our own imaginations. The people we evoke were real people who had real experiences. The question we then have to address is how far that evocation can and should be 'on their terms', as far as that can ever be known (Tarlow 2001b). I shall return to the question of 'ethical representation', not so much to provide a set of answers as to open up some of the problematic and complex issues surrounding our discursive practices.

The foregoing discussion, however, limits the grounds for argument relating to cases I can make on the basis of Western, 'scientific' argument; not considering, for example, religious or spiritual perspectives which might argue that we owe a responsibility to past people because, contrary to our understandings, they are not 'past' at all, but actually present, active and sensible in a theological or spiritual sense. In constructing ethical cases, we proceed from certain culturally specific assumptions about the self, and particular values and ideologies. Williams (1985: 201) makes the point that it is necessary to assume individuals in order to have a philosophy of ethics. But individuals are not always understood the same way, and where our philosophy of ethics requires us to negotiate relationships between people from very different cultural contexts, this limitation is potentially a serious problem. Adherence to particular beliefs about the world and how it works results in specific ideas about how one ought to proceed. For the remainder of this chapter, rather than try to outline any set of principles, responsibilities or practices that 'ought' to constitute ethical practice in relation to past people, I will look at how our particular beliefs about bodies, individuals, life, death, respect, relatedness and other things inform our ethics of practice.

THE SCIENTIFIC, MEDICALISED BODY AND THE TREATMENT OF PAST PEOPLE

One can make a coherent philosophical case that the dead, being insensible of any harm done to their bodies or reputations, need not exercise our ethical scruples; only the living and perhaps those not yet living can be harmed by our actions or utterances. Thus research programmes carried out upon the bodies of past people, or representations constructed of them, can only be unethical if the feelings or interests of living people are in some way harmed by them. Jones and Harris (1998), for example, suggest that archaeologists only need to limit research on the remains of more recently deceased people. Those who are long dead (and therefore do not have descendants who remember them as living individuals) need not concern archaeological ethics; underlying this position, as Scarre (2003) has noted, is the assumption that only the feelings of the living need to be considered in deciding to undertake research on human remains. In contemporary Britain the removal of human remains from cemeteries (to allow development for example) generally only considers the feelings of direct genetic descendants of those buried there and of local religious groups. The expectations those buried in the cemetery would have had during life, and their probable attitudes towards the disinterment and reburial or cremation of their remains, are not considered. Margaret Cox (1996) makes this point forcefully using the example of the clearance of remains from the crypt at Spitalfields church in London. During the eighteenth and nineteenth centuries when the burials were made, cremation was illegal and the majority of English people found it a horrific idea that their bodies might be burned. This, however, was not considered during the crypt clearance exercise and cremation was indeed the ultimate fate of many of the bones; the meaning of cremation for modern people rather than the likely feelings of past people informed practical decisions about the appropriate treatment of human remains.

The attitude that the dead are dead and cannot be harmed or affected by anything done to their bodies or said about them or their lives is based, however, not on universal common sense, but on a specific view of the living and dead body constructed through medical science (e.g. Martin 1990; Shilling 1993), where existence equates unproblematically with a live body identified by biological processes like circulation and respiration. However, this is not the only way to understand what constitutes existence or personhood. Anthropologists and archaeologists have been able to demonstrate that, in some cultures, the 'person' extends beyond the body to include material objects, or the person may have an essence or a number of essences that may exist before and after the life of the body.

The modern body is understood as a 'universal' body, known through medicine and scientific inquiry. A number of assumptions about the modern body are so natural to us that they are not part of most people's discursive consciousness at all: for example, that each person should have ownership of her own body and that things should not be done to it without her consent; that the individual self can be equated with the individual body; and that the death of the body can be clearly located at the moment when the key organs of the body cease to function (although continuing discussion in medical ethics about how the exact moment of death is defined demonstrates that even these taken-for-granteds are not entirely solid). These ideas about the body, living and dead, along with our social values of autonomy, consent, privacy, respect and so on, have a major impact in shaping codes of ethics and codes of practice relating to medical research and to research on human tissue more generally. Beliefs and values evident in the discourse of medical ethics are also apparent in archaeological ethical writing and implicit in our practice, although it is not possible to say how far archaeologists have drawn directly upon medical ethics in constructing their own codes. Some of the key principles are considered below.

Justice and benefit

Modern ethical codes designed to guide research in biological and medical science using tissue from living or newly deceased humans cluster around a number of principles, including professional integrity and competence; informed consent; beneficence; the paramount importance, in principle, of the well-being of the human subject; restriction of commercial and profit-making applications of research; safeguarding the dignity and privacy of human subjects; justice (that those submitting to research stand to benefit from the results of that research); accuracy and honesty in published research results; and others. These principles seem to divide between those which affect the decision to proceed with a given programme of research at all (that is, a judgement on the worth of the research), and measures concerned with safeguarding the interests of the research subjects and minimising or mitigating possible impact on them given that the research is, in principle, justified.

The principles of justice and beneficence, and the paramount concern with the well-being of human subjects, affect the primary decision to carry out research at all. Research on humans should have a demonstrably beneficial consequence and that consequence should be of benefit to the human subjects. It would not be just, for example, if research involving the use of tissue samples from a third world population resulted in a medical treatment that was only available to wealthy Westerners. Nor should it be appropriate for individuals or companies to make huge profits by exploiting genetic properties, such as natural immunities, of people who donated samples and did not stand to benefit from the results of the research.

Common to all medical codes of ethics is a tendency to *refrain* from approving research on human subjects unless its value can be demonstrated in terms of the above criteria. The first guideline produced by the Medical Research Council (Britain) relating to the use of human tissue samples for research says:

Research should only go ahead if the potential benefits outweigh any potential risks to the donors of the samples. The physical risks involved in donating samples for research will usually be minimal, but the risk that information from laboratory tests on a sample might harm the donor or their interests must not be forgotten.

There is thus a presumption that research may be exploitative and prejudicial to its human participants, and only where there is a clear expectation that the good resulting from research will outweigh possible harm to the subjects, and measures have been put in place to minimise any negative impact on the subjects, should it proceed. All medical and bio-science ethical statements emphasise the need for intended outcomes that contribute something worthwhile to the sum of human knowledge, beyond sensationalism or the demonstration of whizzy technique.

Benefit, though it is not made explicit in these statements, is a culturally specific idea and would be considered to be something that materially improves the quality of human life and health. In medical science this is meaningful (although not uncontested), but it is a difficult game for archaeologists to play. We are constantly being asked to defend the worth of the discipline (by funders, the government, our universities and so on). Some archaeologists have tried to justify the pursuit of archaeological knowledge on the basis that it gives us information of material relevance to our understanding of the consequences of human actions in the past and thus has a bearing on decisions that will affect our future (Bahn and Flenley 1992; Barker 1996) or even assist in the resolution of pressing environmental or medical problems in the present (e.g., Erickson 1988; Locock 1998: 13). I have yet to see a positive development in social, environmental or medical policy in which archaeologically derived knowledge was necessary. Most arguments for which archaeology is deployed are more effectively made using contemporary social, political, medical or legal science, and evidence from remote history or prehistory is unlikely to provide a sufficiently close analogy for a modern situation. It is not necessary to consider the archaeology of Easter Island, for example, to demonstrate the result of 'the experiment of permitting unrestricted population growth, profligate use of resources, destruction of the environment and boundless confidence in their religion to take care of the future' (Bahn and Flenley 1992: 213).

However, this does not then mean that archaeology has no value. If we challenge the very instrumental idea of what constitutes a benefit, the 'good' of archaeology can be argued to lie in terms of the generation of knowledge itself as a benefit – to the academic community, and perhaps to other communities too. In some situations archaeological research provides political benefits for nationalist, regionalist or other forms of identity politics, which may or may not be a good thing, depending on the context. Simply recognising the breadth of human difference, a project to which archaeology, along with anthropology, can make a major contribution, is a politically worthwhile goal. There is also a strong argument that says that the increase of knowledge and improvement of understanding are in themselves good and worthy ends. The enhancement of knowledge through archaeological research need not then be instrumental in the production of some immediate social or political good, but can be an end in itself simply because, like all academic endeavour, it is a means by which human potential can be fulfilled.

If archaeology, although inherently neither good nor bad, has the potential to be worthwhile and of value, is the potential for harm occasioned by archaeological research, particularly when it entails the use of human tissue, serious enough to prevent such work proceeding? The harm occasioned to groups in the present largely consists of emotional damage done by offence to people's feelings, principles or values regarding appropriate treatment of the dead. It may also consist in the exacerbation of political and social problems if differential treatment of the dead corresponds to asymmetries in political power. Where no major harm is done to the interests of living or future people, however, can past people themselves be 'injured' by research on their tissue? Physically, 'injury' must result from any destructive technique because the integrity of the remains is compromised. However, removal of tissue samples does not cause corporeal pain to a dead body, so 'injury' must be considered in terms of whether an attack on the integrity or peace of the body offends the beliefs of the deceased. Thus research on human remains involves negotiating between the presumption that the will of the past individual is probably not being carried out, and the benefits that may result from such research in the present. It may be that 'harm' done to past people is less serious than harm done to living people because the potential for injury, although present, is not so great.

The National Statement on Ethical Conduct in Research Involving Humans produced by the National Health and Medical Research Council of Australia is a thorough and excellent statement of principles which should guide the development and approval of research involving human subjects (or 'participants', as the authors prefer). The preamble recognises a number of major principles from which guidelines for professional conduct should grow: essentially beneficence, justice and competence.

Research merit is a related issue, although one that throws up other problems than the identification of meritorious research. Who is to assess the merit of research, particularly in subjects like archaeology where work is not likely to result in lives saved or a just society? Our peers? A committee of worthies? Public concern?

Respect

An implicit recognition of the 'rights' of past people might account for stipulations that human remains should be treated with 'respect' (as in the Vermillion Accord). Of course this need not be on account of the past people themselves; rather it could relate only to the concerns of present-day people who might be shocked, affronted or hurt if human remains were treated inappropriately. However, normal practice in anglophone archaeology is that human remains in the field and in the lab are treated in a way that conventionally denotes 'respect' in the cultural terms of the excavators: 'nicknaming' skeletons is not usually acceptable; bones are not used as props in practical jokes; they are handled with care and used in serious and scholarly contexts (although this has not always been the case). Nevertheless, respectful treatment of human remains reflects contemporary ideas of what is appropriate. 'Respect' is differently constituted in different cultural milieux, however, and what denotes respect in modern Britain or America might not be appropriate elsewhere (Tarlow 2001b). For example, in the modern west 'respect' for the dead is signalled by adopting a demeanour of solemnity and seriousness, dressing soberly and using lugubrious or no music; in many Latin American countries bright colours, festive music, dancing and food may attend the ceremonies of the dead without implying any disrespect. Archaeologically and ethnographically there are many known contexts in which the bodies of the dead are regularly removed from their places of entombment in order to participate in ceremonies (as in the case of dead Incas – Sillar 1992) or dancing (as with the Malagasy ancestors – Bloch 1971), which do not denote any cultural disrespect. It may be that in their culturally situated demonstrations of respect, modern archaeologists are protecting their own feelings from outrage, rather than those of past people.

Consent

The ethical principles by which modern biological research on human tissue is conducted attach great importance to the issue of informed consent. If the person is not in a position to give consent for research on his own tissue (e.g., because of mental incapacity, immaturity, unconsciousness or because they have already died) then consent is obtained from a near relative. Is consent an issue when dealing with people who died some time ago? Assuming that most people who find themselves the subject of archaeological research have not explicitly or implicitly given consent in their lifetimes, is it a reasonable ethical requirement to obtain consent from somebody on their behalf? There are some knotty problems here. Even in the present, the power of next of kin to give consent for medical or research procedures is not uncontested; in many cases there may be a better basis for the representation of an individual's wishes than consanguinity. Nevertheless it is genetic proximity that is valued in medical ethics and the same is true of archaeological codes of ethics and in legal frameworks such as the original formulation of the USA's Native American Graves Protection and Repatriation Act (1990) which gives particular weight to 'the lineal descendants' of the person whose remains are in question, and secondarily to the Indian group who owns the land on which the remains were discovered (NAGPRA 1990). In fact the primacy given to close genetic kinship is not a universal understanding of relatedness or of how ownership or rights over human bodies should operate, and in many cases notions of 'rights' or 'ownership' in relation to human bodies would not be meaningful at all.

Thus, the understanding of relatedness and of the appropriate representative of past people evident in NAGPRA may not always be the most appropriate. In fact, it would not be arrogant to suggest that since archaeologists spend so much time, energy and imagination on knowing past people, they are in a better position to represent past people than most (*contra* the disingenuous position that the views of those who spend their whole lives researching the past are no more authoritative than those of anyone else – see Cooper this volume). Modern ethical codes, moreover, tend to represent consent in highly individualistic terms which may not be appropriate in considering past cultural contexts, or even in the present. This is recognised in the preamble to the Australian National Statement on Ethical Conduct in Research Involving Humans, one of the most nuanced and sophisticated statements of ethical practice:

The basic principles recognised by the authors of the Belmont Report reflect the high value that the dominant Western tradition places on individual autonomy. It is important for researchers to recognise that this is not the only way in which human interaction and responsibilities are conceptualised. In many non-Western societies, and in some communities within Western societies also, the rights and autonomy of the individual are complicated and constrained, to a greater or lesser extent, by those of related individuals and groups with specific authority over that individual. Thus researchers need to be aware of individuals' rights within specific local and national socio-cultural contexts.

It is also the case that non-Western traditions as well as more recent developments in social research practice have often emphasised the importance of community values. Members of societies see value in collective activities well beyond the value of each person's individual share of the benefits.

Consent, then, appears to be a difficult principle to enforce in the case of archaeological samples. Original consent is unobtainable; proxy consent begs the question of who is fit to give or withhold it. Sometimes, however, there are pretty clear archaeological indications that, even though a person did not expressly prohibit archaeological research, they would not have welcomed any post-mortem disturbance: heavy slabs, stones or mounds of earth may cover the entrance to a place of burial; historical sources may reveal an anxiety about preserving the integrity of the corpse (as with Pharaonic Egypt or postmedieval Britain). In these cases research on human tissue surely constitutes pretty flagrant disregard for the wishes of the deceased. That it frequently proceeds regardless (in the case of Egyptology, for example) suggests that, for practising archae-ologists, it is not any desire to act within the wishes of the deceased that drives them to seek permission from descendants, but to avoid political conflict in the present.

Dignity and privacy

A recent paper in *Science* laments the absence of ethical guidelines relating to what the authors call 'biohistory' – scientific research on tissue from human bodies aimed at illuminating significant or sensational aspects of the lives of historical figures (Andrews *et al.* 2004). Considering a number of recent and widely publicised pieces of research, such as testing Albert Einstein's brain to find the source of his genius, or the investigation of a possible line of descent from the illegitimate offspring of Thomas Jefferson and his slave Sally Hemings, the authors worried that the privacy of historical figures was infringed by the release of this information, and were concerned that there were no ethical guidelines to control such work. In fact, there are plenty of ethical guidelines on the treatment of the remains of past people, but sadly none of the eleven authors of this two-page article looked at the ethics codes of the Society of American Archaeology, the World Archaeological Congress or any other major archaeological organisation, instead reviewing codes of bodies such as the Council of American Survey Research Organizations, the Oral History Association and the College Art Association. It is interesting that the authors felt that infringement of privacy or violation of dignity was a serious ethical concern, even when dealing with people from different cultural contexts.

Are there details of past people's lives too intimate to publish? What if archaeological research, for example, can tell us what diseases affected an individual, whether an unmarried woman had children, or a man fathered illegitimate offspring, what food he ate, that he or she wore false teeth or hair, had lice, worms or syphilis, a third nipple or any other deformity? Does it make a difference whether that individual is anonymous? Do we need to know these things and do we need to publish them? Is it ever acceptable to make a person's naked body available to public view? Like respect, our ideas of what threatens human dignity are culturally constructed: while I might find it acceptable to appear bare-headed before strangers, I would not want the world in general to know that I suffered from parasitic infections; for past people with different cultural values it might have been the other way round. Dignity is closely linked in modern Western minds with privacy, and the cultural valorisation of privacy is also evident in modern codes of medical ethics which greatly value the preservation of anonymity. Privacy, though an important value to the modern Westerner, is not a universal priority and there is a good case to be made for saying that, in some contexts, 'fame' or 'celebrity' gained by public display in various media would have been valued positively by those subject to it, and 'privacy' would not have been a meaningful term. Again it seems there can be no universal guideline on when and how privacy and dignity should be respected in the case of past people.

Justice, and accurate and honest representation

I am considering these together because the justice of using past people's remains in research must be assessed on the quality of discourse that arises from that research: past people do not stand to benefit in any other way. A basic principle of medical research using human subjects or human tissue is that the donors of tissue should not be disadvantaged by the result of the research. However, the importance of just representation is not one that has been addressed in the discourse of archaeological ethics. In archaeological ethics our notions of justice and fairness have been restricted to the management of relationships between archaeologists and certain privileged contemporary groups. Thinking through how the principle of justice relates to past people again makes us confront the ideologically specific understandings of what is just, or what is 'true', that we bring to our work.

Can one use archaeological research to construct unflattering depictions of the humans in question? The related issues of accuracy and honesty are easier to address in the sense that, for all sorts of reasons unrelated to the responsibility we might owe to past people, we try to represent our primary research results honestly – i.e., not cheating, fabricating evidence or plagiarising research (and clauses proscribing such behaviour feature in many of the earliest archaeological codes of ethics). However, the results of archaeological inquiry are more ambiguous than the results of a clinical trial: the truth is rarely evident except at the most banal level – interpretation and hypothesising are necessary in the construction of archaeological narratives and accounts; even without the intention of deceit, archaeologists can rarely swear by the accuracy of what they write, so perhaps it is necessary here to uncouple accuracy from honesty and agree that while the latter is a principle to which we should subscribe, the former is hard to assess and impossible entirely to satisfy. It would also be fair to say that the particular 'truths' purveyed by archaeologists will also be shaped and perhaps constrained by the context of publication (readership, germane political or social issues and so on), which is not to say that 'anything goes' in archaeological publication, but that there are many grounds besides accuracy which shape our discourse (Lampeter Archaeology Workshop 1997).

In addition to, and not entirely separate from, the use we make of human remains is the use we make of past people's lives and selves in the stories we tell about them. We invoke their practices, impute to them motivations, emotions, values and deeds in order to fulfil other goals of selling books, pulling in visitors to museums or heritage attractions, and building careers. We necessarily use past people in our representations for our discipline to exist at all (in common with history and all other past-oriented subject areas); at issue here is how we can do this ethically.

The dead cannot answer back and they cannot tell their own stories. All we know of them, their lives and thoughts, is mediated by what they produced or the traces they left, and by the interpretative strategies of those in the present charged with their representation.

Laws of slander and libel protect the reputations of living people from unsubstantiated allegations about their motives, conduct and relationships, but there are no similar legal safeguards protecting past people. As archaeologists the object of our research is to find out about the lives of past people, to identify their practices, and to construct hypotheses about their values, motivations, social relationships and so on. Because of the time differences, often great, between our subjects and ourselves these are necessarily tentative: certainty is not within the capacity of most archaeologists. These days most academic archaeologists would also reject closed and final notions of historical truth in any case, and not just because of the fragmentary nature of archaeological evidence. The stories we tell about past people are always provisional and open rather than fixed truths. Given both the difficulty of uncovering detailed information about past people, especially those who lived in the remote past, and the impossibility of fully recovering, representing or recognising complex historical 'truth', how can responsible representation be attempted?

This topic has been touched on before (Tarlow 2001b). The ethical limits of archaeological representation have recently been considered by the contributors to *The Responsibilities of Archaeologists* (Pluciennik 2001), but although one can identify occasions of 'unethical representation', in the sense that they provoke feelings of wrongness, exactly who is betrayed by partial or inappropriate representation is not always clear. For example, early attempts to 're-create' Colonial Williamsburg as a 'living history' museum were criticised on the grounds that the past they portrayed was an exclusively white one; even after the incorporation of African Americans into the museum, the representation of race there has been considered deficient (e.g., Leone 1981; cf. Blakey 1990). Is this because the interests of *modern* African Americans are not well served by representations that ghettoise or sideline black history, or because the experiences of black Americans *in the past* have been distorted and those past people thus wronged? Another example would be the way that some discussions of the significance of gender in human evolution have attracted criticism for representing women as passive reproducers, in contrast to active men achieving evolutionary developments (Hager 1997). Does this criticism gain its cultural force because it seeks just recognition for the achievements of *past women* or because women *in the present* are affected by prevalent views of the deep past? Of course, the two positions are not exclusive: recognition that representations of the past have contemporary political and social consequences does not preclude a desire to represent past people 'justly'.

One hardly notices the conventions of a discipline until they are broken. For me, this happened when I read Tim Taylor's idiosyncratic book about the archaeology of death, *The Buried Soul* (2002). Discussing Ibn Fadlan's well-known description of a funeral among the Rus, Taylor is obviously outraged by the cultural apologism of most interpretative accounts of the ritual which involved the brutal rape and murder of a young slave girl. Taylor argues that in fact the treatment of the slave girl was aimed at the annihilation of her soul, and that while the dead chief was bound for Valhalla the girl was only an element of the ceremony, ultimately subject to violent destruction of both body and soul. It is, however, rare for an academic archaeologist to take a position of moral censure when discussing past practices. How appropriate is Taylor's insistence that the slave girl's death should be interpreted as the cruel ritual murder of somebody who, as a woman and a foreigner, was a double outsider to the world of the Rus elite? Does our responsibility of representation mean that we have to act as advocates for the people of the past, defending their cultural practices or at least using frameworks of moral relativism to apply different standards to their behaviour than those we would expect of our contemporaries? In the case of Taylor's response to Ibn Fadlan's description, one important issue is that Taylor believes that the interests of the past people involved in the funeral were not homogeneous; they were not practising a ritual in which all willingly participated and from which all benefited. Instead he believes that there were imbalances of power which left women and foreigners at particular disadvantage; he could thus be seen as redressing an injustice which has in the past misrepresented the experience of non-dominant members of society by naturalising them within the conventions of ethnographic relativism and perpetuated a classic masking ideology. For Taylor, the question of how this event should be represented ethically arose because of the heterogeneity of past experiences. A funeral among the Rus was a very different experience for somebody eating and drinking in the party than for the slave girl about to be murdered. Similarly, life in Colonial Virginia was not the same for a well-to-do white towns-man as it was for a slave. Women in the palaeolithic, we may imagine, did not necessarily evaluate their worlds in the same way that their brothers did (or, indeed, their contemporary 'sisters'). One aspect of ethical representation then, keenly experienced if seldom voiced, seems to be that archaeologists should try to ensure that the experiences of a particular and limited set of people in the past are not allowed to represent the whole of their society. This is not, however, to say that archaeologists should only represent the oppressed, or that the life of a small farmer or a slave was in any way more 'authentic' than that of a landowner or a queen. Rather, the past was a complicated place; people were different and their experiences, understandings and evaluations varied. To homogenise that variability surely would be a betrayal of our responsibility of representation.

CONCLUDING COMMENTS

The treatment of past people in archaeological practice is problematic. The ethics on which we depend, either formally constituted as the codes of a particular professional body or alliance, or enacted through professional practice, arise from particular local and limited ideological assumptions. Despite our best intentions (and most practising archaeologists are genuinely concerned to minimise conflict, offence and injustice), our attitudes to past people, based on the principles arising from these shared assumptions, are likely to draw us into conflict with other people whose ethics are differently constructed and are not based on a Western medicophilosophical tradition. In fact, the dependence of ethics on shared cultural beliefs also gives rise to problems in negotiating between groups in the present whose expectations of ethical practice arise from different beliefs. Larry Zimmerman (1987), for example, has demonstrated that incommensurate understandings of time and history handicap negotiations between archaeologists and Native Americans over the issue of research on human remains, and in fact may make a 'compromise' solution to disputes impossible. I have suggested before that the free and open dissemination of knowledge, a core value of most Western archaeologists, can sometimes conflict with other value systems which control and limit the set of people who can have access to knowledge that may be sacred or otherwise special (Tarlow 2001b). Similarly understandings of relatedness, respect, descent and death are culturally variable, as the present discussion has demonstrated, and thus ethics arising from them may vary significantly between societies and over time.

There cannot be comprehensive answers to questions of ethical practice. Even in the present these are hard to maintain, and given the enormous cultural diversity of past peoples, and the number of other groups besides archaeologists who have interests in how past people are represented, no stock answers will be appropriate. This led me in the past to reject the use of codes of ethics to guide our behaviour (Tarlow 2001b). However, Martin Hall recently made the point that rejection of codes of ethics may be easier in politically stable and long-established nations of the north and west; by contrast, in African countries, for example, the institutions and traditions by which social justice can be ensured may be weaker or inaccessible (Hall 2002). Nevertheless, ultimately Hall demonstrates that the implicit or explicit ethics by which African archaeologies have historically operated have differed according to the political and cultural position of the 'reference group' for whom the archaeology is primarily meaningful. Thus a commitment to 'ethical' practice has historically produced very different styles of work, from colonialist and missionary ethics, through instrumental, nationalist ethics to the modern South African valorisation of scientific research deemed 'apolitical' and value-free by its practitioners. Ethics therefore cannot be fixed and final and must be situational, but within this, suggests Hall, there is a place for explicit statements of ethical frameworks. On occasion an explicit statement of consensus about the nature of ethical research may be appropriate to a particular political situation of real difference in social, legal, economic and cultural power. There may therefore be local and limited contingencies in which codes of ethics may be instrumental, but I still see no justification for any code of ethics that pretends to encapsulate global or timeless ethical truth.

ACKNOWLEDGEMENTS

Many thanks to Chris and Geoffrey Scarre for inviting me to contribute to this volume, and particularly to Geoffrey for sharing so freely his thoughts and ideas. The thoughts expressed here have also benefited greatly from discussions with Dave Edwards and Mark Pluciennik. I am very grateful to the Leverhulme Trust for awarding me a Leverhulme Research Fellowship, during which this chapter was completed.

PART IV

The common heritage of humankind?

CHAPTER 13

A plea for responsibility towards the common heritage of mankind

Sandra M. Dingli

Is technological reproduction the way forward for archaeological sites and remains in the future? During past years a number of sites have been, wholly or in part, closed for public viewing, because of the impact that factors such as weather and mass tourism have had on them. However it is not difficult to envisage a scenario in twenty years' time when the only way in which the general public could learn more about archaeological heritage would be either through glass cases in museums or by means of virtual reality trips to the sites.

Is this the way that archaeological sites and artefacts will be made available to the public in the future, as a series of 'experiences', where one's location is irrelevant to the location of the site being 'experienced' and where the negative impact of mass tourism on sites will be diminished or totally eliminated? Or do we prefer another – cleaner but perhaps more 'authentic' – version of present-day reality, a 'see but don't touch' version where what 'we' say is what 'you' must believe and where the public is transported through 'time-carts' and regaled with a univocal version of times past?

These 'experiences' are already evident today and will be even more predominant in the future. They provide easy alternatives to present scenarios where the past has either been buried by previous civilisations – as where we are told, for example, that 'Fort St. Angelo in Malta was built in the 16th century on the site of an old Roman temple which, in turn, had been built on the site of a Phoenician temple' – or where limited underground archaeological remains are available for viewing in old European towns where they were later built over by subsequent civilisations.

My main concern is that archaeology is fast becoming a diminishing resource. Experience over the years has shown that more stringent measures need to be taken to protect and conserve what gives meaning to our lives and tells us more about who we are and where our roots lie. This is important not just for ourselves but also for future generations.

I would like to make a plea based on the premise that archaeological sites and artefacts should be conceived as the common heritage of humankind,[1] a concept to which archaeology often pays lip-service, but the historical significance and implications of which are not always well understood. This will be carried out in full recognition of the fact that a number of conventions and codes of ethics have been drafted and ratified as efforts to prevent the ravages of time, nature and humanity from further destroying that which should be safeguarded because of its vital significance for humankind. I do not wish to claim that this chapter comprehensively covers the whole subject under consideration. My proposal is meant to be taken as an exploratory exercise with the aim of provoking further discussion and research on the subject.

The ideas of John Locke and Hugo Grotius on the concept of property are relevant in this regard. I first discuss their views, following which I review the main points contained in the proposal presented by Malta to the United Nations in 1967 concerning the oceans as common heritage. A summary of the contents of three conventions that I consider to be most relevant where the subject of protection of cultural and natural heritage is concerned follows. I then return to a discussion of my proposal that archaeological heritage should be considered as forming part of the common heritage of humankind, after which I briefly discuss the concept of stewardship.

JOHN LOCKE (1632–1704) AND HUGO GROTIUS (1583–1645) ON PROPERTY

Until recently archaeologists took John Locke's ideas on property in a literal sense and this is how a number of world-famous museums made their acquisitions in the past. John Locke is well known for his ideas on the origin of private property and property rights. In *Two Treatises of Government* Locke states that 'Whatsoever, then, [someone] removes out of the state that Nature hath provided and left it in, he hath mixed his labour with it, and joined to it something that is his own, and thereby makes it his property' (1991: 130). This is described as an 'original

---

1 I use the gender-neutral term 'common heritage of humankind' in this chapter and reserve the use of 'common heritage of mankind' for quotations and historically relevant situations.

law of Nature for the beginning of property, in what was before common' (1991: 131).

Although Locke first applies this law of Nature to produce and animals, he then extends it to land as he states: 'As much land as a man tills, plants, improves, cultivates, and can use the product of, so much is his property.' One proviso Locke includes is that this should not prejudice others, in that 'there was still enough and as good left, and more than the yet unprovided could use' (1991: 132).

Although it is known that Locke had the large undeveloped expanses of the American continent in mind when he wrote the *Two Treatises*, he was also aware of 'surplus' land in Spain, as he states: 'the extent of ground is of so little value without labour that I have heard it affirmed that in Spain itself a man may be permitted to plough, sow, and reap, without being disturbed, upon land he has no other title to, but only his making use of it' (1991: 134).

Property rights play a central role in Locke's ideas on the setting up of civil society, where 'the chief end . . . is the preservation of property' (1991: 158). Today his ideas may provoke a wry smile. Some reflection, however, will reveal that, at least in some parts of the world, Locke's 'original law of Nature' is still in force, in particular in areas where the looting of archaeological sites takes place. It was, up to not very long ago (and perhaps still is in some parts of the world), common practice for those who discovered archaeological treasures to 'help themselves' to whatever they pleased and to apply the saying 'finders keepers' as their maxim. Most major European museums, for example, have built extensive collections in the wake of colonial conquests of other territories.

I clearly remember the situation in Malta just a few decades ago when unique prehistoric sites such as some of the megalithic temples were not protected or enclosed by a boundary wall, access was not controlled, and visitors could 'help themselves' to anything they could lay their hands upon that was easily portable such as potsherds, fossils, carvings and bones. The concerns of the Oxford don, Reverend Professor Sayce, penned in 1883, still rang true. He had deplored the fact that in Malta 'the peasants on whose land [the monuments] are naturally regard them merely as useful quarries for stone and attractive for picnic parties' (Vella and Gilkes 2001: 355).

Times have changed and attitudes have changed too, but Locke's state of nature, where appropriation was equivalent to ownership, raises a number of questions that are relevant where the present situation concerning ownership of archaeological sites and artefacts is concerned.

Although ownership as appropriation nowadays goes against the principles of modern democracy, nobody can deny the fact that pebbles, seaweed and driftwood appropriated from a public beach for the creation of an artistic artefact are not items that anyone would claim to have a property right upon – except for the artist who appropriated them in order to compose her work.

Locke's ideas concerning private property can be contrasted with those of Hugo Grotius or Huig de Groot of Delft, a leading Dutch statesman, scholar and jurist. Grotius was the first to put forward the idea that that which cannot be occupied, 'or which never has been occupied, cannot be the property of anyone, because all property (*properties*) has arisen from occupation' (quoted in Tulley 1980: 70).

Grotius claimed that 'all that which has been so constituted by nature that, although serving some one person, it still suffices for the common use of all other persons, is today, and ought in perpetuity to remain in the same condition as when it was first created by nature'. He applies this to the seas which everyone possesses a claim to use. Since property follows occupation, according to Grotius, the seas belong to no one and may be used, *but not occupied*, by all. His claim is that 'the sea is common to all, because it is so limitless that it cannot become a possession of all' (Tulley 1980: 70). This results in the concept of the sea as forming part of what is now known as the 'common heritage of mankind'.

THE COMMON HERITAGE OF HUMANKIND

In 1967 the Government of Malta proposed the concept of the 'common heritage of mankind' to the United Nations in the context of a new law of the sea. Some of the main elements implied in the concept of common heritage include:

1 non-appropriation by any individual or state, i.e., the right to use resources but not to own them;
2 international management on behalf of the interests of mankind as a whole (including future generations);
3 benefit sharing by mankind as a whole;
4 to be used only for peaceful purposes.

Although the concept of common heritage is generally applied to areas or regions which have not been appropriated by individuals or states, such as the oceans or outer space, I would like to argue that the application of this concept to archaeology could serve a number of useful purposes. If concern is being felt and awareness raised with regards to archaeology as a diminishing resource, why should the concept of responsibility towards archaeological sites and artefacts not be expanded to incorporate a definite (and possibly consensual and international) commitment towards the common heritage or common concern of humankind? This should be viewed in the light of the present unsustainable position where archaeological heritage is concerned.

Archaeologists often ask the question: Who owns the past? If the past can be considered to be owned by no one, it could be seen as representing the cultural heritage of *all beings who have ever lived on earth or will live on it in the future.*

Following the initiative taken by Malta in November 1967, in 1970 the United Nations General Assembly adopted Resolution 2749 declaring the common heritage of mankind as the fundamental principle governing the exploitation of the international seabed. This principle is enshrined in the 1982 United Nations Convention on the Law of the Sea but elements from this concept are also evident in the 1972 UNESCO Convention for the Protection of the World Cultural and National Heritage.

It is to be kept in mind that agreement on the formulation of a global policy for archaeology in this regard would certainly not be an easy task, although efforts in the right direction have already been made by both UNESCO and the Council of Europe. Efforts would certainly have to be made and safeguards formulated to avoid the possibility of stronger nations working only for their own interests and not for the common interest of humankind. Past experience in other areas has demonstrated (for example, in the economic and political spheres) that merely preserving the interests of the most powerful would inevitably prove to be self-defeating.

If archaeological heritage is conceived as the common heritage of humankind, it could be managed at a global, regional, national and local level (1) for the benefit of humankind as a whole, (2) conserved for future generations and (3) reserved for exclusively peaceful purposes, in line with ideas put forward in connection with the concept of the oceans as the common heritage of mankind.

In order for these suggestions to be effective, the principle of subsidiarity should be introduced and those concerned with the management of sites and artefacts should be viewed as stewards, rather than owners, who manage the archaeological resource entrusted to them for present and future generations.

COMMON HERITAGE OR WORLD HERITAGE?

At this point some readers may argue that such a concept is not new and is already enshrined in existing conventions such as the European Convention on the Protection of the Archaeological Heritage (Council of Europe 1992) and the World Heritage Convention (UNESCO 1972). The Society for American Archaeology has a clearly formulated document, 'Principles of Archaeological Ethics', and other conventions exist which are easily accessible in the literature.

The UNESCO 1954 Hague Convention for the Protection of Cultural Property in the Event of Armed Conflict, for example, states that 'damage to cultural property belonging to any people whatsoever means damage to the cultural heritage of all mankind, since each people makes its contribution to the culture of the world' (quoted in Tay 1985: 122). The 1972 UNESCO Convention for the Protection of the World Cultural and Natural Heritage stresses in its preamble that 'the deterioration or disappearance at any time of the cultural or natural heritage constitutes a harmful impoverishment of the heritage of all nations' (UNESCO 1972: Preamble).

Common heritage could be seen as an 'assumption (embedded in legislation pertaining to sites and artefacts) . . . [in] that these constitute the common heritage of all' (McBryde 1985: 2). Mulvaney notes that the 1970 UNESCO Convention on the Means of Prohibiting and Preventing the Illicit Import, Export and Transfer of Ownership of Cultural Property incorporates three notions at the international level:

Firstly, that at one level of 'ownership', the relics of the past belong to the heritage of all people. Secondly, that international understanding and mutual tolerance can be promoted through this common inheritance. The final concept, however, accepts that a national cultural identity is desirable and that it can be fostered through the influence of the individual national inheritance.

(Mulvaney 1985: 90)

Are existing regulations, conventions and ethical codes adequate to protect and conserve archaeological sites? Would the inclusion of the concept of archaeology as the common heritage of humankind in these documents be one move towards better conserving, protecting and sustaining diminishing archaeological resources? The implication is not that existing conventions should be done away with – that would be an unnecessary and useless exercise. What is necessary is an elaboration of three particular factors that are not generally spelt out in sufficient detail in existing conventions, these being (1) the concept of common heritage, (2) the concept of stewardship and (3) suggestions as to how these concepts could be implemented in a practical manner.

It is at this stage pertinent to summarise what I consider to be the three most relevant existing conventions,[2] following which I shall review in more detail the concept of common heritage of humankind as applied to archaeological heritage and briefly discuss the concept of stewardship.

REVISED EUROPEAN CONVENTION ON THE PROTECTION OF THE ARCHAEOLOGICAL HERITAGE (MALTA, 1992)

This significant Convention is applicable to signatory states, members of the Council of Europe. It is mainly concerned with European responsibility for the protection of the archaeological heritage in an attempt to reduce the risk of deterioration and to promote conservation by encouraging exchange of experts and of experience. The Convention is well aware of present threats and problems and its Preamble acknowledges:

that the European archaeological heritage, which provides evidence of ancient history, is seriously threatened with deterioration because of the increasing number of major planning schemes, natural risks, clandestine or unscientific excavations and insufficient public awareness.
(European Convention on the Protection of the Archaeological Heritage [Revised] 1992: Preamble)

The aim of the Convention is 'to protect the archaeological heritage as a source of the European collective memory and as an instrument for historical and scientific study'. Archaeological heritage includes 'structures, constructions, groups of buildings, developed sites, moveable objects, monuments of other kinds as well as their context, whether situated on land or under water' (Article 1, Definition of the Archaeological Heritage).

Measures for the protection of archaeological heritage include mandatory licensing concerning the authorisation and supervision of excavation. The use of metal detectors without specific prior authorisation is prohibited.

---

2 The relevance of other existing conventions that are not discussed in detail here, such as the UNESCO Convention on the Means of Prohibiting and Preventing the Illicit Import, Export and Transfer of Cultural Property (1970), should also be acknowledged.

The Convention claims that 'the archaeological heritage is essential to a knowledge of the history of mankind'. Moreover, it is 'important to institute, where they do not yet exist, appropriate administrative and scientific supervision procedures, and . . . the need to protect the archaeological heritage should be reflected in town and country planning and cultural development policies' (Preamble). It is to be noted that most stipulations are general in nature and precisely how these recommendations should be implemented, what 'appropriate' supervision procedures should cover, or how responsibility should be apportioned is not specified.

In my view, the shortcomings apparent in this Convention are mainly two: (1) the Convention is limited only to signatory states, members of the Council of Europe or other states party to the European Cultural Convention, and not to the global community, and (2) the suggestions, recommendations and stipulations are very general in nature and are not supported by more concrete and practical suggestions or measures which could be implemented by signatory states.

UNESCO (1972) CONVENTION CONCERNING THE PROTECTION
OF THE WORLD CULTURAL AND NATURAL HERITAGE

This Convention is concerned with the conservation of both natural and cultural heritage sites of 'outstanding universal value' in an attempt to conserve them, preserve them for future generations and share responsibility for them among the international community. Such cultural and natural sites will be considered as a common heritage to be treasured, protected and preserved for all humanity as unique testimonies to an enduring past through cooperation among nations.

Archaeology is specifically included in the definition of the cultural and natural heritage. This includes 'archaeological sites which are of outstanding universal value from the point of view of history, art or science' (UNESCO Convention 1972: Section 1, Article 1). The main aims of the Convention are the identification, protection, conservation, presentation and transmission to future generations of the cultural and natural heritage.

Once again, the contents of this Convention are commendable, but most of the articles consist of general statements that are open to interpretation. These include the stipulation that each state, party to the Convention, shall endeavour, in so far as possible, and as appropriate for each country . . . to develop scientific and technical studies and research and to work out such operating methods as will make the State capable of counteracting the dangers that threaten its cultural or natural heritage . . . to take the appropriate legal, scientific, technical, administrative and financial measures necessary for the identification, protection, conservation, presentation and rehabilitation of this heritage; and . . . to foster the establishment or development of national or regional centres for training in the protection, conservation and presentation of the cultural and natural heritage and to encourage scientific research in this field.

(Section 2, Article 5)

No specific suggestions or recommendations are given as to how this could be implemented. Could this be interpreted as an implicit attempt to respect the individual sovereignty of signatory states?

The Convention stipulates the setting up of a World Heritage Committee, to which states will submit inventories of sites suitable for inclusion on the list of World Heritage Sites for consideration by the Committee who, in turn, will establish, update and publish a list of properties considered as being of outstanding universal value.

In a similar manner, the Committee is in duty bound to establish, update and publish a List of World Heritage in Danger, this being composed of natural or cultural heritage for which assistance has been requested owing to various possible threats that include rapid urban or tourist development, accelerated deterioration, the outbreak of an armed conflict or natural disasters such as floods or earthquakes.

The Convention includes the proviso that property forming part of the natural or cultural heritage not included in either of the two lists 'shall in no way be construed to mean that it does not have an outstanding universal value for purposes other than those resulting from inclusion in these lists' (Section 2, Article 12).

EUROPEAN LANDSCAPE CONVENTION (2000)

Although restricted in region to member states of the Council of Europe, this Convention is very broad ranging in content. Landscapes contribute to human well-being and to the consolidation of the European identity and are considered to be an important contribution to the formation of local cultures and as a basic component of the European natural and cultural heritage (European Landscape Convention 2000: Preamble).

The distinction between the UNESCO (1972) World Heritage Convention, which is international in scope, and the European Landscape

Convention, which is regional in scope, is recognised in the following terms:

The Council of Europe convention can be regarded as complementary to the Unesco one. As regards its substantive scope, the Council of Europe Convention covers all landscapes, even those that are not of outstanding universal value, but *does not deal with historic monuments*, unlike the Unesco convention. Similarly, its main objective is not to draw up a list of assets of exceptional universal value, but to introduce protection, management and planning rules for all landscapes based on a set of principles. (Article 12, Clause 78, emphasis added)

It is a pity that 'historic monuments' are excluded from this Convention, as they are provided for under the UNESCO Convention. However it appears as though historic monuments that are *not of exceptional universal value* are excluded from both Conventions. Cooperative action between UNESCO's World Heritage Committee and the European Landscape Convention's Committees of Experts is not excluded.

The Convention acknowledges that 'the quality and diversity of European landscapes constitute a common resource, and that it is important to co-operate towards its protection, management and planning' (Preamble). The exclusion of historic monuments remains, however, unexplained. Such a comprehensive document could easily have built upon the strengths of previous Conventions and attempted to overcome the shortcomings.

The Convention binds parties to undertake 'to recognise landscapes in law as an essential component of people's surroundings, an expression of the diversity of their shared cultural and natural heritage, and a foundation of their identity' (Article 5, clause (a)). Parties to the Convention undertake 'to establish procedures for the participation of the general public, local and regional authorities, and other parties with an interest in the definition and implementation of . . . landscape policies' (Article 5, clause (c)).

These measures are spelt out in detail in Article 6 where the first sub-section is involved with awareness-raising among civil society, private organisations and public authorities of the value of landscapes. Therefore, 'Every citizen has a share in the landscape and in the duty of looking after it, and the well-being of landscapes is closely linked to the level of public awareness. Campaigns for informing and educating the public, elected representatives and associations about the value of present and future landscapes should be organised in this perspective' (B. Explanatory Report, II. Aims and Structure of the Convention, Article 52). Moreover, 'Before any measure is taken for the protection, management and planning of a landscape, it is essential to make clear to the public what objectives are being pursued' (Article 59).

Regular meetings to devise coordinated programmes and the monitoring of the application of the Convention, together with allocation of responsibility for the monitoring, application and subsequent follow-up, are spelt out in detail (Articles 66–70).

Consultation, dialogue and democratic procedures are nowadays essential where the implementation of conventions is concerned. The European Landscape Convention recognises that 'The legal, administrative, fiscal and financial arrangements made in each country to serve the Convention's implementation should fit in as comfortably as possible with that country's traditions' (Article 34). Public authorities are encouraged to adopt policies and measures at a local, regional, national and international level for protecting, managing and planning landscapes throughout Europe (Article 25), and the active role people take in the decision making process is acknowledged.

Rather than placing emphasis on landscape as the common heritage of humankind, the European Landscape Convention acknowledges that, 'In their diversity and quality, the cultural and natural values linked to European landscapes are part of Europe's common heritage, and so European countries have a duty to make collective provisions for the protection, management and planning of these values' (Article 30). The Convention considers European ideals to be common heritage as it states: 'The Council of Europe member States, anxious to promote through international agreements *the ideals which are their common heritage*, possess a precious asset in the landscapes' (Article 36, emphasis added).

Responsibility in the Convention is related to subsidiarity as 'responsibility for action relating to landscape lies with public authorities not only at national and international levels, but also at local and regional levels' (Article 34). Responsibility for the implementation of protection, management and planning of landscapes is recognised as being more effective if this is entrusted '*to the authorities closest to the communities concerned*'. Moreover, 'Each country should set out in detail the tasks and measures for which each level – national, regional or local – is responsible and should lay down rules for inter-level co-ordination of such measures' (Article 49, emphasis added).

The scope of this Convention is broad and wide-ranging. A number of its recommendations could be extended to include archaeological heritage. An extension of its international dimension to incorporate countries other than European and further emphasis on the concept of both landscapes and archaeological heritage as common heritage of humankind could further be included in this Convention.

On a national level Malta's Cultural Heritage Act 2002 (*Suppliment tal-Gazetta tal-Gvern ta' Malta* 2002) makes use of the term 'cultural heritage' to incorporate the idea of natural and man-made landscapes, prehistoric archaeological sites and Baroque heritage, and it incorporates some of the more salient features of the European Landscape Convention to cover historic monuments.

While not wishing to sound paternalistic or defensive of measures that spell out in detail who is responsible for what and how particular problems should be addressed, I believe that the recommendations put forward in the European Landscape Convention could provide a realistic and practical model if adapted to include archaeological heritage.

ARCHAEOLOGICAL HERITAGE CONSIDERED AS THE COMMON HERITAGE OF HUMANKIND

Why should archaeological heritage be considered as common heritage of humankind? Can the concept of ownership be applied to a collective term such as 'humankind'? Is 'ownership' relevant in this context? The concept of common heritage is generally attributed to that which impedes appropriation owing to the physical impossibility of doing so or to legal provisions. Under the heading 'Property, Law of' the *Encyclopaedia Britannica* states:

Apart from human bodies and members or parts thereof, there are things that may not become objects of property rights either because of a physical impossibility of appropriation or because the law so provides. Running waters, the atmospheric air, and the open sea, for example, may not be appropriated in their entirety by an individual or artificial person. According to traditional civilian ideas, these are common things and insusceptible of any ownership.

Although archaeological heritage is not included in the examples cited above of objects that could be considered to be common heritage, Arvid Pardo, Malta's Ambassador to the United Nations in the 1960s and a key player in Malta's proposal to incorporate 'common heritage of mankind' into the law of the sea, includes underwater archaeological heritage as one of the many resources to be found in the depths of the oceans. He states:

It may also be convenient to refer . . . to the archaeological treasures lying on continental shelves and on the ocean floor. I have seen an apparently authoritative statement to the effect that there would appear to be more objects of archaeological interest lying on the bottom of the Mediterranean than exist in the museums of Greece, Italy, France and Spain combined. (Pardo 1975: 5)

The final document states that all archaeological objects found on the ocean floor are to be 'preserved or disposed of for the benefit of mankind as a whole' (United Nations Convention on the Law of the Sea 1982: Articles 149, 303).

Pardo was responding to expressions of suspicion, on the part of a member of the House of Representatives of the United States, that Malta's proposal to the General Assembly of the United Nations concerning the seabed and the ocean floor was premature and rushed, and that the Maltese government's action may have been instigated by the British government.

What motivated the Government of Malta to put forward the proposal that the oceans should be considered as common heritage of mankind? Security and greed on the part of the superpowers were the major considerations, including fear of appropriation and subsequent occupation as a result of advances in science and technology. The realisation of such fears could have led to an escalation of the arms race and increased world tensions, where traditional sea-faring activities would be curtailed and where the growing danger to the marine environment through radioactive and other pollution would be dramatically increased.

The long-term objective that was proposed consisted of the creation of a special agency 'with adequate powers to administer in the interests of mankind the oceans and the ocean floor beyond national jurisdiction'. The concept of sovereignty would be replaced by a form of jurisdiction that would be assumed by the agency that would be empowered to act 'as a trustee for all countries over the oceans and the ocean floor. The agency should be endowed with wide powers to regulate, supervise, and control all activities on or under the oceans and the ocean floor' (Pardo 1975: 39). The result would consist in the practical application of the concept of 'common heritage of mankind' to the seabed and the ocean floor which would be used exclusively for peaceful purposes and for the exclusive benefit of humanity as a whole.

Do these arguments make sense when applied to archaeological heritage? One interesting argument claims that 'Archaeological laws throughout the world have been conceived with an antiquarian, rather than an archaeological, point of view and that is why discussions about cultural property take place. They should be seen as the protection of a world cultural resource and as the defining of fields and subjects for important research' (King 1999: 207). Another argument views archaeological heritage on similar lines to environmentally endangered species – if considered as non-renewable resources, archaeological heritage cannot be replenished or replaced, once destroyed. This would lead to our speaking of 'endangered cultural heritages, endangered cultural pasts, or even, more simply, endangered cultures' (Warren 1999: 19).

In a discussion on cultural property as a non-renewable resource, Warren draws attention to the fact that 'ownership' would not be the right concept to apply, as

they [cultural properties] are not anyone's property and no one can properly be said to own them. Our relationship to them is more like that of a steward, custodian, guardian, conservator, or trustee than of a property owner. Since these cultural properties ought to be preserved yet are no one's property, no one has a right to them. Hence, no one has a claim to their restitution or restriction based on an alleged right (e.g., right of ownership) to them. Their protection and preservation is a collective responsibility of all of us as stewards.

(Warren 1999: 19)

The assertion that 'no one has a claim to their restitution or restriction based on an alleged right' since the concept of 'ownership' is no longer applicable to cases of archaeological heritage may possibly provoke indignation on the part of ethnic groups who claim ownership of what they perceive to be their own cultural heritage and which is conceived to be theirs by right.

Warren notes that the construal of the argument concerning ownership of cultural property is misconceived since there are alternative ways to conceive the debate and 'the dominant perspective seems inadequate by itself as a theoretical framework for understanding and resolving so-called cultural property issues' (Warren 1999: 21).

Archaeology has learnt a great deal from past experience and great strides have been made in this regard. It is now common practice for archaeologists to consult and collaborate with people from the cultures concerned before and during excavations and to respect their wishes especially where human remains and burial objects are concerned. Indigenous cultures may however still find it rather difficult to reconcile local interests with global impositions. It may, in such cases, be pertinent to question whether differences of culture or tradition are being unduly accentuated. A plea to reason concerning excessive ideological claims over the past may be appropriate, and this is cogently expressed by the Samoan scholar Albert Wendt:

It will not do to over-glorify the past. The present is all that we have and we should live it out as creatively as possible. Pride in our past bolsters our self-respect which is necessary if we are to cope as equals with others. However, too fervent or paranoid an identification with one's culture – or what one deems to be that culture – can lead to racial intolerance and the like. This is not to claim that there are no differences between cultures and peoples. Or to argue that we abolish these differences. We must recognise and respect these differences but not use them to try to justify our racist claims to an imaginary superiority.

(quoted in Mulvaney 1985: 27)

Can one speak meaningfully of the concept of the past as common heritage? Can agreement be reached that a relevant common humanity exists? Warren draws attention to the fact that Marxists and feminists would challenge such a claim which would, in their view, presuppose a mistaken ahistorical notion of what it is to be human. She states:

For many Marxists, humans are always historically and materially located; 'human nature' is always a response to the prevailing mode of economic production in a society or culture. On this view, there is no such thing as a 'human nature' or 'common humanity', if by that one means a transcendental ahistorical, asocial 'essence' which all humans have, independent of their particular concrete and historical location. Similarly, many feminists have argued that in contemporary culture, thoroughly structured by such factors as sex/gender, race, and class, there is no such thing as a *human simpliciter*: all humans are humans of some sex/gender, race/ethnicity, class, affectional preference, marital status, etc. (Warren 1999: 5–6)

Arguments in favour of conceiving archaeological heritage as the common heritage of humankind would surely be rejected by Marxists and feminists. Warren however recommends the adoption of an integrative perspective to the understanding and resolution of cultural heritage issues. This would enable us to conceive of the dispute as *one of preservation* rather than as one of ownership of the past, and it would encourage the conception of the resolution of cultural properties conflict from a perspective of a compromise or consensus model of conflict resolution (Warren 1999: 22).

Andrew Selkirk ironically views the UNESCO World Heritage Convention as a 'beauty contest' for individual countries to list as many World Heritage Sites as possible. He draws attention to the fact that a listing on UNESCO's list of World Heritage Sites inevitably carries with it elements of contradiction, as designation ensures listing which, in turn, inevitably increases visitors. Selkirk advises caution in the consideration of the nomination of further World Heritage Sites as this often results in a bureaucratised system where national government takes over responsibility from local management.

Hodder notes that 'European Heritage' assumes a common heritage for all Europeans despite the fact that Europe itself is a historical construction. He further states that 'the term "heritage" conjures up a commercialized world open to the market, a "theme-parking" of history and the past'. This turns history into a distant world which we are protected from and which we are encouraged to visit on vacation where we sit in 'time-cars' in a 'postmodern pastiche of depthlessness' and travel to 'distant worlds miraculously reconstructed for us' (Hodder 1999: 163).

Hodder is aware of the contrasting sense of 'heritage' as relating to ownership, roots and origins. In many countries national heritage is still defined and controlled by the state. The designation of sites as World Heritage Sites may therefore result in the reinforcement of local identities and claims. Hodder recognises the central role of the past in empowerment. He states: 'Throughout the Americas and in Australia, the past is being used to justify claims to land, rights and resources and new alliances are being formed between indigenous peoples. In such cases, marginalized groups are undoubtedly empowered through their engagement with their heritage' (1999: 163).

This is, however, only a short-term perspective which is superficial and temporary. In the longer term, although lip-service is often paid to local culture and traditions, the dominant discourse and methodologies invariably end up moving back to the Western conception of archaeological science. There are very few differences between the Western way of doing science and that of indigenous peoples, and Hodder observes that 'I can think of no example in which minority groups within these societies have developed their own approaches to excavation. In the end, it could be argued that the approaches and techniques of the dominant culture will prevail. Over the long term, there is a homogenization of techniques and terms' (1999: 163). Hodder further states:

Some governments resist world heritage designation since it allows intervention by international agencies in the internal affairs of national heritage programmes. Both the world heritage status and commercial exploitation may lead to the wrenching of a site away from a local meaning and identity. Local people may find traditional understandings of sites denied or disrupted by external agencies. Local heritage identities easily become fragmented by the global process.

(1999: 203)

Both the positive and negative effects which emerge from the relationship between community heritage and the leisure industry are acknowledged by Hodder. He notes that tourism fosters employment and growth in local communities, and may enhance the identity of the community through the management of heritage. Negative aspects include the overriding of local rights, the invasion of external commercial interests and the subsequent trivialisation of community claims and sensitivities.

One final consideration where common heritage is concerned is that of future generations. Emmanuel Agius claims that:

The resources of the earth belong to all generations . . . it is therefore our responsibility to pass them on in good and enhanced condition to posterity. We have an obligation founded on social justice to share the common heritage with all the present population as well as with future generations. (Agius 1994a: 61)

Agius draws attention to the fact that the concept of common heritage does not involve a new theory of property but implies the *absence* of property. He views the key consideration as being *access to common resources* rather than to ownership.

This view reflects that of Karen Warren previously discussed. Warren raises the point that those who have responsibility to preserve cultural heritage could be conceived as stewards of that heritage. Talk of property rights and ownership of that heritage is inappropriate and misguided.

STEWARDSHIP

How could the recommendations that I am suggesting be implemented? I strongly believe in the principle of subsidiarity and that, in line with the European Landscape Convention, responsibility and management of archaeological heritage should be apportioned to entities at the global, national, regional and local level. This would involve the principle of 'stewardship', with preservation and conservation being foremost on their list of priorities.

The concept of 'stewardship' is discussed by other contributors in this volume. Therefore it would be superfluous to rehearse similar arguments.

It is, however, important to mention that an interesting statement concerning 'stewardship' is included in the 'Principles of Archaeological Ethics' of the Society for American Archaeology:

The archaeological record, that is, in situ archaeological material and sites, archaeological collections, records and reports, is irreplaceable. It is the responsibility of all archaeologists to work for the long-term conservation and protection of the archaeological record by practicing and promoting stewardship of the archaeological record. Stewards are both caretakers of and advocates for the archaeological record for the benefit of all people; as they investigate and interpret the record, they should use the specialized knowledge they gain to promote public understanding and support for its long-term preservation.

(Society for American Archaeology: Principle 1)

Archaeologists are moreover urged to 'enlist public support for the stewardship of the archaeological record' (Principle 4) and to treat intellectual property 'in accord with the principles of stewardship' (Principle 5). The Principles acknowledge the fact, where education and outreach are concerned, that:

Many publics exist for archaeology including students and teachers; Native Americans and other ethnic, religious, and cultural groups who find in the archaeological record important aspects of their cultural heritage; lawmakers and government officials; reporters, journalists, and others involved in the media; and the general public. (Principle 4)

Cooperation with such publics and the dissemination of information to such publics is therefore essential.

CONCLUSION

How useful could the application of the concept of common heritage applied to archaeological heritage be? As stated in the introduction, the aim of this chapter is to explore concepts and provoke discussion, rather than comprehensively to resolve the whole issue. It draws on existing conventions in line with the claim that 'UNESCO has always had close links with philosophy and ethics. The ideals underlying its Constitution are drawn from the well-spring of philosophical tradition. And ever since it was founded, the Organisation has had recourse to philosophy in putting them into effect.' In line with this claim, I would like to conclude by proposing six factors that could be considered as valuable in the application of the concept of 'common heritage' to archaeological heritage.[3]

Archaeological heritage is a rapidly diminishing resource

There is no doubt that archaeological heritage is a rapidly diminishing resource. Measures that have been taken so far to safeguard and protect this heritage are commendable but have not resolved chronic problems such as looting, vandalism, overcommercialisation and poor public awareness of its value. We should therefore view archaeological heritage on similar lines to endangered species and, accordingly, ensure that global measures for its protection are taken to safeguard the culturally endangered common heritage of humankind.

The value of archaeological heritage is both local and global

In the local context, Malta has had three nominations included in the UNESCO World Heritage List. These are the city of Valletta, the Hal Saflieni Hypogeum, and the Megalithic Temples which actually consist of six archaeological sites. There have been improved efforts to preserve and safeguard the sites. Improved supervision, access and signage have been incorporated and protective shelters are planned for three sites in the short term.

However, public perception of the value of such heritage leaves a great deal to be desired, as it is generally considered as beneficial only for tourists. But whose archaeological heritage is it really? The authorities are severely challenged by restricted resources and tend to place more emphasis on the role of heritage in attracting revenue through tourism. Anthony Pace recently stated:

Sadly, Malta's heritage has often been characterised exclusively as a most useful attraction for the tourist industry. The benefits of heritage as a factor of social cohesion should not be underestimated. The engagement of the Maltese public in heritage matters is still very uneven. In general there often seems to be a lack of understanding that heritage is primarily 'public heritage'.

(*State of the Heritage Report* 2003: 5)

Heritage is not only 'public heritage' but it should be considered as part of the common heritage of humankind, to be appreciated on both a

---

3 Most of the discussion of the six factors is based on examples drawn from Malta since that is the territory with which I am most familiar and these examples adequately underline the points I wish to make.

global and a local level, in a concerted effort to conserve and protect that which has become a rapidly diminishing resource. It is therefore important to foster better understanding of the values and the benefits of archaeological heritage both on a local and on a global level.

Understanding common heritage leads to economic development and a better quality of life

The *State of the Heritage Report* claims that 'The protection of the cultural and natural environment is rarely seen as an integral element of well-being, a factor of economic growth and an essential ingredient to a quality of life' (2003: 5). It further notes that:

Malta is heavily loaded with responsibility in ensuring adequate conservation for its known heritage . . . The known cultural sites and monuments are not only at risk due to over-development, but also through problems of preservation. To this effect, it is necessary that a monument protection programme be developed to account for the state of conservation of individual sites and monuments.

(2003: 11)

Lack of adequate resources is undoubtedly a problem and

an argument has yet to be articulated to support the view that Malta's economic development has much to gain from enhanced protection and management of the cultural heritage. Economic performance can be improved if the cultural heritage sector is provided with the right resources to develop in a proper way. In essence, economic performance can be enhanced if images of the decay of our heritage are replaced by perceptions of conservation and a general care of the cultural environment. (2003: 47)

Heritage Malta has certainly done a great deal since it was established in 2002. The acceptance and thorough understanding of the application of common heritage to the archaeological heritage can lead to economic gains with benefit to the public as a whole, resulting in a better quality of life.

Acceptance of the concept of common heritage reduces ideological and political motivations

The concept of appropriation of the past has often played a major role in the political and social context. It is well known that 'New visions of the past, or new versions of the past, may serve social and political ends, and a people may be alienated from its past in the process' (McBryde 1985: 8).

Malta, a British colony until 1964, has lived through various shifts in the interpretation of its archaeological heritage. The Germans conceived the megalithic temples as prehistoric in 1901. The British demonstrated interest mainly in their attempts to prevent the Germans from excavating in 1914. Sir Gerald Strickland in 1921 was intent on (mistakenly) demonstrating that the Maltese shared a Phoenician origin with the British, following Caruana's claim in the nineteenth century concerning the Phoenician origin of the Maltese megalithic structures. The Italians sought to demonstrate that Malta was the cradle of the Mediterranean in 1935 (see Vella and Gilkes 2001). Paul Sant Cassia argues that Malta's megalithic temples 'never became a symbol of nationhood' because Christianity 'acted as a barrier to a fuller identification with, and understanding of the pre-Christian period' (Sant Cassia 1993: 358).

It is to be hoped that global acceptance of the concept of common heritage for archaeological sites would go a long way towards eliminating such politically and ideologically slanted tendencies.

The avoidance of the stereotyped 'theme-park' syndrome can come about through understanding archaeological heritage as common heritage

It is important to look towards the future in a serious attempt to address problems where archaeological heritage is concerned. Is the future we wish to move towards composed of stereotypical and bland theme-parks that reproduce sites that have been irreversibly damaged or lost? Or should we aim for a future where archaeological heritage is given its due recognition on all counts, where it is considered to belong to no one, yet where it creates a sense of global solidarity owing to its being considered to be part of the common heritage of humankind? Management of resources would be conducted on a global, national, regional and local level and would incorporate democratic collaboration with interested publics.

The concept of 'common heritage of humankind' creates a shift in mentality from 'global village' to 'global humanity'

Technology and improved means of communication have turned today's world into a global village. This facilitates the use of the term 'humanity' – we all belong to one human species regardless of race or religion. When travelling overseas to visit historical places of interest we often marvel at the achievements that humanity has succeeded in producing. When disaster strikes it is as a collective global humanity that sorrow, anger or indignation are expressed, in particular when, through the irrational action of extremists, yet another archaeological site is irreparably damaged or lost. This sense of 'global humanity' can be translated into the concept of 'common heritage of humankind' also considered as a 'common good'.

Agius defines 'common good' as 'that order in the community by virtue of which every member of society can experience an adequate quality of life' (Agius 1994b: 69). This concept evolved during the sixties from a national to a global level as a result, Agius notes, 'of the newly awakened sense of interdependence which led to the notion of the "family of nations"' (1994b: 68). The holistic perspective of this concept is important as 'Environmental issues have shown that the common good of a particular society cannot be separated, first from the common good of the world community, and secondly from the common good of the human species' (1994b: 69).

Although common good generally refers to the natural environment, Agius maintains that 'We, as a species, need for our survival not only a natural but also a cultural environment. Cultural resources are essential for the well-being of the human species' (1994b: 62). Such cultural resources can and should be conceived as the common heritage of humankind which should also be conserved for future generations. Agius reminds us that:

We, as human species, hold the natural and cultural environment of our planet in common, both with other members of the present generation and with other generations, past and present. At any given time, each generation is both a custodian or trustee of the planet for future generations and a beneficiary of its fruits. This imposes obligations upon us to care for the planet and at the same time gives us certain rights to use it. (1994b: 63)

Property is an important concept — but archaeological heritage that is of value to all humanity should be conceived as the common heritage of humankind as it is a diminishing and endangered resource. Responsibility towards the archaeological heritage conceived as the common heritage of humankind should therefore be assumed at a global, national, regional and local level, and common concern should be accorded to the value of such heritage for the well-being of humankind. If nothing much is done about the present situation, what future lies in store for us?

ACKNOWLEDGEMENTS

The author is grateful to the following persons for commenting on a draft version of this chapter: Professor Joe Friggieri, Dr Nicholas Vella, Professor Peter Serracino Inglott (all from the University of Malta), Ms Antoinette Caruana (Heritage Malta), Ms Patricia Camilleri (The Archaeological Society) and Mr Carmel Bonello. Full responsibility for the opinions and interpretations expressed in this chapter rests solely with the author herself.

CHAPTER 14

The ethics of the World Heritage concept

Atle Omland

[T]he day may yet come when the United Nations flag will fly over cultural sites and natural areas of the World Heritage, constituting a system of international parks and landmarks transferred to the U.N. by member states.

(Meyer 1976: 63)

When the American lawyer Robert L. Meyer in 1976 presented the UNESCO 1972 World Heritage Convention, he expressed the hope that objects of world heritage would one day be transferred from the national state to the international community, reflecting the optimism common at the time that globalisation would encourage the progressive unification of human interests. Developments in media and communications promoted the sense of belonging to a *Global Village* (McLuhan 1962) and the ideal of a *One World Man* (Mumford 1961: 573). The recognition of a global shared present influenced current interpretations of the past. It thus became natural to think that archaeological resources should 'serve as symbols not of nations, but of the common human interest' (Lipe 1984: 10), while the study of general scientific laws in archaeology should remove the political constraints of the past and return the discipline to a 'universal humanism' (Ford 1973: 93).

Although peoples of the world indisputably share a common present, globalisation's discontents have increasingly voiced their concerns during the 1990s. Whilst global economic injustice has been especially in the critics' sights (e.g., Stiglitz 2002), there have also been reactions against the global homogenisation of culture that emphasise the value of diversity and the local dimension (Hall 1991: 33). The World Heritage concept, which initially challenged the national view of cultural heritage, has accordingly been challenged in the name of local and indigenous interests, and pressing questions have been raised about its meaning and ethical status.

THE WORLD HERITAGE CONCEPT: BACKGROUND AND SUCCESS

The World Heritage concept rests fundamentally on the idea that cultural heritage can be held in common (e.g. UNESCO 1960; 1970: 48; 1982: 13), although the term *common heritage* is not used in the Convention text, but rather 'world heritage of mankind as a whole' (UNESCO 1972a: Preamble). This idea of a common heritage is founded on the notion of a relationship of belonging between the preserver and the preserved that was formulated and criticised by, among others, Friedrich Nietzsche (1844–1900): 'By tending with care that which has existed from of old, he [the antiquarian] wants to preserve for those who shall come into existence after him the conditions under which he himself came into existence – and thus he serves life' (Nietzsche 1997 [1874]: 72–3).

UNESCO expressed a similar relationship between the preserver and the preserved two years before the adoption of the Convention: 'as the duty of conserving common property, mankind recognized its own oneness through time and space, through the centuries and the nations, and proclaims the unity of its destiny' (UNESCO 1970: 48).

The concept of a common heritage has been used in the preservation rhetoric since the eighteenth century. The Swiss jurist Emmerich de Vattel (1714–67) applied the common heritage concept in 1758 to protect cultural heritage in cases of war (Jokilehto 1999: 281–2; Williams 1978: 6), and it was employed under the French Revolution to depoliticize art and prevent iconoclasm (Gamboni 1997: 31–6; Jokilehto 1999: 71–2; Sax 1990). John Ruskin claimed in 1849 that buildings belong to 'all the generations of mankind who are to follow us' (Ruskin 1911: 225). The importance of the common heritage concept increased after the establishment of UNESCO in 1945 and the international action to preserve the Nubian remains threatened by the building of the Aswan Dam in the 1960s, while the adoption of the World Heritage Convention in 1972 represented a global acknowledgement of the concept. The Convention is today a definite success story, ratified by 178 States Parties accepting that 'parts of the cultural or natural heritage are of outstanding interest and therefore need to be preserved as part of the world heritage of mankind as a whole' (UNESCO 1972a: Preamble). These States Parties acknowledge the international interest in sites on the World Heritage List, which comprises after the latest additions by the international World Heritage Committee in July 2005 a total of 812 sites located in 137 States Parties. Of these 628 are considered as cultural sites, 160 as natural sites and twenty-four as mixed cultural and natural sites (UNESCO 2005).

Although the World Heritage Convention is globally recognised, the meaning and success of the World Heritage concept are not straightforward to assess. Many archaeologists wrongly view World Heritage designation in terms of a meaningless beauty contest between nations (Cleere 1993a: 123). In contrast, the view to be defended here is that the World Heritage concept is an important one that prompts greater attention to cultural heritage at local, national and international levels. However, the work of UNESCO has in practice clouded the issues by trying to acknowledge at once both the sovereignty of the States Parties that own the sites *and* their status as pieces of World Heritage (cf. UNESCO 1972a: Article 6). Further, the concept has sometimes acquired local and specific resonances that differ from those intended by UNESCO. Consequently the growing literature on the subject embodies a variety of different approaches to the World Heritage concept:

1 *Promotional literature, coffee-table books, glossy magazines, travel literature and newspaper articles* (e.g., Abate 2002; Anker 1997; Cattaneo and Trifoni 2002; Swadling 1992; the periodical *World Heritage Review* published by UNESCO since 1996). These publications provide information that promotes the Convention and often encourages people to visit World Heritage Sites. Designation may seem an innocuous and neutral act, but newspapers can be both proud and critical when they write about sites in their own country.

2 *Literature written independently by people who work in the UNESCO system* (e.g., Cleere 1995, 1996, 2000, 2001; Pressoyre 1996; Prott 1992a, 1992b; Titchen 1995, 1996; cf. Jokilehto 1999: 281–92; Wheatley 1997). This literature critically discusses the Convention and its sustaining ideals, but mainly supports its foundation.

3 *Literature on international cultural heritage law* (e.g., Jote 1994: 245–56; Meyer 1976; Prott and O'Keefe 1989: 31–6; Tanner-Kaplash 1989; Williams 1978: 52–66). Legal consequences of the Convention are discussed, usually highlighting its importance as a successful international conservation tool.

4 *Managers and researchers of World Heritage Sites* often refer to the World Heritage concept. Being proud that 'their' sites are part of a World Heritage, they also discuss local issues and the complex management of the sites (e.g., Woodward 1996). Some get involved in the work of UNESCO or its consultative bodies. An example is the Zimbabwean archaeologist Webber Ndoro who, whilst aware of the problems of the international contra the local interest in World

Heritage Sites (e.g., Ndoro 1994, 2001; Ndoro and Pwiti 2001), still works for improving conservation and the greater representation of Sub-Sahara African cultural heritage on the List.[1]

5 *The independent writer on the World Heritage* (e.g., Ashworth 1998: 117–18; Boniface and Fowler 1993; Carman 2002: 11, 68–70; Dahlström 2003; Eriksen 1996: 81–4, cf. 2001; Fontein 2000; Harrison and Hitchcock 2005; Hewison 1989: 22; Hodder 1999: 162, 202–5; Lowenthal 1998: 239–43; Meskell 2002; Omland 1997, 1998, 1999; Ucko 1990: xviii; cf. Wright 1998). People who are not associated with UNESCO often comment on UNESCO's attempt to create a World Heritage, usually taking a critical stance on the Convention. Scholars doing research on World Heritage sites have also sometimes sounded a cautionary note about international interest in the sites (e.g. Ranger 1999: 287–90; Ucko *et al.* 1991: 255ff).

Since the publications referred to above seldom discuss the ethics of the World Heritage concept in general, it is the various faces of the concept and its ethics that will be scrutinised in the following pages.

THE MANY FACES OF THE WORLD HERITAGE CONCEPT

The view to be defended here is that the World Heritage concept has many different faces, and that what in one context is ethically just may be morally problematic in another. To show this, I will discuss various aspects of the World Heritage concept, interpreting the common World Heritage as a shared heritage (cf. Tanner-Kaplash 1989: 51).

A shared global responsibility YES

A common World Heritage can be interpreted in terms of a shared global moral obligation to protect the cultural heritage of all peoples of the world. The Convention is from this perspective a global ethical solution to the worldwide destruction of sites, expressed in at least two different ways.

International assistance for protecting World Heritage sites NO
Establishing an international fund was an important rationale behind the adoption of the Convention (Titchen 1995: 40ff). The World Heritage Fund fulfils the global moral obligation of international protection, while

---

1 Among other things through the Africa 2009 programme (http://www.iccrom.org/africa2009/ home.asp).

participation under the Convention also allows bi- and multilateral contacts between the States Parties to protect the World Heritage.

It is still doubtful if the Fund is an efficient tool for preserving the World Heritage, and States Parties have had a mixed attitude towards contributions. During the final drafting of the Convention several countries did not support compulsory contribution, in contrast to less wealthy countries (UNESCO 1972b: 1110, 1113, 1117–18). The Fund also had a financial crisis in the mid-1980s (UNESCO 1984: §4), and States Parties have probably sometimes given voluntary donations to influence decisions, e.g., before the controversial nomination in 1987 of the new city of Brasilia (UNESCO 1987: §26). Further, sites are not identified according to the need for international assistance and several are located in wealthy countries.

Respect for the cultural heritage of others YES

A duty of the States Parties to respect and avoid damage to World Heritage sites is a second aspect of the shared global responsibility. The Convention is mainly a tool to protect the cultural heritage in peacetime, but the States Parties are also obliged not to damage World Heritage Sites on the territory of other States Parties (UNESCO 1972a: Article 6).

States Parties do not always acknowledge this obligation, and the US in 1972 expressed the view that the Convention should not attempt to 'impose or govern obligations in cases of armed conflict' (UNESCO 1972b: 1124). World Heritage Sites have also been difficult to protect in cases of war, especially during internal conflicts when, ironically, designation can mark them out for destruction (e.g., Cleere 1992; Chapman 1994; Coningham and Lewer 1999; Gamboni 2001; Meskell 2002; Pressouyre 1996: 10–11; Prott 1992b; Prott, de la Torre and Levin 2001; Šulc 2001).

Another contradiction is that many States Parties have not yet signed up to the 1954 Hague Convention, that aims at protecting the cultural heritage in cases of war, or the 1970 UNESCO Convention on Illicit Export, Import and Transfer of Ownership of Cultural Property. Although unwilling to implement the restrictions of the 1954 and 1970 conventions, these States Parties gladly participate in the World Heritage Convention that gives them prestige and a presence in the global ecumene.

Shared cultural resources

The shared global responsibility has another facet: it reveals itself as an interest (in some cases as a right) of the world community to claim access to shared cultural resources. Some scholars use this internationalist view to defend the international trade in cultural property (e.g., Merryman 1983, 1985, 1996). On the other hand, the illicit trade in cultural property is also viewed as a stealing of the world's cultural resources, which ignores the importance of *in situ* preservation and violates other people's access to the shared resources. The importance of access was a particularly prominent theme during the preliminary work on the Convention in the US in 1965, when it was suggested that 'certain natural, scenic, and historic resources are unique and irreplaceable and *should be shared by all peoples* of the world'. An international fund should then 'help the *host* countries to preserve and maintain these resources for the benefit of present and future generations of all mankind' (Gardner 1966: 142, my emphasis). UNESCO also stressed this interest in an early listing of World Heritage Sites, stating that 'their value cannot be confined to one nation or to one people, but is there to be shared by every man, woman and child of the globe' (UNESCO 1982: 13). This idea of a common World Heritage denoting a shared cultural resource is further explored in what follows.

A means of democratising the World Heritage
The World Heritage is on the one hand being democratised when all the people of the world receive a stake in it, and it is perhaps morally right that sites constructed for elites should become a common heritage and made accessible for tourists and 'common' people. The tourist industry plays in this regard a powerful role, and promotions of the Convention and the List acts can function as a form of marketing for the States Parties. The World Heritage concept has therefore been criticised for symbolising commercial values (Hewison 1989: 22).

Although tourism is a double-edged sword on account of the wear and tear it causes – destruction that challenges the Convention as a tool for global conservation – visitors protect the World Heritage when they spend money at the site, while travels enhance cultural understanding. Inscribing the World Heritage Sites in the personal memories of the visitors further enforces the idea that the sites belong to them, and ICOMOS advises members to write a World Heritage visit report on preservation and accessibility after making private visits.[2] Whilst international standards of conservation and authenticity are scrutinised in the World Heritage work (e.g., Larsen 1995), the international community

---

2 http://www.international.icomos.org/world_heritage/visit.htm.

represented by the Committee can also actively press for the preservation of heritage. The Committee monitors preservation and wields the threat of delisting a site or inscribing it on the List of World Heritage in Danger (on which thirty-three sites have been inscribed by 2005). The desire to avoid such an embarrassment can be a strong stimulus to national authorities to follow the international guidance on preservation.

A mean of obtaining the cultural heritage of others

The inherent danger of the democratisation of the World Heritage is that groups with a special interest in the sites feel alienated and detached from their heritage. Indigenous peoples therefore often criticise the concept of a common heritage as representing potentially a new colonisation (Magga 1990: 120) or an assertion of white rights (Langford 1983: 4) or a device for excluding people with particular interests in the cultural heritage (Bowdler 1988: 521). This critique is not usually directed specifically at the Convention itself, and in fact it can be easily refuted by investigating how the concept functions in other contexts. However, it is important to be aware that the Convention does not tie protection of the cultural heritage to human rights (Schmidt 1996: 20), and sites are only designated if they are of interest to governing elites (Fontein 2000: 57) and the world community (Prott and O'Keefe 1984: 29; cf. O'Keefe 2000). Nevertheless, the cultural heritage of minority groups is represented on the List, but designation has not always recognised their interests. This is because the Convention involves primarily state-to-state cooperation, and the Committee mainly relies on the accounts given by the national delegations and the advisory bodies (that is, IUCN on natural sites, ICCROM and ICOMOS on cultural sites).

The role of minority groups and local people is now on the agenda of the Committee, but was little considered during the early work in the 1970s and 1980s. Only in 1993 did the Committee emphasise the importance of the shared responsibility between local people and the States Parties for protecting sites, though it added that the former 'should not prejudice future decision-making by the Committee' (UNESCO 1993: XIV.2). The Committee later withdrew this statement and stressed from 1995 the important role of local people both in the nomination process and in the maintenance of sites (UNESCO 1995: XVII.I).

Not surprisingly, then, constraints favouring national, local or indigenous people's interests are frequently called for in various parts of the world (cf. UNESCO 2003a: 3–4; Veerkamp 1998). Thus in 2000 a forum of indigenous peoples recommended the creation of a World Heritage Indigenous Peoples Council of Experts (WHIPCOE) to complement the work of the other advisory bodies (Titchen 2001). According to the forum, indigenous peoples are the owners and guardians of 'all their ancestral lands especially those within or comprising sites now designated as World Heritage Areas' (UNESCO 2000: Annex 5). Although the Committee rejected this proposal (UNESCO 2001: xv), there is an emerging understanding of the desirability of restricting outsiders' interests in some World Heritage Sites in order to ensure local control. Whilst I agree that such restrictions can be needed, this view again brings into question the sense and the validity of the World Heritage concept; I shall return to this at the end of the chapter.

A shared world history

A third interpretation of the World Heritage concept construes it as being, first and foremost, not about global obligations to preserve or rights of access but about our shared world history. The World Heritage is taken to consist of memorials to historical periods and events that connect the people of the earth, past and present. This idea can be unpacked in a number of different ways.

Recognising the political, social and cultural evolution of humanity

The evolutionary perspective that lays emphasis on cultural, social and political development represents one possibility for a World Heritage. Criterion (iv) for inscribing cultural sites on the List refers to heritage that illustrates significant stages in human history (UNESCO 2005b: §77). This evolutionary approach gives prehistoric archaeological sites a special role under the Convention: prehistory is a uniting force and the only history that can be common to all civilisations, explored through the medium of archaeology (e.g., Clark 1961, see also 1968 [1939]: 263; 1970: 51; cf. Cleere 1996: 228; Preucel and Hodder 1996: 521).

Despite the potential universality of the sites, only a few World Heritage Sites are of early prehistoric date. Furthermore, prevalent ideas of civilisation and of human progress are contestable on ethical grounds, first because the evolutionary models usually fasten on the progress of Western culture, and represent Western culture as the end of the civilisation process, and second because they tend to be used to legitimise the study of the past in other parts of the world according to Western models.

Recognising contacts in the past between cultures and peoples

World Heritage designation can alternatively use world-system models to highlight past contacts between cultures and peoples (e.g. Wallerstein 1974; Wolf 1982). Thus UNESCO declared in 1966 that 'in the reciprocal influences they [cultures] exert on one another, all cultures form part of the common heritage belonging to all mankind' (UNESCO 1966: Article 1); it further suggested, in 1984, that cultural interaction was a factor that should be considered before designation of sites (Linstrum 1984). Some World Heritage Sites patently have a global significance, for example by virtue of their influence on architecture and building styles elsewhere; hence the Acropolis at Athens has been described as 'symbolizing the idea of world heritage' (UNESCO 2005a). Still, the criteria for identifying sites do not emphasise global contacts. Criterion (ii) cites contact between cultures and proposes that listed heritage sites should 'exhibit an important interchange of human values' but does not insist on these relationships being on a global scale; it is enough if interchanges be 'over a span of time or within a cultural area of the world'. And while Criterion (vi) refers to intangibles such as beliefs, traditions and ideas that may be deemed to be of outstanding universal significance, this criterion is employed only exceptionally (UNESCO 2005: §77).

Creating a meta-heritage that represents human cultures

The UNESCO focus on humanity can also be interpreted as an extension of Hellenistic cosmopolitanism (cf. Kristeva 1991: 56; 1993: 20), or the Renaissance and Enlightenment project of thinking and writing history in terms of humankind (Harbsmeier 1989: 94; cf. Randall 1976 [1926]: 370–2). The World Heritage List from this perspective parallels the ancient wonders of the world or the Renaissance cabinets of curiosity that were meant to 'establish the position of mankind in the grand scheme of things' (Impey and McGregor 1985: 2). Accordingly, the List should be recognised as documenting human historical identity (Michell 1988: 26), a meta-heritage that represents human cultures.

The national dimension of the World Heritage concept is from this perspective ambiguous. The cultural heritage notion represents both a cosmopolitan attitude and a rootedness in the local, a dualism that can be traced back to early Romantic ideas and the fathers of nationalism who also regarded 'the whole of mankind as a greater and higher fatherland' (Kohn 1971: 121–2). This cosmopolitan and national aspect of the List is frequently mentioned in World Heritage work, as when a Tunisian minister argued that World Heritage protection is important to sustain the national identity, but 'within a worldwide context' (UNESCO 1991: §5). Education about World Heritage is often taken to have the dual roles of reinforcing cultural identities and imparting knowledge about other cultures (Khawajike 1990: 15). From this dual perspective the nation continues to be important, and designations often reinforce national and local identities (Hodder 1999: 162, 202; cf. Ashworth 1998: 117–18; Fontein 2000: 28–31); indeed, the simultaneous processes of globalisation and localisation have been termed *glocalisation* (Robertson 1995). Newly independent states are therefore quick to sign the Convention in order to be part of a common World Heritage, and the construction of national cultures continues within the global ecumene (cf. Foster 1991). However, cultural heritage is to be, as far as possible, depoliticised so that it cannot be used to bolster the more unfortunate features of nationalism. To this end, the Committee laid down in 1979 that sites connected with historical events or famous people should be given particular attention, since their selection could be 'strongly influenced by nationalism or other particularisms in contradiction with the objectives of the World Heritage Convention' (UNESCO 1979: §35).

Constructing this meta-narrative of the unity of human culture is a tremendous task in a postmodern era of fragmentation and reluctance to produce grand narratives (cf. Lyotard 1984). The problem of creating a common World Heritage is especially present in the effort of creating a World Heritage that *represents* human culture. The overrepresentation of European and monumental architecture that constitutes the World Heritage is much criticised (e.g., de Cuéllar 1996: 178) as revealing a Eurocentrism also present in the writing of world prehistory (Kohl 1989; Preucel and Hodder 1996: 521) and history (Burke 1989). The issue of representation has been on the Committee's agenda since the first inscriptions on the List in 1978 and high on it since the 1990s, culminating in the 1994 launch of a Global Strategy that would set aside a rigid and restricted List and:

instead take into account all the possibilities for extending and enriching it by means of new types of property whose value might become apparent as knowledge and ideas developed. The List should be receptive to the many and varied cultural manifestations of outstanding universal value through which cultures expressed themselves. (UNESCO 1994: 3)

The issue of representation has become increasingly important in World Heritage work following publication of the Global Strategy. In order to achieve a more representative List there has been a move away from universal standards for evaluating cultural heritage towards the use of more particular and culture-specific ones. Regional World Heritage centres are supported, studies of various types of heritage, regions and heritage themes emphasised (ICOMOS 2004), and regional Global Strategy meetings organised (e.g., Munjeri *et al.* 1995). New kinds of sites are identified, including those exhibiting living cultures and cultural landscapes (e.g., Cleere 1995; Droste *et al.* 1995; Fowler 2003; Titchen 1995, 1996; UNESCO 2003b), although the overall composition of the List has not much changed. Seemingly the postmodern interest in alternative histories is not matched by an equally keen interest in alternative heritages (cf. Byrne 1991).

Creating a common World Heritage for the higher means of peace in the future

The project of creating a World Heritage also aims at a higher end: peace, in accordance with the ultimate purpose of UNESCO. Whereas cultural heritage seen from a national viewpoint tended to divide people, from an international one it is a force for uniting them (Tanner-Kaplash 1989: 201–2), or a new myth that stresses the unity of peoples (cf. Eriksen 1996: 81). In 1972 the Director-General of UNESCO, in launching the international campaign for saving Carthage and speaking about the new World Heritage Convention, argued that the expression 'Carthage must be destroyed' represents hate, while 'Carthage must be saved' represents concord (UNESCO 1972c: 4). At the twentieth anniversary of the Convention it was declared that World Heritage sites should: 'serve to remind humanity of its unity in diversity and thereby contribute powerfully to one of UNESCO's essential goals – the promotion of mutual understanding and solidarity among peoples' (UNESCO 1992: INF 2/4).

This peacemaking objective faces its problems. Too often the World Heritage List represents a cultural prestige contest played out on a global stage, and several European countries seem to compete with each other in order to dominate the List. Nevertheless, some sites are specifically inscribed with a peacekeeping purpose in mind, such as Robin Island where Nelson Mandela was imprisoned (South Africa), the slave Island of Gorée (Senegal), the concentration camp of Auschwitz (Poland) and the nuclear site of Hiroshima (Japan) (UNESCO 2005a). These sites represent *world memories* of colonialism and World War II, although they remind us more about historic cleavages than unity (cf. Smith 1990: 180). Thus both the USA and China objected in 1996 against the designation of Hiroshima (UNESCO 1996: Annex v). The USA was at first positive, but the political climate in the country had changed by the time of the fiftieth anniversary of the end of World War II (as was apparent in the fierce debate concerning the public exhibition of *Enola Gay*, the aircraft that dropped the nuclear bomb) (Wallace 1995, 1996). So the memorial that should symbolise peace became again a political battleground as various groups ascribed various values to the site.

It is sad to note that World Heritage Sites that should symbolise solidarity often signify, to quote the philosopher Hannah Arendt's words from the Cold War era, a '*negative solidarity*, based on the fear of global destruction' (Arendt 1957: 541, my emphasis). In the aftermath of September 11, 2001 the archaeologist Lynn Meskell speaks of *negative heritage*, defined as 'a conflictual site that becomes the repository of negative memory in the collective imaginary' (Meskell 2002: 558). Referring to two examples of a negative heritage – Ground Zero (although not on the World Heritage List) and the Buddhas of Bamiyan (Afghanistan) – Meskell highlights the problem of protecting sites that are ascribed different values:

> For the Taliban, the Buddhist statues represented a site of negative memory, one that necessitated jettisoning from the nation's construction of contemporary identity, and the act of erasure was a political statement about religious difference and international exclusion. For many others today that site of erasure in turn represents negative heritage, a permanent scar that reminds certain constituencies of intolerance, symbolic violence, loss and the 'barbarity' of the Taliban regime.
>
> (Meskell 2002: 561)

Hence, the destructive 'culture' of the Taliban has also become a part of the World Heritage after the designation of Bamiyan in 2003. The World Heritage List has indeed, to paraphrase a Global Strategy statement (UNESCO 1994: 3), become receptive to the many and varied cultural manifestations through which cultures express themselves!

IS THE GLOBAL STRATEGY A MORAL OBLIGATION OR AN ETHICAL PROBLEM?

The foregoing overview of the ethics of the World Heritage concept has aimed at clarifying its various interpretations. The concept has undergone several changes since the adoption of the Convention in 1972. Formulated in terms of a moral obligation to protect the cultural heritage of other countries, the concept is at the same time ethically problematic owing to its underpinning by Western values. UNESCO promulgates the Global Strategy as a solution, but this solution also presents new moral challenges, as we shall see in the final section of this chapter.

Is a fragmentation of the universality of the World Heritage ethically right?

Fragmentation is one of the buzzwords of postmodernism, present in the World Heritage work when the problem of the universality of the cultural heritage is discussed in relation to the Global Strategy, but it is seldom pointed out that fragmentation can also be ethically troublesome. The problem of universality is increasingly an issue when non-Western and non-monumental heritage is discussed, but much less so when European monumental architecture is nominated to the World Heritage List. This may be due to the fact, as Cleere points out, that European cathedrals are easily accepted because they are assessed according to certain aesthetic and art historical standards, while the inscription of less immediately appealing sites are deferred for comparative studies (Cleere 1993b: 11). Other explanations why European cultural heritage easily achieves designation are also plausible. Lowenthal points out that the globalisation of heritage is rooted in chauvinism and imperial self-regard and that: 'These ideas stem above all from Europeans who rate their own national heritage as so superior it *ought* to be global' (Lowenthal 1998: 239, emphasis in original).

Whilst European cultural heritage is regarded as global and universal, other kinds of heritages are seen as being, at best, of regional importance, or as having an exceptional status only in the eyes of the local cultural group. But if Western countries view their own cultural heritage as universal and global, it ought to be legitimate to assess other kinds of heritages from similar points of view, although I still often find the possibility of a cultural heritage embodying universal values problematic.

Implementing the Global Strategy: for whom is living culture preserved?

The Global Strategy, with its identification of new types of heritages, raises the problem of how this heritage can be shared with other people in such a way that its authenticity is preserved. This is particularly pertinent when cultural landscapes, living cultures and sites with spiritual significance are nominated for the List, creating a challenge well known within World Heritage work.[3] Designation can be fraught with problems for indigenous peoples, although, on the plus side, they may see it as

---

3 E.g. discussed at the ICCROM Forum in October 2003 *Conserving the sacred* (http://www.iccrom. org/eng/news/iccrom/2003/10forum.htm).

implying external recognition of the value of their beliefs and practices (e.g. Red Shirt 2002). The case of the Matopos Hills in Zimbabwe, designated in 2003, is an example of the problems that can arise before the designation of a landscape with multiple cultural significances, although in this instance African perception of the landscape was finally prioritised (see Ranger 1989, 1996, 1999; Omland 1998: 58–88; 1999: 91–2; Fontein 2000: 72–84).

The Matopos obtained World Heritage designation after twenty years of national and local discussions stimulated by differing European and African perceptions of the landscape. Parts of the Matopos were designated a national park during the colonial period, when they were cleared of their inhabitants in order to create a wilderness and preserve the geology, ecology and archaeology of the hills. While visitors enjoyed the park, the local people lost ownership over the natural resources and rock-art sites used for rainmaking. The natural values and the 'dead' archaeological landscape were given importance in an early draft nomination of park, while the value of the living culture was first stressed after the launch of Global Strategy. The sacred mountain of Njelele was then identified as an important example of African heritage.

Although the African cultural values of the Matopos were recognised, local concerns were raised about outsiders' interest in the area prior to the designation (Omland 1998: 58–88; 1999: 91–2). The problems were partly due to (1) UNESCO's criterion of securing adequate (which in this case meant traditional) protection of World Heritage Sites and (2) the fact that the sites were expected to keep their distinctive character. The first criterion proved problematic because of an internal conflict about who was the true priest of Njelele. The national authorities represented by the museum had to identify and confirm the rightful custodian before they could transfer decision-making powers. The second problem arose because, while traditional values had to be preserved, traditional values are constantly changing. The local debate focused on the question of the voice of the god Mwari that had in former times been heard from the rocks. When the voice had disappeared from Njelele was disputed, but there was strong local belief that it would be heard again when the right custodian was chosen and the mountain cleansed of colonial and Western remnants.

The project of cleansing the shrine stands in opposition to a process of modernising the uses of the site following World Heritage designation – an issue which has been keenly debated at government level. On one view, people with all kinds of problems were welcome to come to Njelele. This was the position taken by the former vice-president of Zimbabwe, Joshua Nkomo (1917–99), who during the struggle for Zimbabwe's liberation used Njelele for religious and political purposes. In the 1980s and 1990s he supported one of the candidate-priests for the role of custodian and wanted to make Njelele more easily accessible (Ranger 1999: 253–62, 275–9). Some local people and priests also supported this view, stressing that Njelele was important for the whole world, and prepared to welcome visitors on condition they respected local rules.

However, other local inhabitants objected to allowing greater access to the site, urging that visitors should be restricted and the shrine used mainly for rainmaking. On their view, the rival priests were undermining the sacred values of Njelele by accepting visitors. The government's new interest in the shrine was also viewed with suspicion in case it should, from commercial motives, let in a flood of visitors, thereby further threatening the area's sacred significance.

Although the views about access to Njelele remain locally disputed, the World Heritage designation makes it necessary to place constraints on other people's interests in the site, as in the case of sites elsewhere that are sacred to indigenous peoples. However, such restriction of other people's access violates the interpretation of the World Heritage concept as demarcating an essentially shared cultural heritage: what is this 'World Heritage' if other people are not given access to it? Or if the World Heritage concept signals a moral obligation of international protection, is it right to render this protection when it causes local uproar about custodianship and stressful controversy about the distinctive character of the site? Who are then the intended beneficiaries of World Heritage designation and preservation: the site, local people or the conservationists? The asset of being represented on the World Heritage List seems to be an end in its own right after the launch of the Global Strategy, raising the next issue: what is 'culture' that shall be represented?

Cultures, strangers and the World Heritage

The international World Heritage debate has from the mid-1990s increasingly focused on the importance of restrictions of external interests in the cultural heritage. Visitors can enjoy the cultural heritage, but not always participate in the ambient 'culture', by, for example, taking part in sacred and secret rituals. This raises questions about the understanding of the concept of 'culture' in World Heritage work and consequently about the obligations to represent cultures on the List. It also poses a further problem about the right to have a cultural identity versus the right to choose *not* to have a cultural identity and not belong to any place.

The complex concept of 'culture' enjoyed a renaissance after the 1995 UNESCO report *Our Creative Diversity* (de Cuéllar 1996; cf. UNESCO 2002). It has been frequently employed in World Heritage work after the Global Strategy, although the concept has come under critical scrutiny by anthropologists (e.g. Dahlström 2003: 12–15; Eriksen 2001; Wright 1998). Two problems of the concept pertinent to the *Our Creative Diversity* report (Eriksen 2001: 130–2) are also relevant within World Heritage work:

1 'Culture' refers broadly to artistic work and ways of life, and the World Heritage List is from this perspective a catalogue of human activities. But critics complain that the 'culture' of the daily life is typically not included, but only the exotic or the older heritage that points to the roots of the people (Eriksen 2001: 131). However, such exclusion is not intended by the Convention. Whilst it certainly aimed to preserve old cultural heritage, there is nothing to stop newer sites, representing contemporary ways of life, from also being considered for designation.
2 A more serious problem concerns UNESCO's definition of 'culture'. The organisation is criticised for conceiving culture as 'something that can easily be pluralized, which belongs to a particular group of people, associated with their heritage, or "roots"' (Eriksen 2001: 131). On this critique, 'UNESCO, in its vision of a new ethical world order, maps out a world made of "cultures" as discrete entities' (Wright 1998: 12). The practical problem of protection is seen as involving sharp definition of the geographical bounds of cultures, as when the Laponian Area (Sweden) was designated in 1996 on account of the Sámi reindeer herders:

> The World Heritage appointment has meant, in theory, that within the Laponian borders, reindeer herding should be preserved, but outside of these borders there is no such defined goal . . . It is as though it would be possible to point to a certain spot on the culture map and say 'Here this culture begins' and then move the finger to another spot and claim, 'and here it ends', as though we are talking about a tangible, physical reality, that is possible to observe. (Dahlström 2003: 269)

More importantly, the perception of a mosaic of cultures represents an ethical challenge because it is connected to essentialism and the notion of the rootedness of diverse cultures in particular places. Since the Global Strategy, this rootedness is thought of in terms more of groups than of nations, thus helping to counter the national approach to heritage that the World Heritage concept, from its inception, has challenged. This echoes the idea, currently strong in archaeology, that national uses of the past are dangerous, while groups – e.g., indigenous peoples – using the cultural heritage to recover and maintain their identities constitute a superior alternative. Although I concede that indigenous affiliation to and rights over the cultural heritage are often important, I agree with Tarlow that there is a danger in so formulating such general ownership rights to the cultural heritage in that it can sometimes be used to support far right and neo-Nazi claims (Tarlow 2001a: 256).

In so far as the World Heritage concept is formulated, as it increasingly is, in ways that buttress various cultures' sense of their roots and group identities, this risks blurring the sense of the concept. What now happens to individuals who wish *not* to have such a cultural group identity (cf. Eriksen 2001: 135)? I have discussed above how one could approach the World Heritage from a cosmopolitan stance which presupposed a rootedness to one's 'own' past. But there is another form of cosmopolitanism that excludes this kind of affiliation and which does not seem to be present in the World Heritage work: the standpoint of the *stranger* who does not belong to any place. Julia Kristeva refers to this version of cosmopolitanism, quoting Meleager of Gadara writing in the first century BC: 'The only homeland, foreigner, is the world we live in' (Kristeva 1991: 56; 1993: 20).

The idea of the stranger has increasing relevance today with the growing number of refugees, stateless people, immigrants – but also residents in a state or members of a group – who do not consider themselves to be part of the 'culture' of the nation or the group. The World Heritage could be the stranger's heritage, but for the moment it remains national and local, while the diversity of heritages recognised demands restriction of outsiders' interests. The World Heritage continues to prioritise nations and groups, and it is not yet based in the idea of the global ecumene, contrary to some of the hopes entertained in the 1960s and 1970s when the World Heritage concept was formulated (e.g. by Meyer 1976: 63).

CONCLUSIONS: SUPPORTING THE WORLD HERITAGE CONCEPT

This exploration of the World Heritage concept has revealed ambiguities and raised ethical concerns, but I still favour the concept. I support the principles that heritage should be preserved across the territories of the States Parties, that some States Parties need international pressure to preserve the heritage on their territories, and that visitors should be able to explore the World Heritage. However, I acknowledge that international interests in cultural heritage must sometimes be restricted, though I regret that outsiders may thereby be prevented from participating in a 'culture'.

Moreover, the ambiguities we have noted in the concept of a common World Heritage are by no means entirely a negative thing. It can be dangerous to tie a concept down too narrowly, particularly when it grounds a set of specific ethical prescriptions that are liable to be challenged in other contexts. For instance, had archaeologists around 1900 established a code of ethics, it would indubitably have included the principle that cultural heritage belongs to the nation state. As we have seen, the World Heritage concept is also ethically problematic in some contexts, and too strict an interpretation could foreclose or impede discussion on important issues. Whereas, the ambiguous and undefined World Heritage concept has a fruitful role to play in the rhetoric of international cultural heritage protection, as it can be supported, challenged and resisted at local levels all over the world.

ACKNOWLEDGEMENTS

The basic research for this chapter was carried out in the years 1997–98 during stays in Oslo, Cambridge, Harare, Bulawayo, Uppsala and Paris. I am especially grateful to Øivind Lunde, John Carman, Ian Hodder, Sarah M. Titchen and Webber Ndoro for sharing thoughts with me, and to Geoffrey Scarre for considerable improvements to the text.

CHAPTER 15

What value a unicorn's horn? A study of archaeological uniqueness and value

Robin Coningham, Rachel Cooper and Mark Pollard

> The cultural heritage and the natural heritage are among the priceless and irreplaceable possessions, not only of each nation, but of mankind as a whole. The loss, through deterioration or disappearance, of any of these most prized possessions constitutes an impoverishment of the heritage of all the peoples in the world. Parts of that heritage, because of their exceptional qualities, can be considered to be of outstanding universal value and as such worthy of special protection against the dangers which increasingly threaten them.
>
> (UNESCO 1999: 1)

Pressures on the archaeological resource, at both a national and an international level, have never been so great. Increasing population numbers, industrialisation, mechanised cultivation, expanding settlements and an international market for antiquities are causing immense destruction of archaeological sites and their contents. In reaction to this pressure, and the resultant losses, managers of the heritage resource have to make difficult decisions as to the selection and preservation of individual sites at international, national and even local levels. Many of these decisions are guided by national and international legislation such as Britain's Ancient Monuments and Archaeological Areas Act of 1979, its Planning (Listed Buildings and Conservation Areas) Act 1990 and UNESCO's 1972 Convention Concerning the Protection of the World Cultural and Natural Heritage. Despite some voiced misgivings concerning issues of criteria and value (Darvill 1995; Pressoyre 1996; Schaafsma 1989), most managers rely heavily on these instruments. This chapter will investigate the conceptual underpinnings of such legislation.

We will argue that this legislature implicitly accepts that certain sites are 'unique' or 'valuable', and that, because of these characteristics, they should be preserved. We then go on to demonstrate that this apparently unproblematic thought is problematic. Through an analysis of the concepts of 'uniqueness' and 'value' we show that it makes little sense to claim that a particular site is unique, or valuable, *simpliciter*. Rather, sites will only ever be unique in certain respects, and valuable for certain purposes. Using the implementation of the AMAAA 1979, P(LBCA)A 1990 and UNESCO 1972 Convention, we demonstrate that confusion over this point can have practical, and in some cases unfortunate, consequences.

THE LEGISLATION

UNESCO's 1972 Convention Concerning the Protection of the World Cultural and Natural Heritage commits the United Nations to maintaining a list of World Heritage Sites. Sites may be nominated by member states on the basis of their importance to either cultural or natural heritage, or in rare cases both, with only twenty-three sites. Here we are primarily concerned with sites listed as cultural heritage, representing 611 of the 788 sites inscribed on the list. To be added to or inscribed on this list, monuments or groups of buildings must be judged to be of 'outstanding universal value from the point of view of history, art or science' (UNESCO 1972: 2). Archaeological sites may be included if of 'outstanding universal value from the historical, aesthetic, ethnological or anthropological points of view' (1972: 2). Once a site is listed, the state in which it is located is obliged to preserve the site 'to the utmost of its own resources' (1972: 2). In cases where a country cannot afford work essential to the preservation of a Site, the World Heritage Committee may offer various types of assistance. There is thus an assumption that once a Site is included on the World Heritage List it should be preserved indefinitely.

UNESCO also publishes Operational Guidelines to guide decisions as to whether a site should be included on the list of Sites. These state that nominated sites should meet various tests of authenticity, and should also meet one or more of the following criteria:

i represent a masterpiece of human creative genius; or
ii exhibit an important interchange of human values, over a span of time or within a cultural area of the world, or developments in architecture or technology, monumental arts, town-planning or landscape design; or
iii bear a unique or at least exceptional testimony to a cultural tradition or to a civilisation which is living or has disappeared; or
iv be an outstanding example of a type of building or architectural or technological ensemble or landscape which illustrates (a) significant stage(s) in human history; or

v be an outstanding example of a traditional human settlement or land-use which is representative of a culture (or cultures), especially when it has become vulnerable under the impact of irreversible change; or

vi be directly or tangibly associated with events or living traditions, with ideas, or with beliefs, with artistic and literary works or outstanding universal significance (the Committee considers that this criterion should justify inclusion in the List only in exceptional circumstances and in conjunction with other criteria cultural or natural). (UNESCO 1999: 6)

Of UNESCO's cultural conventions, the 1972 Convention is one of the most ratified international conventions by member states as well as most representative, with World Heritage sites listed in 134 of its 190 member states.

At a national level in Britain, the main legislation offering protection to archaeological sites is the Ancient Monuments and Archaeological Areas Act of 1979 (Breeze 1994). This legislation operates in a similar way to the UNESCO Convention, in that it enables the compilation of a list of important sites that then qualify for special protection. The Secretary of State maintains a schedule of those Ancient Monuments and Archaeological Areas that are deemed to be of national importance. In practice, agencies such as English Heritage put forward sites that they think should be protected, although the public is also offered a role in the identification of sites. To aid such agencies, the Secretary of State for Culture, Media and Sport has laid down criteria to be used in judging whether a site is of national importance. These are:

1 extent of survival
2 current condition
3 rarity
4 representivity, either through diversity or because of one important attribute
5 importance of the period to which the monument dates
6 fragility
7 connection to other monuments, or group value
8 potential to contribute to our information, understanding and appreciation
9 extent of documentation enhancing the monument's significance (Breeze 1993).

Once placed on the Schedule, sites enjoy special legal protection. For example, the use of metal detectors is banned on such sites, unless one has written consent from the Secretary of State, and Scheduled Monument

Consent is required before any work on the site can commence. Currently, English Heritage estimates that the Schedule has 18,300 entries but that, once complete, it will include some 30,000 scheduled sites. This is augmented by the Planning (Listed Buildings and Conservation Areas) Act 1990 (Suddards 1993), which provides specific protection for buildings and areas of special architectural or historic interest and compiles a list under three grades:

Grade I buildings are those of exceptional interest
Grade II* are particularly important buildings of more than special interest
Grade II are of special interest, warranting every effort to preserve them (Suddards 1993).

The list currently includes 370,000 sites, 2 per cent of which are listed within the Grade I category, 4 per cent within Grade II* and 94 per cent within the more general Grade II category. Although English Heritage suggests that the older and rarer a building is, the more likely it is to be listed, the stated criteria for listing are:

Architectural interest
Historic interest
Close historical association
Group value
(Suddards 1993).

In both sets of legislation, national and international, the basic reasoning follows similar lines: sites are of varying importance, and may thus be differentiated into categories. Furthermore, those which are of 'outstanding value', 'exceptional interest' or 'national importance' should be preserved, and may be identified on account of 'unique' or 'exceptional' or 'outstanding' characteristics. This reasoning is put most clearly in the introduction to the UNESCO Guidelines for the Implementation of the World Heritage Convention, which state that, 'Parts of that [World] heritage, because of their exceptional qualities, can be considered to be of outstanding universal value and as such worthy of special protection' (UNESCO 1999: 1). However, it is also echoed by English Heritage, which states that Listing will 'protect the best of our architectural heritage' and that it includes 'buildings . . . of outstanding architectural or historic interest and of particularly great importance to the nation's historic environment'. Key concepts in the legislation are thus that of the 'valuable' or 'important', and that of the 'unique', 'exceptional' or 'outstanding'.

UNIQUENESS OR EXCEPTIONALITY

The UNESCO 1972 Convention and the AMAAA 1979 and P(LBCA)A 1990 make much of the supposedly 'scientific' and 'objective' nature of the judgements that are being made. The UNESCO Operational Guidelines state that the World Heritage Committee seeks to make its decisions 'based on considerations that are as objective and scientific as possible' (UNESCO 1999: 1). Seeing as judgements as to whether a site is 'important' or 'valuable' are made (at least partly) on the basis of whether the site is 'unique' or 'exceptional', this implies that judgements of uniqueness must be made on wholly objective grounds. Whether this is so, or whether to say that a site is 'unique' is covertly to make a value-judgement, will be one of the major issues to be dealt with in this section.

As a first step in analysing what it takes for an entity to be unique we can note that the concept of 'uniqueness' is tied to the concept of 'similarity'. To say that an entity is unique in some respect is to say that it is not similar to any other entity in that respect. Noting this is useful, because much philosophical labour has already been expended on analysing 'similarity' – work that we may now hope to make use of in analysing 'uniqueness'.

In his 1957 paper 'Properties and Classes', Anthony Quinton notes that to say 'these things are similar' is equivalent to saying 'these things have a common property'. It is certainly the case that if two entities, say Alex and Bill, possess some common property – both weighing 80 kg, or having spots, or whatever – then they are similar in that respect. However, Quinton's analysis of 'similarity' is not quite right. Suppose Bill weighed 79.5 kg and Alex weighed 80.0 kg, Alex and Bill would weigh different amounts, but we would still judge them to be similar. To cope with such cases, Quinton's analysis must be revised. Quinton claims that two entities, X and Y, are similar if and only if they share a property. Instead we should claim that X and Y are similar if and only if they share a property, *or* if X possesses a property that is similar to, although not identical with, a property possessed by Y. On this analysis, Alex and Bill are similar because the property of weighing 79.5 kg is similar to that of weighing 80.0 kg.

Saying that entities can be similar in virtue of possessing similar, but non-identical, properties prompts the question of what it means to say that two properties are similar to each other. A popular, and plausible, answer is to say that two properties are similar if and only if they endow entities with similar causal powers. Thus, entities that weigh 79.5 and

80.0 kg are similar as they will have similar causal powers – both will tip scales in much the same range of cases, for example. Scientifically, we would use the concept of 'the same within experimental error': on a different day, for example, Bill might appear to weigh 80.0 kg and Alex 79.5 kg, owing to either natural fluctuations in weight or small discrepancies in the accuracy of the weighing scales. It would not, therefore, be unreasonable to regard the two entries as 'similar'.

Whether two properties are similar enough to make the entities that possess them similar will not always be clear-cut. Similarity is a matter of degree. In the example above we claimed that the property of weighing 79.5 kg and that of weighing 80.0 kg are similar, and for most purposes it will be fair to say this. But, what of the property of weighing 75.0 kg and that of weighing 80.0 kg? Whether these should be judged 'similar' depends on the context in which judgements are being made. When pairing boxers, men weighing 75 kg and 80 kg may be similar enough to be classed together. In another context, say precision engineering, metal bars weighing 75 kg and 80 kg may be considered completely unalike.

We can use what we have said about 'similarity' to gain a better understanding of the notion of 'uniqueness'. To say that an entity is unique in some respect is to say that it is not similar to any other entity in that respect. As such, we can say that X is unique if and only if X possesses some property, and there is no entity Y that possesses either that property or one that is significantly similar to it. To illustrate, suppose there are three stone circles remaining from some period. Circle A has a circumference of 40.0 m, Circles B and C have circumferences of 24.0 and 24.2 m. On our analysis, for most purposes, Circle A can be considered unique with respect to its size. It possesses some property (being a stone circle dating from such and such a period with a circumference of 40 m), and there is no entity that possesses either this property or a property significantly similar to it. By contrast, Circles B and C are not unique with respect to their size, because their circumferences are similar.

At this stage we can usefully take on board another point from Quinton's paper. Quinton points out that saying 'these things are similar' and saying 'these things have a common property' are 'indefinite in just the same kind of way and both need the same sort of supplementation before they convey anything very much' (Quinton 1957: 40). In other words, simply to tell you that Alex and Bill are similar would be very odd (as it conveys so little) and would normally be taken as an incomplete statement. More normally one would say that Alex and Bill are similar in build, or have a similar sense of humour, or some such. This point also applies to statements concerning uniqueness. Simply to say that an entity is unique tells us little. An entity might be unique in being the biggest diamond on earth, or in being the dirtiest five pence piece. Only in the former case will its uniqueness be of much interest.

The UNESCO 1972 Convention, the AMAAA 1979 and P(LBCA)A 1990 suggest that if a site is unique then it is valuable and worth saving. However, if we bear in mind that for a site to be unique means only that it differs from all other sites in some respect, whatever that respect might be, we can easily see that this will not necessarily be the case. A site might be unique in being the only monument from a particular period in Britain, or in being the sole surviving building that uses a particular construction technique. However, it might equally be unique in some disvalued or insignificant respect. To say that a standing stone is unique in being the only one that's been defaced by racist graffiti would not, after all, be to give any reason for saving it over others.

To say that a site is unique thus gives no reason to save it. Taking into account space and time, every site is by definition unique – a stone circle dating to the Bronze Age is the only Bronze Age stone circle at that site, and is therefore unique. Only if a site is unique in some valuable respect will its uniqueness be of significance. Perhaps, though, this difficulty can easily be overcome. Rather than claiming that a site should be preserved if it is unique, might we not simply specify that a site should be preserved if and only if it is unique in some *valuable* respect. Now, however, we have come full circle. Both the UNESCO 1972 Convention, the AMAAA 1979 and the P(LBCA)A 1990 sought to determine which sites are valuable by determining which are unique. Now, however, we have reached the conclusion that whether a site is unique in any interesting respect can only be determined once it is known what might make a site valuable. In this scheme, rather than being derivative, judgements about value have to come first. There is thus nothing for it but to tackle the question of what might make a site valuable head-on.

VALUE OR IMPORTANCE

As we have seen, determining whether a site is unique is of little use prior to determining what attributes might make an archaeological site valuable. A site will only be worth saving if it is unique in some valuable respect. Thus, it is necessary to determine what kinds of properties might make a site valuable first. This, however, is far from straightforward, as has been discussed elsewhere by Darvill (1995), Lipe (1984) and McGimsey (1984). There are many different reasons why an archaeological site might be thought valuable, including, but not limited to, Darvill's (1995) threefold categories of use value, option value and existence value:

Use value

archaeological research (archaeologists)
scientific research (scientists other than archaeologists)
creative arts (artists, writers, poets and photographers)
education (children and adults)
recreation and tourism
symbolic representation (frequent use in advertisements)
legitimation of action (present political manipulation of the past)
social solidarity and integrity (bolster social solidarity and promote integrity)
monetary and economic gain (selling books and looting)

Option value

stability (stability, timelessness and tradition)
mystery and enigma (excitement of 'knowledge gaps')

Existence value

cultural identity (feelings of belonging)
resistance to change (protest against change).

This categorisation is very similar to Startin's divisions of academic value, aesthetic value, education value and symbolic value (1993: 185), but it is clear that, depending on the reason why one values (some) archaeological sites, different properties of those sites will be significant. For example, suppose that a site contains well-preserved prehistoric algae. This might well be significant if one values the site for its capacity to provide data for scientific research. However, if one thinks the site is valuable because people like visiting it, or because of its symbolic importance, then the algae will not be of much interest.

It follows that those with different reasons for valuing archaeological sites will end up thinking that different sites are valuable. A site cannot be valuable *simpliciter*, but rather can only be valuable for some specific purpose. Only if one considers that purpose legitimate will one value the site. We can conclude that deciding which sites to save is necessarily tied to determining the reasons why one values archaeological sites. Legislation such as the AMAAA 1979, the P(LBCA)A 1990 and the 1972 UNESCO Convention has obscured this point. Such legislation assumes it is possible to draw up a list of sites that are of importance to Britain or, even more problematically, to the whole world. However, until there is agreement as to the reasons why archaeological sites might be valuable, it is to be expected that it will not be possible to achieve agreement as to which sites should be preserved.

Indeed, academic archaeology has singularly failed to agree on priorities for research, probably for very good reasons. It has not been possible, for example, to reach a consensus academic view that in England the Anglo-Saxon period is 'more important' or 'more interesting' than the Romano-British – each has its own band of devotees and specialists, who would not contemplate competing claims. This is part of the character of archaeology, but like all 'broad churches' it creates weaknesses when attempting to present a coherent view to politicians and other decision-makers (Pollard 2004).

THE CURRENT SITUATION

It is broadly accepted by many of the component bodies and partners of the UNESCO 1972 Convention that there are 'weaknesses and imbalances' in the UNESCO List of World Heritage Sites (WHC-94/CONF.003/INF.6). These can, in part, be attributed to the Convention's 'monumental' definition of cultural heritage but also are created by the additional resources available to member states from the developed world with larger 'cultural' budgets and administrative apparatus. Combined, these factors have led to an overrepresentation of Europe in relation to Sites in the rest of the world, historic towns and religious buildings, Christianity in relation to other religions and beliefs, historic periods in relation to prehistory and the twentieth century, and 'elitist' architecture in relation to vernacular architecture. Finally, it was noted that all living cultures – especially the 'traditional ones' – with their depth, their wealth, their complexity and their diverse relationships with the environment figured very little on the List. In response to these weaknesses and imbalances, and in order to generate a more balanced, representative and credible List, a series of recommendations were made in 1994 (*ibid.*).

These included the consideration of two, largely unrepresented, themes: human coexistence with the land, including the movement of peoples (nomadism, migration), settlement, modes of subsistence and technological evolution; and human beings in society, including human interaction, cultural coexistence, and spirituality and creative expression.

Despite the passing of a decade since these recommendations, the current list of UNESCO World Heritage Sites still clearly displays most of the above weaknesses and imbalances. In particular, these are found within South Asia, which is represented by only fifty-four Sites, less than 7 per cent of UNESCO's List of 788 World Heritage Sites, even though the region contains 20 per cent of the world's population. Whilst the global coverage of Sites is clearly uneven, so is the actual representation within South Asia for cultural heritage sites. Afghanistan, for example, has two monuments, Bangladesh three, Bhutan none, India twenty-six, the Maldives none, Nepal four, Pakistan six, Sri Lanka seven and Iran six. It should be noted that the majority of these inscribed sites were also constructed during a single span of one thousand years – a relatively short time period, between the middle of the first century AD and the middle of the first millennium AD. Furthermore, it should be noted that all but a handful of these sites were built of stone or were excavated from stone outcrops, and that a tiny minority were constructed of brick, with an almost complete absence of timber structures. It is also clear that most are religious structures associated with elites and few from living traditions and none from groups associated with transhumance or nomadism.

This imbalance is met in microcosm within Sri Lanka's UNESCO List, for example, as the inscribed cities of Anuradhapura, Polonnaruva, Sigiriya and Kandy are all stone or brick built, all possess monuments dating to the first millennium AD, and all represent 'elite' architecture (Silva 1989). More worrying, the majority of the island's inscribed Sites are strongly associated with its majority Sinhalese population and none is associated with its Tamil minority (Coningham and Lewer 1999). This has led some commentators to state that although the government of Sri Lanka must feel 'free to sponsor the restoration of Buddhist monuments . . . It would also behove a Sri Lankan government to recognise at the same time that there are monuments . . . that are neither Sinhalese or Buddhist' (Tambiah 1986: 126). This perhaps encouraged extremists to target the UNESCO Temple of the Tooth Site in Kandy in 1997. In this context, the concept of uniqueness must be questioned – what makes each of these sites unique and worthy of inscription but not the island's sacred Hindu sites?

Given the high degree of similarities between each of the inscribed Sri Lankan sites, it is interesting to note that the Pakistani Bronze Age city of Harappa was turned down for inscription in 1980 by UNESCO's World Heritage Committee on the grounds that it was 'the same type of site as Moenjodaro [sic] . . . [and] is less well preserved than Moenjodaro' (CC-80/CONF.017/4). The irony of this decision is that it is now generally agreed that the two cities have very different urban plans, Mohenjo-daro having a citadel mound on the west and a lower town mound on the east whilst Harappa comprises a series of walled mounds around a central depression (Kenoyer 1998). Mohenjo-daro itself was inscribed in 1980 in that it exhibited 'an important interchange of human values' (criterion ii) and bore 'a unique or at least exceptional testimony to a cultural tradition or to a civilisation' (criterion iii), but one has to wonder why the Indus civilisation is represented only by a single city and not by a range of settlements reflecting its smaller, but no less important settlements. Is it more important to preserve the 'exceptional' rather than the representative?

That UNESCO's definition of 'exceptional' and 'unique' is fundamentally flexible (or flawed) in practice is illustrated by the inscription of two new UNESCO World Heritage Sites on the List, even though those characteristics which made them 'exceptional' and 'unique' were destroyed before inscription. The first of these, the Bamiyan Buddhas of Afghanistan, represented some of the largest Buddha images of the ancient world – the larger Buddha was 53m high and its smaller companion 35 m (Tarzi 1977). Built in the first century AD, these rock-cut images were entirely destroyed by iconoclastic Taliban soldiers in 2001 but, representing some of the best-known images of Afghanistan, were inscribed in 2003 having been proposed by the new Afghan government. Despite inscription, debate still surrounds the discussion of the extent to which these monuments should be rebuilt. The second example is the historic city of Bam in south-east Iran, which boasted the most complete mudbrick city in the world. However, the mudbrick citadel and its entire walled town were reduced to rubble by an earthquake in 2003. Despite this human and cultural disaster, or perhaps because of it, the ruined city of Bam and its cultural landscape were inscribed on UNESCO's World Heritage List a year later in 2004. In both these cases, it is clear that UNESCO's own criteria or thresholds of 'uniqueness' and 'outstanding' have been overruled and alternative values, corresponding closely to Darvill's 'existence' or 'symbolic' categories (1995), have been applied in their place.

The case is generally different within the UK, where strategic gu within legislation reflects political directives. Thus as there has be greater emphasis on public value, slowly but surely the list has m... away from 'elite' architecture and more towards areas of greater public interest. For example, English Heritage has been raising awareness of defences of World War II within England and, in parallel, the National Trust has purchased examples of 1950s suburban houses as exemplars. This reflection has even affected the UK's UNESCO World Heritage listings where early properties represented concepts of 'Britishness' and predictably included Stonehenge, Durham cathedral and castle, Studley Royal Park and Fountains Abbey, Blenheim Palace, Westminster Palace and the Tower of London but which now have been widened to include the textile towns of Saltaire in Bradford and New Lanark in Scotland.

However, there is even an example of a 'unique' monument, described by the Chairman of English Heritage as 'one of the most enthralling archaeological discoveries of our time', being dismantled by English Heritage in 1999 rather then being scheduled *in situ*. The site, Seahenge, comprised a circle of fifty-five oak timber posts encircling an upturned oak tree in the centre, and was exposed on a Norfolk beach as the sea washed peat away from around the monument. As other timber circles have rotted away leaving only post holes, the state of preservation at Seahenge made it unique. However, English Heritage decided that the monument would be better dismantled, and studied and conserved else-where before it was destroyed by a storm. Subsequent studies have yielded much information concerning Bronze Age woodworking techniques, and analysis of the timbers have identified that they were all felled in 2050 BC. The accompanying research notwithstanding, this 'unique' monument was dismantled, and its context destroyed, because the permanent conser-vation of its constituent timbers, the 'academic' value, was valued more highly by English Heritage than the 'aesthetic' and 'symbolic' value of its limited survival as a whole monument *in situ*.

CONCLUSION

To sum up, the AMAAA 1979, the P(LBCA)A 1990 and the 1972 UNESCO Convention claim that judgements as to which sites are important can be made 'scientifically' or 'objectively'. However, we have shown that this is not the case. Judgements as to which sites are 'import-ant' or 'valuable' are necessarily linked to value judgements. Whilst archaeologists and heritage managers cannot agree about definitions of values themselves (Darvill 1995; Lipe 1984; McGimsey 1984; Schaafsma 1989), it is unlikely that this situation will change in the near future. Indeed, it might be more helpful if those involved in the nominations and approval system were to explicitly identify the non-exceptional values more clearly. For example, if the valley and Buddhas of Bamiyan have been inscribed as a symbol of resistance against those who would destroy art, and the ruins of Bam inscribed as a symbol of the suffering of its modern inhabitants following the earthquake, both would have marshalled global support. However, being inscribed for lost 'unique' and 'exceptional' characteristics surely weakens the consistent application of the 1972 Convention. The example of Seahenge also highlights the tension between the value of the context and the value of the constituent parts. Finally, we must acknowledge the fact that even our concepts and definitions of the 'nature' and 'value' of cultural heritage have changed over time, as demonstrated by Choay (2001). Thus whilst country houses, palaces, castles and cathedrals might have been inscribed on the United Kingdom's UNESCO list in the past, new sites, such as Saltaire, are presented as reflecting the contribution of the masses. Only more explicitly articulated and expressed values will allow managers of heritage resources to select sites more confidently for national or international preservation, rather than relying on concepts of international or national uniqueness.

References

Abate, M. (ed.) 2002. *World Heritage: Archaeological Sites and Urban Centres.* Milan and Paris: Skira and UNESCO.

Abungu, G. 2001. 'Examples from Kenya and Somalia', in N. Brodie, J. Doole and C. Renfrew (eds.), *Trade in Illicit Antiquities: The Destruction of the World's Archaeological Heritage*, pp. 37–46. Cambridge: McDonald Institute for Archaeological Research.

Addyman, P. 2001. 'Antiquities without Archaeology in the United Kingdom', in N. Brodie, J. Doole and C. Renfrew (eds.), *Trade in Illicit Antiquities: The Destruction of the World's Archaeological Heritage*, pp. 141–4. Cambridge: McDonald Institute for Archaeological Research.

Agius, E. 1994a. *Problems in Applied Ethics.* Malta: Malta University Publishers Ltd.

1994b. 'What Future for Future Generations', in M. Moskowitz (ed.), *Thinking about Future Generations*, pp. 56–78. Kyoto: Institute for the Integrated Study of Future Generations.

Alexander, E. P. 1996. *Museums in Motion: An Introduction to the History and Functions of Museums.* Walnut Creek, CA: AltaMira Press, in cooperation with the American Association for State and Local History.

Alva, W. 2001. 'The Destruction, Looting and Traffic of the Archaeological Heritage of Peru', in N. Brodie, J. Doole and C. Renfrew (eds.), *Trade in Illicit Antiquities: The Destruction of the World's Archaeological Heritage*, pp. 89–96. Cambridge: McDonald Institute for Archaeological Research.

American Anthropological Association 1998. 'Code of Ethics of the American Anthropological Association'. *Anthropology Newsletter*, 39(6). Available at http://www.aaanet.org/committees/ethics/ethcode.htm.

Anderson, Terry L. 1995. *Sovereign Nations or Reservations: An Economic History of American Indians.* San Francisco: Pacific Research Institute for Public Policy.

Andrews, L., N. Buenger, J. Bridge, L. Rosenow, D. Stoney, R. E. Gaensslen, T. Karamanski, R. Lewis, J. Paradise, A. Inlander, and D. Gonen 2004. 'Constructing Ethical Guidelines for Biohistory'. *Science* 304 (5668) (9 April 2004): 215–16.

Anker, L. 1997. *Our Nordic Heritage: World Heritage Sites in the Nordic Countries.* Kristiansund: KOM.

Anscombe, G. E. M. 1958. 'Modern Moral Philosophy'. *Philosophy* 33: 1–19.

Archaeological Institute of America 1990. 'Archaeological Institute of America Code of Ethics', in Karen D. Vittelli (ed.), *Archaeological Ethics*, pp. 261–3. Walnut Creek, CA: AltaMira Press.

Arendt, H. 1957. 'Karl Jaspers: "Citizen of the world"', in Paul Arthur Schilpp (ed.), *The Philosophy of Karl Jaspers*, pp. 539–49. New York: Tudor Publishing Company.

Aristotle. 1954. *Nicomachean Ethics*, trans. Sir David Ross. London: Oxford University Press.

Ashworth, G. 1998. 'Heritage, Identity and Interpreting a European Sense of Place', in D. Uzzell and R. Ballantyne (eds.), *Contemporary Issues in Heritage and Environmental Interpretation: Problems and Prospects*. London: HMSO.

Atwood, R. 2003. 'Guardians of the Dead'. *Archaeology* 56 (1): 42–9.
  2004. *Stealing History: Tomb Raiders, Smugglers, and the Looting of the Ancient World*. New York: St Martin's Press.

Ayau, E. H. 2002. '*Ka Huaka'i O Na 'Ōiwi*: The Journey Home', in C. Fforde, J. Hubert and P. Turnbull (eds.), *The Dead and Their Possessions: Repatriation in Principle, Policy and Practice*, pp. 171–89. London and New York: Routledge.

Bahn, P. 1984. 'Do Not Disturb? Archaeology and the Rights of the Dead'. *Journal of Applied Philosophy* 1: 213–26.

Bahn, P. and J. Flenley 1992. *Easter Island, Earth Island*. London: Thames and Hudson.

Baier, A. 1994. *Moral Prejudices*. Cambridge, MA: Harvard University Press.
  1997. 'What do Women Want in a Moral Theory?' in R. Crisp and M. Slote (eds.), *Virtue Ethics*, pp. 263–77. Oxford: Oxford University Press.

Bailey, D. W. 1996. 'The Looting in Bulgaria', in K. D. Vitelli (ed.), *Archaeological Ethics*, pp. 112–16. Walnut Creek, CA: AltaMira Press.

Bannister, K. and K. Barrett 2004. 'Weighing the Proverbial "Ounce of Prevention" versus the "Pound of Cure" in a Biocultural Context: A Role for the Precautionary Principle in Ethnobiological Research', in T. Carlson and L. Maffi (eds.), *Ethnobotany and Conservation of Biocultural Diversity. Advances in Economic Botany* 15, pp. 307–39. Bronx: New York Botanical Garden Press.

Barakat, S., C. Wilson, V. S. Simcic and M. Kojakovic 2001. 'Challenges and Dilemmas Facing the Reconstruction of War-Damaged Cultural Heritage: The Case Study of Pocitelj, Bosnia-Herzegovina', in R. Layton, P. Stone and J. Thomas (eds), *The Destruction and Conservation of Cultural Property*, pp. 168–81. London: Routledge.

Barker, A. B. 2003. 'Archaeological Ethics: Museums and Collections', in L. J. Zimmerman, K. D. Vitelli, and J. Hollowell-Zimmer (eds.), *Ethical Issues in Archaeology*, pp. 71–83. Walnut Creek, CA: AltaMira Press.

Barker, G. 1996. 'Castles in the Desert', in G. Barker, D. Gilbertson, B. Jones and D. Mattingly, *Farming the Desert: The UNESCO Libyan Valleys*

Archaeological Survey, pp. 1–20. Paris, Tripoli and London: UNESCO, the Department of Antiquities (Tripoli) and the Society for Libyan Studies.

Barringer, T. and Flynn, T. F. (eds.) 1998. *Colonialism and the Object: Empire, Material Culture and the Museum.* London: Routledge.

Barron, A. 1998. 'No other law? Authority, Property and Aboriginal Art', in L. Bentley and S. Mamatis (eds.), *Intellectual Property and Ethics*, pp. 37–88. London: Sweet and Maxwell.

Battiste, M. and J. Y. Henderson 2000. *Protecting Indigenous Knowledge and Heritage.* Saskatoon: Purich.

Bauer, A. 2003. [WAC] Proposition 15, 20th December. Available at https:// listserver.flinders.edu.au/mailman/private/wac/2003-December/000181. html.

Becker, H. S. 1982. *Art Worlds.* Berkeley: University of California Press.

Beech, H. 2003. 'Stealing Beauty: Asia's Looted Treasures'. *Time* 162 (17) (27 October): 58–66.

Bell, S. *et al.* 2004. 'Integrated Management of European Wetlands Project (Contract # EVK2-CT2000–22001)'. Final Report to the European Commission. www.dur.ac.uk/imew.ecproject.

Belmont Report 1979. *The Belmont Report: Ethical Principles and Guidelines for the Protection of Human Subjects of Research.* The National Commission for the Protection of Human Subjects of Biomedical and Behavioral Research. http://ohrp.osophs.dhhs.gov/humansubjects/guidance/belmont.htm (accessed 30 May 2004).

Bendremer, J. C. 1996. 'Investigations of the Old Mohegan Reservation (1663–1869): Reconciling Tradition, Archaeology and the Ethnohistoric Record'. Paper presented at the 95th Annual American Anthropological Association Meeting, San Francisco.

   1998. 'A New Approach to Native American Archaeology: An Approach to Applied Archaeology or Making a Contribution at Mohegan'. Paper presented at the 14th International Congress of Anthropological and Ethnological Sciences, Williamsburg.

Bendremer, J. C. and M. J. Fawcett 1995. 'Mohegan Field School: A Model for the Future'. Paper presented at the 1995 Conference of New England Archaeology, Old Sturbridge Village, Massachusetts.

Bendremer, J. C. and D. F. Wozniak 2000. 'Who Are We Working For? A New Paradigm for Professional Relationships between Anthropologists and Native Americans'. Paper presented at the American Anthropological Association Meeting, San Francisco.

Bendremer, J. C., D. F. Wozniak and E. L. Thomas 2002. 'Mohegan Field Research: A Case Study in Applied Archaeology'. Paper presented at the Ethics and the Practice of Archaeology Symposium, University of Pennsylvania.

Bentz, M. 1997. 'Beyond Ethics: Science, Friendship and Privacy', in T. Biolsi and L. J. Zimmerman (eds.), *Indians and Anthropologists: Vine Deloria, Jr.*

and the Critique of Anthropology, pp. 120–32. Tucson: University of Arizona Press.

Biolsi, T. 1997. 'The Anthropological Construction of "Indians": Haviland Scudder Mekeel and the Search for the Primitive in Lakota Country', in T. Biolsi and L. J. Zimmerman (eds.), *Indians and Anthropologists: Vine Deloria, Jr. and the Critique of Anthropology*, pp. 133–59. Tucson: University of Arizona Press.

Blair, B. 1979. 'Indian Rights: Native Americans versus American Museums – A Battle for Artefacts'. *American Indian Law Review* 7: 125–54.

Blakey, M. 1990. 'American Nationality and Ethnicity in the Depicted Past', in P. Gathercole and D. Lowenthal (eds.), *The Politics of the Past*, pp. 38–48. London: Routledge.

Bloch, M. 1971. *Placing the Dead*. London: Seminar Press.

Blumt, Orly 2002. 'The Illicit Antiquities Trade: An Analysis of Current Antiquities Looting in Israel'. *Culture without Context* 11 (Autumn): 20–3.

Boas, F. 1940. *Race, Language and Culture*. New York: Macmillan.

Boniface, P. and P. J. Fowler 1993. *Heritage and Tourism in 'the Global Village'*. London: Routledge.

Bordewich, F. M. 1996. *Killing the White Man's Indian: Reinventing Native Americans at the End of the Twentieth Century*. New York: Anchor Books Doubleday.

Bourdieu, P. 1977. *Outline of a Theory of Practice*, trans. R. Nice. Cambridge: Cambridge University Press.

  1984. *Distinction: A Social Critique of the Judgement of Taste*, trans. R. Nice. Cambridge, MA: Harvard University Press.

  1990. *The Logic of Practice*, trans. R. Nice. Stanford: Stanford University Press.

Bowdler, S. 1988. 'Repainting Australian Rock Art', *Antiquity* 62: 517–23.

Bradshaw, E. 2000. 'Mining and Cultural Heritage Management: the Hamersley Iron Experience', in I. Lilley (ed.), *Native Title and the Transformation of Archaeology in the Postcolonial World*, pp. 10–23. Sydney: Oceania Publications.

Brandt, R. B. 1954. *Hopi Ethics: A Theoretical Analysis*. Chicago: University of Chicago Press.

Bray, T. L. and T. W. Killion (eds.) 1994. *Reckoning with the Dead: The Larsen Bay Repatriation and the Smithsonian Institution*. Washington and London: The Smithsonian Institution.

Brecher, B. 2002. 'Our Obligations to the Dead'. *Journal of Applied Philosophy* 19: 109–19.

Breeze, D. J. 1993. 'Ancient Monuments Legislation', in J. Hunter and I. Ralston (eds.), *Archaeological Resource Management in the UK: An Introduction*, pp. 184–96. Stroud: Sutton.

Brent, M. 1994. 'The Rape of Mali'. *Archaeology* 47 (3): 26–35.

  1996. 'A View inside the Illicit Trade in African Antiquities', in P. R. Schmidt and R. J. McIntosh (eds.), *Plundering Africa's Past*, pp. 63–78. Bloomington: Indiana University Press.

Brodie, N. and J. Doole 2001. 'Illicit Antiquities', in N. Brodie, J. Doole and C. Renfrew (eds.), *Trade in Illicit Antiquities: The Destruction of the World's Archaeological Heritage*, pp. 1–6. Cambridge: McDonald Institute for Archaeological Research.

Brodie, N., J. Doole and C. Renfrew (eds.) 2001. *Trade in Illicit Antiquities: The Destruction of the World's Archaeological Heritage*. Cambridge: McDonald Institute for Archaeological Research.

Brodie, N., J. Doole and P. Watson 2000. *Stealing History: The Illicit Trade in Cultural Material*. Report for the Museums Association and ICOM-UK. Cambridge: McDonald Institute for Archaeological Research.

Brodie, N., M. Kersel, C. Luke and K. W. Tubb (eds.) in press. *Archaeology, Cultural Heritage and the Trade in Antiquities*. Gainesville: University Press of Florida.

Brodie, N. and K. W. Tubb (eds.) 2002. *Illicit Antiquities: The Theft of Culture and the Extinction of Archaeology*. London: Routledge.

Brown, M. 1998. 'Can Culture be Copyrighted?' *Current Anthropology* 39: 193–222. 2003. *Who Owns Native Culture?* Cambridge, MA: Harvard University Press.

Burke, P. 1989. 'New Reflections on World History'. *Culture and History* 5: 9–18.

Byrne, D. 1991. 'Western Hegemony in Archaeological Heritage Management'. *History and Anthropology* 5: 269–76.

Canouts, V. and F. P. McManamon 2001. 'Protecting the Past for the Future: Federal Archaeology in the United States', in N. Brodie, J. Doole and C. Renfrew (eds.), *Trade in Illicit Antiquities: The Destruction of the World's Archaeological Heritage*, pp. 97–110. Cambridge: McDonald Institute for Archaeological Research.

Carleton, M.-H., M. Zubeidi and M. Garen 2004. 'The War within the War'. *Archaeology* 57 (4): 28–31.

Carman, J. 2002. *Archaeology and Heritage: An Introduction*. London: Continuum.

Carter, C. E. 1997. 'Straight Talk and Trust', in N. Swidler, K. E. Dongoske, R. Anyon and A. S. Downer (eds.), *Native Americans and Archaeologists: Stepping Stones to Common Ground*, pp. 151–5. Walnut Creek, CA: AltaMira Press.

Carter, H. 1923. *The Tomb of Tut-ankh-Amen, Discovered by the Late Earl of Carnarvon and Howard Carter*. New York: George H. Doran Company.

Cassell, J. and S.-E. Jacobs (eds.) 1987. *Handbook on Ethical Issues in Anthropology*. Special Publication of the American Anthropological Association 23. Washington, DC: American Anthropological Association.

Cattaneo, M. and J. Trifoni 2002. *The World Heritage Sites of UNESCO: The Treasures of Art*. Vercelli: White Star.

Champe, J. L., D. S. Byers, C. Evans, A. K. Guthe, H. W. Hamilton, E. B. Jelks, C. W. Meighan, S. Olafson, G. I. Quimby, W. Smith and F. Wendorf 1961. 'Four Statements for Archaeology'. *American Antiquity* 27: 137–8.

Chapman, J. 1994. 'Destruction of a Common Heritage: The Archaeology of War in Croatia, Bosnia and Hercegovina'. *Antiquity* 68: 120–6.

Chippendale, C. and D. M. Pendergast 1995. 'Intellectual Property: Ethics, Knowledge and Publication', in M. J. Lynott and A. Wylie (eds.), *Ethics in American Archaeology: Challenges for the 1990's*, pp. 45–9. Washington, DC: American Anthropological Association.

Choay, F. 2001. *The Invention of the Historic Monument*. Cambridge: Cambridge University Press.

Clark, G. 1968 [1939]. *Archaeology and Society*. London: Methuen.

    1961. *World Prehistory: An Outline*. Cambridge: Cambridge University Press.

    1970. *Aspects of Prehistory*. Berkeley: University of California Press.

Clavir, M. 2002. *Preserving What Is Valued: Museums, Conservation, and First Nations*. Vancouver: UBC Press.

Cleere, H. 1992. 'Editorial'. *Antiquity* 66: 3–9.

    1993a. 'British Archaeology in a Wider Context', in J. Hunter and I. Ralston (eds.), *Archaeological Resource Management in the UK. An Introduction*, pp. 115–24. London: Alan Sutton.

    1993b. *The World Heritage Convention 1972: Framework for a Global Study (Cultural Properties)*. Paris: ICOMOS.

    1995. 'Cultural Landscapes as World Heritage'. *Conservation and Management of Archaeological Sites* 1: 63–8.

    1996. 'The Concept of "Outstanding Universal Value" in the World Heritage Convention'. *Conservation and Management of Archaeological Sites* 1: 227–33.

    2000. 'The World Heritage Convention in the Third World', in Francis P. McManamon and Alf Hatton (eds.), *Cultural Resource Management in Contemporary Society: Perspectives on Managing and Presenting the Past*, pp. 99–106. One World Archaeology 33. London: Routledge.

    2001. 'The Uneasy Bedfellows: Universality and Cultural Heritage', in Robert Layton, Peter G. Stone and Julian Thomas (eds.), *Destruction and Conservation of Cultural Property*, pp. 22–9. One World Archaeology 41. London: Routledge.

Clifford, J. 1988. *The Predicament of Culture: Twentieth-Century Ethnography, Literature, and Art*. Cambridge, MA: Harvard University Press.

Clifford, J. and G. Marcus (eds.) 1986. *Writing Culture: The Poetics and Politics of Ethnography*. Berkeley: University of California Press.

Coe, M. D. 1993. 'From Huaquero to Connoisseur: The Early Market in Pre-Columbian Art', in E. H. Boone (eds.), *Collecting the Pre-Columbian Past*, pp. 271–90. Washington, DC: Dumbarton Oaks Research Library and Collection.

Coggins, C. 1972. 'Archeology and the Art Market'. *Science* 175 (4019): 263–6.

Cohen, J. and N. Swidler 1995. 'Integrated Methodologies: Cultural Resource Management on the Navajo Nation'. Paper presented at the Society for Applied Anthropology meetings, Albuquerque.

Cole, D. 1985. *Captured Heritage: The Scramble for Northwest Coast Artifacts*. Seattle: University of Washington Press.

Coleman, E. B. 2004. 'Property, Ownership and Rights'. Lecture given in the Department of Anthropology, University of New York.

Collingwood, R. G. 1993. *The Idea of History*. Oxford: Oxford University Press.

Colwell-Chanthaphonh, C. 2004. 'Those Obscure Objects of Desire: Collecting Cultures and the Archaeological Landscape in the San Pedro Valley of Arizona'. *Journal of Contemporary Ethnography* 33 (5): 571–601.

Colwell-Chanthaphonh, C. and T. J. Ferguson 2004. 'Virtue Ethics and the Practice of History: Native Americans and Archaeologists along the San Pedro Valley of Arizona'. *Journal of Social Archaeology* 4 (1): 5–27.

Common Rule 1981. Code of Federal Regulations. Title 45 2001: §46.102.

Coningham, R. A. E. and N. Lewer 1999. 'Paradise Lost: The Bombing of the Temple of the Tooth – a UNESCO World Heritage Site in Sri Lanka'. *Antiquity* 73: 857–66.

Cooper, D. E. and S. P. James 2005. *Buddhism, Virtue and Environment*. Aldershot: Ashgate.

Cox, M. 1996. 'Crypt Archaeology after Spitalfields: Dealing with Our Recent Dead'. *Antiquity* 70: 8–10.

Crisp, R. and M. Slote (eds.) 1997. *Virtue Ethics*. Oxford: Oxford University Press.

Crosby, A. 2002. 'Archaeology and *Vanua* Development in Fiji'. *World Archaeology* 34 (2): 363–79.

Crowell, A. 1985. *Archaeological Survey and Site Condition Assessment of St. Lawrence Island, Alaska, 1984*. Washington, DC: Smithsonian Institution and Sivuqaq Native Corporation.

Cunliffe, B., W. Davies and C. Renfrew (eds.) 2002. *Archaeology: The Widening Debate*. Oxford: Oxford University Press.

Dahlström, Å. N. 2003. *Negotiating Wilderness in a Cultural Landscape: Predators and Saami Reindeer Herding in the Laponian World Heritage Area*. Uppsala Studies in Cultural Anthropology 32. Uppsala: Uppsala University.

Darvill, T. 1995. 'Value Systems in Archaeology', in M. A. Cooper, A. Firth, J. Carman and D. Wheatley (eds.), *Managing Archaeology*, pp. 40–50. London: Routledge.

Davis, H. A. 1984. 'Approaches to Ethical Problems by Archaeological Organizations', in E. L. Green (ed.), *Ethics and Values in Archaeology*, pp. 13–21. New York: Free Press.

2003. 'Creating and Implementing a Code and Standards', in L. J. Zimmerman, K. D. Vitelli and J. Hollowell-Zimmer (eds.), *Ethical Issues in Archaeology*, pp. 251–60. Walnut Creek, CA: AltaMira Press.

Day, M. 1990. 'Archaeological Ethics and the Treatment of the Dead'. *Anthropology Today* 6: 15–16.

de Cuéllar, J. P. 1996. *Our Creative Diversity: Report of the World Commission on Culture and Development*. Second edition. Paris: UNESCO.

Deloria Jr., Vine 1969. *Custer Died for Your Sins: An Indian Manifesto*. New York: Avon.

1973. *God Is Red: A Native View of Religion*. New York: Delta Press.

1980. 'Our New Research Society: Some Warnings for Social Scientists'. *Social Problems* 27 (3): 265–71 (special issue, *Ethical Problems of Fieldwork*, ed. J. Cassell and M. Wax).

1989. 'A Simple Question of Humanity: The Moral Dimensions of the Reburial Issue'. *Native American Rights Fund Legal Review* 14 (4): 1–12.

1992. 'Indians, Archaeologists and the Future'. *American Antiquity* 57 (4): 595–8.

1995. *Red Earth, White Lies: Native Americans and the Myth of Scientific Fact.* New York: Scribner's.

1999. 'A Flock of Anthros', in B. Deloria, K. Foehner and S. Scinta (eds.), *Spirit and Reason: A Vine Deloria, Jr. Reader*, pp. 123–6. Golden, CA: Fulcrum Publishing.

2000. 'Secularism, Civil Religion, and the Religious Freedom of American Indians', in D. A. Mihesuah (ed.), *Repatriation Reader: Who Owns American Indian Remains?*, pp. 218–28. Lincoln: University of Nebraska Press.

Dippie, B. W. 1982. *The Vanishing American: White Attitudes and U.S. Indian Policy.* Middletown, CT: Wesleyan University Press.

Dombrowski, K. and G. M. Sider 2002. 'Series Editors' Afterword', in K. S. Fine-Dare, *Grave Injustice: The American Indian Repatriation Movement and NAGPRA*, pp. 189–97. Lincoln: University of Nebraska Press.

Dominguez, V. R. 1986. 'The Marketing of Heritage'. *American Ethnologist* 13 (3): 546–55.

Downer, A. S. 1997. 'Archaeologist–Native American Relations', in N. Swidler, K. E. Dongoske, R. Anyon and A. S. Downer (eds.), *Native Americans and Archaeologists: Stepping Stones to Common Ground*, pp. 23–34. Walnut Creek, CA: AltaMira Press.

Droste, B. von, H. Plachter and M. Rössler (eds.) 1995. *Cultural Landscapes of Universal Value: Components of a Global Strategy.* Jena: Gustav Fischer Verlag.

Dummett, Michael 1986. 'The Ethics of Cultural Property'. *Times Literary Supplement* 4347 (25 July 1986), 809–10.

Durkheim, E. 1915. *The Elementary Forms of the Religious Life*, trans. J. W. Swain. London: Unwin.

Early, A. M. 1999. 'Profiteers and Public Archaeology: Antiquities Trafficking in Arkansas', in P. Messenger (ed.), *The Ethics of Collecting Cultural Property: Whose Culture? Whose Property?*, pp. 39–50. Albuquerque: University of New Mexico Press.

Echo-Hawk, R. 1997. 'Forging a New Ancient History for Native America', in N. Swidler, K. E. Dongoske, R. Anyon and A. S. Downer (eds.), *Native Americans and Archaeologists: Stepping Stones to Common Ground*, pp. 88–102. Walnut Creek, CA: AltaMira Press.

2000. 'Ancient History of the New World: Integrating Oral Traditions and the Archaeological Record in Deep Time'. *American Antiquity* 65: 267–90.

Echo-Hawk, R. C. and W. R. Echo-Hawk 1994. *Battlefields and Burial Grounds: The Indian Struggle to Protect Ancestral Graves in the United States.* Minneapolis: Lerner Publications.

Elia, R. J. 1997. 'Looting, Collecting, and the Destruction of Archaeological Resources'. *Nonrenewable Resources* 6 (2): 85–98.

2001. 'Analysis of the Looting, Selling, and Collecting of Apulian Red-Figure Vases: A Quantitative Approach', in N. Brodie, J. Doole and C. Renfrew (eds.), *Trade in Illicit Antiquities: The Destruction of the World's Archaeological Heritage*, pp. 145–54. Cambridge: McDonald Institute for Archaeological Research.

Epicurus 1926. *The Extant Remains*, ed. C. Bailey. Oxford: Clarendon Press.

Erickson, C. 1988. 'Raised Field Agriculture in the Lake Titicaca Basin'. *Expedition* 30 (3): 8–16.

Eriksen, Thomas Hylland 1996. *Kampen om fortiden: et essay om myter, identitet og politikk*. Oslo: Aschehoug.

2001. 'Between Universalism and Relativism: A Critique of the UNESCO Concept of Culture', in J. K. Cowan, M.-B. Dembour and R. A. Wilson (eds.), *Culture and Rights. Anthropological Perspectives*, pp. 127–48. Cambridge: Cambridge University Press.

European Convention on the Protection of the Archaeological Heritage (Revised) (1992), Valletta, 16.1.1992, www.tufts.edu/departments/fletcher/multi/www/bh997.html.

European Landscape Convention 2000 (2000), http://www.nature.coe.int/english/main/landscape/conv.html.

Fagan, B. 1996. 'Archaeology's Dirty Little Secret', in K. D. Vittelli (ed.), *Archaeological Ethics*, pp. 247–52. Walnut Creek, CA: AltaMira Press.

Featherstone, M. 1991. *Consumer Culture and Postmodernism*. London: Sage Publications.

Fechner, F. G. 1998. 'The Fundamental Aims of Cultural Property Law'. *International Journal of Cultural Property* 7: 376–94.

Ferguson, T. J. 1991. 'Return of War Gods Sets Example for Repatriation', in *Zuni History: Victories in the 1990s*. Zuni History Repatriation Project. Seattle: Institute of the American West.

1996. 'Native Americans and the Practice of Archaeology', *Annual Review of Anthropology* 25: 63–79.

Ferguson, T. J., R. Anyon and E. J. Ladd 2000. 'Repatriation at the Pueblo of Zuni: Diverse Solutions to Complex Problems', in D. A. Mihesuah (ed.), *Repatriation Reader*, pp. 239–65. Lincoln: University of Nebraska Press.

Ferris, N. 1998. '"I Don't Think We're in Kansas Anymore . . .". The Rise of the Archaeological Consulting Industry in Ontario', in P. Smith and D. Mitchell (eds.), *Bringing Back the Past: Historical Perspectives on Canadian Archaeology*, Museum of Civilization, Archaeological Survey of Canada, Mercury Series, Paper 158. Gatineau, Quebec: Museum of Civilization.

2003. 'Between Colonial and Indigenous Archaeologies: Legal and Extra-legal Ownership of the Archaeological Past in North America'. *Canadian Journal of Archaeology* 27: 154–90.

Fforde, C., J. Hubert and P. Turnbull (eds.) 2002. *The Dead and Their Possessions: Repatriation in Principle, Policy and Practice*. London and New York: Routledge.

Fichte, J. G. 1988. *Early Writings*, trans. D. Breazeale. Ithaca, NY: Cornell University Press.

Filer, C. 1996. 'The Social Context of Renewable Resource Depletion in Papua New Guinea', in R. Howitt, J. Connell and P. Hirsch (eds.), *Resources, Nations and Indigenous Peoples*, pp. 289–99. Melbourne: Oxford University Press.

Fine-Dare, K. S. 2002. *Grave Injustice: The American Indian Repatriation Movement and NAGPRA*. Lincoln: University of Nebraska Press.

Fingarette, H. 1996. *Death: Philosophical Soundings*. Chicago and La Salle: Open Court.

FitzHugh, W. W. 1994. 'Foreword', in T. L. Bray and T. W. Killion (eds.), *Reckoning with the Dead: The Larsen Bay Repatriation and the Smithsonian Institution*, pp. v–x. Washington and London: The Smithsonian Institution.

Fluehr-Lobban, C. (ed.) 2003. *Ethics and the Profession of Anthropology: Dialogue for Ethically Conscious Practice*. Walnut Creek, CA: AltaMira Press.

Fontein, J. 2000. *UNESCO, Heritage and Africa: An Anthropological Critique of World Heritage*. Centre of African Studies, Occasional Papers 80. Edinburgh: Edinburgh University Press.

Ford, R. I. 1973. 'Archaeology serving humanity', in Charles L. Redman (ed.), *Research and Theory in Current Archaeology*, pp. 83–93. New York: Wiley.

Forsman, L. A. 1997. 'Straddling the Current: A View from the Bridge over Clear Salt Water', in N. Swidler, K. E. Dongoske, R. Anyon and A. S. Downer (eds.), *Native Americans and Archaeologists: Stepping Stones to Common Ground*, pp. 105–111. Walnut Creek, CA: AltaMira Press.

Foster, R. J. 1991, 'Making National Cultures in the Global Ecumene'. *Annual Review of Anthropology* 20: 235–60.

Foucault, M. 1972. *The Archaeology of Knowledge*, trans. A. M. Sheridan Smith. London: Tavistock.

   1977. *Discipline and Punish: The Birth of the Prison*, trans. A. Sheridan. London: Penguin.

Fowler, P. J. 2003. *World Heritage Cultural Landscapes 1992–2002*. World Heritage Paper 6. Paris: UNESCO World Heritage Center.

Fuchs, A. E. 1990–91. 'Posthumous Satisfactions and the Concept of Individual Welfare'. *Journal of Philosophical Research* 16: 345–51.

Fullagar, R. and L. Head 2000. 'Archaeology and Native Title in Australia: National and Local Perspectives', in I. Lilley (ed.), *Native Title and the Transformation of Archaeology in the Postcolonial World*, pp. 24–34. Sydney: Oceania Publications.

Fuller, R. 1997. 'Aspects of Consultation for the Central Sierran Me-Wuk', in N. Swidler, K. E. Dongoske, R. Anyon and A. S. Downer (eds.), *Native Americans and Archaeologists: Stepping Stones to Common Ground*, pp. 181–7. Walnut Creek, CA: AltaMira Press.

Gado, B. 2001. 'The Republic of Niger', in N. Brodie, J. Doole and C. Renfrew (eds.), *Trade in Illicit Antiquities: The Destruction of the World's Archaeological Heritage*, pp. 57–72. Cambridge: McDonald Institute for Archaeological Research.

Galtung, J. 1967. 'After Camelot', in I. Horowitz (ed.), *The Rise and Fall of Project Camelot: Studies in the Relationship between the Social Sciences and Practical Politics*, pp. 281–312. Cambridge, MA: MIT Press.

Gamboni, D. 1997. *The Destruction of Art: Iconoclasm and Vandalism since the French Revolution*. London: Reaktion Books.

2001. 'World Heritage: Shield or Target?'. *The Getty Conservation Institute Newsletter* 16 (2): 5–11.

Gardner, R. N. (ed.) 1966. *Blueprint for Peace: Being the Proposals of Prominent Americans to the White House Conference on International Cooperation*. New York: McGraw-Hill.

Garza, C. E. and S. Powell 2001. 'Ethics and the Past: Reburial and Repatriation in American Archaeology', in T. Bray (ed.), *The Future of the Past: Archaeologists, Native Americans and Repatriation*, pp. 37–56. New York: Garland Publishing.

Geach, P. 1969. *God and the Soul*. London: Routledge and Kegan Paul.

Gerstenblith, P. 1995. 'Identity and Cultural Property: The Protection of Cultural Property in the United States'. *Boston University Law Review* 75: 559–688.

Gill, D. W. J. and C. Chippindale 1993. 'Material and Intellectual Consequences of Esteem for Cycladic Figures'. *American Journal of Archaeology* 97: 601–59.

Goldstein, L. and K. Kintigh 1990. 'Ethics and the Reburial Controversy'. *American Antiquity* 55: 585–90.

Golvan, C. 1992. 'Aboriginal Art and the Protection of Indigenous Cultural Rights'. *European Intellectual Property Review* 7: 227–32.

Gombrich, R. and G. Obeyesekere 1988. *Buddhism Transformed: Religious Change in Sri Lanka*. Princeton, NJ: Princeton University Press.

Goodale, G. 1996. 'Central American Sleuths Target a Hot Black Market'. *Christian Science Monitor* 88 (230), 23 October: 1.

Goodman, N. 1968. *Languages of Art*. New York: Bobbs-Merrill.

Graburn, N. (ed.) 1976. *Ethnic and Tourist Arts*. Berkeley: University of California Press.

Green, E. L. (ed.) 1984. *Ethics and Values in Archaeology*. New York: The Free Press.

Green, L. F., D. R. Green and E. G. Neves 2003. 'Indigenous Knowledge and Archaeological Science: The Challenges of Public Archaeology in the Reserva Uaça'. *Journal of Social Archaeology* 3 (3): 366–98.

Greenawalt, K. 1998. 'Thinking in Terms of Law and Morality'. *International Journal of Cultural Property* 7: 7–20.

Greenwood, D. 1989. 'Culture by the Pound: An Anthropological Perspective of Tourism as Cultural Commoditization', in V. L. Smith (ed.), *Hosts and Guests: The Anthropology of Tourism*, pp. 171–86. Philadelphia: University of Pennsylvania Press.

Grimes, R. L. 2001. 'Desecration: An Interreligious Controversy', in T. L. Bray (ed.), *The Future of the Past: Archaeologists, Native Americans and Repatriation*, pp. 91–105. New York: Garland Publishing.

Groarke, L. 2001. 'Over My Dead Body: Archaeology *versus* Aboriginals on Ancient Skeletal Remains', Paper presented at *Grave Concerns: The Ethics of the Dead*. The Second Annual Laurier Brantford Interdisciplinary Conference. Brantford: Wilfrid Laurier University.

Grobsmith, E. S. 1997. 'Growing Up on Deloria: The Impact of His Work on a New Generation of Anthropologists', in T. Biolsi and L. J. Zimmerman (eds.), *Indians and Anthropologists: Vine Deloria, Jr. and the Critique of Anthropology*, pp. 35–49. Tucson: University of Arizona Press.

Gupta, A. K. 1998. 'Rewarding Local Communities for Conserving Biodiversity: The Case of the Honey Bee', in L. D. Guruswamy and J. A. McNeely (eds.), *Protection of Global Biodiversity: Converging Strategies*, pp. 180–9. Durham, NC: Duke University Press.

Hager, L. 1997. 'Sex and Gender in Paleoanthropology', in L. Hager (ed.), *Women in Human Evolution*, pp. 1–28. London: Routledge.

Hall, M. 2002. 'Beyond Ethics: Anthropological Moralities on the Boundaries of the Public and the Professional'. Mexico, March 2002. http://www.meg.uct.ac.za/martin/beyond_ethics.htm. Accessed May 2004.

Hall, S. 1991. 'The Local and the Global: Globalization and Ethnicity', in A. D. King (ed.), *Culture, Globalization and the World-System: Contemporary Conditions for the Representation of Identity*, pp. 19–39. London: Macmillan.

Hamann, B. 2002. 'The Social Life of Pre-sunrise Things: Indigenous Mesoamerican Archaeology'. *Current Anthropology* 43 (3): 351–82.

Hamilakis, Y. 1999. 'La trahison des archéologues? Archaeological Practice as Intellectual Activity in Postmodernity'. *Journal of Mediterranean Archaeology* 12 (1): 60–79.

Hamilton, C. E. 1995. 'A Cautionary Perspective', in M. J. Lynott and A. Wylie (eds.), *Ethics in American Archaeology: Challenges for the 1990's*, pp. 57–63. Washington, DC: Society for American Archaeology.

2000. 'A Cautionary Perspective', in M. J. Lynott and A. Wylie (eds.), *Ethics in American Archaeology: Challenges for the 1990's*, pp. 64–70. 2nd rev. edn. Washington, DC: Society for American Archaeology.

Hampshire, K., S. Bell, F. Stepukonis and G. Wallace 2003. '"Real" Poachers and Predators: Shades of Meaning in Local Understandings of Threats to Fisheries'. *Society and Natural Resources* 17 (4): 305–18.

Handler, R. 1991. 'Who Owns the Past?', in B. Williams (ed.), *The Politics of Culture*, pp. 63–74. Washington, DC and London: Smithsonian Institution Press.

Hantman, J. L., K. Wood and D. Shields 2000. 'Writing Collaborative History: How the Monacan Nation and Archaeologists Worked Together to Enrich our Understanding of Virginia's Native Peoples'. *Archaeology Magazine* 53 (5): 56–61.

Harbsmeier, M. 1989. 'World Histories before Domestication. The Writing of Universal Histories, Histories of Mankind and World Histories in Late Eighteenth Century Germany', *Culture and History* 5: 93–131.

Hardy, S. 2003. [WAC] 'Looting Replies, 20 December'. Available at https://listserver.flinders.edu.au/mailman/private/wac/2003-December/000185.html.

2004. 'Is There a Human Right to Loot?' Manuscript in the possession of the author.

Harrington, S. P. M. 1991. 'The Looting of Arkansas'. *Archaeology* 44 (3): 22–31.

Harrison, D. and M. Hitchcock 2005. *The Politics of World Heritage: Negotiating Tourism and Conservation.* Current Issues in Tourism 4. Clevedon, Buffalo and Toronto: Channel View Publications.

Harrison, R. 2000. 'Challenging the "Authenticity" of Antiquity: Contact Archaeology and Native Title in Australia', in I. Lilley (ed.), *Native Title and the Transformation of Archaeology in the Postcolonial World*, pp. 35–53. Sydney: Oceania Publications.

Hastings, J. (ed.) 1912. *Encyclopaedia of Religion and Ethics.* Edinburgh: T. and T. Clark.

Haugerud, A., M. P. Stone and P. D. Little, (eds.) 2000. *Commodities and Globalization: Anthropological Perspectives.* Lanham, MD: Society for Economic Anthropology; Rowman and Littlefield.

Heath, D. B. 1973. 'Economic Aspects of Commercial Archeology in Costa Rica', *American Antiquity* 38 (3): 259–65.

Heidegger, Martin 1962. *Being and Time,* tr. Macquarrie, John and Robinson, Edward. Oxford: Blackwell.

Herle, A. 1994. 'Museums and First Peoples in Canada', *Journal of Museum Ethnography* 6: 39–66.

Hewison, Robert 1989. 'Heritage: An Interpretation', in *Heritage Interpretation. Volume I. The Natural & Built Environment.* Edited by David Uzzel. London: Belhaven Press.

Hinsley, Curtis M. 2002. 'Digging for Identity: Reflections on the Cultural Background of Collecting', in D. A. Mihesuah (ed.), *Repatriation Reader: Who Owns American Indian Remains?*, pp. 37–59. Lincoln: University of Nebraska Press.

Hodder, I. 1999. *The Archaeological Process. An Introduction.* Oxford: Blackwell.

Hollowell, J. 2002. (Hollowell-Zimmer) 'The Legal Market in Archaeological Materials from Alaska's Bering Strait'. *Journal of American Archaeology (Revista de Arquelogia Americana): Special Issue on Heritage* 21: 7–32 (published by the Instituto Panamericano de Geografia e Historia).

2004. '"Old Things" on the Loose: The Legal Market for Archaeological Materials from Alaska's Bering Strait'. PhD dissertation. Bloomington: Indiana University.

Hollowell, J. and R. R. Wilk 1995. 'Are Practices of Archaeological Field Projects Related to Positive Relationships with Local Communities? A Quantitative Analysis of 84 Cases.' Paper presented at the Society for American Archaeology (March), Chicago, Illinois.

Hollowell, J. 2003 (Hollowell-Zimmer). 'Digging in the Dirt-Ethics and "Low-End Looting"', in L. Zimmerman, K. Vitelli and J. Hollowell-Zimmer (eds.), *Ethical Issues in Archaeology*, pp. 45–56. Walnut Creek: AltaMira Press.

Hosmer, Charles B., Jr. 1965. *Presence of the Past.* New York: Putnam Press.

Hoving, T. 1978. *Tutankhamun: The Untold Story.* New York: Simon and Schuster.

Howell, C. J. 1996. 'Daring to Deal with Huaqueros', in K. D. Vitelli (ed.), *Archaeological Ethics*, pp. 47–53. Walnut Creek, CA: AltaMira Press.

Huang, Y. 2003. 'Cheng Brothers' Neo-Confucian Virtue Ethics: The Identity of Virtue and Nature'. *Journal of Chinese Philosophy* 30: 451–67.

Hurst Thomas, D. 2000. *Skull Wars: Kennewick Man, Archaeology, and the Battle for Native American Identity.* New York: Basic Books.

Hursthouse, R. 1999. *On Virtue Ethics.* Oxford: Oxford University Press.

Hutt, S., E. W. Jones and M. McAllister 1992. *Archaeological Resource Protection.* Washington, DC: The Preservation Press.

ICOMOS 2004. *The World Heritage List: Filling the Gaps – An Action Plan for the Future. An Analysis by ICOMOS.* Paris: ICOMOS.

Impey, O. and A. MacGregor (eds.) 1985. *The Origins of Museums: The Cabinet of Curiosities in Sixteenth- and Seventeenth-Century Europe.* Oxford: Clarendon.

Janke, T. 1998. *Our Culture: Our Future. Report on Australian Indigenous Cultural and Intellectual Property Rights.* Canberra: Australian Institute of Aboriginal and Torres Strait Islander Commission, and Michael Frankel and Company, Surrey Hills, NSW.

Johnson, E. 1973. 'Professional Responsibilities and the American Indian'. *American Antiquity* 38 (2): 129–30.

Jokilehto, J. 1999. *A History of Architectural Conservation.* Oxford: Butterworth-Heinemann.

Jolles, C. Z. with E. M. Oozeva 2002. *Faith, Food, and Family in a Yupik Whaling Community.* Seattle: University of Washington Press.

Jones, D. G. and R. Harris 1998. 'Archaeological Human Remains: Scientific, Cultural and Ethical Considerations'. *Current Anthropology* 39 (2): 253–64.

Jones, S. 2003. *Early Medieval Sculpture and the Production of Meaning, Value and Place: The Case of Hilton of Cadboll.* Edinburgh: Historic Scotland.

in press. 'Making Place, Resisting Displacement: Conflicting National and Local Identities in Scotland', in J. Littler and R. Naidoo (eds.), *The Politics of Heritage: Commemoration, Hybridity and National Stones*, pp. 97–117. London: Routledge.

Jote, K. 1994. *International Legal Protection of Cultural Heritage.* Stockholm: Juristförlaget.

Joyce, R. A. 2002. 'Academic Freedom, Stewardship and Cultural Heritage: Weighing the Interests of Stakeholders in Crafting Repatriation Approaches', in C. Fforde, J. Hubbert and P. Turnbull (eds.), *The Dead and Their Possessions*, pp. 99–107. New York: Routledge.

Kant, Immanuel 1909 [1785]. *Fundamental Principles of the Metaphysic of Morals*, in *Kant's Critique of Practical Reason and Other Works on the Theory of Ethics*, trans. T. K. Abbott. London: Longmans.

1959 [1785]. *Foundations of the Metaphysics of Morals*, trans. L. W. Beck. Indianapolis: Bobbs-Merrill.

Karoma, N. J. 1996. 'The Deterioration and Destruction of Archaeological and Historical Sites in Tanzania', in P. R. Schmidt and R. J. McIntosh (eds.), *Plundering Africa's Past*, pp. 191–200. Bloomington: Indiana University Press.

Keane, W. 2001. 'Money Is No Object: Materiality, Desire, and Modernity in an Indonesian Society', in F. R. Myers (ed.), *The Empire of Things: Regimes of Value and Material Culture*, pp. 65–90. Santa Fe: School of American Research.

Kenoyer, J. M. 1998. *Ancient Cities of the Indus Valley Civilisation*. Karachi: Oxford University Press.

2002. 'Challenges in Pakistan: Efforts to Combat a Taliban Mentality' (Interview by Susan Kepecs). *Archaeology* 55 (2): 19–21.

Keon-Cohen, B. A. 1993. 'Some Problems of Proof: The Admissibility of Traditional Evidence', in M. A. Stephenson and S. Ratnapala (eds.), *Mabo: A Judicial Revolution. The Aboriginal Land Rights Decision and Its Impact on Australian Law*, pp. 185–205. St Lucia: University of Queensland Press.

Kersel, M. 2002. 'A Double Edge Sword: Are Managed Antiquities Markets an Ethical Solution to the Trade in Antiquities?' Paper presented at the Symposium on Ethics and the Practice of Archaeology, University of Pennsylvania Museum of Archaeology and Anthropology, 28 September, Philadelphia.

in press. 'From the Ground to the Buyer: A Market Analysis of the Illegal Trade', in N. Brodie, M. Kersel, C. Luke and K. W. Tubb (eds.), *Archaeology, Cultural Heritage and the Trade in Antiquities*. Gainesville: University Press of Florida.

Kersel, M. and C. Luke 2003. 'Comment: The Battle for the Past'. *Culture without Context* 13, Autumn 2003: 28–31. Available at http://www.mcdonald.cam.ac.uk/IARC/cwoc/issue13/comment-reply.htm.

Khawajike, E. 1990. 'The Study of Our Universal Cultural Heritage through the Unesco Associated Schools Project', in P. Stone and R. MacKenzie (eds.), *The Exluded Past: Archaeology in Education*, pp. 15–23. London: Unwin Hyman.

King, C. 1997. 'Here Come the Anthros', in T. Biolsi and L. J. Zimmerman (eds.), *Indians and Anthropologists: Vine Deloria, Jr. and the Critique of Anthropology*, pp. 115–19. Tucson: University of Arizona Press.

King, J. L. 1999. 'Cultural Property and National Sovereignty', in P. M. Messenger (ed.), *The Ethics of Collecting Cultural Property*, pp. 199–208. Albuquerque: University of New Mexico Press.

King, T. 2003. [WAC] Proposition 15, 18th December. Available at https://listserver.flinders.edu.au/mailman/private/wac/2003-December/000173.html.

King, T. F. 1985. 'The Whiddah and the Ethics of Cooperating with Pothunters: A View'. *SOPA News* 9 (3–4): 1–3.

1991. 'Some Dimensions of the Pothunting Problem', in G. S. Smith and J. E. Ehrenhard (eds.), *Protecting the Past*, pp. 83–92. Boca Raton, FL: CRC Press.

King, T. F., P. P. Hickman and G. Berg 1977. *Anthropology in Historic Preservation: Caring for Culture's Clutter*. New York: Academic Press.

Kirkpatrick, S. D. 1992. *Lord of Sipan: A Tale of Pre-Inca Tombs, Archaeology, and Crime*. New York: William Morrow and Company.

Kluth, R. and K. Munnell 1997. 'The Integration of Traditional and Scientific Knowledge on the Leech Lake Reservation', in N. Swidler, K. E. Dongoske, R. Anyon and A. S. Downer (eds.), *Native Americans and Archaeologists: Stepping Stones to Common Ground*, pp. 112–19. Walnut Creek, CA: AltaMira Press.

Knudson, R. 1991. 'The Archaeological Public Trust in Context', in G. S. Smith and J. E. Ehrenhard (eds.), *Protecting the Past*, pp. 3–8. Boca Raton: CRC Press.

Kohl, P. L. 1989. 'World Prehistory. Comments on the Development, Peculiarities and Requirements of a Forgotten Genre'. *Culture and History* 5: 133–44.

 2004. 'Making the Past Profitable in an Age of Globalization and National Ownership: Contradictions and Considerations', in Y. Rowan and U. Baram (eds.), *Marketing Heritage: Archaeology and the Consumption of the Past*, pp. 295–301. Walnut Creek, CA: AltaMira Press.

Kohl, P. and C. Fawcett (eds.) 1995. *Nationalism, Politics and the Practice of Archaeology*. Cambridge: Cambridge University Press.

Kohn, H. 1971. 'Nationalism and Internationalism', in W. W. Wagar (ed.), *History and the Idea of Mankind*. Albuquerque: University of New Mexico Press.

Krech, S. and B. A. Hail (eds.) 1999. *Collecting Native America, 1870–1960*. Washington, DC: Smithsonian Institution Press.

Kristeva, J. 1991. *Strangers to Ourselves*. New York: Columbia University Press.

 1993. *Nations without Nationalism*. New York: Columbia University Press.

Krupnik, I. 1993. *Arctic Adaptations: Native Whalers and Reindeer Herders of Northern Eurasia*. Hanover and London: University Press of New England.

LaBelle, J. 2003. 'Coffee Cans and Folsom Points: Why We Cannot Continue to Ignore the Artifact Collectors', in L. J. Zimmerman, K. D. Vitelli and J. Hollowell-Zimmer (eds.), *Ethical Issues in Archaeology*, pp. 115–127. Walnut Creek, CA: AltaMira Press.

Lal, B. B. 2001. 'The Excavations at Ayodhya with Reference to the Mandir-Masjid Issue', in R. Layton, P. Stone and J. Thomas (eds.), *The Destruction and Conservation of Cultural Property*, pp. 117–26. London: Routledge.

Lampeter Archaeological Workshop 1997. 'Relativism, Objectivity and the Politics of the Past'. *Archaeological Dialogues* 4 (2): 164–84.

Langford, R. F. 1983. 'Our Heritage – Your Playground'. *Australian Archaeology* 16: 1–6.

Larsen, K. E. (ed.) 1995. *Nara Conference on Authenticity in Relation to the World Heritage Convention. Nara, Japan. 1–6 November 1994, Proceedings*. Paris: UNESCO.

Lawler, A. 2003. 'Looting Savages New Site'. *Science* 302 (5647): 974–5.

Leone, M. 1981. 'Archaeology's Relationship to the Present and the Past', in R. Gould and M. Schiffer (eds.), *Modern Material Culture: The Archaeology of Us*, pp. 5–14. New York: Academic Press.

Lepper, B. T. 2000. 'Working Together – or Serving Two Masters?'. *SAA Bulletin* 18 (4): 22–5.

Lewis-Williams, D. 2002. *The Mind in the Cave: Consciousness and the Origins of Art*. London: Thames and Hudson.

Lilley, I. (ed.) 2000. *Native Title and the Transformation of Archaeology in the Postcolonial World*. Oceania Monograph 50. Sydney: Oceania Publications.

Linstrum, D. 1984. 'An Alternative Approach? An Interview with Anne Reidl'. *Monumentum* (Special Issue): 50–5.

Lipe, W. D. 1984. 'Value and Meaning in Cultural Resources', in H. Cleere (ed.), *Approaches to the Archaeological Heritage: A Comparative Study of World Cultural Resource Management Systems*, pp. 1–10. Cambridge: Cambridge University Press.

Lippert, D. 1997. 'In Front of the Mirror: Native Americans and Academic Archaeology', in Nina Swidler *et al.* (eds.), *Native Americans and Archaeologists: Stepping Stones to Common Ground*, pp. 120–70. Walnut Creek, CA: AltaMira Press.

Locke, J. 1991. *Two Treatises of Government*, with an Introduction by W. S. Carpenter. London: J. M. Dent and Sons Ltd.

Locock, M. 1998. 'Dignity for the Dead'. *The Archaeologist* 33: 13.

Loring, S. 2001. 'Repatriation and Community Archaeology: The Smithsonian Institution's Arctic Studies Center', in T. Bray (ed.), *The Future of the Past: Archaeologists, Native Americans and Repatriation*, pp. 185–200. New York: Garland.

Lowe, E. J. 2002. *A Survey of Metaphysics*. Oxford: Oxford University Press.

Lowenthal, D. 1998. *The Heritage Crusade and the Spoils of History*. Cambridge: Cambridge University Press.

Lurie, Nancy O. 1988. 'Relations Between Indians and Anthropologists', in W. Washburn (ed.), *History of Indian-White Relations*, Handbook of North American Indians, vol. 4. Washington, DC: Smithsonian Institution Press.

Lynott, M. J. 1997. 'Ethical Principles and Archaeological Practice: Development of an Ethics Policy'. *American Antiquity* 62 (4): 589–99.

Lynott, M. J. and A. Wylie 1995. 'Stewardship: The Central Principle of Archaeological Ethics', in M. J. Lynott and A. Wylie (eds.), *Ethics in American Archaeology: Challenges for the 1990's*, pp. 28–32. Washington, DC: Society for American Archaeology.

2000a. 'Stewardship: The Central Principle of Archaeological Ethics', in M. J. Lynott and A. Wylie (eds.), *Ethics in American Archaeology: Challenges for the 1990's*, pp. 28–32. 2nd rev. edn. Washington, DC: Society for American Archaeology.

Lynott, M. J. and A. Wylie, (eds.) 2000b. *Ethics in American Archaeology*. 2nd rev edn. Washington, DC: Society for American Archaeology.

Lyotard, J. F. 1984. *The Postmodern Condition: A Report on Knowledge.* Manchester: Manchester University Press.

McBryde, I. (ed.) 1985. *Who Owns the Past?* Melbourne: Oxford University Press.

McEwan, C., C. Hudson and M.-I. Silva 1994. 'Archaeology and Community: A Village Cultural Center and Museum in Ecuador'. *Practicing Anthropology* 16 (1): 3–7.

McGimsey, C. R. 1984. 'The Value of Archaeology', in E. L. Green (ed.), *Ethics and Values in Archaeology*, pp. 171–4. New York: The Free Press.

McGuire, R. H. 1994a. 'Do the Right Thing', in T. L. Bray and T. W. Killion (eds.), *Reckoning with the Dead: The Larson Bay Repatriation and the Smithsonian Institution*, pp. 180–3. Washington, DC: The Smithsonian Institution.

1994b. 'The Sanctity of the Grave: White Concepts and American Indian Burials', in R. Layton (ed.), *Conflict in the Archaeology of Living Traditions*, pp. 167–84. London: Routledge.

1997. 'Why Have Archaeologists Thought the Real Indians Were Dead and What Can We Do About It?', in T. Biolsi and L. J. Zimmerman (eds.), *Indians and Anthropologists: Vine Deloria, Jr. and the Critique of Anthropology*, pp. 63–91. Tucson: University of Arizona Press.

2003. 'Foreword', in L. J. Zimmerman, K. D. Vitelli and J. Hollowell-Zimmer (eds.), *Ethical Issues in Archaeology*, pp. vii–ix. Walnut Creek, CA: AltaMira Press.

McIntosh, R. J. 1996. 'Just Say Shame: Excising the Rot of Cultural Genocide', in P. R. Schmidt and R. J. McIntosh (eds.), *Plundering Africa's Past*, pp. 45–62. Bloomington: Indiana University Press.

MacIntyre, A. 1966. *A Short History of Ethics: A History of Moral Philosophy from the Homeric Age to the Twentieth Century.* New York: Macmillan.

McLaughlin, R. H. 1998. 'The American Archaeological Record: Authority to Dig, Power to Interpret'. *International Journal of Cultural Property* 7 (2): 342–75.

McLeod, M. 2002. 'Archaeology is New Target for Ukraine's Mafia Gangs'. *Scotland on Sunday*, 13 October.

McLuhan, M. 1962. *The Gutenberg Galaxy.* Toronto: University of Toronto Press.

McManamon, F. P. 1991. 'The Many Publics for Archaeology'. *American Antiquity* 56: 121–30.

Magga, O. H. 1990. 'Samiske kulturminner og samisk kulturarbeid'. *Kulturminnevernets teori og metode. Status 1989 og veien videre. Seminarraport fra Utstein Kloster 8.–11. mai 1989.* Oslo: Rådet for humanistisk forskning/ Norges Allmennvitenskapelig Forskningsråd.

Mandal, D. 1993. *Ayodhya: Archaeology after Destruction.* London: Sangam; Hyderabad: Orient Longman.

Mapunda, B. 2001. 'Destruction of Archaeological Heritage in Tanzania: The Cost of Ignorance', in N. Brodie, J. Doole and C. Renfrew (eds.), *Trade in Illicit Antiquities: The Destruction of the World's Archaeological Heritage*, pp. 47–56. Cambridge: McDonald Institute for Archaeological Research.

Martin, E. 1990. 'Science and Women's Bodies: Forms of Anthropological Knowledge', in M. Jacobus, E. Fox Keller and S. Shuttleworth (eds.), *Body/ Politics: Women and the Discourses of Science*, pp. 69–82. London: Routledge.

Matsuda, D. J. 1998a. 'The Ethics of Archaeology, Subsistence Digging, and Artifact "Looting" in Latin America: Point, Muted Counterpoint'. *International Journal of Cultural Property* 7 (1): 87–97.

1998b. *Subsistence Digging in and around Belize*. Ann Arbor, MI: University Microfilms.

May, W. F. 1980. 'Doing Ethics: The Bearing of Ethical Theories on Fieldwork'. *Social Problems* 27 (3): 358–70.

Meighan, C. W. 1984. 'Archaeology: Science or Sacrilege?', in E. L. Green (ed.), *Ethics and Values in Archaeology*, pp. 208–23. New York: The Free Press.

1992. 'Some Scholars' Views on Reburial'. *American Antiquity* 57: 704–10.

Merenstein, A. 1992. 'The Zuni Quest for Repatriation of the War Gods: An Alternative Basis for Claim'. *American Indian Law Review* 17: 589–637.

Merrill, W. L., E. J. Ladd and T. J. Ferguson 1993. 'The Return of the *Ahayu:da*: Lessons for Repatriation from Zuni Pueblo and the Smithsonian Institution'. *Current Anthropology* 34: 523–68.

Merriman, N. 2002. 'Archaeology, Heritage and Interpretation', in B. Cunliffe *et al.* (eds.), *Archaeology: The Widening Debate*, pp. 540–65. Oxford: Oxford University Press.

Merryman, J. H. 1983. 'International Art Law: From Cultural Nationalism to a Common Cultural Heritage'. *Journal of International Law and Politics* 15: 757–63.

1985. 'Thinking about the Elgin Marbles'. *Michigan Law Review* 83: 1881–1923.

1986. 'Two Ways of Thinking about Cultural Property'. *The American Journal of International Law* 80: 831–53.

1996. 'A Licit International Trade in Cultural Objects', in Martine Briat and Judith A. Freedberg (eds.), *Legeal Aspects of International Trade in Art*, pp. 3–45. International Sales of Works of Art 5. The Hague: Kluwer Law International.

Meskell, L. 2002. 'Negative Heritage and Past Mastering in Archaeology'. *Anthropological Quarterly* 75 (3): 557–74.

Messenger, P. M. (ed.) 1999. *The Ethics of Collecting Cultural Property: Whose Culture? Whose Property?* Albuquerque: University of New Mexico Press.

Meyer, K. E. 1973. *The Plundered Past*. New York: Atheneum.

Meyer, R. L. 1976. '*Travaux préparatoires* for the UNESCO World Heritage Convention'. *Earth Law Journal* 2: 45–81.

Michell, G. 1988. 'Time Regained. A Historical Perspective on Cultural Sites and Monuments'. *The UNESCO Courier* (August): 16–26.

Migliore, S. 1991. 'Treasure Hunting and Pillaging in Sicily: Acquiring a Deviant Identity'. *Anthropologica* 33: 161–75.

Mihesuah, D. A. 1996. 'American Indians, Anthropologists, Pothunters, and Repatriation: Ethical, Religious, and Political Differences'. *American Indian Quarterly* 20 (2): 229–37; reprinted in D. A. Mihesuah (ed.), *Repatriation*

Reader: Who Owns American Indian Remains? pp. 95–106. Lincoln: University of Nebraska Press.

Mihesuah, D. A. (ed.) 2000. *Repatriation Reader: Who Owns American Indian Remains?* Lincoln: University of Nebraska Press.

Moody-Adams, M. 1997. *Fieldwork in Familiar Places: Morality, Culture, and Philosophy.* Cambridge, MA: Harvard University Press.

Morphy, H. 2000. 'Elite Art for Cultural Elites: Adding Value to Indigenous Arts', in C. Smith and G. K. Ward (eds.), *Indigenous Cultures in an Interconnected World*, pp. 129–44. Toronto: University of British Columbia Press.

Mortensen, L. 2001. 'The Local Dynamics of Global Heritage: Archaeotourism at Copán, Honduras'. *Mesoamerica* 42: 104–34.

Moulin, R. 1987. *The French Art Market: A Sociological View*, trans. A. Goldhammer. New Brunswick, NJ: Rutgers University Press.

Moustakas, J. 1989. 'Group Rights in Cultural Property'. *Cornell Law Review* 74: 1179–1227.

Muirhead, J. H. 1912. 'Ethics', in J. Hastings (ed.), *Encyclopedia of Religion and Ethics*, vol. 5, pp. 414–25. Edinburgh: T. and T. Clark.

Mulvaney, J. 1985. 'A Question of Values: Museums and Cultural Property', in I. McBryde (ed.), *Who Owns the Past?*, pp. 86–98. Melbourne: Oxford University Press.

1991. 'Past Regained, Future Lost: The Kow Swamp Pleistocene Burials'. *Antiquity* 65: 12–21.

Mumford, L. 1961. *The City in History.* London: Secker and Warburg.

Munjeri, D., C. Sibanda, G. Saouma-Forero, L. Lévi-Strauss and L. Mbuyamba (eds.) 1995. *African Cultural Heritage and the World Heritage Convention. First Global Strategy Meeting, Harare (11–13 October 1995).* Harare: The National Museums and Monuments of Zimbabwe.

Munson, C. A. and M. Jones 1995. 'The GE Mound: An ARPA Case Study'. *American Antiquity* 60 (1): 131–49.

Murray, T. 1992. 'Aboriginal (Pre)History and Australian Archaeology: The Discourse of Australian Prehistoric Archaeology', in B. Atwood and J. Arnold (eds.), *Power, Knowledge, and Aborigines*, pp. 1–19. *Journal of Australian Studies* special issue 35. Victoria: LaTrobe University Press in association with National Centre for Australian Studies.

2000. 'Conjectural Histories: Some Archaeological and Historical Consequences of Indigenous Dispossession in Australia', in I. Lilley (ed.), *Native Title and the Transformation of Archaeology in the Postcolonial World*, pp. 65–77. Sydney: Oceania Publications.

Myers, F. 2002. *Painting Culture: The Making of an Aboriginal High Art.* Durham, NC: Duke University Press.

Nagel, T. 1979. 'Death', in T. Nagel (ed.), *Mortal Questions*, pp. 1–10. Cambridge: Cambridge University Press.

NAGPRA 1990. *Native American Graves Protection and Repatriation Act.* http://www.cr.nps.gov/nagpra/MANDATES/25USC3001etseq.htm. The full text of NAGPRA is provided as an appendix in Fine-Dare 2002. NAGPRA

Review Committee Minutes are posted at www.cast.uark.edu/other/nps/ nagpra/rcm.html *Native American Rights Fund Legal Review*, 14 (4): 1–12.

Nason, J. D. 1997. 'Beyond Repatriation: Cultural Policy and Practice for the Twenty-First Century', in B. Ziff and P. V. Rao (eds.), *Borrowed Power: Essays on Cultural Appropriation*, pp. 291–312. New Brunswick, NJ: Rutgers University Press.

Ndoro, W. 1994. 'The Preservation and Presentation of Great Zimbabwe'. *Antiquity* 68: 616–23.

2001. *Your Monument Our Shrine: The Preservation of Great Zimbabwe.* Studies in African Archaeology 19. Uppsala: Uppsala University.

Ndoro, W. and G. Pwiti 2001. 'Heritage Management in Southern Africa. Local, National and International Discourse'. *Public Archaeology* 2 (1): 21–34.

Nicholas, G. and K. Bannister 2004. 'Copyrighting the Past? Emerging Intellectual Property Rights Issues in Archaeology'. *Current Anthropology* 45: 327–50.

Nichols, D. L., A. L. Klesert and R. Anyon 1999. 'Ancestral Sites, Shrines, and Graves: Native American Perspectives on the Ethics of Collecting Cultural Properties', in P. M. Messenger (ed.), *The Ethics of Collecting Cultural Property: Whose Culture? Whose Property?*, pp. 27–38. Albuquerque: University of New Mexico Press.

Nietzsche, Friedrich 1997 [1874]. 'On the Uses and Disadvantages of History for Life', in *Untimely Meditations*, D. Breazeale, trans. R. J. Hollingdale, 2nd edn, pp. 57–124. Cambridge: Cambridge University Press.

2001 [1882]. *The Gay Science*, trans. J. Naukhoff. Cambridge: Cambridge University Press.

Norton, P. 1989. 'Archaeological Rescue and Conservation in the North Andean Area', in H. Cleere (ed.), *Archaeological Heritage Management in the Modern World*, pp. 142–5. London: Unwin Hyman.

Nuttall, M. 1997. 'Packaging the Wild: Tourism Development in Alaska', in S. Abram, J. Waldren and D. Macleod (eds.), *Tourists and Tourism: Identifying People with Places*, pp. 223–38. Oxford: Berg.

1998. *Protecting the Arctic: Indigenous Peoples and Cultural Survival.* Amsterdam: Harwood Academic Publishers.

NWHO 1999. *Sustainable Tourism and Cultural Heritage: A Review of Development Assistance and Its Potential to Promote Sustainability.* Oslo: Nordic World Heritage Office.

O'Brien, S. 1989. *American Indian Tribal Governments.* Norman: University of Oklahoma Press.

Office for Human Research Protections 1993. *Institutional Review Board Guidebook*, http://ohrp.osophs.dhhs.gov/irb/irb_guidebook.htm (accessed 30 May 2004).

O'Keefe, P. 1997. *The Trade in Antiquities: Reducing Destruction and Theft.* London and Paris: Archetype Publications and UNESCO.

1998. 'Codes of Ethics: Form and Function in Cultural Heritage Management'. *International Journal of Cultural Property* 7: 32–51.

2000. 'Archaeology and Human Rights'. *Public Archaeology* 1 (3): 181–94.

Omland, A. 1997. 'World Heritage and the Relationship between the Global and the Local'. Unpublished MPhil thesis, Department of Archaeology, University of Cambridge.

    1998. 'UNESCOs Verdensarv-konvensjon og forståelsen av en felles verdensarv'. Unpublished Cand. philol. thesis, Department of Archaeology, University of Oslo.

    1999. 'Kulturminnevern og demokrati: problematikk omkring meningskontroll og vestliggjøring av kulturminner'. *Primitive Tider* 2: 82–98.

Ouzman, S. 2003. [WAC] Proposition 15, 18th December. Available at https://listserver.flinders.edu.au/mailman/private/wac/2003-December/000175.html.

Paddaya, K. and P. Bellwood 2002. 'South and Southeast Asia', in Cunliffe *et al.* (eds.), *Archaeology: The Widening Debate*, pp. 295–316. Oxford: Oxford University Press.

Padgett, T. 1989. 'Walking on Ancestral Gods: Using Mayan Ruins for Patios and Pigstys'. *Newsweek* 9 October, 83.

Pardo, A. 1975. *The Common Heritage: Selected Papers on Oceans and World Order 1967–1974*. IOI Occasional Papers 3. Malta: Malta University Press.

Pardoe, C. 1991. 'Competing Paradigms and Ancient Human Remains: The State of the Discipline', *Archaeology in Oceania* 26: 79–85.

Paredes-Maury, S. 1998. *Surviving in the Rainforest: The Realities of Looting in the Rural Villages of El Peten, Guatemala*. The Foundation for the Advancement of Meso-American Studies. Available at www.famsi.org/reports.paredesmaury/paredesmaury.html.

Partridge, E. 1981. 'Posthumous Interests and Posthumous Respect', *Ethics* 91: 243–64.

Pearce, S. M. 1995. *On Collecting: An Investigation into Collecting in the European Tradition*. New York: Routledge.

Pearce, S. M. (ed.) 1997. *Experiencing Material Culture in the Western World*. London and Washington, DC: Leicester University Press.

Peers, A. 1989. 'Some Players in Art Market Find "Exhibition Effect" Spells Profit'. *Wall Street Journal* 14 August, sec. C:1.

Peers, L. and A. K. Brown 2003. *Museums and Source Communities: A Routledge Reader*. London: Routledge.

Pels, P. 1999. 'Professions of Duplexity: A Prehistory of Ethical Codes in Anthropology'. *Current Anthropology* 40: 101–36.

Pendergast, D. M. 1991. 'And the Loot Goes On: Winning Some Battles, but Not the War'. *Journal of Field Archaeology* 18: 89–95.

    1994. 'Looting the Maya World: The Other Losers'. *Public Archaeology Review* 2 (2): 2–4.

Plato 1992. *The Republic*. Indianapolis: Hackett.

Pluciennik, M. 2001. 'Archaeology, Advocacy and Intellectualism', in M. Pluciennik (ed.), *The Responsibilities of Archaeologists: Archaeology and Ethics*, pp. 19–30. BAR International Series 981. Oxford: Archaeopress.

Pokotylo, D. and N. Guppy 1999. 'Public Opinion and Archaeological Heritage: Views from Outside the Profession', *American Antiquity* 64 (3): 400–16.

Politis, G. 2002. 'South America: In the Garden of Forking Paths', in B. Cunliffe *et al.* (eds.), *Archaeology: The Widening Debate*, pp. 193–236. Oxford: Oxford University Press.

Pollard, A. M. 2004. 'Putting Infinity Up on Trial: A Consideration of the Role of Scientific Thinking in Future Archaeologies', in J. Bintliff (ed.), *A Companion to Archaeology*, pp. 380–96. Oxford: Blackwell.

Posey, D. A. 1990. 'Intellectual Property Rights and Just Compensation for Indigenous Peoples'. *Anthropology Today* 6 (4): 13–16.

Powell, S., Garza, C. E. and Hendricks, A. 1993. 'Ethics and the Ownership of the Past: The Reburial Controversy'. *Archaeological Method and Theory* 5: 1–42.

Pressoyre, L. 1996. *The World Heritage Convention, Twenty Years Later.* Paris: UNESCO.

Preucel, R. W. and I. Hodder 1996. *Contemporary Archaeology in Theory.* Oxford: Blackwell.

Price, J. 2003. [WAC] Proposition 15, 19th December. Available at https://listserver. flinders.edu.au/mailman/private/wac/2003-December/000179.html.

Prott, L. V. 1992a. 'A Common Heritage: The World Heritage Convention', in L. Macinnes and C. P. Wickham-Jones (eds.), *All Natural Things: Archaeology and the Green Debate*. Oxford: Oxbow Books.

1992b. 'From Admonition to Action: UNESCO's Role in the Protection of Cultural Heritage'. *Nature and Resources* 28 (3): 4–11.

2003. [WAC] Proposition 15, 21st December. Available at https://listserver. flinders.edu.au/mailman/private/wac/2003-December/000182.html.

Prott, L. V. and P. J. O'Keefe 1984. *Law and the Cultural Heritage*, vol. 1: *Discovery and Excavation*. London: Butterworths.

1989. *Law and the Cultural Heritage*, vol. 111: *Movement*. London: Butterworths.

Prott, L. V., M. de la Torre and J. Levin 2001. 'Cultural Heritage and International Law. A Conversation with Lyndel Prott'. *The Getty Conservation Institute Newsletter* 16 (2): 12–15.

Pyburn, K. A. 2003. 'Archaeology for a New Millennium: The Rules of Engagement', in L. Derry and M. Molloy (eds.), *Archaeologists and Local Communities: Partners in Exploring the Past*, pp. 167–84. Washington, DC: Society for American Archaeology Press.

Quick, P. (ed.) 1985. *Proceedings: Conference on Reburial Issues.* Washington, DC: Society for American Archaeology.

Quinton, A. 1957. 'Properties and Classes'. *Proceedings of the Aristotelian Society* 48: 33–58.

Raab, L. M. 1984. 'Achieving Professionalism through Ethical Fragmentation: Warnings from Client-Oriented Archaeology', in E. Green (ed.), *Ethics and Values in Archaeology*, pp. 51–61. New York: The Free Press.

Randall, J. H. Jr. 1976 [1926]. *The Making of the Modern Mind.* New York: Columbia University Press.

Ranger, T. 1989. 'Whose Heritage? The Case of the Matobo National Park'. *Journal of Southern African Studies* 15 (2): 217–49.

1996. 'Great Spaces Washed with Sun. The Matopos and Uluru Compared', in K. Darian-Smith, L. Gunner and S. Nuttall (eds.), *Land, Literature and History in South Africa and Australia.* London: Routledge.

1999. *Voices from the Rocks: Nature, Culture & History in the Matopos Hills of Zimbabwe.* Harare: Baobab.

Rao, N. and R. Reddy 2001. 'Ayodhya, the Print Media and Communalism', in R. Layton, P. Stone and J. Thomas (eds.), *The Destruction and Conservation of Cultural Property*, pp. 139–56. London: Routledge.

Red Shirt, D. 2002. *Cultural Heritage and Sacred Sites: World Heritage from an Indigenous Perspective 15 May 2002 – New York University.* Available at: http://www.dialoguebetweennations.com/N2N/PFII/English/DelphineRed-Shirt.htm.

Register of Professional Archaeologists 2004. 'Code of Conduct and Standards of Research Performance', http://www.rpanet.org/.

Renfrew, C. 1993. 'Collectors are the Real Looters'. *Archaeology* 46 (3): 16–17.

2000. *Loot, Legitimacy and Ownership: The Ethical Crisis in Archaeology.* London: Gerald Duckworth.

Richman, K. A. 2002. 'Responsible Conduct of Research is All Well and Good'. *American Journal of Bioethics* 2 (4): 62–3.

Riding In, J. 1996. 'Repatriation: A Pawnee's Perspective'. *The American Indian Quarterly*, Special Issue on Repatriation 20 (2): 238–50.

2000. 'Repatriation: A Pawnee's Perspective', in D. A. Mihesuah (ed.), *Repatriation Reader: Who Owns American Indian Remains?*, pp. 106–22. Lincoln: University of Nebraska Press.

Robertson, R. 1995. 'Glocalization: Time–Space and Homogeneity–Heterogeneity', in M. Featherstone, S. Lash and R. Robertson (eds.), *Global Modernities*, pp. 25–44. London: Sage.

Rose, M. and Ö. Acar 1996. 'Turkey's War on the Illicit Antiquities Trade', in K. Vitelli (ed.), *Archaeological Ethics*, pp. 71–89. Walnut Creek, CA: AltaMira Press.

Rosenwig, R. M. 1997. 'Ethics in Canadian Archaeology: An International, Comparative Analysis'. *Canadian Journal of Archaeology* 21: 99–114.

Rowan, Y. and U. Baram (eds.) 2004. *Marketing Heritage: Archaeology and the Consumption of the Past.* Walnut Creek, CA: AltaMira Press.

Ruben, D.-H. 1988. 'A Puzzle about Posthumous Predication'. *The Philosophical Review* 97: 211–36.

Ruskin, J. 1911. *The Seven Lamps of Architecture.* Second edition. London: Ward Lock.

Russell, A. J. and Wallace, G. 2004. 'Irresponsible Ecotourism'. *Anthropology Today* 20 (3): 1–2.

SAA, *see* Society for American Archaeology.

Salmon, M. H. 1997. 'Ethical Considerations in Anthropology and Archaeology, or Relativism and Justice for All'. *Journal of Anthropological Research* 53 (1): 47–63.

1999. 'Ethics in Science: Special Problems in Anthropology and Archaeology'. *Science and Engineering Ethics* 5 (3): 307–18.

Sandler, L. 2004. 'The Thieves of Baghdad'. *Atlantic Monthly* 294 (4): 175–82.

Sant Cassia, P. 1993. 'The Discovery of Malta: Nature, Culture and Ethnicity in Nineteenth Century Painting' (review article). *Journal of Mediterranean Studies* 3: 354–77.

Sax, J. L. 1990. 'Heritage Preservation as a Public Duty: The Abbé Grégoire and the Origins of an Idea'. *Michigan Law Review* 88: 1142–69.

1999. *Playing Darts with a Rembrandt*. Ann Arbor: Michigan University Press.

Scarre, G. 2003. 'Archaeology and Respect for the Dead'. *Journal of Applied Philosophy* 20: 237–49.

Schaafsma, C. F. 1989. 'Significant until Proven Otherwise: Problems versus Representative Samples', in H. F. Cleere (ed.), *Archaeological Heritage Management in the Modern World*, pp. 38–51. London: Unwin Hyman.

Schmidt, P. R. 1996. 'The human right to a cultural heritage. African Applications', in P. R. Schmidt and R. J. McIntosh (eds.), *Plundering Africa's Past*. Bloomington and Indianapolis: Indiana University Press.

Schmidt, P. R. and R. J. McIntosh (eds.) 1996. *Plundering Africa's Past*. Bloomington and Indianapolis: Indiana University Press.

Selby-Bigge, L. A. (ed.) 1897. *British Moralists*. Oxford: Clarendon Press.

Selkirk, A. (n.d.). *Who Owns the Past? A Grassroots Critique of Heritage Policy*, http://www.archaeology.co.uk.gateway/thinktank/who/welcome.htm.

Sharma, Y. D., K. M. Srivastava, S. P. Gupta, K. P. Nautiyal, B. R. Grover, D. S. Agrawal, S. Mukherji and S. Malayya 1992. *Ramajanma Bhumi: Ayodhya. New Archaeological Discoveries*. New Delhi: Historians' Forum.

Shilling, C. 1993. *The Body and Social Theory*. London: Sage.

Sillar, B. 1992. 'The Social Life of the Andean Dead'. *Archaeological Review from Cambridge* 11 (1): 107–24.

Silook, S. 1999. 'St. Lawrence Island "Digs" Resource Management'. *Nome Nugget*, 22 July: 15.

Silva, R. 1989. 'The Cultural Triangle of Sri Lanka', in H. F. Cleere (ed.), *Archaeological Heritage Management in the Modern World*, pp. 221–6. London: Unwin Hyman.

Sim, R. and D. West 1999. 'Prehistoric Human Occupation in the Bass Strait Region, Southeast Australia: An Aboriginal and An Archaeological Perspective', in P. Ucko and R. Layton (eds.), *The Archaeology and Anthropology of Landscape: Shaping Your Landscape*, pp. 423–38. London: Routledge.

Singer, P. 1975. *Animal Liberation*. New York: New York Review of Books.

Smith, A. 1897 [1759]. *The Theory of Moral Sentiments*, excerpted in L. A. Selby-Bigge (ed.), *British Moralists*, vol. 1, pp. 255–336. Oxford: Clarendon Press.

Smith, A. D. 1990. 'Towards a Global Culture?' in M. Featherstone (ed.), *Global Culture. Nationalism, Globalization and Modernity*, pp. 171–91. London: Sage.

Smith, C., H. Burke and G. K. Ward 2000. 'Globalisation and Indigenous Peoples: Threat or Empowerment?', in C. Smith and G. K. Ward (eds.), *Indigenous Cultures in an Interconnected World*, pp. 1–26. Toronto: University of British Columbia Press.

Smith, C. and H. Burke 2003. 'In the Spirit of the Code', in L. J. Zimmerman, K. D. Vitelli and J. Hollowell-Zimmer (eds.), *Ethical Issues in Archaeology*, pp. 177–97. Walnut Creek, CA: AltaMira Press.

Smith, G. and J. Ehrenhard 1991. *Protecting the Past*. Boca Raton, FL: CRC Press.

Smith, K. L. 2005. 'Looting and the politics of Archaeological Knowledge in Northern Peru'. *Ethnos* 70 (2): 149–70.

Smith, L. T. 1999. *Decolonizing Methodologies: Research and Indigenous Peoples*. London: Zed Books.

Smith, M. 1998. 'Challenging the Law: Two Lengthy Battles over Cultural Patrimony'. *The Houston Chronicle* 22 February 1998.

Society for American Archaeology (SAA).
   1996. 'Principles of Archaeological Ethics'. *Society for American Archaeology Bulletin*, 14 (3).
   2000. Society for American Archaeology Ethics in Archaeology Committee, 'Principles of Archaeological Ethics', in M. J. Lynott and A. Wylie (eds.), *Ethics in American Archaeology*. pp. 11–12. 2nd rev. edn. Washington, DC: Society for American Archaeology.
   2004. 'Principles of Archaeological Ethics', http://www.saa.org/aboutSAA/ethics.html.

Society of Professional Archaeologists (Register of Professional Archaeologists) 1995. 'Code of Conduct and Standards of Research Performance', in K. D. Vittelli (ed.), *Archaeological Ethics*, pp. 253–8. Walnut Creek, CA: AltaMira Press.

Staley, D. P. 1993. 'St. Lawrence Island's Subsistence Diggers: A New Perspective on Human Effects on Archaeological Sites'. *Journal of Field Archaeology* 20: 347–55.

Stark, M. T. and P. Bion Griffin 2004. 'Archaeological Research and Cultural Heritage Management in Cambodia's Mekong Delta: The Search for the "Cradle of Khmer Civilization"', in Y. Rowan and U. Baram (eds.), *Marketing Heritage: Archaeology and the Consumption of the Past*, pp. 117–42. Walnut Creek, CA: AltaMira Press.

State of the Heritage Report 2003. The Superintendence of Cultural Heritage, Malta.

Suppliment tal-Gazetta tal-Gvern ta' Malta (2002), No. 17,232, 26 April 2002, Cultural Heritage Act, Act No. VI of 2002, enacted by the Parliament of Malta.

Stiglitz, J. E. 2002. *Globalization and Its Discontents*. New York: W. W. Norton and Co.

Stocker, M. 1976. 'The Schizophrenia of Modern Ethical Theories'. *Journal of Philosophy* 73: 453–66.

Stoffle, R. W., L. Loendorf, D. E. Austin, D. B. Halmo and A. Bulletts 2000. 'Ghost Dancing in the Grand Canyon. Southern Paiute Rock Art, Ceremony and Cultural Landscapes'. *Current Anthropology* 41: 11–38.

Strauss, R. *et al.* 2001. 'The Role of Community Advisory Boards: Involving Communities in the Informed Consent Process'. *American Journal of Public Health* 91 (12): 1938–43.

Suddards, R. W. 1993. 'Listed buildings', in J. Hunter and I. Ralston (eds.), *Archaeological Resource Management in the UK: An Introduction*, pp. 77–88. Stroud: Sutton.

Šulc, B. 2001. 'The Protection of Croatia's Heritage during War 1991–95', in R. Layton, P. Stone and J. Thomas (eds.), *The Destruction and Conservation of Cultural Property*, pp. 157–67. London: Routledge.

Sutton, P., P. Jones and S. Hemming 1988. 'Survival, Regeneration and Impact', in P. Sutton (ed.), *Dreamings: The Art of Aboriginal Australia*, pp. 180–212. New York: Asia Society Galleries and George Brazillier.

Swadling, M. (ed.) 1992. *Masterworks of Man and Nature: Preserving our World Heritage*. Patonga: Harper Mac-Rae.

Swidler, N., K. E. Dongoske, R. Anyon and A. S. Downer (eds.) 1997. *Native Americans and Archaeologists: Stepping Stones to Common Ground*. Walnut Creek, CA: AltaMira Press.

Tambiah, S. J. 1986. *Sri Lanka: Ethnic Fratricide and the Dismantling of Democracy*. New Delhi: Oxford University Press.

Tanner, M. 1997. *Croatia: A Nation Forged in War*. New Haven: Yale University Press.

Tanner-Kaplash, S. 1989. 'The Common Heritage of All Mankind: A Study of Cultural Policy and Legislation Pertinent to Cultural Objects'. Unpublished PhD thesis, Department of Museum Studies, University of Leicester.

Tarlow, S. 2001a. 'Decoding Ethics'. *Public Archaeology* 1: 245–59.
　　2001b. 'The Responsibility of Representation', in M. Pluciennik (ed.), *The Responsibilities of Archaeologists: Archaeology and Ethics*, pp. 57–64. BAR International Series 981. Oxford: Archaeopress.

Tarzi, Z. 1977. *L'architecture et le décor rupestre des grottes de Bamiyan*. Paris: Mémoires de la Délégation Archéologiques en Afghanistan.

Tay, A. E. S. 1985. 'Law and the Cultural Heritage', in I. McBryde (ed.), *Who Owns the Past?*, pp. 107–38. Melbourne: Oxford University Press.

Taylor, T. 2002. *The Buried Soul*. London: Fourth Estate.

Thoden van Velzen, D. 1999. 'The Continuing Reinvention of the Etruscan Myth', in A. Gavin-Schwartz and C. Holtorf (eds.), *Archaeology and Folklore*, pp. 175–95. London: Routledge.

Thomas, D. H. 2000. *Skull Wars: Kennewick Man, Archaeology and the Battle for Native American Identity*. New York: Basic Books.

Thompson, J. 2003. 'Cultural Property, Restitution and Value'. *Journal of Applied Philosophy* 20: 251–62.

Thompson, M. 1979. *Rubbish Theory: The Creation and Destruction of Value.* Oxford: Oxford University Press.

Thornton, R. 1998. *Studying Native America.* Madison: University of Wisconsin Press.

2001. 'Who Owns Our Past? The Repatriation of Native American Human Remains and Cultural Objects', in S. Lobo and S. Talbot (eds.), *Native American Voices,* pp. 303–17. Upper Saddle River, NJ: Prentice Hall.

Thwe, P. K. 2003. Review of A. Green and T. R. Blurton (eds.), *Burma: Art and Archaeology, Times Higher Education Supplement,* 21 February 2003.

Titchen, S. M. 1995. 'On the Construction of Outstanding Universal Value. UNESCO's World Heritage Convention (Convention concerning the Protection of the World Cultural and Natural Heritage, 1972) and the Identification and Assessment of Cultural Places for the Inclusion in the World Heritage List'. Unpublished PhD thesis, The Australian National University, Canberra.

1996. 'On the Construction of "Outstanding Universal Value". Some Comments on the Implementation of the 1972 UNESCO World Heritage Convention'. *Conservation and Management of Archaeological Sites* 1: 235–42.

2001. 'Recognizing Indigenous Values, Rights and Interests'. *World Conservation* 2: 19.

Tonder, M. and J. Jurvelius 2004. 'Attitudes towards Fishery and Conservation of the Saimaa Ringed Seal in Lake Pihlajavesi, Finland'. *Environmental Conservation* 31 (2): 1–8.

Toussaint, S. (ed.) 2004. *Crossing Boundaries: Cultural, Legal, Historical and Practice Issues in Native Title.* Carlton: Melbourne University Press.

Trigger, B. 1980. 'Archaeology and the Image of the American Indian'. *American Antiquity* 45 (4): 662–76.

1989. *A History of Anthropological Thought.* Cambridge: Cambridge University Press.

Trope, J. F. and W. R. Echo-Hawk 2001. 'The Native American Graves Protection and Repatriation Act: Background and Legislative History', in T. L. Bray (ed.), *The Future of the Past: Archaeologists, Native Americans and Repatriation,* pp. 9–33. New York: Garland Publishing.

Tsosie, R. 1997. 'Indigenous Rights and Archaeology', in N. Swidler, K. E. Dongoske, R. Anyon and A. S. Downer (eds.), *Native Americans and Archaeologists: Stepping Stones to Common Ground,* pp. 64–76. Walnut Creek, CA: AltaMira Press.

Tubb, K. W. (ed.) 1995. *Antiquities Trade or Betrayed: Legal, Ethical and Conservation Issues.* London: Archetype Publications.

Tulley, J. 1980. *A Discourse on Property: John Locke and his Adversaries.* Cambridge: Cambridge University Press.

Ucko, P. J. 1990. 'Foreword', in P. Stone and R. MacKenzie (eds.), *The Excluded Past: Archaeology in Education,* pp. ix–xxiv. London: Unwin Hyman.

Ucko, P. J., M. Hunter, A. J. Clark and A. David 1991. *Avebury Reconsidered: From the 1660s to the 1990s.* London: Unwin Hyman.

UNESCO 1960. *International Campaign to Save the Monuments of Nubia. Official inaguration 8 March 1960.* Paris: UNESCO. [Most UNESCO documents are available from the UNESCO World Heritage Centre: http://whc.unesco.org/.]

1966. *Declaration of the Principles of International Cultural Co-operation.* Paris: UNESCO.

1970. *Protection of Mankind's Cultural Heritage. Sites and Monuments.* Paris: UNESCO.

1972a. *Convention concerning the Protection of the World Cultural and Natural Heritage.* Paris: UNESCO.

1972b. *Records of the General Conference: 17th session, Paris 1972. Vol. III. Proceedings.* 17c. Paris: UNESCO.

1972c. *Saving Carthage: Address by Mr. René Maheu, Director-General of UNESCO.* DG/72/9. Paris: UNESCO.

1979. *World Heritage Committee. CC-79/CONF.003/13.* Paris: UNESCO.

1982. *A Legacy for All: The World's Major Natural and Historic Sites.* Paris: UNESCO.

1984. *Bureau of the World Heritage Committee. SC-84/CONF.001/9.* Paris: UNESCO.

1987. *Bureau of the World Heritage Committee. SC-87/CONF.004/11.* Paris: UNESCO.

1991. *The World Heritage Committee. SC-91/CONF.002/15.* Paris: UNESCO.

1992. *The World Heritage Committee. WHC-92/CONF.002/12.* Paris: UNESCO.

1993. *The World Heritage Committee. WHC-93/CONF.002/14.* Paris: UNESCO.

1994. *Expert Meeting on the 'Global Strategy' and Thematic Studies for a Representative World Heritage List. WHC-94/CONF.001/INF.6.* Paris: UNESCO.

1995. *The World Heritage Committee. WHC-95/CONF.203/16.* Paris: UNESCO.

1996. *The World Heritage Committee. WHC-96/CONF.201/21.* Paris: UNESCO.

2000. *The World Heritage Committee. WHC-2000/CONF.204/21.* Paris: UNESCO.

2001. *The World Heritage Committee. WHC-01/CONF.208/24.* Paris: UNESCO.

2002. *Cultural Diversities: Common Heritage, Plural Identities.* Paris: UNESCO.

2003a. *Conclusions and Recommendations of the Conference. Linking Universal and Local Values: Managing a Sustainable Future for World Heritage, Amsterdam, 22–24 May 2003.* Amsterdam: The Netherlands National Commission for UNESCO.

2003b. *Cultural Landscapes: The Challenges of Conservation.* World Heritage Papers 7. UNESCO World Heritage Centre, Paris.

2005a. *The World Heritage List.* Paris: UNESCO.

2005b. *Operational Guidelines for the Implementation of the World Heritage Convention.* Paris: UNESCO.

United Nations Convention on the Law of the Sea 1982. Signed 10 December 1982, United Nations Document A/Conf. 62/122.

Veerkamp, A. 1998. 'World Heritage Site Designation: A Threat to U.S. Sovereignty?' *Historic Preservation Forum* 12 (3): 18–22.

Vella, N. and Gilkes, O. 2001. 'The Lure of the Antique: Nationalism, Politics and Archaeology in British Malta (1880–1964)'. Reprinted from *Papers of the British School at Rome*, vol. LXIX, pp. 353–84. Oxford: Alden Press.

Vermillion Accord 1989. www.wac.uct.ac.za/archive/content/vermillion.accord. html.

Vitelli, K. D. 1996a. 'Introduction', in K. D. Vitelli (ed.), *Archaeological Ethics*, pp. 17–28. Walnut Creek, CA: AltaMira Press.

2000. 'Looting and Theft of Cultural Property: Are We Making Progress?' *Conservation* (The GCI Newsletter) 15 (1): 21–4.

Vitelli, K. D. (ed.) 1996b. *Archaeological Ethics.* Walnut Creek, CA: AltaMira Press.

Waldram, J. 1988. *As Long as Rivers Run: Hydroelectric Development and Native Communities in Western Canada.* Winnipeg: University of Manitoba Press.

Wallace, G. 2002. 'The Contribution of Cultural Tourism to the Development of Sustainable Tourism', in P. Kakouros (ed.), *Tourism in Protected Areas in Greece: Symposium Proceedings, Sitia, Crete, October 15 & 16 2001.* Thermi: Greek Biotope/Wetland Centre.

Wallace, G. and A. Russell in press. 'Eco-cultural Tourism as a Means for the Development of Culturally Marginal and Environmentally Sensitive Regions in Europe'. *Tourist Studies* 5.

Wallace, M. 1995. 'On the Warpath'. *Museums Journal* (June): 32–4.

1996. 'The Battle of the Enola Gay', in his *Mickey Mouse History and Other Essays on American Memory.* Philadelphia: Temple University Press.

Wallerstein, I. 1974. *The Modern World-System.* London: Academic Press.

Warren, K. J. 1999. 'A Philosophical Perspective on the Ethics and Resolution of Cultural Property Issues', in P. M. Messenger (ed.), *The Ethics of Collecting Cultural Property: Whose Culture? Whose Property?* pp. 1–25. Albuquerque: University of New Mexico.

Watkins, J. 1999. 'Conflicting Codes: Professional, Ethical, and Legal Obligations in Archaeology'. *Science and Engineering Ethics* 5 (3): 337–45.

2000a. 'Archaeological Ethics and American Indians', in L. J. Zimmerman, K. D. Vitelli and J. Hollowell-Zimmer (eds.), *Ethical Issues in Archaeology*, pp. 129–42. Walnut Creek, CA: AltaMira Press.

2000b. *Indigenous Archaeology.* Walnut Creek, CA: AltaMira Press.

2001. 'Yours, Mine or Ours: Conflicts between Archaeologists and Ethnic Groups', in T. L. Bray (ed.), *The Future of the Past: Archaeologists, Native Americans and Repatriation*, pp. 57–68. New York: Garland Publishing.

2003. 'Archaeological Ethics and American Indians', in L. J. Zimmerman, K. D. Vitelli and J. Hollowell-Zimmer (eds.), *Ethical Issues in Archaeology*, pp. 129–41. Walnut Creek, CA: AltaMira Press.

2004. 'Becoming American or Becoming Indian? NAGPRA, Kennewick and Cultural Affiliation'. *Journal of Social Archaeology* 4 (1): 60–80.

Watkins, J., L. Goldstein, K. Vitelli and L. Jenkins 2000. 'Accountability: Responsibilities of Archaeologists to Other Interest Groups', in M. J. Lynott and A. Wylie (eds.), *Ethics in American Archaeology: Challenges for the 1990's*, pp. 33–7. Washington, DC: Society for American Archaeology.

Watkins, J., A. Pyburn and P. Cressey 2000. 'Community Relations: What the Practicing Archaeologist Needs to Know to Work Effectively with Local and/or Descendant Communities', in S. J. Bender and G. Smith (eds.), *Teaching Archaeology in the Twenty-First Century*, pp. 73–81. Washington, DC: Society for American Archaeology.

Wax, M. L. 1991. 'The Ethics of Research in American Indian Communities'. *American Indian Quarterly* 15 (4): 431–56.

1993. 'Comments'. *Current Anthropology* 40 (2): 128–30.

1997. 'Educating an Anthro: The Influence of Vine Deloria, Jr.', in T. Biolsi and L. J. Zimmerman (eds.), *Indians and Anthropologists: Vine Deloria, Jr. and the Critique of Anthropology*, pp. 50–60. Tucson: University of Arizona Press.

Weatherson, B. n.d. 'Intrinsic-Extrinsic'. *Stanford Encyclopaedia of Philosophy*, http://plato.stanford.edu/entries/intrinsic-extrinsic/.

Wheatley, G. 1997. *World Heritage Sites*. London: English Heritage.

White Deer, G. 1997. 'Return of the Sacred, Spirituality and the Scientific Imperative', in N. Swidler, K. E. Dongoske, R. Anyon and A. S. Downer (eds.), *Native Americans and Archaeologists: Stepping Stones to Common Ground*, pp. 37–43. Walnut Creek, CA: AltaMira Press.

Whitely, P. 1997. 'The End of Anthropology (at Hopi)?', in T. Biolsi and L. Zimmerman (eds.), *Indians and Anthropologists: Vine Deloria, Jr. and the Critique of Anthropology*, pp. 177–208. Tucson: University of Arizona Press.

Wildesen, L. E. 1984. 'The Search for an Ethic in Archaeology: An Historical Perspective', in E. L. Green (ed.), *Ethics and Values in Archaeology*, pp. 3–12. New York: The Free Press.

Wilk, R. R. 1999. 'Whose Forest? Whose Lands? Whose Ruins? *Journal of Science and Engineering Ethics* (special issue edited by M. Salmon) 5: 367–74.

Wilkens, D. E. and K. T. Lomawaima 2002. *Uneven Ground: American Indian Sovereignty and Federal Law*. Norman: University of Oklahoma Press.

Wilkinson, T. M. 2002. 'Last Rights: The Ethics of Research on the Dead'. *Journal of Applied Philosophy* 19: 31–41.

Williams, B. 1973. 'A Critique of Utilitarianism', in J. J. C. Smart and B. Williams, *Utilitarianism For and Against*, pp. 77–150. Cambridge: Cambridge University Press.

1985. *Ethics and the Limits of Philosophy*. London: Fontana.

2002. *Truth and Truthfulness: An Essay in Genealogy.* Princeton, NJ: Princeton University Press.

Williams, S. A. 1978. *The International and National Protection of Movable Cultural Property: A Comparative Study.* New York: Oceana Publications.

Wittgenstein, L. 1979. *Remarks on Frazer's* Golden Bough, trans. A. Miles. Retford: Brynmill.

Wolf, E. R. 1982. *Europe and the People without History.* London: University of California Press.

Woodall, J. N. (ed.) 1990. *Predicaments, Pragmatics, and Professionalism: Ethical Conduct in Archaeology.* Special Publication 1. Washington, DC: Society of Professional Archaeologists.

Woodvard, L. (ed.) 1996. *World Heritage Managers Workshop. Ravenshoe April 11–15 1996. Papers and Proceedings.* Canberra: Department of Environment, Sport and Territories, World Heritage Unit.

World Archaeological Congress 1991. 'World Archaeological Congress First Code of Ethics (Members' Obligations to Indigenous Peoples)'. *World Archaeological Bulletin* 5: 22–3. http://www.wac.uct.ac.za/archive/content/ethics.html. Accessed April 2002.

Wright, S. 1998: 'The Politicization of "Culture"'. *Anthropology Today* 14 (February): 7–15.

Wylie, A. 1996. 'Ethical Dilemmas in Archaeological Practice: Looting, Repatriation, Stewardship, and the (Trans)Formation of Disciplinary Identity'. *Perspectives on Science* 4 (2): 154–94; reprinted in Lynott and Wylie 2000.

1997. 'Contextualizing Ethics: Comments on Ethics in Canadian Archaeology by Robert Rosenwig'. *Canadian Journal of Archaeology* 21: 115–20.

1999. 'Science, Conservation, and Stewardship: Evolving Codes of Conduct in Archeology'. *Science and Engineering Ethics* 5 (3): 319–36.

2000. 'Ethical Dilemmas in Archaeological Practice: Looting, Repatriation, Stewardship and the (Trans)formation of Disciplinary Identity', in M. J. Lynott and A. Wylie (eds.), *Ethics in American Archaeology*, pp. 138–57. 2nd rev. edn. Washington, DC: Society for American Archaeology.

2003. 'On Ethics', in L. J. Zimmerman, K. D. Vitelli and J. Hollowell-Zimmer (eds.), *Ethical Issues in Archaeology*, pp. 3–16. Walnut Creek, CA: AltaMira Press.

2004. 'Why Standpoint Matters', in S. Harding (ed.), *The Feminist Standpoint Reader: Intellectual and Political Controversies*, pp. 339–51. New York: Routledge.

in press. 'The Promise and Perils of an Ethic of Stewardship', in L. Meskell and P. Pells (eds.), *Embedding Ethics: Shifting Boundaries of the Anthropological Profession.* London: Berg Press.

Yablo, S. 1999. 'Intrinsicness'. *Philosophical Topics* 26: 479–505.

Yellowhorn, E. 2000. 'Indians, Archaeologists, and the Changing World', in M. J. Lynott and A. Wylie (eds.), *Ethics in American Archaeology*, pp. 126–37. 2nd rev. edn. Washington, DC: Society for American Archaeology.

Young, E. 1995. *Third World in the First: Development and Indigenous Peoples.* London: Routledge.

Zimmer, J. 2003. 'When Archaeological Artifacts are Commodities: Dilemmas Faced by Native Villages of Alaska's Bering Strait', in T. Peck and E. Siegfried (eds.), *Indigenous People and Heritage*, pp. 298–312. Alberta: University of Calgary Archaeological Association.

Zimmerman, L. J. 1987. 'The Impact of Concepts of Time and the Past on the Concept of Archaeology: Some Lessons from the Reburial Issue'. *Archaeological Review from Cambridge* 6 (1): 42–50.

1995. 'Regaining Our Nerve: Ethics, Values and the Transformation of Archaeology', in M. Lynott and A. Wylie (eds.), *Ethics in American Archaeology: Challenges for the 1990's*, pp. 64–7. Washington, DC: Society for American Archaeology.

1996a. 'A New and Different Archaeology?' *The American Indian Quarterly*, Special Issue on Repatriation, 20 (2): 297–306.

1996b. 'Sharing Control of the Past', in K. D. Vitelli (ed.), *Archaeological Ethics.* Walnut Creek, CA: AltaMira Press.

1997a. 'Anthropology and Responses to the Reburial Issue', in T. Biolsi and L. J. Zimmerman (eds.), *Indians and Anthropologists: Vine Deloria, Jr. and the Critique of Anthropology*, pp. 92–112. Tucson: University of Arizona Press.

1997b. 'Remythologizing the Relationship Between Indians and Archaeologists', in N. Swidler, K. E. Dongoske, R. Anyon and A. S. Downer (eds.), *Native Americans and Archaeologists: Stepping Stones to Common Ground*, pp. 44–56. Walnut Creek, CA: AltaMira Press.

2000. 'Regaining Our Nerve: Ethics, Values, and the Transformation of Archaeology', in M. J. Lynott and A. Wylie (eds.), *Ethics in American Archaeology*, pp. 71–4. 2nd rev. edn. Washington, DC: Society for American Archaeology.

2001. 'Usurping Native American Voice', in T. Bray (ed.), *The Future of the Past*, pp. 169–83. New York: Garland Publications.

2002. 'A Decade after the Vermillion Accord', in C. Fforde, J. Hubert and P. Turnbull (eds.), *The Dead and Their Possessions: Repatriation in Principle, Policy and Practice*, pp. 91–8. New York: Routledge.

Zimmerman, L. J., K. D. Vitelli and J. Hollowell-Zimmer 2003a. 'Introduction', in L. J. Zimmerman, K. D. Vitelli and J. Hollowell-Zimmer (eds.), *Ethical Issues in Archaeology*, pp. xi–xvi. Walnut Creek, CA: AltaMira Press.

Zimmerman, L. J., K. D. Vitelli and J. Hollowell-Zimmer (eds.) 2003b. *Ethical Issues in Archaeology.* Walnut Creek, CA: AltaMira Press.

Index